D1594057

War in Social Thought

War in Social Thought

HOBBES TO THE PRESENT

Hans Joas and Wolfgang Knöbl

translated by Alex Skinner

CABRINI COLLEGE LIBRARY
610 KING OF PRUSSIA ROAD
RADNOR, PA 19087

PRINCETON UNIVERSITY PRESS

Princeton & Oxford

777327504

First published in Germany under the title *Kriegsverdrängung:
Ein Problem in der Geschichte der Sozialtheorie* © Suhrkamp Verlag,
Frankfurt am Main, 2008.

English translation © 2013 by Princeton University Press

Published by Princeton University Press, 41 William Street, Princeton,
New Jersey 08540
In the United Kingdom: Princeton University Press, 6 Oxford Street,
Woodstock, Oxfordshire OX20 1TW

press.princeton.edu

Jacket Art: Gerhard Richter, *Bombers*, 1963, Oil on canvas 51-1/8 x 70-7/8 in.
Courtesy of the artist.

All Rights Reserved

Library of Congress Cataloging-in-Publication Data
Joas, Hans, 1948–
 [Kriegsverdrängung. English]
 War in social thought : Hobbes to the present / Hans Joas and Wolfgang
  Knöbl ; translated by Alex Skinner.
  p. cm.
 "First published in Germany under the title Kriegsverdrängung: Ein Problem
  in der Geschichte der Sozialtheorie, [published by] Suhrkamp Verlag,
  Frankfurt am Main, 2008."
 Includes bibliographical references and index.
 ISBN-13: 978-0-691-15084-0 (cloth : alk. paper)
 ISBN-10: 0-691-15084-2 (cloth : alk. paper) 1. War and
  society. 2. Sociology—History—19th century. 3. Sociology—History—
  20th century. I. Knöbl, Wolfgang, 1963– II. Skinner, Alex. III. Title.
 HM554.J6313 2013
  303.6'6—dc23   2012005612

British Library Cataloging-in-Publication Data is available

This work is published with support from the Max Weber Center for
Advanced Cultural and Social Studies at the University of Erfurt, the Albion
Small fund of the Sociology Department at the University of Chicago, and the
University of Göttingen.

This book has been composed in Sabon

Printed on acid-free paper ∞

Printed in the United States of America

 10 9 8 7 6 5 4 3 2 1

CONTENTS

PREFACE

In 2009 WE PUBLISHED a book called *Social Theory*, which attempts to provide a comprehensive overview of developments in sociological theory and adjacent fields in the German-, English-, and French-speaking worlds since the Second World War. Our latest joint effort is another book of theory and history of thought. This book goes much further back in history but has a narrower thematic focus. We are concerned here with the history of social theorizing on war and peace. The period in question extends from the early modern revolution in thinking about political issues in the work of Thomas Hobbes to the immediate present. There was of course an extensive philosophical, theological, and historiographical discourse on war and peace before Hobbes. By beginning with Hobbes, however, we are following a well-founded convention common within philosophy and the social sciences, one evident in the work of authors from Leo Strauss to Talcott Parsons. Our account revolves around the development of sociological theory, though supplemented by consideration of those thinkers whose writings—whatever their specific disciplinary affiliation—have exercised and continue to exercise a great influence on the development of sociology and the social sciences. We have not been concerned to achieve encyclopedic completeness, but we have tried to write a coherent narrative presenting a history of theory rather than the history of a discipline.

The key justification for our project is that, particularly when it comes to the topic of war and peace, we can fully comprehend and evaluate arguments only in their historical contexts. A historical account enables us to observe current assumptions and conclusions, as it were, *in statu nascendi*. We are not advocating a historical reductionism here, as if every contemporary idea were merely a lingering echo of classical thinking. But the practice of analyzing arguments in context helps us take a step back and gain perspective when thinking about the present.

We decided to organize the mass of relevant material on an essentially chronological basis. One alternative would have been to structure our account around paradigms, whether still emerging or with a lengthy tradition often extending over vast stretches of time (such as "power-political realism"). We decided against this because it would have forced us to indulge in numerous schematizations and repetitions; it is seldom possible to confine the most interesting thinkers within the clear-cut boundaries of "paradigms."

Like our previous joint effort, this book too is based partly on academic courses;[1] in this case, political motifs play a greater role. But we should mention that the origins of this book project also lie in a plan partially pursued but eventually abandoned. Years ago we made the decision to write a better and more comprehensive version of Günther Wachtler's (1983) commendable but diminutive volume with its brief excerpts from important social scientific analyses of the armed forces. The introduction to this planned volume grew exponentially, far beyond our original intentions; we now present it, in expanded form, as a publication in its own right. Both authors have already published various texts on parts of this history. We have taken the liberty of drawing on our earlier work for some of the passages in this new book. This applies especially to passages from Hans Joas's book *War and Modernity* (2003), though there the history of theory was just one motif among others and the focus was on the relationship between the experiences that constitute values and experiences of violence; it applies also to the introduction by Wolfgang Knöbl and Gunnar Schmidt to their jointly edited volume *Die Gegenwart des Krieges* (2000, The Presence of War) and the essay by Wolfgang Knöbl on the paradoxes of markets in violence: "Krieg als Geschäft" (2006b, War as Business).

We have sought to highlight one *leitmotiv* of our history of the relationship between social thought and war by using a term not used before as far as we know, namely the "suppression of war." This choice of term is rooted in the observation that throughout the period examined here—from Hobbes to Habermas as it were—wars are often constitutive of theory construction, as the informative background to ideas, yet they do not appear in theories themselves at all or only to a small extent. This at least raises the suspicion that there is a mechanism at work here of the kind described by Sigmund Freud. According to him, frightening and threatening experiences perceived as negative are the very ones the conscious mind is likely to shut out—without robbing them of their potency. As our account shows, wars and periods of escalating tensions are often times of intensive interpretive production, featuring a highly positive mythologization of "us" in contrast to an equally negative mythologization of "them." Once hostilities have abated, these interpretations are often discarded or denied with much shame. This may apply to the relevant thinkers and scholars themselves or to their successors and admirers. In any case, wars represent a special affective challenge to our thinking, to which people often react with strategies of avoidance or mythologization or with historical self-consolation, as when a particular war is interpreted as the last that will be waged before the rise of a peaceful world.

But it would be a misunderstanding of our choice of terminology to imagine that we wish to psychoanalyze theory production. We are neither qualified nor motivated to do so. We will not be tracing the consequences of the suppression of war in the work of those authors in which it is most strikingly evident. Our focus is on the thematization of war, whatever marginal or distorted forms this may take. In-depth exploration of how social theory has approached the topic of war over the centuries can and should contribute to overcoming the "suppression of war" and to making the contemporary social sciences more realistic in this regard.

This book, originally published in German in 2008, has been slightly revised and expanded for the English-language edition. The Freiburg Institute for Advanced Studies (FRIAS, School of History), at which both authors are presently fellows, has offered excellent working conditions that have made it easy for us to complete that work.

Hans Joas
Wolfgang Knöbl
Freiburg im Breisgau, Germany
January 2012

1

Introduction

IF WE SURVEY post-1945 sociology, which has claimed for itself chief if not sole responsibility for the field of social theory, it is striking how little it has been influenced by violence and war. This pattern applies both to the recent violent past, in other words the era of world wars and state-organized mass murder that ended in 1945, and to the dangers of the contemporary era, by which we mean both the tensions between the two superpowers during the Cold War and the unstable international situation of the early twenty-first century. Neighboring subjects or analytical approaches, such as the theory of international relations or interdisciplinary conflict and peace studies, have produced important studies on states' capacity for peace and the stability of the global power system (Galtung 1996; Senghaas 2001). But these studies had very little impact on the overall development of social theory. A truly in-depth engagement with the problems of war or the threat of war that might have driven theoretical developments is absent both from the oeuvre of Talcott Parsons, the most influential sociologist during the first few decades after the Second World War, and from the grand theories of the 1970s, 1980s, and 1990s. Authors such as Jürgen Habermas and Niklas Luhmann in Germany and Pierre Bourdieu and Alain Touraine in France all produced a more or less systematic theory of society without seriously examining the problem of war and associated phenomena. This absence is all the more remarkable given that war undoubtedly played a formative role in their biographies. There are exceptions. In early postwar sociology, the key figure here is Raymond Aron and later, above all, Anthony Giddens (1985), who produced a comprehensive social theory at around the same time as the previously mentioned French and German authors, in which historical analyses of war and collective violence played a major role. But Giddens quite abruptly lost sight of this topic in the early 1990s. Surprisingly, then, the vast majority of past and present theorists—even if they attempted to produce a systematic interpretation of "modernity"—have almost always sidestepped the phenomenon of war, either completely or to a great extent. All too often, if they show any interest at all in historical analyses rather than restricting themselves to snapshots of society or cursory diagnoses of the contemporary world, they approach the history of the past few centuries as a more or less linear process of differentiation and rationalization, as if social change had always been a matter of peaceful if not harmonious progress, as if modernity hadn't been characterized by repeated phases of large-scale violence between states (see Knöbl/Schmidt 2000).

In brief, most contemporary social theory has failed to adequately express the internal contradictions, the Janus face, of the modern era. A substantial number of social scientists are still caught up in the peaceful-utopian mood of the European Enlightenment and continue to dream the "dream of a non-violent modernity" (Joas 2003). From this perspective, it is easy to dismiss wars as extreme exceptions, as temporary disturbances in the civilizational equilibrium. What are the reasons for this blindness of contemporary sociology and, above all, social theory with regard to war or—more generally—to violence?

It is no doubt significant in this context that violence, whether within societies or between states, has *never* been a central topic within the discipline. Certainly, the founders and classical figures of sociology referred to the causes, course, and impact of wars, class struggles, or other violent conflicts in their commentaries on current affairs and historical surveys— but the relationship between these commentaries and the systematic core of their theories is mostly quite unclear. They always paid far more attention to economic, social, and political inequality than to the phenomena of violence in general and war in particular. Even the legitimate institutions of the state monopoly on violence (police and armed forces) received fairly scant attention, which is remarkable in view of their size and significance in the age of the greatest rivalry between nation-states and massive social conflicts on the cusp of the twentieth century. It is this past lack of interest that has resulted in the theoretical problems of the present. While criminology and the sociology of deviant behavior have become established research fields, with notable findings on *individual* violence, far too little attention continues to be paid to the genesis and forms of *collective* and *state* violence (of whatever kind), and thus we find the greatest theoretical shortcomings here as well. Analyses of collective violence are often plagued by the misleading application of models presenting the genesis of individual violence and tend to fluctuate between rationalistic and irrationalistic overstatement. Whereas some authors attempt to understand violence as an instrument coolly selected and deployed to further the interests of a nation or class, a phenomenon about which we can say little beyond noting its instrumentality, others view violence solely as the collapse of all social order, the consequence of a loss of normative orientation and individual rationality (for an excellent survey, see Pettenkofer 2010). Dramatic public events such as the racial unrest in the United States during the 1960s did lead to a temporary increase in scholarly interest and to solid reports by expert commissions; and it is true that recently some authors (mostly from the field of historical sociology) have produced theoretically ambitious studies of the genocidal violence that has proliferated since the 1990s (see, e.g., Mann 2005). Yet just as the public, and social scientists, quickly lost interest in the commissions' findings in the past, even a broad social theoretical interest in genocidal violence or the so-called New Wars is likely to tail off again rapidly as soon as other phenomena become the flavor of the month. The deeply anchored relevance structures of sociology have tended to obstruct engagement with the topic of collective violence and will likely continue to do so in future.

There are good reasons to believe that this peculiar apportioning of attention is due to the Western social sciences' attachment to the worldview of liberalism. There is of course no such thing as liberalism in the singular; we would probably be best advised to refer to a family of "liberalisms." Nonetheless it is fair to say that in this worldview violent internal conflicts and especially wars inevitably appeared as relics of an era nearing its end, an era not yet illuminated by the Enlightenment (Williams 2006). Early liberalism regarded contemporary wars as a consequence of the aristocrats' martial spirit or despots' mood swings, and even the First World War was perceived by American liberal intellectuals of the day as a sign of European backwardness in comparison with American modernity. The martial spirit of the aristocracy, and despotism, were themselves considered remnants of primitive developmental stages of humanity; civilized life should also be a civil life in which martial characteristics and needs are not merely prohibited by religion and morality, but genuinely toned down and alleviated, or redirected into sporting and economic competition ("le doux commerce"). Although this might not quite amount to an age of nonviolence, enlightened liberals at least seemed to discern the path ahead and the steps that must be taken in order to achieve a perfectly rational order. Just as torture, including its publicly celebrated forms, must be eliminated from the field of criminal justice, so must war and all forms of violence against individuals and things vanish from modern—in other words, bourgeois—society. In the modernization theory of the period after 1945, nonviolent conflict resolution even became part of the definition of modernity. Thus, in this worldview, the sharp rejection of violence goes hand in hand with a certain downplaying of its presence. As liberals kept their eyes fixed firmly on the bright future to come, they looked on the bad old ways, now on their way out, with impatience, and without much real interest. The theories of globalization so fashionable at present, incidentally, have often simply adopted certain premises of the old modernization theory (see Knöbl 2007, 54ff.); they too see the occurrence of conflicts and wars merely as a sign of a lack of cosmopolitanism, and there is therefore no need to subject them to further scrutiny.

Even classical Marxism is a descendant of the liberal worldview when it comes to this faith in the future. Its exponents, it is true, emphasized the violent enforcement of the capitalist mode of production, the unrelenting material constraints concealed behind freely made contracts, and the class rule underlying the equality of individuals. So it didn't weigh heavily on their conscience that class rule could probably be overcome only by violent means or that, even well after the victory of the revolution, the "dictatorship of the proletariat" would have to suppress its opponents by force. But, in a sense, classical Marxism merely pushed the liberal worldview one era further: *after* the violence-necessitating global upheavals, Marxists envisaged the rise of a social order with no place for violence—in the shape of the universal and free association of producers. Thus, for Marxism, the end of violent social conflicts would ultimately result from the disappearance of all divergent interests in a totally just, spontaneously self-regulating system. As all wars or ethnic conflicts were understood as the expression of class contradictions, they would vanish when class conflicts came to an end.

Since the nineteenth century, then, (Western) social theory has largely been characterized by fundamental and deep-seated liberal assumptions, as a result of which violence has been ignored. Examination of the topic of war in the modern era—and thus the unavoidable questioning of those fundamental assumptions—is bound, therefore, to result in theoretical revisions and reorientations. It is also clear that getting to grips with forms of international violence is not something we might safely leave to the subdiscipline of "military sociology" and thus "exoticize" with respect to its significance to social theory. Rather, we can expect detailed consideration of the topic of war to advance the discipline's *theoretical* development, or at least to provide pointers to the construction of a more empirically convincing sociological theory and theory of modernity. For if we fail to take account of war, we can understand neither the constitution of modernity through the *nation-state*—rather than transnational processes—nor many of the social and cultural changes that have occurred in the modern age. Revolutions, shifts in class structures, and the extension and universalization of rights or upheavals in artistic and aesthetic fields are phenomena that have often been very closely bound up with the consequences of wars. Ignoring the question of the role played by military conflicts in the genesis and form of modernity inevitably results in sociological blind spots. Wars, which will not, presumably, be disappearing any time soon, can then be understood—as liberal theorists have suggested time and again—merely as a barbaric relic, as the "relapse" of civilized societies into cultural stages believed long since overcome rather than a *constitutive* element of the modern age, as momentous events that *change* the course of history. If sociology continues to argue in this way, if it fails to grasp the significance of wars and continues to suppress them, it will be squandering major opportunities to analyze the contemporary era—with far-reaching consequences for the future of the discipline.

So war is a field well worth researching, especially from a theoretical standpoint. But why should examination of the *history* of social theory be such a promising source of insight if (as indicated above) since its foundation sociology has never seemed to get very far with the topic of war? The answer begins to emerge from the following facts. The discipline, it is true, has never featured a stable and long-standing focus on "war" comparable to that on "social inequality," for example. Yet it has produced individual analyses here and there that are worth looking at if we want to understand why the social sciences in general and sociology in particular, with all their blind spots, have become what they are—but especially if we are in search of ideas that might still be a source of inspiration today. Such analyses are not simply sitting there ripe for the picking; there is no canon of classical texts on war and peace by social theorists, let alone genuine sociologists, that would provide a rapid and representative overview of the field. If we want to uncover *this* aspect of the sociological inheritance, we really have to look for it, setting off along seemingly remote paths as well as those that lead deep into the prehistory of social theory; only then will we understand why modern-day social scientists answer questions about war and peace just as they do. Four conceptual or methodological remarks are necessary at this point in order to avoid misunderstandings from the outset.

1. We quite consciously do *not* refer to "sociology" or "social sciences" in the title of this book. Instead, we use the terms "social thought" and "social theory." This choice of terminology has at least two consequences. "Social theory" (see Joas/Knöbl 2009, ix ff.) refers to systematic reflection on social realities and putative regularities of social life; but there is also an element of (critical) theoretical strategy to the term, which was after all coined and deployed toward the end of the nineteenth century (in the Anglo-American world) as a means of questioning overt and covert utilitarian premises in the social sciences. Social theory and—with an even broader meaning—social thought are thus essentially the analysis of social action, social order, and social change (1ff.); at the same time, such analysis inevitably comes up against normative questions, and those engaged in it are compelled to take some kind of position on these questions. This is plainly apparent, for example, in the "genre" of sociological analyses of the contemporary world (such as theories of modernity). All of this means (to turn to those consequences we mentioned) that, *first,* examination of the relationship between social theory and war must be both wide-ranging and focused. It must be wide-ranging because ideas about social action, social order, and social change on the one hand and war on the other were never limited to just one discipline. Analyses of these things have been produced (and are produced still) within economics and political science, history and philosophy—though we should bear in mind that before the nineteenth century disciplinary boundaries were blurred anyway. In what follows, therefore, we are not concerned to keep strictly within the confines of the discipline of sociology, though we are both sociologists. We feel that debates on who is or is not a genuine sociological pioneer are quite unhelpful: sociology is certainly active in the domain of social theory but is not alone there. So we discuss a number of authors not usually counted among the subject's ancestral lineage. Our approach is inter- or transdisciplinary and thus "wide-ranging" in the sense of a "post-disciplinary history of disciplines" (Joas 1999a). *Second,* however, the notion of "social theory" compels us to focus our attention. Because we are concerned with the abstract problems of action, order, and change, we are not interested in every social scientific analysis ever published on the topic of war: detail-rich findings by military sociologists on the ethnic or class composition of ground forces are of as little interest

to us here as analyses of key players' decision-making behavior in crisis situations by international relations scholars. Only those research findings, observations, and reflections that touch on the field of social theory, defined in abstract terms above, are of relevance to us here, which is why we feel free to ignore large swathes of the social scientific literature on war. We do discuss a fair number of thinkers of the seventeenth and eighteenth centuries in particular who are also key figures in social philosophy and/or political philosophy. But we believe that our social theory focus on the problems of action, order, and change provides new insights into the often quite peculiar highways and byways of thinking on war and peace. If we therefore opt not to consider certain issues or adopt a different perspective, this is not a matter—to use Max Weber's terms—of a value judgment (*Werturteil*) but merely a value relation (*Wertbeziehung*); the problems with which we are concerned are simply different from those dealt with in parts of the literature or the various disciplines mentioned above.

2. This should also make it clear that our intention here is not to put forward a novel social theory that is "sensitive to war." Our project is reconstructive and thus far more modest. Of course, there may be implications for social theory. As our jaunt through the history of social theories on war will show, attempts to trace war back to single factors (whether premodern values, economic interests, or actors' irrational actions) have always been doomed to failure. It is instead those theoretical approaches that eschewed historical teleologies or overly simplistic models of action that have proved closer to reality. We might put it like this. Reflections on war and peace throughout history not only feature arguments of remarkable contemporary relevance that indicate why some of the models of peace and strategies for avoiding war much discussed at present—whether they refer to the peace-promoting effects of democracy or global trade—should be viewed with skepticism; analysis of the debates on war also opens our eyes to the whole range of human motives for action and the complexity of processes of social change, enabling insights that deserve greater emphasis within contemporary social theory (see Joas/Knöbl 2009).

This brings us to the question of the relationship between our project and recent efforts within the discipline of international relations to forge links with sociology, with some referring to a "social theory of international politics" and "sociological turn" (Wendt 2010, 20) in this context. The point of departure for this shift toward sociology is the insight that proceeding solely on "realist" or "neorealist" premises, in other words

assuming the rationality of state actors in the face of an allegedly anarchic state system, is very unlikely to further advance our understanding
(for an overall survey, see Menzel 2001). So a species of thought enriched
by institutionalism, constructivism, and cultural theory has now arrived
in international relations, and as a result the normative premises and
values of actors *in* institutions have received increasing emphasis. It remains doubtful, however, whether this opening and sociologization of the
theory of international relations has gone far enough. Has full account
really been taken of the wealth of action motives discussed in social theory? Or have international relations scholars, while making reference to
the institutional and cultural shaping of actors and their intentions, focused on simple alternatives such as "instrumentally rational vs. value
rational action" or dichotomies such as "materialism vs. idealism," "structure vs. action," or "individualism vs. holism" (see Wendt 2010), thus precipitately narrowing the debate? In addition, for disciplinary reasons, even
theorists of international relations that see themselves as close to sociology tend to view "domestic factors" in the formation of state identities as
the concern of other disciplines (Wendt 2010, 11), leading to the neglect
of key issues in social theory—such as social order and social change.

Remarkably enough, similar questions can also be posed regarding
sociologists' attempts to move closer to international relations. Here, it is
chiefly authors in the field of historical sociology who have striven to incorporate ideas from international relations (see Hobden 1998; Hobson
2000; Sindjoun 2002; Hobden/Hobson 2002). This move, however, has
also failed to go far enough. What these authors have taken up, first and
foremost, are "realist" positions and thus ones that favor an instrumentally rational model of action; as a result, they have in fact fallen behind
the efforts currently being made to sociologize international relations
(Hobson 2000, 181ff.; Knöbl 2011). We believe, therefore, that only a
thorough analysis of the history of thinking about war can cast light on
these foreshortened efforts, that it is only by reconstructing this substantial, though sometimes half-hidden legacy of social theory that we can lay
the foundations for the construction of empirically adequate theories.

3. Our interests here are limited in another sense as well. However
narrowly or broadly the social sciences may be defined and however
great the theoretical aspirations that are linked with our historical exploration—what we are doing here does not come close to being a comprehensive discourse analysis of war. But because a young German historian
has taken on this hugely ambitious task more or less concurrently with

our own efforts here, it may be helpful to make a few remarks on how our aims relate to his.

We are referring to Jörn Leonhard's extensive study on the interpretation of war and definition of the nation in Europe und the United States between 1750 and 1914 (Leonhard 2008). In contrast to many authors influenced by Michel Foucault, his discourse analysis is not conceived as the mere "observation" of texts and their structures, as if it were possible to rise above the specific arguments in the source texts without adopting any sort of position on them. For him, discourses are relations "between speakers and addressees concerned with the appropriation of experience" (18). These relations are of course facilitated or limited by structural parameters but still retain their core communicative quality. A discourse analysis of this kind must address the arguments themselves. In this sense it also differs from conceptual history, as it deals not only with specific concepts or conceptual fields but with the interplay of perceptions and experiences, their interpretation and how they serve to guide actions.

A historical discourse analysis of this kind must attempt not only to interpret revealing texts but to attain a representative material basis. A discursive history must therefore systematically seek out all texts relevant to the selected topic. This includes not only books and journal articles but also newspapers, leaflets, sermons, and much more besides. Such a history must develop a high degree of awareness of the mediality of these texts, of anticipated readers and the constraints of the selected genre. It must pay attention to any national peculiarities the material may contain while always bearing in mind how much various national developments are mutually entangled. In European history especially, the interactions between "nations"—if we can use the term at all without lapsing into anachronism—has been intensive. Perceptions have often been mutual in character; the roots of many instances of self-definition have lain in a conscious need for one group to mark itself off from others; and the processing of experiences has rarely remained limited to those immediately involved. But however interested we may be in the diversity of national paths, we must not neglect the internal plurality of thought in the different nations.

Approaching things as Leonhard does, it becomes evident that if we want to grasp the true dynamics of the (always situational) processing of war experiences and their translation into political action, schematic descriptions of different national attitudes to war are quite inadequate. Just one example will suffice to illustrate this. The intensity of war experiences tends to result in the self-sacralization of the combatants, as well as the collective that faces annihilation. But this self-sacralization must always be related to living religious traditions and their interpretive offerings. In France, for example, this took the form of the militant anti-Christian self-sacralization of the nation, though there were always other forms at large in France as well. In Germany, the very struggle against Napoleon was stylized as a holy war, and the idea of a Protestant legitimation of the German nation was born. In Great Britain, the dominant self-image from the nineteenth century was of a culturally superior nation called to a global civilizing mission. In the United States, a universalist sense of mission was developed out of Protestant-Christian and classical republican motives (Leonhard 2008, 823f.).

This example demonstrates that even the most sophisticated scholarly contributions to the discourse of war can never be entirely detached from their context of origin. In this sense, the theory-oriented thematic history that we are presenting here and a historical discourse analysis are complementary. In the spirit of history of science, we will constantly be examining the conditions constitutive of theories; conversely, it is clear that a discourse analysis that turns, as Leonhard's study does, into a history of arguments cannot entirely eschew consideration of the persuasiveness of the arguments transmitted in historical texts.

4. A quick glance at the contents page reveals that we are dealing in some detail with the "early history" of social theories on war. Our reconstruction does not begin with Thucydides, as it might conceivably have done, but with Thomas Hobbes. But even this starting point is quite early compared, for example, with reconstructions of the disciplinary history of sociology, which often start with the subject's classical figures and thus the nineteenth century, generally treating earlier authors as immature precursors. Our point of departure is a different one, at least with respect to the topic of "social theory and war"—and this is mostly due to the following consideration. If liberalism played a decisive role in the formation or perhaps even *de*formation of social theories on war, then we are faced with the pressing question of what form such thinking took *before* the liberal age (if there really was a "liberal century," then it was surely the nineteenth)—in other words, what liberalism strengthened, neglected, or marginalized. It is in fact the case that our reconstruction of social theories of war places significant emphasis on the era of the Enlightenment; here, as we shall see, in an often covert but nonetheless exact manner, arguments were developed for the first time that were both extended

and suppressed by the liberalism of the nineteenth century and which often reappear only much later in social theoretical debates. Our aim here, if you will, is to satisfy the demand made by Ernst Cassirer in his reconstruction of the *Philosophy of the Enlightenment* (1932)—that we grasp and take seriously the internal contradictions, the highly disparate strands of the Enlightenment era, because this is the only way to gain an adequate understanding of the debates of subsequent centuries. Especially in the case of social theories on war, it would be wrong to imagine that the Enlightenment era merely saw an imperfect and ultimately failed groping toward insights that were only fully expressed later by the classical figures of sociology.

The "postdisciplinary history of disciplines"—as we understand it—is aware that the past of the social sciences and humanities is more than just a dumping ground of obsolete ideas, which is why we should be very hesitant about using the term "progress" when writing such history. The irony in this case is that examination of the Enlightenment era, one supposedly so obsessed with progress, makes it particularly clear how impossible it is to write the story of social theory's engagement with war as a history of progress. This is apparent in the next chapter ("War and Peace before Sociology: Social Theorizing on Violence from Thomas Hobbes to the Napoleonic Wars")—which brings us to a brief survey of the structure of this book. This chapter provides an overview of the key arguments in the debate on war and peace carried on during this period between philosophers, political economists, and political thinkers. Anyone who studies this era, which was bookended by the names of Thomas Hobbes and Carl von Clausewitz, will be surprised by at least two things. *First*, it is revealing that those doctrines that defined the later discipline of international relations were already being expressed in a mature and differentiated form. Thomas Hobbes anticipated the key arguments of the "realist" school of foreign policy as brilliantly as Montesquieu articulated the thinking of the later neo-institutionalism; hopes of the pacifying effects of trade (a central doctrine of the later liberal thought of the nineteenth century), based on utilitarian premises, and Immanuel Kant's ideas on the close relationship between a republican constitution, or the rule of law, and peace were both born in this era. *Second*, and this is the other surprise, debates were carried on in this historical era that were viewed as over and done with in the later nineteenth century—yet they are of much interest from a social theory perspective and help shed light on the narrowing of political and social thought that took place in the nineteenth and twentieth centuries, with substantial consequences for the relationship between social theory and war.

The third chapter ("The Long Peace of the Nineteenth Century and the Birth of Sociology") goes on to show how the progressive optimism nourished by liberal doctrines gradually began to take hold, though this was not a unilinear process either. Toward the end of the eighteenth and during the first third of the nineteenth century, utilitarians such as Jeremy Bentham and later James and John Stuart Mill were already singing the praises of free trade and its peace-promoting effects (though, it should be emphasized, this particular "song" often featured sharp criticisms of colonialism). This laid the foundations for at least one strand of liberal thought in the nineteenth century, on which early "sociologists" such as Auguste Comte and Herbert Spencer, with their sharp typological opposition between a premodern bellicose and a peaceful modern (industrial) society, could then build. At the same time, however, we should not forget that "liberal thought" could also take quite different forms, by no means always in favor of free trade and by no means always anticolonial or anti-imperial. What is more, despite the hegemonic status of liberal doctrines, other views were always present beneath the surface. We are thinking here not so much of Marxism, which, as underlined above, shared certain premises of classical liberalism. What we have in mind are very different authors in a variety of countries, who—whatever their motivation—incorporated arguments into their theories that could lead to a high regard for battle and war, to, in other words, a bellicist position. Bellicist thought of this kind is to be found in the work of Hegel at the beginning of this long nineteenth century as well as that of William Graham Sumner at its end. This bellicism prefigures the interpretation of the First World War by those who lived through that great seminal catastrophe of the twentieth century, during which (at least temporarily) war became a dominant theme for sociologists and social theorists—though from a very specific perspective.

The fourth chapter ("The Classical Figures of Sociology and the Great Seminal Catastrophe of the Twentieth Century") deals with the intellectual prehistory and history of what was later called the First World War. Toward the end of the nineteenth and in the early twentieth century, German social scientists in particular had already attempted to theorize the connection between war and capitalism, or war and democracy, with authors such as Werner Sombart and Otto Hintze playing the leading role here. One might have assumed that these promising approaches would have been further advanced during and by the war; but this was not in fact the case. Many European and American intellectuals, including, incidentally, most of the classical figures of sociology, did feel called to give their views on the question of war. In many cases, however, their writings did them little credit. How easily social theory can be led astray is plain for all to see in many of the statements made at the time, in that the bellicist arguments already to be found in the nineteenth century were often shamelessly deployed to denounce the enemy. Just a few prominent social theorists such as Durkheim, Tönnies, and Max Weber managed to exercise a degree of self-restraint. On the other hand, however, this period saw the appearance of serious analyses, including the first comparative interpretations, such as those of Thorstein Veblen, that inquired into the specific social causes of the war that Germany had started; Marxist interpretations of imperialism were developed further (by Lenin, among others), and these in turn were criticized not much later, by Joseph Schumpeter in 1919 for example, and attempts began—quite hesitantly, but still—to analyze the societal consequences of war, with Emil Lederer being the outstanding figure here.

As chapter 5 ("Sociology and Social Theory from the End of the First World War to the 1970s") shows, however, social theory's engagement with the phenomenon of war (however critically we may view it), which had already begun before the First World War, did not continue in any substantial way after 1918. War quickly vanished from the radar of those subjects in which social theories find their home. Anyone who looks at the period of around fifty years between the Peace of Versailles and the beginning of the policy of détente between the two superpowers of the United States and Soviet Union in the 1970s will be amazed to discover that the suppression of war within social theory is more or less constant. Regardless of regime, national context, public mood, wars, or other outbreaks of violence: the social science disciplines always managed to stonewall any inclusion of war in social theory. War was unable to awaken any general theoretical interest within the individual subjects. It was always isolated figures, if not outsiders, who formed the exception here. It is to them that we must generally turn to find texts on war of relevance to social theory. Reading the relevant social scientific journals, meanwhile, gets us almost nowhere.

In Germany between the world wars it was constitutional law scholar Carl Schmitt, who was well to the right politically, who provided the most provocative ideas on the problem of war; in France, it was the work of Roger Caillois, a member of the theoretically idiosyncratic, Paris-based

"Collège de Sociologie," who took on the topic in a theoretically innovative way; and in the United States, it was initially political émigrés, once again outsiders, who—like Hans Speier—produced the first significant studies of militarism and "total war." When military sociology then boomed in the United States during the Second World War, it seemed as though social theorists' interest in war might become institutionalized. Again, though, appearances were deceptive. Military sociology saw itself as an almost exclusively *applied* sociological specialism that was scarcely in a position to reflect on war to the enrichment of social theory, though there were exceptions to this rule (see, for instance, the work of Morris Janowitz and Edward Shils). Paradoxical though it sounds, it may even be that the very establishment of military sociology caused sociology in general, and sociological theory in particular, to turn away from war once again, as it was assumed that this topic was being dealt with adequately by that subdiscipline and serious theoretical efforts were thus unnecessary.

So it is no surprise that after 1945 the experience of war or the possibility of nuclear annihilation rarely formed the focus of social theoretical debates. Again, just a few individuals tackled the subject, though without managing to say anything really *new*. The key figures here are Raymond Aron and C. Wright Mills, whose work is of relevance to social theories of war and peace and who, alongside a small number of outstanding authors in the field of military sociology (which continued to exist in a state of isolation), actually regarded war as relevant to social theory in the first place. Otherwise, the dominance of modernization theory and its optimistic worldview obstructed any serious engagement with the phenomenon of war during this period.

This neglect of war came to an end in the 1970s, which saw the meteoric rise of historical sociology in the Anglo-American world. Here, the connections between war and modernity were explored in systematic fashion. However—as chapter 6 ("After Modernization Theory: Historical Sociology and the Bellicose Constitution of Western Modernity") reveals—its insights remained sealed off within the subdiscipline of "historical sociology," which never really managed to rid itself of this status and struggled to make its findings known within the discursive framework of the discipline as a whole. Outside of Britain and the United States, in any event, historical sociology never managed to play much of a role. As far as Germany and France (as well as other European countries) are concerned, sociologists there either never really took a historical approach (Germany) or adopted a historical perspective molded by the dominant figure of Michel Foucault, a perspective from which war was of no special interest.

This was evident in the debate on the "democratic peace" that took off in the 1980s and early 1990s, the debaters (especially in Germany) being almost exclusively philosophers and political scientists; this was a debate of great relevance to social theory, though it was carried on for the most part without the involvement of sociologists (see chapter 7, "After the East-West Conflict: Democratization, State Collapse, and Empire Building"). It remains to be seen (and this is the focus of the final section of chapter 7), whether the recent discussion of so-called new wars and the peace-stabilizing functions of "imperia" can stimulate a renewed turn to the topic of war on the part of social theorists.

The book ends with some remarks on what we see as a convincing conception of enduring peace and on the need to move beyond monothematic diagnoses of the contemporary world and of social change.

War and Peace before Sociology

SOCIAL THEORIZING ON VIOLENCE FROM THOMAS
HOBBES TO THE NAPOLEONIC WARS

REFLECTIONS ON WAR AND PEACE, and even the beginnings of *social theories* about them, did not of course appear only in the modern era (for an excellent survey, see Johnson 1987). They stretch much further back into the past. So there is some justification for the claim that such works as Thucydides' (460–396 BC) *History of the Peloponnesian War* or Plato's (427–347 BC) *Republic* already featured a large number of ideas of great importance to early modern European philosophy (Münkler 1987, 24f.). But in searching for the forerunners of social theoretical ideas on war and peace, there are good reasons to resist going all the way back to antiquity. We should instead concentrate on the period since the sixteenth century, given that the classical figures of sociology and many of those nineteenth- and twentieth-century authors whom we might broadly describe as social theorists drew crucial inspiration from this early modern thought.

It was during the time of the emerging European state system and absolutism, that is, the period lying roughly between the sixteenth and eighteenth centuries, that authors such as Franciscus Suarez (1548–1617), Albericus Gentilis (1552–1608), Hugo Grotius (1583–1645), and Samuel Pufendorf (1632–94) laid the foundations of European international law, thus establishing a new standard of conduct for interstate relations. This could not have happened without systematic reflection on issues of war and peace (see Münkler 1987, 203–59). British political scientist Hedley Bull is surely right to claim that three competing schools of thought have been crucial to the theory of the modern state system: "the Hobbesian or realist tradition, which views international politics as a state of war; the Kantian or universalist tradition, which sees at work in international politics a potential community of mankind; and the Grotian or internationalist tradition, which views international politics as taking place within an international society" (1977, 24). These three traditions of thought undoubtedly molded all subsequent accounts of the nature and dynamics of the international state system and thus also influenced the behavior of those in power. And Bull is right to insist that the ideas found in Grotius's *On the Law of War and Peace* (1625) have made a particularly important contribution to the development of international law and to the form of modern-day international intergovernmental organizations. Nonetheless, the point of departure for *social theoretical* ideas was Hobbes's *Leviathan* (1651).[1] If we remain for now within the categories put forward by Bull, thinkers clearly moved away from the realist position of a Hobbes toward the universalist stance of a Kant—while neglecting the intermediate position of Grotius. More cautiously, we might state that they moved toward liberal stances in the widest sense, though, it is important to emphasize, this development was anything but inevitable or unilinear. So social theory—and not just the kind that dealt with war—began in response to or reacted against a thinker whose writings were still being used by twentieth-century theorists to argue for a nonliberal power-political realism.

Thomas Hobbes (1588–1679) broke more radically with classical natural law than any other philosopher of his time (Skinner 1966, 314ff.), erecting his philosophy and political theory on strictly individualist premises. The theories of natural law developed by Stoicism and Scholasticism all assumed the existence of a natural and social world governed by a clear normative framework, a world in which individuals are embedded and whose laws they can understand and must obey (see Euchner 1979, 14ff.). Hobbes, meanwhile, rid himself of this notion and now recognized the individual's right to self-preservation as the only natural right. It is not just that references to God fade almost entirely from view within Hobbes's theoretical framework. More important to the social theoretical discussion is the fact that he abandons the idea of the human being's natural sociability, still common in classical natural law. This forces Hobbes, building on an anthropology of mutual indifference (Tuck 2002, 65), to derive social order from the selfish pursuit of individual interests. Hobbes's reduction of the human capacity for action to the realization of passions and interests was quite understandable. As already evident in the work of Grotius, to whom Hobbes owed a great deal, it was possible to believe that the notion of the individual right to self-preservation provided an unquestionable foundation for the construction of a universally recognized ethics. We might describe Hobbes's line of thought here as follows: A readily understandable "minimalist theory of natural rights" (29) would provide solid arguments for the construction of a political community. This would avoid the relativist-skeptical conclusions of the likes of Montaigne (1533–92), conclusions that—at least in the view of Hobbes, writing against the background of the English Civil War—would lead to perpetual ideological conflicts.[2] The construct of the state of nature was intended to demonstrate *more geometrico* how and why those individuals described as selfish might nonetheless agree on a generally accepted order.

So the famous thought experiment in Thomas Hobbes's *Leviathan* (1651) was a key influence as the sociology of war and peace got off the ground. Hobbes posited a state of nature[3] in which each person exclusively pursues his own interests and makes ready use of violence and deception ("force and fraud"), but one in which he faces the ever-present risk of falling victim to violation and deception and can therefore never enjoy his life and property in peace. How was a peaceful and stable social order to emerge from this state of nature? Hobbes's solution was universal submission, motivated by the fear of death, to a strong state or to the will of a generally accepted ruler. This solution now became one of the basic models for modern political thought. As often noted, highly illiberal conclusions were drawn from the premises of a highly individualist or rather atomistic theory. What has gone largely unnoticed, interestingly, is the way in which Hobbes's solution to this problem created a major new problem. Domestic peace might be guaranteed by strong and centralized states—but it is these very states that give rise to the risk of a conflict between leviathans. The consequences of interstate conflicts constitute a new threat to the security of the individual citizen, partially removing the rationale for a strong state, namely the dangers of civil war—if we assume that there might be less risk of conflicts between weak states. Hobbes's own response to this problem—in other words, to the fact that his preferred means of overcoming the state of nature *within* a given society actually brings about the state of nature *between* states—was not entirely consistent. By no means did he disregard the fact of war between states. He used this fact as much more than mere metaphor, namely as empirical evidence that the state of nature he had described was a real-world problem rather than merely a fictitious hypothesis. But while he brought out the explosive domestic significance of this problem like no one before him, he tended to play it down at the intersocietal level, though it must be conceded that for Hobbes interstate behavior certainly ought to obey certain rules (see the interpretation put forward by Willms 1987, 187f.). For as Hobbes underlines in *Leviathan*, states still live "in the condition of a perpetual war, and upon the confines of battle, with their frontiers armed, and cannons planted against their neighbours round about" (Hobbes 1996, 142/43). But the state of nature between states, according to Hobbes, is less dreadful and more readily avoidable than that between individuals. States, he thought, are better able to constrain themselves, such that there is no need for the entire population of a state to take part in a war; states are also stronger than individuals and therefore less concerned with further increasing their power. Military competition between states also "uphold[s] ... the industry of their subjects," which is why "there does not follow from it that misery which accompanies the liberty of particular men" (85). All of this is said to alleviate the dilemma of security between states and to facilitate a state of equilibrium between them.

Whatever we might think of Hobbes's rationale here and whether we still think it valid in the age of total war, it is plain that he envisages a quite different solution to conflicts between states as opposed to those within states. He neither expects the emergence of a centralized world state in an empirical sense nor does he argue in favor of one politically. Instead he advocates the suppression of all domestic efforts toward expansion and the "confining of war to an affair between states" (Koselleck 1988, 44). This, however, is neither a particularly consistent nor a very convincing argument, especially as it takes Hobbes a great deal of effort to disguise the fact that his line of argument clearly shifts when he moves from the domestic to the interstate context:

> Hobbes's concept of peace between states builds on those elements on which the survival strategy of the individual living in the state of nature also depends. All of these elements can be brought down to the common denominator of armed rational distrust, which is rational only in that it recognizes that others are also justified in feeling distrust. For the instrument that *individuals* perceived as inadequate to ensure coexistence in the state of nature must now be sufficient *for the state*, along with other states, to ensure the absence of war. The idea at the core of this concept is to prevent war by making anyone who might attempt to end the war-free state pay such a high price that no one could rationally expect to gain from doing so. So the core idea is mutual deterrence. (Kersting 2002, 176; emphasis added)

In other words: the strategy that obviously did not work between individuals, namely that of deterrence, is supposed to work tolerably well between states, which Hobbes happens to conceive of explicitly as individuals!

Further, the power-political realism that draws on Hobbes conceives of states as coherent actors with clear-cut interests. It is striking how loaded with premises but ultimately unclear this idea actually is. What the interests of a state or large-scale collectivity are, who defines these interests, how this process of definition occurs, which worldviews these interests reflect, and whether power and security are conceived in expansive or defensive terms and are mutually compatible in a given case—all of this remains unresolved. What is clear is that because of the idea of the state of nature and the particular way in which he plotted the supposed route out of the war of all against all, Hobbes (and all subsequent power-political realists followed his lead) was soon to unceremoniously dismiss the topic of just war as well. For if Hobbes refuses to concede that there is any difference, when it comes to the freedom of citizens, between Lucca and Constantinople, between republics and monarchies (according to him the social contract is always and everywhere an identical form of domination devoid of moral connotations, see Hobbes 1996, 142f.), it is only logical for him to present similar arguments about interstate relations. According to Hobbes, a state has every right to do whatever "that man, or assembly that representeth it, shall judge . . . most conducing to [its] benefit" (142)—and that includes waging wars, as long as certain formalities are respected, such as the obligation to comply with treaties. Just as Hobbes, in his initial analysis, reduces the diverse motives, passions, and interests to that of self-preservation, thus leveling out any differences between them, this demoralization also spills over into his view of interstate relations. Here again, we may speak only of interests as such, no longer of justified or unjustified interests (see also Kersting 2002, 177; Hanson 1984).

So however much it may underline its own purchase on reality, this power-political realism, still one of the key theoretical currents within international politics, is by no means a simple reflection of reality.[4] It emerged out of a programmatic demoralization undertaken in a specific historical situation and out of an empirically problematic abstraction from the normative and interpretative character of reality. So it is no surprise that this standpoint was very quickly countered with conceptions that claimed to be not only more optimistic and normatively appealing but also more empirically tenable than power-political realism. From a social theory perspective it is not so much the fact that authors in the period after Hobbes put forward alternative conceptions of how to maintain peace, painted a different picture of the international state system, and placed greater emphasis on the danger of war than did Hobbes that is of key interest. It is primarily the theory and history of the discipline of international relations that must grapple with these aspects. What is more interesting in the present context is that those authors to whom we shall now be turning spurred the development of alternative models of action, and in some cases it was precisely *because of this* that they produced alternative ideas on how to achieve peace. This remark is not intended to imply that authors' theories of social order and ideas on war and peace can always be derived straightforwardly from their concepts of action. Individual authors' processes of reflection were of course more complicated than that; their arguments generally advanced from individual action to an anticipated peaceful or warlike macro-order via a wide variety of intermediate stages. We must not forget, for example, that the thinkers in question all developed their concepts in specific social historical contexts that exercised a profound influence on these concepts. But their social theories of action, order, and change make themselves felt again and again at various points as they develop their arguments. It seems that it is only by decoding these social theories that we can achieve a realistic assessment of what is owed to the "logic" of particular arguments on establishing peace and what is due to the more or less contingent circumstances in which they were formulated.

Regardless of this, it is clear that Hobbes's work threw up a whole number of questions on the problem of peace for subsequent generations of thinkers to struggle with. Their answers by no means always dealt with Hobbesian questions as such, not least because the social historical context was constantly changing. But it is fair to say that Hobbes paved the way for discussions revolving chiefly around the anthropological question of the human capacity for action, the form of relations between subjects and head of state (which had a direct influence on the instruments of military power available to the state), and—in connection with this—the specific features of the international order. However, new questions not anticipated by Hobbes were also raised, so that social theories on war and peace in the eighteenth century were pervaded by both continuities and discontinuities.

■ ■ ■

Eighteenth-century ideas on how to maintain peace can be explained largely in light of the fact that the philosophers and thinkers of this era had a quite different notion of freedom from that found in the work of Hobbes. As mentioned above, Hobbes produced his account of the state of nature on the basis of a radical reworking of natural law: all that remained was the individual right to self-preservation. In light of this, he could reduce human motives for action to the pursuit of self-interest. But the emphasis on "interests" as such was not the radically new aspect of Hobbesian theory. We have already pointed out that in this respect Hobbes borrowed a great deal from Grotius, though we should add—as Johan Heilbron (1998) has shown—that the discourse of interests also had quite different roots (such as Jansenism). The radical thing about Hobbes was that he made self-interest (whether instrumentally rational or driven by blind passions) the *exclusive* motive for action. He thus consciously ignored other forms of social motivation. In solving the problem of the war of all against all in the state of nature, his only option was now to fall back on the "leviathan," vis-à-vis which citizens could assert no rights. And this also explains his thesis that freedom exists in both Lucca and Constantinople—but freedom now understood as the mere absence of mortal terror and the risk of death.

Such ideas were by no means shared by most thinkers of the late seventeenth and eighteenth centuries. They could not reconcile themselves to Hobbes's understanding of freedom (see Pettit 1997, 44; Skinner 1998, 59ff.). Nor were they prepared to declare the pursuit of self-interest the sole criterion informing human action or accept it as an adequate anthropological description of human life. Yet the pursuit of self-interest was increasingly ascribed an outstanding role, particularly in the preservation of peace. This brought a new idea into play that was to become one of the central premises of liberal thinking on war and peace. This complex discursive landscape, which led to the appearance of seemingly highly contradictory motives in the writings of the same thinker, is probably nowhere more evident than in the work of Charles Louis de Secondat, Baron de Montesquieu (1689–1755) (on the "ruptures" in Montesquieu's work, which gave rise to very different interpretations, see the anthology by Carrithers/Coleman, 2002). His ideas were in fact the point of departure for a significant alternative to Hobbesian power-political realism. Montesquieu developed his ideas in contradistinction to Hobbes, as evident even in the first few pages of his great work *The Spirit of the Laws* (1748). In book I, chapter 2, he contradicts Hobbes's account of the state of nature, instead underlining that war is a consequence of human sociation. And for him, war between states was anything but unregulated, in fact being hedged in by positive rules in the form of international law, which is "founded on the principle that the various nations should do to one another in times of peace the most good possible, and in times of war the least ill possible, without harming their true interests" (Montesquieu 1989 [1748], 7). In *Spirit of the Laws*, Montesquieu deals in depth with wars, concluding among other things that international law prohibits wars of annihilation but allows defensive wars and wars of liberation (book X, chs. 2–4). But what is crucial for us here is not the fact that Montesquieu, building on the work of Grotius and others, might be described as one of the forerunners of the institutionalist stream of international relations, but rather the fact that he makes famous a (long-standing) argument that was entirely absent from the work of Hobbes. It was to become crucially important to the later *liberal* conception of peace and then, especially in the nineteenth century, to a nascent sociology. We are referring to the notion of the pacifying effects of trade.

But Montesquieu is anything but a typical liberal, despite the fact that he was later often interpreted as a leading intellectual light of liberalism and democracy with reference to his theory of the division of powers. Montesquieu was loyal to the basic political and social values of the aristocracy (Kondylis 1996, 10); his definition of political freedom has very little to do with social equality or the abolition of privileges; and he made statements to the effect that democracies are not automatically free and consequently that freedom can also be found in other forms of government. Rather than a typical bourgeois liberal, all of this indicates that what we are dealing with here is more of a thinker and pamphletist who argued against absolutist despotism in light of the aristocratic conception of freedom. His arguments, moreover, were deeply influenced by a positive view of the early Roman republic, a view that provided the normative background to his assessment of contemporary developments. This tendency to look to Rome allowed him to produce innovative insights but also forced him to come to conclusions that later authors influenced by him sought to avoid.

Over the past few decades the view has increasingly taken hold that the era of the Enlightenment was anything but a one-dimensional bourgeois project, that it was more than just the age in which property-based individualism (C. B. MacPherson) or an individualist legal discourse broke through.[5] In fact, this era featured a whole number of motifs that build on ancient ideas. Here the (Roman) republic and its virtues were taken as the normative model, thereby defending other ideas of freedom than those associated with the notion of "negative freedom" (see Pettit 1997 and Skinner 1998). This means that trade alone could scarcely be viewed as providing redemption from the many evils of the world, as was subsequently the case in the English utilitarianism of the late eighteenth and especially nineteenth centuries.

The first point to note here is that the implications of trade for peace had rarely been emphasized as strongly as they were in Montesquieu's text. *The Spirit of Laws* contains a brilliant defense of trade of much significance to the politics of peace and to sociology: "No landed aristocrat ever sang its praises more enthusiastically" (Shklar 1987, 107). And Montesquieu does in fact ascribe to trade two astonishing effects (see also Hirschman 1977, 70ff.), the first of which is unintentional and tends to operate gradually and imperceptibly. The laws of trade eliminate prejudices—as traders come into contact with one another—and calm and "perfect mores" (Montesquieu 1989, 338), because the spirit of trade awakens the "feeling for exact justice" (339). To put it a little differently, for Montesquieu trade has a civilizing effect and *unconsciously* strengthens the peaceful impulses of individuals and peoples. But trade also has peaceful implications for human coexistence—and this might be described as Montesquieu's second, basically *utilitarian* argument for the expansion of trade—because two peoples that trade with one another become dependent on one another, and thus recognize that trade is in their own best interest. They will therefore take care not to wage war on one another (ibid.). Here, then, peace is the result of a safeguarding of interests on both sides.[6] In light of this—if one or even both of these arguments were taken seriously—it was possible to imagine a time in which all armed conflict would have disappeared through the expansion of trade. Such expansion could then even be promoted as *the* key means of establishing peace.

But Montesquieu does not go that far—for the reasons indicated above. He was not enough of a bourgeois to see the positive effects of trade in an exclusive and unqualified way. Neither—as his attacks on Hobbes quoted above indicate—was he a Hobbesian content to denormativize the concept of freedom. It is true that Montesquieu praised trade, but not all trade at any cost. Montesquieu's key argument in *The Spirit of Laws* was in principle a relativist one, an awkward one for every Enlightenment liberal, a "subversive" one—as Isaiah Berlin (2001, 148) rightly put it. Montesquieu conceived of societies as purposeful wholes and saw different forms of society and state, *all of which he believed had a right to exist*, as determined by certain inner forces and principles—the monarchy by honor, the aristocracy by restraint, the republic by virtue. And whatever strengthens or weakens the various principles also causes the polity to grow stronger or decline. So Montesquieu discusses the republican form of society against the background of the key principle of virtue. And, in his view, trade as well must be justified in light of this key principle. When he asserts that rather than corrupting, trade in fact encourages moderation, work, and order (Montesquieu 1989, 48), he does so in the context of a discussion of republican virtues. Trade may even promote civic virtues—but only to the extent that it serves to *satisfy people's needs*. Excessive trade on the other hand, trade that leads only to luxury, is of dubious value to citizens' virtuousness and thus tends to be harmful (see Keohane 1972, 388). This also seems to be the reason why Montesquieu was unable to fully develop the argument that trade has a civilizing effect and promotes peace in the way it was developed later in the work of the English liberals of the late eighteenth and nineteenth centuries. For Montesquieu holds virtue in such high esteem that he cannot simply neglect, let alone criticize, such things as the *military* and *martial* virtues of ancient Rome. It is true that Montesquieu often condemned the brutality of the wars waged by the young Roman republic. But, as he also admired the simplicity and uniformity of this form of society, he does not categorically condemn martial virtues (Russo 2002, 114).[7] Montesquieu, then, does not want peace at any cost. Just as trade is to be judged in the context of the virtues, so is peace. So for Montesquieu a republic based on martial virtues is not per se a bad thing that must be eliminated at all costs through specific measures—such as the expansion of trade. This was certainly not a bourgeois-liberal stance.

So ironically Montesquieu's *liberal* reference to the pacifying effect of trade became influential through an author whom we cannot straightforwardly describe as a liberal. But, as Montesquieu's work was hugely successful, it is reasonable to date the beginning of a *liberal* conception of peace to the first half of the eighteenth century, a conception that—as we have seen—rested on two compatible but quite different arguments. Nonetheless, we must be wary of the assumption that liberalism had a clearly defined meaning in the eighteenth century (Pocock 1985a, 111) or that it was a monolithic block in the nineteenth century (Pocock 1985b, 71). The advance of "liberalism" was not so straightforward or rapid, and this applies to its conception of how best to establish peace as well. This is confirmed by Ernst Cassirer's insight, cited earlier, that the era of Enlightenment was more contested than is generally assumed. This was an era characterized by a number of tendencies, *only one* of which pointed the way toward "classical" liberalism. Our wariness of teleological assumptions must extend to both Enlightenment and liberalism.

■ ■ ■

We should keep this last point in mind as our search for a sociology of war and peace brings us to the Scottish moral philosophy that was to have such a great impact. It flourished in the second half of the eighteenth century and developed into a "natural history of society" in this period, forming the seedbed, among other things, for Adam Smith's *Wealth of Nations*, the foundational text of what was later called "political economy" and something of a "Bible" for all later liberals. Many representatives of this intellectual movement have now been forgotten. But four of the key authors can still be counted among the forefathers or classical figures of sociology, philosophy and economics, namely Adam Ferguson (1723–1816), John Millar (1735–1801), David Hume (1711–76), and of course Adam Smith (1723–90).

This temporal and spatial concentration of outstanding philosophical and political-economic thinkers in what was—from a continental perspective—a rather remote region of Europe inspired and continues to inspire interpretive conflicts with far-reaching consequences for the history of ideas. It is in fact impossible to overlook this astonishing spatial concentration of intellectual creativity: "For a period of nearly half a century, from about the time of the Highland rebellion of 1745 until the French Revolution of 1789, the small city of Edinburgh ruled the Western intellect. For nearly fifty years, a city that had for centuries been a byword for poverty, religious bigotry, violence and squalor laid the mental foundations for the modern world" (Buchan 2003, 1; see also Herman 2002).[8] This perhaps overstated but not inaccurate account suggests at least three very different historical interpretations, with significant consequences for the history of social theory and for the history of ideas on war and peace. This account may form the point of departure for a thesis of *discontinuity*: there are good reasons for the assertion that the origins of sociology in fact lie in Scotland rather than France. Raymond Aron's (1965, 13) thesis that Montesquieu was the first modern sociologist is probably less convincing than Werner Sombart's reference to Ferguson as sociology's progenitor (Sombart 1923). This is because, in contrast to Montesquieu's work, the focus of the Scottish Enlightenment (and not just in the work of Ferguson) was not so much on types of political rule whose "essence" must be explained, but on actual social processes. It is not just that Scotland was the setting for the first real attempts to conceptualize social stratification and class formation theoretically and explain them historically. In the works of Smith and Ferguson, for example, social conflicts were concurrently studied in terms of their constitutive significance to societies (see Swingewood 1970, 170ff.; for a critical take, see Hill 1996, 204). The emergence of genuine intimacy in social relations was celebrated by these thinkers, in that it was the market that undid clientelist-feudal ties, thus making space for relations of friendship largely free of self-interest (Silver 1990, 1480f.). So there is undoubtedly some justification for describing Hume and Smith, Ferguson and Millar as the founding fathers of a *novel* way of thinking.

But we might also underline the significance of the Scottish Enlightenment—and this would be the second interpretation—in support of the thesis of *continuity*, because the ideas of Hobbes and Locke were merely *taken further*, subsequently leading to the modern political economy of the nineteenth century. On this view the "Scots" would be important intermediate figures who certainly had some new ideas but ultimately did no more than continue the individualist-liberal project initiated by Hobbes and Locke. This is how the traditional Whig historiography has always attempted to interpret things (for a critical perspective, see Winch 1988, 361).

But neither of these interpretive tendencies seems particularly convincing. There was neither an abrupt rupture nor mere continuity. It is more appropriate to think in terms of a hotchpotch of attempts to preserve tradition on the one hand and intellectual innovation on the other. So what we propose is a thesis of *transformation*. The transformation of traditional ideas under conditions of unprecedented novelty was apparent in this Scottish Enlightenment not least in the treatment of topics such as war and armies. Partly for reasons of theoretical systematicity, however, these topics were the subject of much dispute. For even the work of Adam Smith, that seeming "arch liberal," is pervaded by arguments that point to the previously mentioned "neo-Roman understanding of liberty," to the fact, in other words, that even in the second half of the eighteenth century the ideals of the ancient (Roman) republic were being upheld. We cannot fully understand the work even of the founder of political economy without recourse to the intellectual tradition of "civic humanism" (Pocock 1975). And we must also avoid writing the emergence of a self-confident liberal utilitarianism in the England of the late eighteenth and early nineteenth centuries as a simple story of intellectual progress. It was in fact a process of narrowing and suppressing, for a variety of reasons, arguments formerly considered important.

For as differently as they may have argued in the detail—all the authors discussed here who contributed substantial social theories on war (Hume, Smith, and Ferguson)[9] were faced with a key question, which may be expressed as follows: How can the model of the citizen borrowed from Roman republican traditions be reconciled with the new conditions of a large-scale capitalist society based on the division of labor? (Batscha/ Medick 1986, 13; for a slightly different focus, see also Bohlender 1999)

The abstract problem of the division of labor, discussed with particular intensity during this period, threw up the significant and far more concrete problem of military specialization. There was a passionate debate in Scotland on the question of a "citizens' militia versus professional army." This debate was so complicated partly because Great Britain had long ceased to be a relatively straightforward polity. It had become an imperial power with possessions of a size that recalled the Roman empire, in which the ideal of virtuous self-government had been lost, a loss—according to the widespread and pessimistic contemporary interpretation—that had marked the beginning of Rome's decline (Armitage 2002).[10] In any case, *virtue* was one of the key words in this debate, which of course recalls Montesquieu's remarks. And, in fact, Montesquieu was in contact with Hume, and parts of Ferguson's famous *Essay on the History of Civil Society* are crucially dependent on Montesquieu (on Montesquieu's influence, see also Allan 2006, 49 or Berry 1997, 7). But Montesquieu was of course not the only supporter and disseminator, let alone the key or typical representative, of a political ideal developed chiefly in the Italian city-republics of the Renaissance, an ideal whose roots lay in the ancient world and which was then developed further in modern England, particularly by James Harrington (1611–77). This ideal was spread by many intellectuals and was interpreted differently in different "national" contexts. Generally, though, what they had in mind was a polity that lives and functions through the active participation of all citizens, which would avoid the widespread despotism of the few and thus the decline and corruption of the political community. It is no surprise that there were vehement disputes over questions of military virtue, and thus those of war and peace, in this context.

The Scottish thinkers now set about discussing the crucial question, mentioned above, of the potential for these ideals of virtue to live on, and they did so in a quite new way. What distinguished them quite fundamentally from Montesquieu is that all of them made the idea of progress the "guiding principle that organized and integrated" their intellectual output (Medick 1973, 149, n. 48; Berry 1997, 7). They thus left behind them the static perspective of Montesquieu, who had worked on the assumption of the more or less erratic rise and fall of states and empires. Some of them (especially Ferguson [see Hill 2006, 193, 199] but also Smith [see Pitts 2005, 32]) were far from having blind faith in this progress. Nonetheless, their arguments were geared toward this idea—so typical of the Enlightenment—in that they tried, in a fairly systematic and historically well-founded way, to investigate the developmental conditions and stages of humanity and thus to understand their own time.

What is striking here, *first*, is that the stages of historical development conceived in this context (such as the distinction between hunting, pastoral, agricultural, and more developed societies in the work of Smith) arose from a serious interest in "earlier" or "outmoded" forms of society, yet there was no sweepingly negative assessment of earlier stages—something that was to change significantly in the work of nineteenth-century thinkers. While Ferguson was one of the first eighteenth-century authors to refer to the concept of (modern) "civilization" at the start of his *Essay on the History of Civil Society*, this was not associated with any denigration of earlier or non-European cultures. And this is not just because Ferguson had a generally more pessimistic view of progress than, for example, Adam Smith. For even Smith's historical accounts are largely devoid of arrogance toward past or "premodern" social formations. For all the talk of "barbaric societies," the era of Enlightenment as a whole[11]—and we return to this point later—probably had too much "feeling" for the fragility and problematic nature of contemporary "society" to disparage other models of sociation and make them the object of imperialism.[12]

Second, though this applies quite specifically to the Scottish authors and by no means to Enlightenment thought as such, there was a conscious refusal to think in terms of a *pre*social state of nature, however conceived, as a result of which our Scottish thinkers were not tempted—on the basis of a theoretical construct erected on a purely fictional foundation as in the case of Hobbes—to produce a reductionist anthropology (see Hill 1998, 50). Scottish Enlightenment philosophers were too empirically oriented to even attempt such a thing. Instead their analyses were alert to the varying motives for action and the different habits of (real) people, which in turn had consequences for their analysis of war and military forces (Berry 1997, 31ff.).

The significance of David Hume's (1711–76) contributions should not be underestimated in this context. Through the publication of concisely formulated essays (e.g., "Of the Balance of Power," 1987a [1741]), Hume was one of the first theoreticians to address this problem, of increasing importance to European foreign policy, and think it through systematically. What is more, in this brief essay, Hume places the idea of the balance of power in historical perspective, remarking that it could develop only under circumstances of military competition between states of essentially equal strength. At the same time, Hume underlines the necessity for cold, rational consideration in pursuing such a politics of equilibrium. Passions and sympathy had no role to play here. Yet Hume is far from sure how the instruments of military power should ultimately be related to the state as a whole: it was still quite apparent, from looking at the major monarchies, that the military genius of the conquest phase evaporated all too rapidly, that military security had to be entrusted to mercenaries, and that as a result these monarchies always went into political decline sooner or later. So despite the denormativized policy of equilibrium that he recommended, Hume is no advocate of a power-political realism that unquestioningly ascribes primacy to foreign policy, one that could simply ignore the interplay of domestic and foreign policy by falling back on the concept of supposed "state interests." Quite the opposite. Hume's work is still very much located within the tradition of "civic humanism," which means that he was in search of a political and military constitution approaching a (republican) ideal of freedom, one geared toward ancient models. So Hume was much more than a mere theoretician of "international relations." He evidently had a profound interest in social theory, as apparent above all in his essay "Idea of a Perfect Commonwealth" (1964 [1752]) published more than ten years later. It is clear here that, partly for the reasons mentioned above, his ideas on a future ideal "state" rely on the presence of a militia: "The militia is established in imitation of that of Swisserland, which being well known, we shall not insist upon it. It will only be proper to make this addition, that an army of 20,000 men be annually drawn out by rotation, paid and encamped during six weeks in summer; that the duty of a camp may not be altogether unknown" (1964 [1752], 486). Hume sees power politics in isolation as undesirable. It must always be linked back to a republican ideal of freedom, with which military institutions must also comply, as clearly evident in Hume's preference for a militia rather than standing army.[13]

But the fact that the republican tradition was no longer being continued in undiluted form, and indeed that Hume's social theories were already located *on the margins* of "civic humanism" (see also Robertson 1983b, 455), is bound up with the evolving reevaluation of societal wealth in the Scottish Enlightenment—and it was precisely this reevaluation that was to have repercussions for ideas on war and peace (Hont 1983, 271). It was after all Hume himself who drove forward this reevaluation, opening the way for new thinking in the debate on how best to establish peace. Particularly important here are the essays, generally known only to specialists today, published in 1752 in a volume entitled

Political Discourses. The most instructive of these for our purposes is "Of Refinement in the Arts,"[14] in which Hume's aim is to do away with the tension, which formerly tended to receive heavy emphasis, between the requirements and structures of a "commercial society" and the concept of virtue derived from ancient ideals. He attempts to demonstrate that "the ages of refinement are both the happiest *and most virtuous*" (Hume 1987b [1752], 269; emphasis added).[15] So it is only logical for him to emphasize that "industry, knowledge *and* humanity" (271; emphasis added) go very much hand in hand, that increasing trade and increasing economic activity are generally of benefit to the state, that the resulting luxury by no means inevitably leads to the decline of the polity and "corruption" (the opposite of virtue), but in fact helps maintain a free political community. Furthermore, ever-accumulating knowledge—Hume thought—would have a certain restraining effect on political action, an effect that would be felt even in the waging of war as "foreign wars" would become less cruel as a result (274).

So Hume's ideas marked a change of course, one that inevitably seemed paradoxical from a traditional perspective (Hont 1983, 272; see also Robertson 1983a, 175). It was on these new ideas that Adam Smith was to build. He was satisfied with Hume's resolution of the supposed dilemma thrown up by virtue and commerce, and he was even to take Hume's position a stage further. But not all the Scottish Enlightenment thinkers, Adam Ferguson perhaps least of all, were happy with this.

Ferguson, perhaps the most underestimated but actually the most brilliant theoretician in this group when it comes to action theory, produced an assessment of war that differed from Smith's later stance. In the first part of his *Essay on the History of Civil Society*, published in 1767, Ferguson offers an analysis—in terms of action theory—that still seems incredibly modern today. The crucial point for our purposes is that in grappling with the concept of "interest" he mounts a sharp attack on all conceptions of action that might be described as utilitarian. In connection with this, he develops a kind of philosophy of the "act." By taking action, by achieving goals, though these should not be understood solely in terms of instrumental rationality, the human being achieves happiness, which should not be mistaken merely for the gratification of the senses. Community-related activities (in contrast to self-seeking ones) are also and particularly likely to make people happy. But there is more to the spectrum of human action than this; people also take action for the sake of honor and recognition. It is no surprise that Ferguson takes a skeptical view of the consequences of "commercial society" and the coldness resulting from the division of labor, because in principle such a society curtails human potential. Neither is it surprising that he does not condemn war in any clear-cut way. Quite the reverse. According to Ferguson (2006 [1767], 30), war does not come about solely as a result of wicked motives or reasons. Human beings' "best qualities" may in fact find expression in war. War is not an instrumentally rational event; it is bound up with emotionality and hate, but also with honor. War, or the willingness to wage it, is also the guarantor of virtue: "Without the rivalship of nations, and the practice of war, civil society itself could scarcely have found an object, or a form. Mankind might have traded without any formal convention, but they cannot be safe without a national concert. . . . To overawe, or intimidate, or, when we cannot persuade with reason, to resist with fortitude, are the occupations which give its most animating exercise, and its greatest triumphs, to a vigorous mind; and he who has never struggled with his fellow creatures, is a stranger to half the sentiments of mankind" (35; cf. Hill 2006, 126ff.).[16] Ferguson is certainly not the first thinker to underline the connection between bourgeois society and armed conflict, the "dialectic" between the domestic and foreign relations of a society. But he was the first intellectual with great international appeal to do so, his thinking here owing much to the "neo-Roman understanding of history" to which we have referred several times already. As we shall see, however, this particular dialectic was also developed within other traditions, not least in Germany, where for a wide variety of reasons "civic humanism" failed to take hold as firmly as in Great Britain and France. While Hegel—who is of most relevance in this regard—knew Ferguson's work, he was to develop Ferguson's "dialectic" using quite different conceptual means, taking it much further than did Ferguson, something we return to in the next chapter.

But we would be doing Ferguson an injustice if we were to see *nothing but* the legacy of ancient concepts of virtue in the statements quoted above. Ferguson's writings are also pervaded with praise for conflict *within* societies—an idea that contradicts at least certain ancient ideas of the citizen as embedded unquestioningly in the polis (Geuna 2002, 190; on Ferguson as conflict theorist, see also Hill 1996, 215ff.; Kalyvas/ Katznelson 1998, 182ff.). Nevertheless, these republican ideals do play a huge role in Ferguson's thought, as was to become apparent in the "standing army versus militia" debate (see also Mizuta 1980; Sher 1989).

Ferguson accepts the ever-advancing division of labor—though, to repeat, with reluctance; but despite this he is keen to sound out the limits of the economic sphere, prompting him to ask which forms of the division of labor can in fact be reconciled with the ideal of virtue (Geuna 2002, 185). Precisely because Ferguson advocates virtue, because he advocates a republican political ideal, he takes a skeptical view of the possible division between citizen and soldier. He therefore criticizes the establishment of a professional army, interpreting it as a "breach . . . in the system of national virtues" (Ferguson 2006, 167). This institution cuts citizens off from an important dimension of the republican experience (see Robertson 1985, 201ff.). Only a citizens' militia—and not an army of professional soldiers—is capable of reconciling the need to defend the polity with its need for virtue.[17] Ferguson's call for a militia was consistent given his theoretical premises, because it allowed him to uphold the republican ideal of virtue. But it was also in tune with the circumstances of the time, particularly given that when *An Essay on the History of Civil Society* was published, as well as later on, the achievements of standing armies were anything but uncontested: "Indeed, given Britain's own increasingly parlous position, with the shattering loss of the American colonies . . . , and with a fatal combination of luxury and corruption widely believed to be overwhelming the constitution at home, these eternal lessons about the sustaining link between virtue, virility and military vigour had at least in the eyes of many of Ferguson's contemporaries, never been more germane" (Allan 2006, 106).

It is against this theoretical and political background and in clear contrast to Ferguson's views that we must see Adam Smith's remarks on the development of the standing army through the process of the division of labor. For Ferguson—as for many other representatives of "civic humanism"—the republican concept of politics and virtue was based on the sharp division, rooted in antiquity, of the inhabitants of a political community into mere producers (slaves in the ancient world) and citizens. For Ferguson, only the latter were capable of participation in the state because of their economic independence (Kalyvas/Katznelson 1998, 179), making them both entitled and obliged to help defend the polity militarily. Smith did not share Ferguson's ideas on society; he marginalized republican ideals of virtue or—at least to some extent—reinterpreted them (Berry 1997, 134f.). Smith, like Hume before him, placed greater emphasis on economic development than on the ancient ideal of politics, and because economic development demands an unrestrained division of labor, it is necessary to ensure the freedom of the individual and therefore to abandon the categorical distinction between free or full citizens and slaves, servants, or mere producers (see also Robertson 1983b). But this means that Smith is anything but a typical nineteenth-century *laissez-*

faire liberal, as his enemies (such as socialists and Marxists) or his alleged friends (modern free-market liberals and libertarians) have often wished to have it (Haakonssen 2006; Long 2006). Neither was he a self-satisfied bourgeois who wanted peace only so that the members of his class could go about their economic activities undisturbedly. While he was the founder of bourgeois political economy, he was also an Enlightenment moral and historical philosopher *of his time* (Medick 1973, 173). The final objective of his *Wealth of Nations* (1776) was not to achieve the wealth of nations. In the functional mechanisms of market society, Smith in fact saw a kind of trick of reason through which society's wealth could be created and distributed most efficiently. But he did not view market society as the realization of reason as such (Medick 1973, 224f.). For him the ideal of virtue continued to play a certain role; it included military and martial virtues. As a result—in contrast to Ferguson and because of his faith in the superior efficiency of the division of labor—he favored a standing army over a militia, but at the same time he called for a state education to cultivate the military spirit among lower-class youths, who were particularly affected by the negative impact of the division of labor. In the *Wealth of Nations* Smith states: "Even though the martial spirit of the people were of no use towards the defence of the society, yet, to prevent that sort of mental mutilation, deformity, and wretchedness, which cowardice necessarily involves in it, from spreading themselves through the great body of the people, would still deserve the most serious attention of government" (2007 [1776], 509). It would be quite wrong, in light of this call for the military education of the lower classes, to impute to Smith merely a desire for social discipline. In fact the discourse of virtue inspired by the ancient Roman republic, to which we have referred so often, can still be felt in the background, however weakly. In the eighteenth century, this discourse exercised a direct influence on almost every debate on how best to establish peace.

It is no surprise that Smith by no means supported every form of economic development and all its (possible) results. Smith's political-economic analyses were very much informed by the ideal of a society of petty capitalists, and this applies to both his *Theory of Moral Sentiments* and *Wealth of Nations*. As John Dwyer (1998, 25ff.) puts it, Smith was the advocate of a small-scale, overwhelmingly agrarian capitalism who saw the "yeomanry" as the class most crucial to economic and social stability. And it was largely because of this that he was never afraid to criticize rapacious businessmen and industrialists (ibid.). It is no coincidence that Smith—and this aspect of his work was also to play an important role in the debate on how best to achieve peace—always underlined the highly detrimental effects of colonies, because the *monopoly* profits made there only rarely benefited those who show themselves to be good (virtuous) citizens (70).

However, and here Smith builds on Hume, while he by no means disregarded the republican discourse of virtue, his central concern differed from that of Ferguson. It was not the problem of virtue with which he was most concerned, but that of justice. Smith believed that the division of labor could no longer be avoided and that therefore a synthesis of the productive worker, political citizen, and citizen-soldier—as envisaged by Ferguson and above all by those authors influenced by "civic humanism"—was no longer possible. In line with this, Smith defined freedom not solely but nonetheless primarily as a negative, passive type of freedom, as the freedom to enjoy one's property (Hont/Ignatieff 1983, 43). This is the way in which Smith also discusses military matters, the relevant remarks in *Wealth of Nations* pointing to two aspects that were highly innovative at the time.

First, in the first chapter of the fifth book, Smith presents his above-mentioned stage theory of history, featuring hunting, pastoral, agricultural, and developed societies, linking this political-economic line of argument with the question of the military structures possible in each case. In just a few pages, Smith delivers an analysis that both probes, from a functional point of view, the socioeconomic conditions facilitating specific forms of warfare and discusses the causal relationship between the development of military technology and military structures: "The number of those who can go to war, in proportion to the whole number of the people, is necessarily much smaller in a civilized than in a rude state of society. In a civilized society, as the soldiers are maintained altogether by the labor of those who are not soldiers, the number of the former can never exceed what the latter can maintain, over and above maintaining, in a manner suitable to their respective stations, both themselves and the other officers of government and law, whom they are obliged to maintain" (Smith 2007, 454). Here Smith takes a big step towards a sociological analysis of the link—as Otto Hintze was later to put it—between "state constitution" and "military constitution." Although his analysis of the embeddedness of military institutions within an overall social structure may not be particularly systematic, it at least makes a good start. And it is in light of this analysis that he attempts to draw conclusions about the waging of war in various "social formations."

But Smith does not stop there. He goes on to take this line of argument, which itself suggests that a professional army is the only military structure workable under "commercialized" conditions, as the starting point for a discussion of the "standing army or militia" issue from an efficiency perspective. And here he comes to a clear conclusion. The efficiency-driven specialization of the art of warfare and concomitant division of labor in war make armies unavoidable, which is why the future belongs to the army rather than the militia (see also Battistelli 1989, 24). For Smith, it is this point that settles the debate on a Scottish militia, stirred up again and again by Ferguson: the militia is rejected. He sweeps aside the debate, led by Ferguson, on the connection between virtue, republic, and war with the aid of efficiency arguments. At the same time, he is clear that these efficiency arguments have political consequences, though these are no longer comprehensible in light of the discourse of virtue borrowed from antiquity. In the chapter of *Wealth of Nations* mentioned earlier, Smith points out that a professional army may have positive political effects. Such an army not only facilitates comprehensive enforcement of the laws of the land; we can also expect a standing army—Smith tells us—to have liberalizing effects. "To a sovereign . . . who feels himself supported, not only by the natural aristocracy of the country, but by a well regulated standing army, the rudest, the most groundless, and the most licentious remonstrances, can give little disturbance. He can safely pardon or neglect them, and his consciousness of his own superiority naturally disposes him to do so" (2007, 461).[18] But this argument was not especially convincing—and it did not convince all of Smith's contemporaries, as evident in Ferguson's ongoing advocacy of a militia. This is just one more indication that, as modern political economy was getting off the ground, efficiency arguments were by no means entirely dominant: there were other ideas in the background.

If we summarize the Scots' debate on the militia and army with respect to its significance to social theory, it is clear that their analyses were underpinned by a model of action quite different from that found in the work of Hobbes. Like Montesquieu, the Scots did not see self-preservation as the only reasonable principle of action. They investigated, more or less empirically, the various possible forms of human action, while being careful—in drawing on the ancient discourse of virtue—not to rashly privilege a limited model of action. Of course, as we have seen, there were also significant differences between Smith, Ferguson, and Hume in this regard. But it is fair to say that this still relatively open concept of action made it possible to conduct a serious debate on the army-or-militia issue. Even Smith, who voiced clear opposition to a militia oriented toward the ancient ideal of the citizen with efficiency arguments, nonetheless saw the need for an education in virtue. In other words, these concepts of action had substantial consequences for theories of order and society. But it was also clearly apparent from the Scottish debate that this broad concept of action and the concomitant notions of order might come under pressure. The influence of political economy and its discourse of efficiency had already grown too strong. How would this affect prevailing ideas on how to maintain a peaceful social order? And how would these perhaps quite different notions of order be shaped by specific national political contexts? We must bear in mind that the debate in Scotland revolved less around war itself than around the instruments of war, perhaps in part because at the time the Scots felt removed from the incessant armed conflicts between the states of the European continent. The continental Enlightenment paid more attention to war as such or to mechanisms and processes conducive to peace, and this inevitably showed up in the specific national focus characteristic of the discourse on war and peace.

■ ■ ■

As a result of the palpable influence of "civic humanism," a critique of the consequences of "commercial society" was always evident in the Scottish school. At the very least, particularly in the work of Ferguson, but also that of Smith, there was still a *feeling* for the partly negative consequences of the division of labor and commercial industriousness. This was no longer self-evident for many of their successors (on what follows, see Ignatieff 1983, 343). The development of the academic disciplines spelled the end of the unity of history, economics, "sociology," moral philosophy, and politics still present in the work of the Scots, including that of Adam Smith, with consequences for all associated problems of social theory, morality, and politics (see Heilbron 1995, 19ff.). This meant that the later discipline of economics in particular was cleansed of criticism of the "commercial spirit." Subsequently, in Great Britain, such criticism was often articulated only in religious circles or in literature, but not in the academic disciplines. The exclusion of the questions that had been asked of economics—as well as other disciplines—in light of "civic humanism" almost always resulted in a narrower concept of action.

This was first apparent not in the nineteenth century but already by the late eighteenth century. In the shape of the group later referred to as the "philosophic radicals" (Bentham, James and John Stuart Mill), English philosophy began to be molded by a school of thought that advanced an antiaristocratic, liberal program of sociopolitical reform and discussed human action chiefly with respect to utility maximization and the weighing up of "pleasure and pain." This tradition, which exercised a significant influence on key figures in British political economy such as David Ricardo and helped pave the way for the later theory of marginal utility in economics, also included the discussion of war. But those working in this tradition relied overwhelmingly on the liberal argument made famous by Montesquieu that trade helps promote peace, though other arguments were certainly present as a kind of background music. The work of Bentham and his successors, however, focused not so much on the thesis of a tacit disciplining effect, which Montesquieu had also brought into play, but on the *utilitarian* argument: expanding trade between nations enhances utility, so sooner or later, at least when everyone has grasped this fact, war will be no more. Wars are wasteful and pointless and—according to this particular prophecy—will therefore disappear. Jeremy Bentham's (1748–1832) essays, collectively entitled "Principles of International Law," written between 1786 and 1789, though some were published only in 1843, said much the same thing. These four essays ("Objects of International Law," "Of Subjects, or of the Personal Extent of the Dominion of the Laws," "Of War, Considered in Respect of Its Causes and Consequences," and "A Plan for an Universal and Perpetual Peace") give us a sense of Bentham's early ideas on the maintenance of peace, their origins lying—particularly in the case of the last of these texts—in the Enlightenment search for perpetual peace. They are interesting because here we have an author who is advancing his theoretical program with great radicalism and trying to achieve an enduring conception of how best to maintain peace solely on the basis of utilitarian premises. Some of Bentham's successors were to tone down this radicalism while bringing new arguments into play, leading them to different political consequences in some cases. Despite this, the logic of Bentham's arguments was to resurface frequently in the ideas on how best to achieve peace produced by nineteenth-century European liberalism, making an in-depth examination of his work very worthwhile.

Whereas the first three essays feature an unmistakable condemnation of war, propose a very general definition of war,[19] and reflect on the causes of war (Bentham 1843b, 544), the fourth essay offers a program for peace based essentially on utilitarian arguments. For Bentham the Englishman, who was writing against the background of the British-French wars of hegemony, disarmament treaties between the two states and the establishment of a European congress or international tribunal to regulate competition between nations were key measures intended to cement peace. At the same time however he made it quite plain that the real cause of armed conflict, particularly that between France and Britain, lay

primarily in a false understanding of economics and that the decisive solution must therefore be sought elsewhere. Free trade between nations
would be the ultimate breakthrough on the way to peace. Everyone profits from trade, but rulers in particular have yet to understand this; because of their ignorance of economics, they impose all kinds of restrictions on trade, which is precisely what provokes armed conflicts. In truth,
"All trade is in its essence advantageous—even to that party to whom it
is least so. All war is in itself ruinous; and yet the great employments of
government are to treasure up occasions of war, and to put fetters upon
trade" (552). In his "Plan for an Universal and Perpetual Peace," it is true,
Bentham makes a number of suggestions as to how nations' foreign
policies, particularly those of France and Britain, might be improved.
Alongside the previously mentioned measures, he calls for state and international transactions to be made entirely public, in order to make it impossible for governments to wage war in a way that goes against the interests of their citizens (558f.). Yet his central argument is that it is only
when the advantageous nature of the free exchange of goods has become
common knowledge (particularly among rulers) that a lasting peace can
be achieved. Trade civilizes, but it must also be understood by everyone if
it is to have its full civilizing effect.

In view of this argument, it is no accident that Bentham immediately
comes up against the problem of the colonies. It was after all in the mercantilist interests of the European colonial powers—again, particularly
France and Britain—to gear economic processes in the colonies solely
toward the "mother country," which also meant curtailing their trade.
And this—so Bentham tells us—was a cardinal error on the part of the
rulers, one that entailed not only economic drawbacks but also political
ones—namely war. Bentham was subsequently to take an ever harder line
on colonies, though it is probably fair to say that his positions on the
subject were never entirely consistent (Conway 1989, 85; Winch 1997,
154). In any case, the year 1793, and thus the period of the revolutionary
wars, saw the appearance of two notable publications by Bentham setting
out a compelling anti-imperial vision of peace. In *A Manual of Political
Economy*—the first of these publications—Bentham does not dispute
that the emergence of European settler colonies, predominantly in America, had brought an increase in the wealth of humanity (1843c, 53); nor
does he dispute that processes of colonization might be useful as a means
of reducing population pressure in Europe (56). But the wealth generated
in the colonies belonged to the colonists and settlers, not the mother
country, prompting Bentham to call explicitly for the "emancipation" of

the colonies (ibid.). For Bentham, such emancipation is necessary for reasons of justice but also, and above all, for economic reasons. For the colonies are essentially useless to the mother country. Trade—Bentham argues—is always proportional to the available capital, so it is quite irrelevant where the trade is conducted. The key thing in trade is the quantity of available capital, not additional markets (colonies).[20] Because of this, according to Bentham's argument, which was later subject to criticism (not least his own) (see also below, p. 69ff.), the colonial mother countries would gain nothing whatever from their overseas possessions. Quite the reverse. The colonies would greatly intensify the risk of war, prompting him to exhort: For goodness sake, free the colonies!

In his *Wealth of Nations*, Adam Smith was still describing the colonies as a profitable venture for Great Britain and merely warned against colonial *monopoly* trade, which he thought led to an unnatural shift and use of capital in the mother country because of the likely monopoly profits (see 2007, 387/88), thus hurting the interests of large sections of the population.[21] Bentham extended this argument in an intriguing way (see Halévy 1972, 115), integrating it—from a consistently utilitarian and laissez-faire perspective—into a program for peace. In his view, conflicts incessantly occur solely because of a pointless struggle over the supposedly profitable colonies and, therefore, because of pointless attempts by states to restrict trade in order to secure the supposed profitability of these colonies. But this is an endeavor as harmful as it is futile. This is why Bentham urges the following approach in "A Plan for an Universal and Perpetual Peace": "1. Give up all the colonies. 2. Found no new colonies" (Bentham 1843b, 548). And this was also the watchword of Bentham's petition to the French National Convention: "Emancipate Your Colonies!"—as it was titled, the second of his publications to appear in 1793. Here again, Bentham begins with appeals to justice. The settlers in the non-European world had a right to self-government, to freedom, and the French revolutionaries' hesitation with respect to the colonies' role was a clear violation of the "rights of men." "Are you the only men who have rights?" Bentham asks (1843d, 408). Interestingly, Bentham also warns of the dangers of a messianic revolutionary creed that wants colonial possessions specifically in order to establish democratic conditions in them and abolish the aristocracy: "'Oh, but they are aristocrats.' Are they so? Then I am sure you have no right to govern them: then I am sure it is not their interest to be governed by you: then I am sure it is not your interest to govern them. Are they aristocrats? They hate you. Are they aristocrats? You hate them. For what would you wish to govern a people who hate you? Will they hate you the less for governing them? Are a people the happier for being governed by those they hate?'" (409). Bentham continues by referring once again to the economic and political disadvantages of any kind of colonial policy, to the fact that "trade is the child of capital," which is why any (colonial) restriction on trade not only entails immediate economic disadvantages but also undermines the possibility of a lasting peace (411).

We have presented Bentham's stance in a fair amount of detail here because of his palpable influence on the nineteenth-century British peace movement, in which both religious and utilitarian motifs played a part (Conway 1990). But more importantly we did so because the literature on the history of the social sciences often goes too far in conflating Bentham's project with that of James as well as John Stuart Mill. This conflation is far from absurd given that it was they who formulated a utilitarian theory of action (as pointed out by Talcott Parsons). But this closeness is then unjustifiably carried across to other discursive contexts, overlooking the fact that with respect to certain political and economic issues Bentham belongs to an older discursive universe than the Mills, namely that of the Enlightenment era, in which a clear skepticism about colonial or imperial policies prevailed—a stance that was to fade away in the nineteenth century. It is true that there was a connection between mercantilism and imperialism (Schuyler 1922, 440), but this should not lead us to conclude that the authors of classical political economy, as successors to and opponents of the mercantilists—from Smith and Bentham to Ricardo, Malthus, and James and John Stuart Mill—necessarily had an anti-imperialist attitude, as authors such as Schuyler (465) suppose. It is true that all these authors' work was characterized by an economically inspired condemnation and critique of war and military policies. Bentham's successors were as clear about the disastrous consequences of all wars as he was. But this does not mean that they simply adopted Bentham's position on issues such as the colonies. They by no means supported his call for their "emancipation" in the same unambiguous way. We have more to say on this in the next chapter. What matters for now (Muthu 2003; Pitts 2005) is that, whatever fashionable "postmodern" critiques may have to say about Enlightenment philosophy, in comparison to the ideas that were to follow in the nineteenth century it was fundamentally anti-imperialist in character.[22] Condorcet and Diderot, Johann Gottfried Herder, branded a "nationalist" by some, and even the "reactionary" Edmund Burke, along with Smith, Bentham, Rousseau, and Kant—all criticized the European conquests in various ways, though of course they were not the only ones to do so. Their skepticism toward colonies and colonial policies was widely shared around 1780, but this had already changed fifty years later, in other words in the first third of the nineteenth century and not only in the period of high imperialism. This applies not just to quite unliberal Germany but also to the liberal paragons of England and France. "The liberal turn to empire in this period was . . . accompanied by the eclipse of nuanced and pluralist theories of progress as they gave way to more contemptuous notions of 'backwardness' and a cruder dichotomy between barbarity and civilization" (Pitts 2005, 2). Such crude notions were not yet widespread in the Enlightenment era, as we have seen so clearly in the case of Scottish Enlightenment philosophy and as still evident in the work of Bentham. In contrast to the self-righteousness of the nineteenth century, his essay "Of the Influence of Time and Place in Matters of Legislation" (1843a [1782]) adopts a skeptical, almost ironical tone with respect to the potential for applying British (or European) laws to other peoples; there is as yet no sign of any clear civilizing mission, for as Bentham concludes so succinctly: "If my taste is a sufficient reason for me, an opposite taste may be as sufficient a reason for another" (181). Tastes and cultures are different, which is why one must be wary of rash attempts to intervene in other cultures, and particularly wary—we might add—of civilizing missions pursued through military means.[23]

There was very little left of this position, which we might describe as relativist, by the end of the eighteenth century. A new political attitude to colonies and empires was to prevail. This also changed the social theory debate on war, as was to become evident in the work of the "liberal" authors. But conversely this means (Pitts 2005, 4) that it is not liberal thought as such that is susceptible to imperial and military temptations. Instead, at *specific historical moments*, authors of varying liberal provenance made a decisive turn toward imperialism and war. This occurred because they were no longer persuaded by the utilitarian argument of the pacifying effects of trade and, above all, because they did not view the democratic-universalist tradition in liberalism as a convincing option either. It is to this other tradition that we now turn.

▪ ▪ ▪

The beginnings of the "*utilitarian*" tradition of thought on how best to maintain peace, as we have seen, are associated with the names of Montesquieu and especially Bentham in the eighteenth century. This tradition must still be taken seriously today as a means of explaining states' capacity for peace. But it did not remain uncontested within liberalism. Another stream of thought (no less influential and of equal contemporary salience) developed in parallel to it. The key name here is Immanuel Kant (1724–1804), and we might refer to this as the "*democratic-universalist*" tradition in liberalism. Kant composed his text "Perpetual Peace" (1795) in the context of a variety of eighteenth-century debates in philosophy and the politics of peace, which of course Bentham had also followed closely and commented on. The work of Jean-Jacques Rousseau (1712–78) played a crucial role for Kant. But we must immediately add that the reception history here is hugely complicated, as a fair number of Rousseau's texts dealing with foreign policy or international matters were not published during his lifetime; in other cases, it was unclear which passages of the published texts can be attributed to Rousseau.

As early as the mid-1750s, Rousseau had written a number of texts that show him to be a highly independent thinker on the topic of wars, one who made a very serious attempt to uncover the hidden social roots of these periodic outbreaks of collective violence. Rousseau considered mere analysis of the circumstances surrounding war to be insufficient, as evident in the fact that he does not believe that the international state system is capable of limiting war, let alone abolishing it.[24] In contrast to many Enlightenment thinkers, he was not content to dream up plans for peace between nations that were intended merely to contain or mitigate the risk of war; eliminating the external causes of war was not enough for him. So he saw no point in making a sharp distinction between foreign and domestic policies or historical and contemporary issues. If we start with his social theoretical premises, the problem of war can be dealt with appropriately, as he was soon to realize, only if we consider more than just relations between states. In "Discourse on Political Economy" (1997a [1758]), he had no illusions as he concluded that even what he thought of as "well-governed republic[s]" may very well wage unjust wars against one another (8). While this was not a consequence of the general will of a given nation, such wars could never be ruled out. And of course, the less the states making up a given state system lived up to Rousseau's ideal in terms of their internal structures, the greater the risk of war. This insight drove Rousseau almost inevitably to think ever more radically about the (sociohistorical) causes of war.

So war was already a core feature of Rousseau's ideas at a relatively early stage. As Olaf Asbach (2002) has pointed out, it was more than just a marginal topic within a theoretical approach supposedly concerned solely with the internal reality of societies. This is evident in the fact that, for Rousseau, the consequences of war are devastating in the truest sense of the term. For him, in contrast to Hobbes's stance, they cannot be marginalized. As Rousseau was to write a little later in "The State of War" (1997b [1755/56]) on the madness of traditional foreign policies and the fatalistic acceptance of their bloody consequences, "And all this is done quietly and without resistance. It is the peace of Ulysses and his comrades, imprisoned in the cave of the Cyclops and waiting their turn to be devoured. We must groan and be silent. Let us for ever draw a veil over sights so terrible. I lift my eyes and look to the horizon. I see fire and flame, the fields laid waste, the towns put to sack. Monsters! Where are you dragging those hapless wretches? I hear a hideous noise. What a tumult and what cries! I draw near; before me lies a scene of murder, ten thousand slaughtered, the dead piled in heaps, the dying trampled under foot by horses, on every side the image of death and the throes of death" (162).[25] Anyone who describes war in this way as the scourge of humanity, but at the same time can see no foreign policy means of ending war, is compelled to reflect on fundamentals. Rousseau does so—and is forced to acknowledge that his ideas ultimately result in aporias.

In the Enlightenment era, those who constructed their arguments in terms of theoretical fundamentals (the exception here being Scottish Enlightenment thinkers) almost always brought in the state of nature, which meant grappling with the work of Hobbes. Rousseau was no exception. Initially, he objected to Hobbes's account of the state of nature not because he felt it entailed an erroneous view of the human being but because he thought it had failed to explain what exactly we mean by "war." Rousseau clarifies that there was no "war of all against all" in the state of nature for the simple reason that war can be meaningfully referred to only as a very specific and infinitely terrible form of (socially organized) conflict. War is more than just a conflict between individuals or small groups. In other words, in contrast to Hobbes and in much the same way as Montesquieu, Rousseau is attempting to come up with a precise definition of war. In "The State of War," Rousseau explicitly criticizes Hobbes as he asserts that war emerges out of peace: "Let us briefly contrast these ideas with the horrible system of Hobbes; and we will find that, altogether contrary to his absurd doctrine, the state of war, far from being natural to man, is born of peace, or at least of the precautions men have taken to secure a lasting peace" (1997b [1755/56], 163). So Rousseau gives Hobbes's argument a very specific and quite plausible twist. The "true" state of nature is not warlike; it is only the sociation of human beings, as political communities take shape, that engenders a (Hobbesian) state of nature, a state of incessant war (see Asbach 2002, 219).

But if this is the case, then we are immediately confronted with the question of the origin of the state, which itself gives rise to the problem of war. In *Discourse on the Origin of Inequality* (2004a [1755]), Rousseau had argued that it was only the "invention" of private property that destroyed human beings' formerly harmonious relations, bringing about enduring conflicts that could be curtailed only by political bodies. The state is the result of an unwarranted rupture of original harmony in that it came into being in order to protect a distribution of property that is in principle illegitimate. As Christine Jane Carter has summed up so precisely, Rousseau's reflections on the genesis of the state are in essence a description of injustice. On this view, the rich manage to cast their superiority in the form of laws. So order is produced through repression, and this is clearly apparent in the state—in every state. "In Rousseau's view it is inequality which gives rise to the pact by which the dominant few secure and legitimise their position: 'usurpation' is cleverly converted into 'un droit irrévocable'" (Carter 1987, 78).

This derivation of the state leads to a number of conclusions, and Rousseau develops these in a highly compelling way. First—like Hobbes, but for very different reasons—he does away with the distinction between just and unjust wars (on the following, see the excellent study by Asbach 2002, 252ff.). As there are no lawlike relations within the international state of nature, this distinction is simply meaningless within the foreign policy context. There is no right *to* war! However, Rousseau tells us, this does not mean that statements about the legitimate way of waging war (about law *in* war) have become impossible. Rousseau regards states as artificial bodies and thus war as a conflict between artificial bodies. It follows from this that only the enemy state may be fought, but not its population. In the first version of his *Contrat social*, Rousseau was to state that a war without victims among the population is quite conceivable. "War is not a relation between men, but between powers, in which the private individuals are enemies only by accident, less as citizens than as soldiers. The foreigner who robs, pillages, and detains subjects without declaring war on the prince is not an enemy but a brigand; and even in the midst of war a just prince seizes everything in an enemy country that belongs to the public, but respects the person and goods of private individuals. He respects the rights on which his own power is based. The end of war is the destruction of the enemy State. One has the right to kill its defenders as long as they are armed, but as soon as they lay down their arms and surrender, they cease to be enemies, or rather instruments of the enemy, and one no longer has a right to their lives. One can kill the state without killing a single one of its members. War confers no right that is not necessary to its end" (Rousseau 1994, 124/25).[26]

In line with this, war is solely a state of affairs that exists between states, but—and Clausewitz was later to take up this idea—we can speak of war only if the attacked state enters into the fray: "If I wanted to get to the bottom of the notion of the state of war, I would easily show that it could only arise from the free choice of the belligerents, that if one attacked and the other chose not to defend himself there is only violence and aggression" (Rousseau 1991a, 50; for an overall survey, see Hoffmann 1963; Hoffmann/Fidler 1991b; Roosevelt 1987).

Whereas Rousseau's texts and arguments quoted so far seem to have remained largely unknown and thus without influence during his lifetime, this does not apply to the text to be discussed now. From now on, Rousseau goes over to discussing the question of how, under the conditions of *already existing* statehood—and, after all, there is no way back to a genuine propertyless and nonbelligerent state of nature—any kind of reasonably peaceful relations might be maintained. The occasion for these reflections was his study of the peace plan set out by the Abbé de Saint-Pierre.

Of the treatises on how to achieve lasting peace circulating in the final third of the eighteenth century (Bentham's text cited earlier was just one of several), Charles Irenée Castel de Saint-Pierre's (1658–1743) *Projet pour rendre la paix perpétuelle en Europe* from 1713 achieved the greatest fame at the time—in Rousseau's revised and annotated version. At the request of "Abbé" Saint-Pierre's relatives, Rousseau revised his vast text, finally producing a readable version in 1756. The result was a treatise with a rather complicated genesis. The first half, consisting of a summary of Saint-Pierre's ideas, was widely read and thus enhanced Saint-Pierre's fame. The second half, however, "Judgement of the Plan for Perpetual Peace," was first published after Rousseau's death and therefore remained unknown to his contemporaries. With a critical assessment of Saint-Pierre's views, it expressed Rousseau's own thinking on the problem of peace (see Mori 1989, 62, and Asbach 2002, 204ff.).

To achieve an enduring peaceful order in Europe, Saint-Pierre had proposed the establishment of a "form of federal government as shall unite nations by bonds similar to those which already unite their individual members, and place the one no less than the other under the authority of the law" (Rousseau 1991b [1761], 55). According to Saint-Pierre's the-sis—still salient to present-day debates on the European Union—a Euro-pean federation of this kind must be achievable because there are already economic and cultural ties between the European powers that make this *political* project possible.

> Thus the priesthood and the Empire wove a bond between various na-tions which, without any real community of interest, of rights, or of mutual dependence, found a tie in common principles and beliefs, the influence of which still survives even after its foundation is withdrawn. The venerable phantom of the Roman Empire has never ceased to unite the nations which once formed part of it; and as, after the fall of the Empire, Rome still asserted her authority under another form, Eu-rope, the home of the temporal and spiritual powers, still retains a sense of fellowship far closer than is to be found elsewhere. The nations of the other continents are too scattered for mutual intercourse; and they lack any other point of union such as Europe has enjoyed. (58)

Though well disposed toward Saint-Pierre's goal of establishing peace, Rousseau quickly demolishes these hopes in the second (but unpub-lished) part of this text, the "Judgement of the Plan for Perpetual Peace." He cannot see why the currently existing states, particularly the self-seeking rulers who disguised their egotistical and expansive interests with pleasing phrases, should subordinate themselves to such a Euro-pean federation. "Now I ask whether there is in the world a single sover-eign who, limited in this way forever in his dearest plans, would without indignation put up with the mere idea of seeing himself forced to be just, not only with foreigners, but even with his own subjects" (Rousseau 2005 [1761], 54). Under the conditions of the day—so Rousseau ar-gued—the general interest could not be reconciled with the differing in-terests of the various states, which is why the establishment of a Euro-pean federation in the general interest could be achieved only through violence, an unpalatable option for reasons of humanity. As desirable as it might be, in contrast to the Abbé Rousseau saw no feasible way of es-tablishing such a European federation, let alone a world republic (see also Gallie 1978, 18).

With these arguments, Rousseau found himself compelled to draw radical conclusions. On the one hand, he believed that the state system (and, indeed, every state system) fostered war. In "The State of War," in an argument close to power-political realism, he refers to international law as mere illusion (1997b [1755/56], 163). Thus, as we have seen, he presents the problem of the state of nature between states in an even sharper form than Hobbes (see Hoffmann 1963, 324). On the other hand, as he considers a world state or world federation impossible, he is left with no option but to propose a solution that seems obvious to him in any case for "domestic reasons": the establishment of small autarkic republics, which should establish a militia, to be used at most defensively, in order to minimize the risk of war, a risk ever present within the international state system. Rousseau's stance here finds its clearest expression in his constitutional projects for Corsica (2004b [1765]) and Poland (1997c [1772]). Sharply rejecting any notion—of the kind propagated by Montesquieu and further disseminated later on by the utilitarians—that trade is conducive to peace, Rousseau asserts that the exchange of goods engenders greed rather than harmony, further destabilizing a state system already prone to violence (see also Hassner 1997, 214; Hoffmann 1963, 321). Trade and an extreme money economy are obstacles not only to democracy but also to peace, which is why autarkic republics living mainly from agricultural production still offer the surest guarantee of peace. Rousseau is not being naive here. By no means does he believe that the kind of state and society he has in mind and which he proposes for Poland would be easy to establish. He is all too aware that Poland is in a geostrategically unfavorable position, surrounded by power-hungry neighbors that would be only too happy to conquer it. But he believes that a small republic fortified by great civil spirit and defended by a militia could be a rather disagreeable opponent for any assailant, especially given that under such conditions a "small war," a guerrilla war, is also conceivable. With respect to the military units to be formed in Poland, Rousseau's advice, among other things, is to "train primarily for speed and lightness, to break formation, disperse, and regroup without strain or confusion; to excel in what is known as guerrilla warfare, all the maneuvers appropriate to light troops, the art of sweeping over a country like a torrent, to strike everywhere without ever being struck" (1997c, 237). And he hopes for a kind of "domino effect" in which the establishment of an autarkic republic inspires other nations to follow suit and adopt the same type of constitution, so that gradually more stable conditions might prevail within the international state system. But even then—as emphasized above—peace will presumably be less than perpetual,[27] and the goal of a world federation unachievable. This is so for the simple reason that Rousseau—and again this links him with the republican tradition—can imagine a virtuous polity only on a small scale and found no use for cosmopolitan dreams.[28] It was his view of human beings and his philosophy of history that led him to conclude that the "transformation of the child of nature into a moral individual . . . is the work of states, that is, small political communities. It is states that help individuals achieve mastery over their own unsociable passions (characteristic of *amour propre*)" (Fetscher 1990, 124). In keeping with this, Rousseau can envisage a more or less peaceful state of affairs only in the form of the coexistence of small autarkic republics (125). But even republics will wage war on one another from time to time. So the causes of war, which have proved impossible to eliminate since the emergence of states, can at best be mitigated—if a nation seals itself off and withdraws into a state of autarky. Asbach is quite right to describe this as an aporetic moment in Rousseau's writings, because—as Rousseau himself sees—the problem of war cannot really be resolved: "Peace *is established* when states seal themselves off from one another entirely, and this process therefore signifies the exact *opposite of the establishment of a political-legal framework*. For while the establishment of a social contract signifies the institutional foundations of political life and conduct, with respect to relations between states this results in a total 'evasion of politics'" (Asbach 2002, 286; emphasis in original). Rousseau thought this situation through to its ultimate conclusions, which he committed to paper. But he seems not to have made them public, probably in part because, as Asbach (289) underlines, he seems to have given up hope of coming up with a genuine solution to the problem of war. He was always to view overcoming the state of nature between nations as unrealistic.

Rousseau's reflections on war and peace are so remarkable because they blend the arguments in social theory developed since Hobbes in a fascinating way. Rousseau has no time at all for Hobbesian reductionism, in which human action must be understood chiefly in terms of self-preservation. Rousseau's conception of action can be described as decidedly antiutilitarian. He strongly rejects the argument, made famous by Montesquieu and then disseminated by Bentham and others, of the peace-promoting effects of trade. For him, trade and the excessive societal wealth that goes along with it aggravate conflicts. This is because they merely increase greed, thus putting ever greater emphasis on the considerations of utility that are undoubtedly also part and parcel of human action.

Rousseau uses these antiutilitarian premises to develop his vision of how to attain peace, deploying arguments very close to the Scottish discourse on virtue. Rousseau too upholds the ideal of a virtuous republic, but one in which—in contrast to Ferguson's ideas—martial virtues would play no role at all. His abhorrence for war is too great. And Rousseau, a citizen of Geneva, is normatively oriented toward *small* autarkic communities as it is only there that virtue can truly bear fruit. It was quite impossible for the "Scots," as generally proud members of the burgeoning British world empire, to consistently adopt such an orientation. Rousseau insists on such small communities as the embodiment of the political realm, his thesis being that true political identity can develop only in manageable republics, not in large territorial states, let alone a cosmopolitan world state. But as a result he is tied to the assumption that there will inevitably be numerous republics or states. And this in turn means that stable, comprehensive, in some sense community-establishing and thus peace-preserving norms and regulations cannot exist *between* the republics and states, for there is no one to uphold such norms. Surprisingly, this brings Rousseau close to the Hobbesian or realistic interpretation of international politics. War, as Rousseau sees it, is possible at any time and may at best be mitigated through defensive militias.

It is at this point that Immanuel Kant intervenes in the discussion, quite consciously taking up arguments from the preceding debate and placing himself cleverly within it, though his thoughts here are highly complex and he needed two attempts to get it right. We may perhaps best understand Kant's viewpoint by discussing it against the background of Saint-Pierre's peace plan. Even during his lifetime, Saint-Pierre attracted fairly sharp criticism (see Hassner 1961, 653), with most Enlightenment thinkers highlighting the improbability of the European rulers volunteering to give up their power in favor of a European federation that would then place constraints upon them. And this critique was still just as sharp when—as mentioned earlier—Rousseau republished a condensed version of Saint-Pierre's peace plan in 1756. Typical responses included the caustic satire penned by Voltaire in 1761 (*De l'empereur de la Chine à l'occasion du projet de paix perpétuelle*), which—making no distinction between Saint-Pierre and Rousseau[29]—has the emperor of China proclaim in astonishment:

> We knew that the monarchy of France, which is the foremost of monarchies; the anarchy of Germany, which is the foremost of anarchies; Spain, England, Poland, Sweden, which are, according to their historians, each in its kind, the foremost power of the universe, are all required to accede to the treaty of Jean-Jacques. We have been edified to see that our dear cousin the empress of all Russia was similarly required to furnish her contingent. But great was our imperial surprise

when we searched in vain for our name in the list. We judged that, being such a near neighbour of our dear cousin, we should have been named along with her; that the Great Turk, neighbour of Hungary and of Naples, the king of Persia, neighbour of the Great Turk, the Great Mogol, neighbour of the king of Persia, similarly have the same rights, and that it would be doing a flagrant injustice to Japan to forget it in the general confederation. (Voltaire 2005 [1761], 50)

Voltaire's critique may have been particularly malicious,[30] but it expressed a widely shared understanding present in the work of most Enlightenment authors. On this view, Saint-Pierre's notions of peace might sound wonderful in theory but are of no use in practice, as they are unenforceable in the context of real-world power relations.

What makes Kant special is that he does *not* accept this disparaging opinion. At the very least, he is unwilling to shelve Saint-Pierre's goal of peace, which he regards as normatively desirable, merely by labeling it impracticable.[31] Instead, Kant adopts this ideal—and he does so quite consciously, in what was for him the most difficult way possible, by not only accepting the premises of Saint-Pierre's critics but going far beyond them in some cases and adopting a Hobbesian premise, which even many of Saint-Pierre's critics presumably did not share. The point of Kant's argument was that it is possible, with the help of arguments based in philosophy of history as well as political and sociological thought, to arrive convincingly at the shining vision of a Saint-Pierre even on the basis of the gloomy, pessimistic premises of a Thomas Hobbes (see Hassner 1961, 652 and 666). Right from the outset, however, it was clear to Kant that this endeavor would overcome or cut down to size both Hobbes's and Saint-Pierre's ideas on war and peace.[32]

He began his first major though still "tentative" attempt to develop an argument of this kind in 1784 in "Idea for a Universal History with a Cosmopolitan Purpose." "Conjectures on the Beginning of Human History" (1786) and "On the Common Saying: 'This May be True in Theory, but It Does Not Apply in Practice'" (1793) were intermediate steps preceding his reflections on how best to achieve peace, which found full expression in the 1795 treatise "Perpetual Peace: A Philosophical Sketch" and in the—rather short—passages on international law in the "Metaphysics of Morals" (1797).

In "Idea," Kant attempts to weave together arguments and viewpoints expounded by Hobbes and Saint-Pierre (and Rousseau)—a hopeless task at first sight. As he states explicitly, he sees no reason at all to "ridicule" the supposedly "fanciful . . . idea" put forward by Saint-Pierre and Rous-seau—two authors whom, as mentioned above, he believes to be of the same opinion (1991a [1784], 47). At the same time, however, he immedi-ately makes it clear that he also wishes to work with the Hobbesian con-cept of the state of nature—a far from peaceful, violent state. Kant refers to the fact that the human being is an animal that requires a master; he describes the human being as a "warped wood," out of which "nothing straight can be constructed" (46), thus approaching the description of the human being in the state of nature, recalling, probably quite consciously, passages in Hobbes's *Leviathan*. Like Hobbes (though with a different conceptual thrust), Kant assumes that only the sociation of the human being frees him from the far from pleasant—in fact, unbearable—state of nature.

But the argumentational approaches of Kant and Hobbes then diverge. Whereas the latter is content with the state of domestic peace brought about (by the Leviathan) and—as we have seen—accepts the state of na-ture between states and societies as a simple fact or marginalizes its war-like consequences, Kant is unwilling to accept this premise. It is true that Kant describes the state of nature between states with an almost Hobbes-ian vocabulary. As he underlines, "each commonwealth, in its external relations (i.e. as a state in relation to other states), is in a position of un-restricted freedom. Each must accordingly expect from any other pre-cisely the same evils which formerly oppressed individual men" (47).[33] But for Kant the state of nature is deeply immoral—and indeed *every* state of nature, including that pertaining *between* states—so that the aim must always be to overcome this as well (see Hassner 1961, 649; Hurrell 1990, 187). Furthermore—his thinking far more sociological than that of Hobbes—he is convinced that a "civil constitution is subordinate to the problem of a law-governed external relationship with other states" (1991a [1784], 47), in other words, that the state's domestic conditions cannot be analyzed independently of its foreign relations. This is why, however much certain aspects of his position may have changed in subse-quent years, Kant was always to call for the establishment of a federation of nations on moral grounds—in order to bring to an end the state of nature (between states). It is only when this has been achieved that we might speak of a true, in other words complete, form of civic sociation.

The question of course is *how* such a peace-bringing federation be-tween states can be created without succumbing to the arguments that had already been made against Saint-Pierre, who was constantly accused of naiveté. To do so, Kant requires a mechanism that, behind the backs of the actors, who are cut of that "warped wood," produces unexpected, that is, peaceful results. And he believes he has pinned down such a mechanism, which is in fact—and here again Kant's mode of argument is ingenuous—a *Hobbesian* mechanism. According to Kant, it is the human species' "unsociable sociability" (44) that, sooner or later, will force it to make a consistent effort to escape the *inter*national state of nature. "Wars, tense and unremitting military preparations, and the resultant distress which every state must eventually feel within itself, even in the midst of peace—these are the means by which nature drives nations to make initially imperfect attempts, but finally, after many devastations, upheavals and even complete inner exhaustion of their powers, to take the step which reason could have suggested to them even without so many sad experiences—that of abandoning a lawless state of savagery and entering a federation of peoples" (47). Ultimately, then, it is a trick of a (bloody and belligerent) history that brings about peace: in the end, conflict will bring about the triumph of reason. This is because conflict—that between states in particular in view of its terrible consequences—forces people to the rational conclusion that peace is a necessity. So Kant ascribes to conflict, and war especially, an altogether positive and productive impact.[34] In the past and even in the present, (military) competition between states has promoted freedom because states must always ensure their subjects' loyalty and are therefore compelled to grant them certain freedoms. Competing states, thought Kant, were particularly keen to bolster trade, as soon as they had understood its advantages, because it had augmented their (military) strength (50). But as such trade could truly blossom only within a framework of liberty, it was necessary to concede certain freedoms to the citizenry. Kant was to repeat his positive assessment of the liberalizing effects of war again and again in subsequent writings. Two years later he refers to war as an "indispensable means" of bringing dynamism to societies, prompting him to warn of the dangers of a unified empire, citing China as a case in point: "We need only look at China, whose position may expose it to occasional unforeseen incursions but not to attack by a powerful enemy, and we shall find that, for this very reason, it has been stripped of every vestige of freedom. So long as human culture remains at its present stage, war is therefore an indispensable means of advancing it further; and only when culture has reached its full development—and only God knows when that will be—will perpetual peace become possible and of benefit to us" (1991b [1786], 232).

And yet, however productive the impact of armed conflicts may have been, Kant still asserts that war is working toward its own abolition, that there is an unmistakable trend toward a gradual end to war, to a "universal cosmopolitan existence" (1991a [1784], 51). War will cease because, owing to the spirit of freedom that war itself has done so much to promote, a spirit that has made itself felt in individual states, an enlightened self-interest will become dominant in *all* actors, the ruled as well as the rulers. People will find war increasingly pointless, especially given that this enlightenment will lead them to understand the "good" (51): "[E]ventually, war itself gradually becomes . . . a very dubious [undertaking] . . . the effects which an upheaval in any state produces upon all the others in our continent, where all are so closely linked by trade, are so perceptible that these other states are forced by their own insecurity to offer themselves as arbiters, albeit without legal authority, so that they indirectly prepare the way for a great political body of the future, without precedent in the past" (51). So it is the ever-advancing interlinkage of people and societies (brought about by war and other factors) that leads to the moralization of relations within a society. What is more, it ultimately forces both individual and collective actors to act in line with their enlightened (not least economic) self-interest and to found something quite new, a "great political body," a confederation of states.

In the "Idea for a Universal History with a Cosmopolitan Purpose," published in 1784, Kant thus deploys an argument anchored in both moral theory and utilitarianism to undergird his philosophy-of-history thesis that a future peaceful age is in the offing. His argument as a whole shows quite obvious weaknesses, which Kant no doubt admitted to himself and which Otfried Höffe (2006, 174/75) describes as follows: If we rely too much on utilitarian arguments to explain those developmental tendencies driving the shift to peace, we cannot rule out the possibility that they will result not in a universal league of nations, but in a league of the *most powerful* nations, which enter into a coalition at the expense of the weaker primarily for reasons of utility. So self-interest (however enlightened it may be) by no means guarantees a *universal* union. Rather than ensuring peace, this would merely mean the perpetuation of the state of nature on a higher level. If this argument is correct, it automatically imposes an enormous burden of justification on the moral argument in Kant's construction (through enlightenment, the moralization of relations within a society spills over to the organization of states' foreign relations). And it is precisely here that Kant leaves himself vulnerable to the same accusations of naiveté directed at Saint-Pierre's project. This is not—as Kant too must have recognized—the way to build a bridge between Hobbes and Saint-Pierre. In this form, Kant's project must be considered a failure.

But Kant changed his thinking, notably under the influence of the French Revolution and his positive interpretation of it. He now introduced an argument in political sociology, making him the father of the "democratic-universalist" tradition of liberal thinking on war and peace. In 1793, in the essay "On the Common Saying: 'This May Be True in Theory, but It Does Not Apply in Practice,'" Kant deployed an argument that was to find full expression two years later in his text on "Perpetual Peace." This was the argument of the peaceable nature of nations, though Kant—and this is the novel and crucial aspect—makes a clear distinction between the nations on the one hand and the rulers (to date) on the other (1991c [1793], 91). In other words, Kant abandons his hopes, still present in the "Idea," of a moralization of international relations through enlightenment, hopes directed in significant part at the rulers. Instead— while fully retaining the utilitarian argument on the pacifying effects of trade—he now emphasizes that it is in the interests of the self-governing political entities, the republics, to keep well away from wars, and that this will prepare the ground for a robust peace. The state of nature between political entities will come to an end—according to Kant—when every citizen is involved in all decision-making processes (including those related to foreign policy). As Kant himself says, peace will not be enforced through (enlightened) "good will" but through "powerless[ness]" (ibid.), namely the powerlessness of the (hitherto irresponsible) heads of state. Whereas the wars triggered by the rulers formerly cost them nothing (the subjects bearing the burdens of war), the situation changes fundamentally as soon as the former subjects, now responsible citizens, govern themselves. If the people have the "deciding vote" as to "whether war is to be declared or not," there will be very few wars "out of a mere desire for aggrandisement, or because of some supposed and purely verbal offence" (91). States with a republican constitution express the interests of the citizens, in other words of the nation, and pursue a foreign policy leading ultimately to the treaty-based integration of states and thus to their global sociation. This will guarantee an enduring peace, in any case a more enduring peace than the major powers' traditional balance-of-power approach sought to establish.[35]

So what was still being justified in 1784 in the "Idea" solely in philosophy-of-history terms receives backing from a political sociology perspective almost a decade later—in 1793, under the influence of the French

Revolution and, undoubtedly, the revolutionary wars as well. Despite the wars raging at the time, Kant still wished to adhere to Abbé Saint-Pierre's objective of peace, though this forced him to structure his arguments differently. His study "Perpetual Peace" (1991d [1795]) brought together all these arguments into a great synthesis, which Kant had attempted in the previous decade, though it is his new argument in political sociology that now takes center stage.

Taking up his earlier ideas, Kant does not condemn war per se in "Perpetual Peace." He takes the view that wars had positive consequences in the early stages of humanity, because they disseminated human beings across the globe while compelling them to leave the state of nature. All the same he believes that social progress has made this positive impact of war increasingly negligible and that—during his lifetime—it has in fact rendered war obsolete (see Mori 1989, 54ff.).[36] He draws on utilitarian arguments when he refers to the communitizing effect of world trade, which makes war increasingly improbable: "[T]he spirit of commerce sooner or later takes hold of every people, and it cannot exist side by side with war. And of all the powers (or means) at the disposal of the power of the state, financial power can probably be relied on most. Thus states find themselves compelled to promote the noble cause of peace, though not exactly from motives of morality" (1991d [1795], 114). But the civilizing effect of world trade is not—as the final clause of this quotation makes clear—Kant's real argument. He takes a different approach, and this is why we may describe Kant as the founder of a "democratic-universalist" tradition within the liberal discourse of peace.[37]

This is evident in the argumentational structure of the treatise "Perpetual Peace," whose first section consists of five Preliminary Articles and second section of three Definitive Articles: "While the Preliminary Articles [outline] the prerequisites for peace between states . . . , the Definitive Articles indicate those conditions that must in principle apply always and everywhere in order to enforce peace *definitively*, in other words without reservation" (Gerhardt 1995, 79; emphasis in original). And the Preliminary Articles do in fact tend to present norms and recommendations with respect to international law (e.g., a prohibition on the conclusion of peace treaties whose actual goal is the waging of future wars, the gradual abolition of standing armies, no violent intervention in the affairs of other states), whereas the arguments put forward in the Definitive Articles and associated remarks (as well as the addenda) tend to be sociological in nature.

In the First (and crucial) Definitive Article, Kant links states' capacity for peace with their internal political structure, characterizing republics as peaceful.[38] This is due not least to the fact that the experience of equal rights *within* republics affects the external relations between them, with all the pacifying effects that we might expect. But more important here is Kant's argument discussed above (which is true political sociology). If only they are taken into consideration in foreign policy making—whether in a democratic republic or constitutional monarchy—it is the well-understood interests of the citizens that facilitate the avoidance of war and the establishment of mutually beneficial relations between states and that lead to these states' unification, whatever form this may take. But, of course, this immediately leads on to the question of just what form the relations between states ought to take. Is a mere loose federation desirable? Or should there be a kind of global confederation holding executive powers vis-à-vis the constituent states? Kant is unsure on this point and his stance fluctuates, as apparent in the fact that his arguments in "Perpetual Peace" (1795) differ from those in "Metaphysics of Morals" (1797).[39] The one thing he is sure of is that the aim is *not* to establish a true unified world republic, a world state. He identifies the key reasons for this as the linguistic and cultural differences among nations and the fact that "the laws progressively lose their impact as the government increases its range, and a soulless despotism, after crushing the germs of goodness, will finally lapse into anarchy" (1991d [1795], 113; see also Gerhardt 1995, 96). It is just such an ultimately despotic world government that Kant wishes to avoid.

So what Kant would like to see is a *Völkerbund* in the sense of a union of states, not a universal world state (Second Definitive Article). For Kant, the legal reality pertaining *between* states is *enough* to ensure the prerequisites for each individual to live in accordance with the demands of reason, even in the domestic context, while—as we have seen—a world state always entails the risk of universal despotism (on the debate on Kant's idea of peace, see Lutz-Bachmann/Bohman 1996 and Doyle 1997). What Kant did not see, but what his critics in the age of nationalism—at the latest—explicitly drew attention to, was the fact that his notion of a *Völkerbund* or league of nations was rather vague. Kant did not want to transfer sovereign powers to this league (because of the risk, just mentioned, of a leveling out of cultural and religious differences and the emergence of a universal despotism), in other words the power to coerce members should they misbehave. But this ultimately left the problem of

peace unresolved (see Höffe 2006, 15/16). It is precisely if—like Kant—
one refers, quite rightly, to nations' religious and cultural peculiarities,
that one finds oneself unable to rule out conflicts between nations. Those
who believe in peace under these conditions must also have confidence
that the costs of any war will always be viewed (in republics) as greater
than the benefits one might hope to attain from the violent pursuit of
cultural or religious objectives. Whether this is a realistic assumption,
whether overblown notions of citizens' rationality are at work here—
such questions could perhaps be suppressed during Kant's lifetime but
not, as we shall see, in the late nineteenth century.

But the debate that followed on directly from Kant did not focus primarily on the question of citizens' rationality but on the equally important issue of the specific character of the *Völkerbund* imagined by Kant,
the question of whether, by introducing the idea of such a league, Kant
had truly thought his peace project through to its conclusion. Though
virtually all of those involved in the incipient debate on peace were beholden to the brilliance of Kant's ideas,[40] the critique of Kant's vision or
of comparable "democratic-universalist" arguments within liberalism
began immediately, whereas the critique of "utilitarian" conceptions was
to begin on any scale only in the 1840s, its main thrust very different
from that found in the work of Rousseau (see p. 69ff.). In the decade following the publication of Kant's text, dozens of in-depth, often profound
analyses were published in the German-speaking world alone (for an excellent survey, see Dietze/Dietze 1989). We can examine only a few of
them here.

In his respectful and sympathetic review of 1796, the young Johann
Gottlieb Fichte defended Kant's text against the criticism that it was
merely the expression of a pious wish or pleasant dream; he saw its central idea as progressing logically from the "essence of reason" and viewed
the text as a whole as a comprehensive account of the results of Kantian
philosophy of law (2001 [1796], 313f.). But even at this early stage he
was pushing beyond Kant in two respects. First, he did not accept Kant's
skepticism toward a universal state; in line with this, he interpreted the
idea of a treaty-based league as no more than an "intermediary condition"—in other words, a transitional stage on the way to a comprehensive "state of nations" (319). Second, reflecting his Jacobin proclivities, he
placed more emphasis than Kant did on the need for just conditions
within a country as the precondition for states' ability to engage in peaceful relations with one another, "since a state that is internally unjust must
necessarily aim at robbing its neighbors, in order to provide some respite

for the old citizens it has bled dry and open up access to new resources" (321, translation corrected; on the further development of Fichte's ideas on war and peace, see Münkler 1999).

To what extent can we make do, like Kant, with a process of legalization between states with differing constitutional arrangements—this the ever more urgent critical question—if we take seriously the political sociology argument that it is the citizens' well-understood interests that bring about peace? What does this mean in concrete terms as long as these well-understood interests cannot yet be articulated in all states—because not all states are truly republican and democratic? To bring about perpetual peace as quickly as possible, is it not necessary—as Johann Joseph von Görres (1776–1848) and Friedrich Schlegel (1772–1829)[41] asked—to press for the external imposition of new internal conditions, ignoring the international legal principle of nonintervention in a state's internal affairs? "But as long as there are still despotic states and unpoliticized nations there will still remain cause for war"—as Schlegel put it in his "Essay on the Concept of Republicanism" (1996 [1796], 109). The young Görres had the same thing in mind two years later, when he argued that it was imperative to "republicanize as many despotic (regulatory) states as the circumstances of time and place allow" in "Der allgemeine Frieden, ein Ideal" (Universal Peace, an Ideal, 1979 [1798], 168). Görres, the young Koblenz-based Jacobin, was "ultimately [concerned to] reshape states' internal conditions as the precondition for a new international order" (Dülffer 1990, 55), which could be fostered through war. So there is a problem inherent in Kant's idea of peace, which—if solved in a radical way—lays bare the sinister side of the "democratic-universalist" version of liberalism. Kenneth Waltz (1959, 103ff.) is right to point out that, if one believes that social progress is not proceeding quickly enough, Kant's optimistic noninterventionism may quickly become "messianic interventionism" or—to use a different terminology—a peace-endangering missionary universalism. In the absence of such progress—as Kant's previously mentioned critics underlined—it may well appear legitimate to help this progress along through violent intervention in other countries, in other words to impose democratic arrangements in order to eliminate despotism once and for all as the primary cause of all armed conflicts.[42]

By no means was it only in the German-speaking world of the day that this problem was viewed in such terms. Before Kant published his text "Perpetual Peace," the radical Anglo-American democrat Thomas Paine (*The Rights of Man*, 1792) had espoused the view that Kant's critics were to take even further: Paine (1737–1809) had promised Marquis de La

Fayette, the "foreigner" who provided assistance in the American War of Independence and later general in the French revolutionary armies, to whom he dedicated the second part of *The Rights of Man*, that he would have his support should it prove necessary for France to snuff out "German despotism" and establish freedom throughout Germany in order to ensure lasting peace and security (Paine 1992 [1791/92], 115; see also Waltz 1959, 109).[43] And in the nineteenth century—now in a rather different context—this argument could again be deployed in almost identical form, at a time when the issue was no longer democracy alone but rather democracy *and national self-determination*: "Is it enough," asked Giuseppe Mazzini with rhetorical intent in 1847 in his struggle for Italian unity, "to preach peace and non-intervention, and leave Force unchallenged rule over three-fourths of Europe, to intervene, for its own unhallowed ends, when, where, and how, it thinks fit?" (quoted in Waltz 1959, 107/8). Was it not necessary, Mazzini implied, to intervene by force to support the self-determination of oppressed nations? Without such self-determination, as a component of true democracy, would not every attempt to establish genuine and lasting peace be in vain? And to what extent are such justifications for intervention safe from abuse? Are republics more peaceful in themselves or only in their relations with one another? These questions were debated more vigorously than ever in the 1990s with the tools of modern social research (see chapter 7 of this book).

▪ ▪ ▪

So in the shape of the liberal conception of how to achieve peace, the eighteenth century left the nineteenth a legacy that could lead to very different theoretical approaches to the issues of war and peace.[44] There was an inherent tension in this legacy between a "utilitarian" and a "democratic-universalist" tradition. The power-political realist school also lived on, playing a key role in both the theory of international relations and the practice of political rulers.[45] In addition, at the start of the long peace of the nineteenth century (1815–1914), there appeared an outstanding and highly influential work on war that basically defied this schematization of the theoretical landscape. In terms of its origins, it can clearly be placed amid the turmoil resulting from the French Revolution.[46] Carl von Clausewitz's *On War* was written between 1816 and 1830 and dealt with the author's military experiences in the turbulent period between 1792 and 1815—the duration of his active service as an officer in the Prussian army (Howard 1983, 5; Aron 1983, 9–60). It was the first truly systematic attempt to define war and describe it "phenomenologically" in all its complexity, to distinguish the extreme case of absolute war from that of a war genuinely "limited" by a variety of circumstances and factors and to clarify the relationship between military and political goals. This clear-eyed perspective on the phenomenon of war was possible not only because the author was a military man. It was also possible because Clausewitz (1780–1832), who was well versed in philosophy, broke with the conceptions of peace typical of the Enlightenment and did not condemn war as a matter of principle (on the following, see Münkler 1992, 56ff., and Förster 2000). In contrast to many (though *not* all) Enlightenment thinkers, Clausewitz, who had lived through the nationalistic fervor of the masses in the revolutionary and Napoleonic Wars, was reluctant to interpret war as a mere conspiracy of the monarchs to the detriment of the people. Instead, he ascribed moral qualities to war itself, qualities that must be grasped conceptually. We can get at the roots of the political and military escalation of war in the age of the French Revolution, he thought, only by reflecting on the phenomenon of war itself in a comprehensive and general way. But interpreting Clausewitz's work is no easy task because the posthumously published manuscript *On War* contains passages from different creative periods, featuring interpretations of different wars. Andreas Herberg-Rothe distinguishes between an early and late Clausewitz, as his arguments shifted between a number of extremes:

> 1. The primacy of military force versus the primacy of politics. 2. Existential warfare, or rather warfare related to one's own identity, which engaged Clausewitz most strongly in his early years, as against the instrumental view of war that prevails in his later work. 3. The pursuit of military success through unlimited violence embodying "the principle of destruction," versus the primacy of limited war and the limitation of violence in war, which loom increasingly large in Clausewitz's later years. 4. The primacy of defense as the stronger form of war, versus the promise of decisive results that was embodied in the seizure of offensive initiative. (Herberg-Rothe 2007, 3/4)

But if we leave aside the philological issues here—though they should certainly be taken seriously—and dare to simplify our argument, then for Clausewitz, inasmuch as war may be regarded as an extension of politics, it is undoubtedly governed *in part* by instrumental rationality, though this does not constitute a full account of the nature of war. Wars, Clausewitz tells us, are always characterized to some degree by accidents and unpredictable elements, by situations of chaos and dissolution in which it is the creative energies of the generals and of the army that come into play. In the end, of course, violent confrontations between states are also a matter of passion and blind hate. So Clausewitz described war with the help of his "trinitarian" formula, according to which it is a combination of "blind instinct" and passion, creative spirit and chance, and of pure intellect, in other words reason, with the first quality tending to characterize the people, the second the general and the army, and the third the government. "War is, therefore, not only chameleon-like in character, because it changes its colour in some degree in each particular case, but it is also, as a whole, in relation to the predominant tendencies which are in it, a wonderful trinity, composed of the original violence of its elements, hatred and animosity, which may be looked upon as *blind instinct*; of the play of probabilities and chance, which make it a *free activity of the soul*; and of the subordinate nature of a political instrument, by which it belongs *purely to the reason*" (Clausewitz 1968, 44; emphasis in original). To the extent that war approaches the category of absolute war—according to one of Clausewitz's key theses, expressed here in much abbreviated form—passion will increase and the rational element naturally decrease.

With this "trinitarian" formula, critics asserted, Clausewitz had reproduced the division, still strict in the age of absolutism, between army, government, and people, such that his ideas could no longer be applied to the age of total war with its mobilization of all resources and its extreme interlinkage of society, economy, and politics (see Roxborough 1994; for a similar critique, though with a quite different thrust, see van Creveld 1991). We shall leave aside the question of whether this criticism is correct. What is beyond dispute is that Clausewitz's ideas had laid the conceptual foundations for all substantial reflections on the political dynamics inherent to wars, as well as for the phenomenological description of violent events: he was one of the first authors to *at least begin* to approach war in its sanguinary aspect, and not merely with regard to its consequences (again, see Howard 1983, 46). Like no one before him, Clausewitz described how the circumstances and conditions of war—the violence, fear, and power that prevail when two states go to war—might very well lead to the curtailment of war, such that the stage of absolute war does not occur. Yet, at the same time, Clausewitz had to concede that these very conditions might also make things worse, with every use of violence being met with even greater violence;[47] in other words, fear of the enemy[48] and the struggle to gain the upper hand[49] may drive the protagonists to extremes (Herberg-Rothe 2007, 66/67). So absolute war is a possibility, but Clausewitz—and this distinguishes him from later advocates of total war—does not yet see the possibility of war for war's sake. For him, the aim of a radical escalation in the means of violence is merely the successful waging of war; in other words, outdoing one's opponent in the use of violence should at most be a means of steering war back into a more moderate form (42, 76). That such escalation was viewed differently and even propagated by some intellectuals at the time of the First and Second World Wars makes the study of his statements on the dynamics of violence no less fruitful.

So this chapter ends with a thinker who, not least because he directly analyzed the dynamics of armed violence, was something of an exception and perhaps for this reason continues to be of great contemporary relevance. This is not something that can be claimed of all the theorists dealt with in this chapter, though at least certain aspects of their arguments can be found in the discourse on how to maintain peace in the late twentieth and early twenty-first century. But there are good reasons why the modern-day social sciences still refer to a neo-Clausewitzian approach, but not, for instance, to a "neo-Benthamian" one.

If we wish to sum up this chapter while leaving aside Clausewitz's position, it is fair to say that in the seventeenth and eighteenth centuries the debate on how best to achieve peace revolved essentially around three topics: the form of the supra- or international order, with increasing attention being paid to the dialectic between a state's domestic constitution and its foreign policies; the potential of markets to promote peace; and the significance of the citizen-soldier ideal, which touched in particular on the relationship between the state and its subjects. Attention was also paid to other aspects such as the legitimation of wars and the connection between imperialism and war, but they were intertwined with the three topics identified above.

We can discern four highly disparate theoretical standpoints from which authors explored these topics. There is the power-political realist position, associated with the name of Thomas Hobbes; the utilitarian-liberal conception, directly linked with the name of Bentham, but which undoubtedly has roots in the work of Montesquieu as well; the republican-universalist stance that goes back to Kant, though certain arguments can be found in the work of Rousseau; and finally the position linked with the "neo-Roman understanding of history" and the associated emphasis on the ideal of virtue, which we dealt with mainly in connection with the Scottish Enlightenment. It is difficult to identify this last position with any of the three approaches mentioned above, and it can therefore claim to be significant in its own right. We discussed the three thematic complexes in light of these four basic positions, though we should immediately add that the various theories did not all pay equal attention to these topics. Overall it is fair to say that our authors' differing theoretical standpoints led them to very different conclusions in their analyses of war and peace. As we shall see, the nineteenth century saw shifts within the debate on how to achieve peace. Certain basic standpoints (as well as certain topics) received more attention than others, some disappeared entirely, while new ones appeared. This was not always a matter of theories' varying purchase on reality. Often, it was due to contingent reasons, with consequences that extend to modern-day social theory. And here the establishment of the discipline of sociology, which differed from country to country, is of crucial significance.

3

The Long Peace of the Nineteenth Century and the Birth of Sociology

THE NINETEENTH CENTURY is often referred to, for good reasons, as a liberal century. No one would dispute, however, that this liberalism could take on very different forms and that socialism, liberalism's great adversary, was beginning to gain ground. But even this countercurrent shared more than a few of liberalism's premises. How did the manifold upheavals of the nineteenth century impact on social theoretical debates on war and peace? Which new topics were examined? Which were abandoned? Were socialist ideas on peace the only significant alternatives to the liberal utopia? And how did Kantian thought and that associated with the discourse of virtue develop? These are the questions we shall be exploring now. We should bear in mind here that liberal thinking on war and peace (no less than its socialist counterpart) constantly came up against its own (economic and political) limitations—that historical reality refused to conform to the various conceptions of history that were put forward. As a result, the liberal discourse on peace was frequently marked by surprising about-turns, and we must pay attention to these as well. The equally apparent constancy and fragility of liberal discourse is evident even in the work of the classical figures of British liberalism.

James Mill (1773–1836) is one of those nineteenth-century liberals who continued the utilitarian-liberal tradition of thought on war and peace. But we can discern in his work clear modifications of Bentham's views, which were to become even more apparent in the work of his son, John Stuart Mill (1806–73). In the case of Mill senior at least, his arguments on how best to achieve peace are largely an elaboration of the views of Bentham, his friend and teacher: they amount to a vigorous plea for (free) trade, which he defended throughout his oeuvre against critics who claimed that it resulted in increased conflict (see Silberner 1946, 37–40). As James Mill sets out in *Commerce Defended* (1808),

> [W]here industry is free, and where men are secure in the enjoyment of what they acquire, the greatest improvement which the government

can possibly receive is a steady and enlightened aversion to war. While such a nation remains at peace, the faults of the government can hardly ever be so great, that the merits of the nation will not more than compensate them, and that society from its own beneficent tendency will not improve. Nothing however can compensate the destruction of war. The creative efforts of individuals can never equal its gigantic consumption, and the seeds of prosperity are eaten up. (1808, 120/21)

War, he (and Bentham) asserted, is a great evil. It has nothing to do with trade but in fact does terrible harm to national economies.

Given this assessment of war, it is unsurprising that James Mill, like his teacher Bentham before him, devoted considerable energy to identifying the most effective political means of achieving enduring peace. The long article "Law of Nations," which appeared in 1825 as a supplement to the *Encyclopaedia Britannica*, is essentially a reflection on the opportunities and risks inherent in an international legal system. Like Hobbes and many later Enlightenment authors, Mill is highly skeptical about the effectiveness of international law. According to him, within the international state system there is little prospect of punishing violations of international law, precisely because there is no supreme executive authority at the global level. Indeed, Mill underlines that every attempt to seriously implement the "laws of nations" might increase the risk of war, especially if individual nations take it upon themselves to administer and enforce a law for the whole world, a point already thrown up in the debate on Kant's peace plan (see p. 59ff.): "A nation is often but too easily stimulated to make war in resentment of injuries done to itself. But it looks with too much coolness upon the injuries done to other nations, to incur the chance of any great inconvenience for the redress of them" (1825, 5). So Mill is forced to conclude that the international state system offers very little scope for the effective enforcement of laws. But this does not lead him to consider the subject closed. He states that it is entirely possible to attain greater authority for international law if it is endowed with a commensurate degree of "moral power." And this is the point of departure for his specific proposals. According to Mill, it is necessary, first, to codify existing international law in a clear and transparent way and, second, to establish a tribunal to identify infringements by applying this law (9). This tribunal would have no way of implementing its judgments by force (32), but Mill believed this would not render it powerless. The creation of a public realm for the purposes of "shaming" would surely have an impact: "In this manner a moral sentiment would grow up, which would, in time, act as a powerful restraining force upon the injustice of nations, and give a wonderful efficacy to the international jurisdiction. No nation would like to be the object of the contempt and hatred of all other nations, to be spoken of by them on all occasions with disgust and indignation" (ibid.).

Mill is fairly optimistic about his proposals' chances of success, first because all nations gain from trade (1825, 24), which means that a stable peace is greatly in their interest, for reasons of utility as it were. Second, by no means every nation in the world must be involved in establishing such a tribunal. It would be enough for the "more civilized and leading nations" (29) to take the initiative, particularly given that under these circumstances it seems likely that other nations would eventually follow suit.

So there are undoubtedly great similarities to Bentham's arguments on how to achieve peace, though James Mill sets out his proposals for a world tribunal with greater clarity than Bentham ever did. Like Bentham, he identifies the colonies as one of the (remaining) key causes of bellicose dynamics. As evident particularly in his 1824 article "Colony," James Mill took the view that colonial administrative costs always greatly exceed the utility accruing to the national economy of the "mother country." Free trade would be far better and more beneficial—to all parties—not only economically but also politically, precisely because the trade barriers that colonies inevitably entail intensify rivalries between nations and cause wars. But why do the major European nations not refrain from founding more colonies? Mill's answer is simple—and in line with the arguments put forward by the early political economists (see, e.g., Bentham's arguments, and those of Adam Smith in *Wealth of Nations*, 2007, 395–99): colonies and the resulting armed conflicts are in the interest of the "ruling few." There is a governing class that benefits from positions within the administration and army and which therefore wishes to keep alive the existing colonial system. "Now wars, even in countries completely arbitrary and despotical, have so many things agreeable to the ruling few, that the ruling few hardly ever seem to be happy except when engaged in them" (Mill 1824, 272). This problem can be solved only if the *interests of the majority* prevail in a given country. Only then will the danger of war be eliminated. And in the view of Mill senior, these interests of the majority find perfect expression in a worldwide free-trade system, an argument later deployed to great effect by one of the great English political propagandists of the nineteenth century, Richard Cobden (see Greenleaf 1988, 32ff.).

It is striking, however, that in contrast to Bentham Mill senior pays almost no attention to moral arguments in his article on the colonies (Pitts 2005, 123ff.). No mention is made of the political rights of the colonized or their self-determination. As apparent in his earlier publication, *History of British India* (1817), Mill had never believed that British rule in India was reasonable or efficient enough, yet despite all his criticisms of British law and British policies, he believed it was Britain's obligation, as a civilized nation, to rule India. Not much later and despite his criticisms of the East India Company, Mill was hired as an expert adviser by this very company. This did not cause him to change his views. He repeatedly emphasized that Great Britain must maintain its rule in India for the sake of the Indians: "[T]his English government in India, with all its vices, is a blessing of unspeakable magnitude to the population of Hindustan. Even the utmost abuse of European power, is better, we are persuaded, than the most temperate exercise of Oriental despotism" (Mill, quoted in Pitts 2005, 125).

Pitts argues persuasively that there was a discernible shift within the utilitarian camp. In a far more self-evident way than in the work of Bentham (let alone the Scottish Enlightenment thinkers),[1] a clear hierarchy of societies begins to emerge in the work of Mill senior, a hierarchy in which the European nations in general and Great Britain in particular are viewed as the summit of humanity. We begin to see a clear contrast between civilization and "rudeness," which his son John Stuart was to elaborate theoretically (see below). In light of this contrast, it appeared possible to legitimize a colonial policy that seemed impossible to justify on economic grounds. In India, the empire would even prove itself capable of establishing peace.

As set out by Edmund Silberner (1946), the great historian of economic thought, the arguments put forward by Mill senior on how best to achieve peace, which were predominantly utilitarian in character, were plausible, *at first sight*, as long as one was willing to think in purely economic categories. But Mill's (highly ambivalent) plea against colonies could not convince those keen on obtaining or preserving colonies for political and strategic reasons. And as we shall see, by the mid-nineteenth century nationalists and liberal imperialists were in fact to push this argument, endorsing the struggle for colonies even if there are no economic benefits, because the *political gains* accrued through colonies outweigh the economic losses. And in the age of nationalism, this was no longer the kind of argument—as Mill senior had still assumed—that would reflect the dividing line between the avaricious "ruling few" and a pacifist majority. We might describe this as the dark side of the "utilitarian" version of liberalism, which emerged chiefly in the second half of the nineteenth century—namely, the ease with which liberal thinkers accommodated themselves to imperialist policies.

But this accommodation with imperialist policies did not necessarily occur solely on power-political grounds. As quickly became apparent in the wake of the utilitarian debate around Bentham and the older Mill, arguments for colonies rooted in *economics* and a corresponding power politics were also ready to hand, and here the question arose as to whether, on these premises, war should be rejected as categorically as it still tended to be in the eighteenth century.

Various supplementary arguments paved the way for or accompanied this economic accommodation. Notably, the genuine interest in other peoples still found in the Enlightenment era gradually began to disappear, giving way to a sharp and value-laden dichotomization. This was already discernible in the work of James Mill, but John Stuart Mill's article "Civilization" from 1836 is the first significant milestone. As we have seen, Adam Ferguson had already coined the term "civilization." But Mill now deploys it *in a sharply dichotomous way* by distinguishing between civilization and barbarism (1977c [1836]). Though Mill cannot help mentioning a few negative aspects of (modern) civilization, the loss of importance suffered by individuals and the rise of the masses, the decline of heroism, and the middle classes' exclusive focus on monetary matters (130ff.), he favors civilizations in normative terms: these are societies featuring a highly developed division of labor that are clearly superior to the barbarian peoples, not least when it comes to war, as a result of the discipline and cooperation that prevails within them (122; see also Parekh 1995, 93f., and Robson 1998).

This high regard for (European) civilization went hand in hand with argumentational shifts in the field of political economy—with far-reaching consequences for the debate on how to achieve peace. In the early 1960s, Bernhard Semmel had already pointed out that the skepticism toward any kind of colonial policy still discernible in the work of Smith, Bentham, and—in embryonic form—James Mill, and generally justified in economic terms, had begun to change by the mid-1830s at the latest. Arguments (fueled by Edward Gibbon Wakefield) now appear according to which it is not capital—as Bentham still thought—that is decisive to capitalist growth but rather the markets in which capital can be invested. New land for the surplus population to settle and new investment opportunities for accumulated capital were said to make an empire necessary. Wakefield obviously managed to convince even the aged Bentham of his views and thus of the utility of colonies (see Semmel 1961, 518). But of even greater importance was the fact that John Stuart Mill adopted this position, advancing in a highly influential way the emerging economically inspired accommodation between imperialism and liberalism. He provided free-trade imperialism with a theoretical foundation, as it were.[2]

In the *Principles of Political Economy* (1848), Mill junior underlines that Adam Smith was clearly laboring to some extent under a misapprehension in his account of the role of foreign trade, which he often considered solely in terms of its function as an outlet for surplus goods (1965 [1848], 592). According to Mill, this view is wrong or one-sided. In fact, foreign trade benefits the consumer; market expansion as a whole entails major positives and, where applicable, stimulates an "industrial revolution" (593) in any country that makes this market expansion a permanent state of affairs. But this line of argument puts Mill in an ambivalent position. He continues to make the well-known utilitarian argument that foreign trade promotes increasing contact between strangers and thus produces moral, in other words pacifying, effects, which ultimately guarantee progress. Increasingly, Mill tells us, trade replaces war: "And it may be said without exaggeration that the great extent and rapid increase of international trade, in being the principal guarantee of the peace of the world, is the great permanent security for the uninterrupted progress of the ideas, the institutions, and the character of the human race" (594). But in his view an anticolonial and anti-imperial policy based on free-trade principles can no longer be justified in a straightforward way—and the old Benthamian argument that wars are caused by colonies also becomes problematic. As Mill (735) states with explicit reference to Wakefield, in civilized countries there is a risk that the rate of profit will sink to a minimum, that accumulating capital will lead to a kind of "stationary state" that can be remedied only by investing in foreign countries or colonies. Prosperity can be assured only through investment outside of England—and colonies, among other things, provide an opportunity for such investment:

> It is to the emigration of English capital, that we have chiefly to look for keeping up a supply of cheap food and cheap materials of clothing, proportional to the increase of our population; thus enabling an increasing capital to find employment in the country, without reduction of profit, in producing manufactured articles with which to pay for this supply of raw produce. Thus, the exportation of capital is an agent

of great efficacy in extending the field of employment for that which remains: and it may be said truly that, up to a certain point, the more capital we send away, the more we shall possess and be able to retain at home. (746)

All of this has clear repercussions for Mill's thought with respect to democratic theory, as is only too apparent in his *Considerations on Representative Government* (1861), especially chapter 18 ("Of the Government of Dependencies by a Free State"). John Stuart Mill, who like his father James worked for the East India Company, presents his argument in an astonishingly open way. Distinguishing between mature and immature colonies, he makes no bones about defending the British Empire while emphasizing that immature nations, among which he specifically identifies India, can do without full political representation (1977b [1861], 563ff.). In fact, what was needed was a "vigorous despotism" to educate these immature peoples, "a good despot" (565) who would not even require supervision by the British Parliament, as the British public lacked an understanding of the colonies' problems (570; see also Parekh 1995, 94; Robson 1998, 360ff.). The concept of freedom—Mill junior concluded—cannot be appropriately applied to barbarian (in other words, noncivilized) peoples. It makes sense only within the context of the civilized nations: "Those who are still in a state to require being taken care of by others must be protected against their own actions as well as against external injury. For the same reason, we may leave out of consideration those backward states of society in which the race itself may be considered as in its nonage. The early difficulties in the way of spontaneous progress are so great, that there is seldom any choice of means for overcoming them; and a ruler full of the spirit of improvement is warranted in the use of any expedients that will attain an end, perhaps otherwise unattainable" (Mill 1977a [1858], 224; on this issue, see Mehta 1999, 102). This point in the argument of one of the forefathers of liberalism is not only surprising from a democratic theory perspective. What seems even more remarkable (though entirely logical on utilitarian premises) is how quickly economic arguments could render obsolete the aversion to war and colonial policies still present in the early days of classical political economy. As Mill explains in "A Few Words on Non-Intervention" (1984 [1859]), Britain is often simply forced to wage war by the (non-European) barbarians, whether it itself has been attacked or not: "But there assuredly are cases in which it is allowable to go to war, without having been attacked, or threatened with attack; and it is very important that nations should make up their minds in time, as to what these cases are" (1984 [1859], 118). Though determining these "cases" may be difficult in the detail, it is nonetheless clear that there is no requirement for wars against barbarian peoples and lower civilizations to be fought on the basis of international law or an international morality: "[T]he rules of ordinary international morality imply reciprocity. But barbarians will not reciprocate" (ibid.). Barbarians have no rights *as* nations, so the emergent critique of the actions of the colonial powers of France and Britain in Algeria or India rests on false premises: "A civilized government cannot help having barbarous neighbors: when it has, it cannot always content itself with a defensive position, one of mere resistance to aggression. After a longer or shorter interval of forbearance, it either finds itself obliged to conquer them, or to assert so much authority over them, and so break their spirit, that they gradually sink into a state of dependence upon itself" (ibid.).[3] But this did not invalidate the universal rules of morality. Mill considers intervention justifiable in principle if it aids a people's struggle for liberation from a foreign yoke or a tyranny based on foreign military power, or contributes to struggles against cruel regimes that enslave their own populations, though only if other ways of influencing events have been exhausted and the means are proportionate.

So free trade, justified in economic terms, was seemingly able to enter smoothly into a symbiosis with imperialism (see also Semmel 1970), though the danger of war between the European nations and between the colonial masters and the colonized was now ignored or viewed as morally insignificant. Ultimately, this led to an ironic turn in liberal thought on war and peace, or at least certain aspects of it. In their sociopolitical ideas, James and John Stuart Mill—like Bentham before them—had abandoned all suggestion of a concept of the citizen informed by Roman virtues. They could now regard the debate—which Adam Smith and Adam Ferguson still thought necessary and which revolved around the citizen's active participation in the republican polity—as outmoded. In this context, there was no longer any question of the ideal of the citizen-soldier—so important to Ferguson in light of his praise for virtues, particularly martial ones—continuing to play a significant role. At least in England, the sociopolitical thought of liberalism moved away from any direct concern with war and the armed forces. The process of historical development was understood as in principle nonviolent, because of a faith in the (disciplining) effects of the economy and an assumption that individual and collective actors (such as states) would submit to the logic of the economy and thus refrain from violence and war. The "ironic" aspect is that it was nonetheless impossible to bid farewell to war as an intellectual possibility. It returned, in the colonial areas beyond Europe. However, these areas were far away, far enough away at least to allow influential liberal thinkers to marginalize war as a topic of relevance to social theory. This made both the Scottish debate on the role of the citizen-soldier ideal and the debate provoked by Kant on the relationship between a democratic republican constitution and war seem no longer relevant. In any event—see the reflections of James Mill (see p. 65ff.)— liberal thinkers were still quite willing to consider the "law of nations" and an international tribunal, though it was unclear what mechanisms, beyond the moral pressure applied by a transnational public and the pacifying function of markets, were to produce a peaceful settlement between the (European) nations. It is not to underestimate the significance of the transnational public sphere, which was flourishing during this era as a result of the struggle to abolish slavery (Keck/Sikkink 1998), to describe this as insufficient.

In the first half of the nineteenth century, it was only from a British perspective that the pacifying function of markets was still viewed in such unambiguous terms. Intellectuals in other nations, which faced quite different economic problems, developed highly critical views on this subject. These thinkers quickly understood that arguments for free trade were not disinterested but in fact intended to help *Britain* assume a leading role in the world with the minimum of violence and expense.[4] They also understood that British propagandists of free trade were quite consciously concerned with the industrial superiority of Britain, its products, production methods, and prospects for innovation. In fact, in the thought of most British liberal free-trade enthusiasts, the link between free trade and Britain's superiority did not occur as an afterthought or, as it were, a contingent outcome. It was consciously factored in and intended (see Semmel 1970). So it is quite understandable that, in the early 1840s, the German Friedrich List (1789–1846) responded to free-trade ideas with the argument that the universal spread of free trade would mean the perpetuation of most countries' inferiority to the leading producing, trading, and naval powers and that the American Henry Carey (1793–1879) endorsed his view in the 1850s. The arguments put forward by both these thinkers certainly captured the intentions of the British free-trade theorists.[5] There were good reasons for List's (and Carey's) plea for protectionism, and their views clearly helped weaken the utilitarian-liberal conception of peace outside Britain. If one believed that free trade merely served British interests, then the notion of the pacifying effects of trade no longer held much plausibility, because on this view economic conflicts between nations would be a likely occurrence, conflicts that might—and might have to—be fought out with military means.

Arguments espousing free trade as a means of achieving peace ran into particular difficulties in light of the non-European colonies, at least if one believed in the need to "conquer markets" in order to maintain the dynamism of capitalism. It is no coincidence that the liberal discourse changed markedly with respect to colonies. The early liberal argument that colonies could trigger wars was no longer maintained on these premises, so a strictly anti-imperialist position no longer followed automatically from liberal economic arguments. All of this points up the fact that, apart from hopes of a transnational public sphere, there were few pacifying mechanisms left within liberal thinking on war and peace if even the economy and trade offered no guarantees in this regard (on liberal economic theories' affinity to peace, see the brief account in Burkhardt 1997, 561).

So the weakness of utilitarian-liberal arguments on peace, their openness to attack—on *economic* grounds—were already apparent at a very early stage, and there was no telling whether liberal premises might also come under pressure on the basis of decidedly *political* considerations. However much liberals might believe in trade as a mechanism that brings about peace, they were soon to face the far more pressing question of what sort of stability and, above all, what kind of reach liberal principles ultimately have against the background of nationalism, and whether liberal principles in themselves guarantee peace.

▪ ▪ ▪

This skeptical question quickly rose to prominence even in those countries in which liberalism seemed firmly rooted. And it is telling that the answers to it, which can hardly be called "liberal," can be found even in the work of those authors one would least expect to offend against liberal principles.

Historical research has demonstrated—chiefly with reference to the history of *German* liberalism in the Bismarck period and mainly in the Wilhelmine era—that only a small number of thinkers produced a free-trade-based critique of the negative economic impact of a state's colonial acquisitions and of the wasteful character of militarism. It has also been correctly observed that this critique pushed such critics to a marginal position within the spectrum of opinion. Even those who maintained a skeptical distance from imperialist tendencies had no objections to state support for economic expansion through export policies. But this era was in fact marked by syntheses of liberalism and imperialism. We need only mention the names of Friedrich Naumann and Max Weber to illustrate this. As a liberal role model, Britain's political, economic, and cultural ability to lead a world empire was viewed as exemplary. The "liberal imperialists" in particular regarded a German imperialism as the fulfillment and logical continuation of the policy of founding the Reich. For them, domestic liberal reforms were not justified primarily in terms of the values of freedom and popular sovereignty. Instead, reforms were intended to lay the groundwork for imperialist policies, not least because liberals were more aware of the link between the domestic and external spheres and supported this connection more vigorously than did conservative forces. We shall have more to say about this era later on. For now we wish to underline that similar ideas had in fact been expressed far earlier, not in Germany but France, in the work of an author whose name is not usually mentioned in connection with imperialist or belligerent policies— Alexis de Tocqueville.

Though the first half of the nineteenth century in particular was deeply influenced by liberal optimism about progress, this liberalism was by no means monolithic. There were (still) intellectuals who sought to reconcile "civic humanism" with liberal ideas, and who can therefore scarcely be described as "classical" liberals. *The Strange Liberalism of Alexis de Tocqueville* is the title of a summary of the basic political views of a thinker who brought new elements to the debate on how best to achieve peace, but who undoubtedly deployed arguments in his texts reminiscent of "civic humanism."[6]

In his social theorizing on war, Tocqueville (1805–59) shared, at least in embryonic form, the premise that economic progress has a civilizing effect: "The ever-increasing numbers of men of property, [who are] lovers of peace, the growth of personal wealth which war so rapidly consumes, the mildness of manners, the gentleness of heart, those tendencies to pity which are engendered by the equality of conditions, that coolness of understanding which renders men comparatively insensible to the violent and poetical excitement of arms—all these causes concur to quench the military spirit" (Tocqueville 2007 [1835/40], 563). But Tocqueville's position went far beyond this. Though he emphasized the civilizing effects of modern economic life, this did not cause him to believe in a final end to the age of war, referring as he did to the need for future national defense. But this is not the key difference from the Scottish Enlightenment thinkers, who quite explicitly took this need for granted as well, even if they were at odds over the "standing army versus militia" issue. What made

Tocqueville different was the fact that he—two generations younger than the main figures in the Scottish Enlightenment—was more attentive to, and had a more sophisticated grasp of, the effects of mass democracy on the institutional structure of societies than many of his liberal contemporaries, particularly the social and cultural effects. The aristocrat Tocqueville, who grew up in the era of Napoleon and was familiar with the turmoil of the mass mobilized French public of the 1820s and 1830s, became acquainted with Jackson-era American democracy on his one-year trip through America, which he began in 1831. However highly he regarded this democracy, he was very sensitive to the dark sides of democratization. And he was able to bring this sensitivity to his theoretical analyses of the position of the army in democracies (analyses almost entirely removed from the American case). These are chiefly to be found in the third section (and esp. chapters 22–26) of the second volume of *Democracy in America* (see also Kernic 2001, 27ff.).

Tocqueville saw clearly that if aristocratic supremacy in society was to cease, this would also put an end to aristocratic dominance in the various national armies. The (democratic) opening of the army brings a new dynamic to it. Because military hierarchies were no longer cemented by class privileges, and were instead structured according to (democratic) principles of performance, Tocqueville thought it possible that this would make the armed forces more aggressive toward other countries. Military performance can best be demonstrated in war, so there would probably be a greater willingness to launch military adventures within an army structured according to the performance principle. From this perspective, Tocqueville believes he can discern a rift between a democratic army always ready and willing to wage war and a more peacefully inclined democratic polity: "We thus arrive at this singular consequence, that of all armies those most ardently desirous of war are democratic armies, and of all nations those most fond of peace are democratic nations" (Tocqueville 2007 [1835/40], 564). Regardless of whether Tocqueville's prophecy here regarding the dichotomy between army and people has been borne out by history, Tocqueville was touching on a sore point, still relevant today, of any "armed" democracy. Tocqueville's prediction, which applies equally to conscript and professional armies, that the richest, most educated, and most able citizens are unlikely to pursue a career in (democratic) armed forces,[7] has unquestionably been proved correct, and the problem of representativity is still a live one today. The question of whether a basically unrepresentative army or army leadership can impose its own particular goals on politics is still as relevant as the question of which social strata or classes have to put their necks on the line in wars in order to achieve goals that may never have been theirs.

If we look primarily at Tocqueville's main works, *Democracy in America* (1835/40) and *On the State of Society in France before the Revolution of 1789* (1856), we might conclude that, while he was a highly sensitive, indeed brilliant observer or analyst of processes within societies (whether in America or France), he paid little attention to the international dimension of social processes—and thus to war itself. Ultimately, as we have seen, he discusses the upheavals that follow in the wake of democratic armies, but not war and its dynamics as such. Such a view, however, would be highly one-sided, if not wrong, though it never ceases to find exponents. As recently as 1985, Bruce James Smith came close to attributing a kind of pacifist tenor to Tocqueville's thought: "And while Tocqueville never doubted that love of country and political liberty often called for the highest sacrifices from the patriot, he was inclined to view the war-like patriotism of the Imperial Republic as a perversion of more generous affections and a positive danger to civic vitality. . . . That war sustained the virtue of the ancient city (which to Machiavelli had appeared true) was, to Tocqueville's mind, a dubious proposition" (Smith 1985, 160/61). But this is a gross distortion, which can probably be explained only in light of the way in which, overcome with enthusiasm for Tocqueville's democratic ideals, certain writers plainly forget that there is another quite different side to him, evident in his treatment of the "Algeria question." The literature on Tocqueville often carefully sidesteps this issue,[8] preventing us from grasping how easily liberal thought could be seduced by imperialism *before the mid-nineteenth century* and suppressing how rapidly liberal thought could lead to a seemingly unproblematic justification of war.

Tocqueville was interested in Algeria even before his trip to America and—after his return—he even thought seriously about relocating there (Jardin 1962, 62). He was also a very enthusiastic supporter of France's Africa policy in this connection, a policy that, for rather trivial reasons, led to the capture of Algiers in 1830 and subsequently to the full-scale occupation of the area, previously under Ottoman supremacy, by huge numbers of French troops (see Richter 1963, 368ff., and Hereth 1986, 145ff.). Tocqueville was a keen observer of Algeria and published his thoughts on events there. In preparation for his entry into politics, he ultimately became a sought-after expert on the country, though at this point he knew it solely from his reading of administrative documents. As a shareholder in the local newspaper *Journal de Seine-et-Oise*, he pub-

lished two long letters on Algeria in that publication in 1837 to make
himself known to his potential voters. Here he provides a kind of long-
range analysis of the sociostructural conditions of Algerian "society," describing the different cultures of Kabyle and Arabs, the role of religion,
the effects of centuries-long Turkish rule on the prevailing mentality, and
the sometimes disastrous consequences of the rapid abolition of Turkish
administrative structures by the new French colonial masters (Tocqueville
2001b [1837], 14–17). For our purposes, this is of relevance only insofar
as his proposals on French colonial policy and French settlement are
very cautious in nature. Tocqueville is doubtful that every part of the
country can be penetrated to the same degree—in his opinion, the Kabyle area seems unsuited to French settlement, and the same probably
applies even to parts of the majority-Arab regions. The area around Algiers, meanwhile, provided suitable structures. And here Tocqueville
states optimistically that an amalgamation of the French and Arab population is quite possible—in fact, he suggests that a blending of the inhabitants, so disparate ethnically and religiously, is a probability, in part
because of processes of secularization (24ff.). So Tocqueville, who was
already writing against the background of the Abd-el-Kader Arab upris-
ing against the French colonial masters, still hopes in good liberal fashion that the ethnoreligious and sometimes violent conflicts can be resolved through a reasonable—in other words, moderate—settlement
policy and that the expansion of trade structures will also ultimately alleviate these conflicts.

But his first trip to Algeria in May–June 1841 seems to have brought
about a significant shift in his views, at least if we consult his roughly
fifty-page "Essay on Algeria" from the same year, a result of this trip that
was never published during his lifetime. Here, Tocqueville emerges as a
convinced nationalist, who—like the later liberal imperialists in Germany—calls without reservation for French expansion and supports a
merciless war against the Algerian population. The aversion to colonies
still common in the eighteenth century has disappeared, and his nationalism is so aggressive that even John Stuart Mill, who corresponded with
Tocqueville, was highly irritated by his remarks on the Algeria question.
Tocqueville—as he states at the start of "Essay on Algeria"—wants the
colonies to bolster the greatness of France! The difficult political and
military situation should not cause France to conclude that it ought to
withdraw from Algeria, as giving up this colony could only be interpreted
as weakness on the part of France. "Any people that easily gives up what
it has taken and chooses to retire peacefully to its original borders pro-

claims that its age of greatness is over" (Tocqueville 2001c [1841], 59). France must hold on to Algeria because only colonies guarantee influence in world politics, and rule over the North African coast guarantees geo-strategically important control of access to the Mediterranean. The specific actions to be taken by the French colonial administration and the French troops in Algeria must be determined in light of these premises. Since—in contrast to 1837—Tocqueville no longer considers it possible to amalgamate the French and non-French populations, as he sees no prospect of assimilating the latter to the French way of life and the Arabs' social structures clearly cannot be changed,[9] now the only aim must be to systematically populate the country with French settlers. Under no circumstances must an Arab nation be allowed to emerge in this context (67), which is why the ultimate goal must be France's "total domination" in Algeria (66). And this domination can be achieved only through massive use of force, and Tocqueville is quite specific here: "What type of war we can and must wage on the Arabs" (69) is the heading of one section. Tocqueville calls for a military strategy that destroys the foundations of the Arab way of life. Crops should be destroyed, foodstuffs confiscated or withheld, women and children placed under detention, and a ban on trade implemented (70f.). "Small mobile corps" must do their utmost to lay waste to the country—though while safeguarding "humanity and . . . the law of nations"—and destroy Arab cities (71f.): "I think it is of the greatest importance not to let any town remain or rise in Abd-el-Kader's domain" (72).

To repeat, Tocqueville does not justify this belligerent policy toward Algeria with reference to economic benefits. He is quite emphatic that *political* considerations eclipse all conceivable *economic* interests: "I know that metropolitan commerce and industry will protest that we are sacrificing them; that the principal advantage of a colony is to provide an advantageous market for the mother country and not to compete with it. All of this may be true in itself, but I am not moved by it. In the current state of things, Algeria should not be considered from the commercial, industrial or colonial point of view: we must take an even higher perspective to consider this great question" (92). And as we have seen, for Tocqueville this "higher perspective" means endorsing whatever will enhance the power and greatness of France; it is these that must be promoted, by every possible means, even means that Tocqueville himself subsequently seemed to fear. In a quite prophetic way—and here he can build on his observations on "military sociology" in *Democracy in America*—he warns of the political consequences if the leaders of an African army estranged from French society should one day demonstrate their will to power *in France*: "God save France from ever being led by officers from the African army!" (78).

In his later years, Tocqueville found his way back to a more moderate stance on Algeria (see Richter 1963, 392f.); but the problem remains of how the understanding of liberalism and democracy articulated in his key texts can be reconciled with those his "Essay on Algeria" expressed so vehemently in 1841. In the 1960s, in one of the first major political science analyses of Tocqueville's writings on Algeria, Melvin Richter put forward the irreconcilability thesis, asserting the existence of an inexplicable rupture between his liberal and nationalist arguments. "Tocqueville's stand on Algeria was inconsistent with the *Democracy*. When this issue forced him to choose, he placed nationalism above liberalism; the interests of 'progressive' Christian countries above the rights of those that were not" (1963: 364; emphasis in original). But this view has recently been questioned by a number of authors (see the remarks by Fredrickson 2000, 112ff.; Bohlender 2005; Pitts 2005, chs. 6 and 7) who believe that it may in fact be possible to identify parallels with *Democracy in America*.

Toward the end of the first volume of this work (in the chapter "The Present and Probable Future Condition of the Three Races That Inhabit the Territory of the United States"), Tocqueville comments on the ethnic minorities in the United States and is highly skeptical about the prospects for integration of black and native Americans. Tocqueville, who rejects slavery on Christian grounds (see Gershman 1976, 470), believes that the United States will face great problems if it is abolished,[10] prompting him to call for a process of gradual change. Tocqueville's remarks on the integration of the nonwhite population are marked by melancholy and irony, an attempt to conceal the fact that he is unable to put forward any political solutions (Bohlender 2005, 527ff.). Tocqueville had no answer to the question of how the different cultures and ethnic groups might live together in harmony. He could be sharply critical of the British or European settlers' behavior towards the indigenous population and slaves; but this criticism is frequently mixed with understanding for the settlers' brutality, as he saw westward expansion and its economic foundations as indispensable to the political vitality of the United States: "He presents a complex historical argument about the causes of Amerindians' suffering that enables him at once to defend and to deplore European expansion, as well as to refrain from offering any more just alternative" (Pitts 2005, 197). With respect to Algeria as well, in view of the difficulties of social integration in this multiethnic colonial society, Tocqueville could do no more than fall back on his ultimate value, the greatness of France. And this is what gives his argument its particular bite.

We must bear in mind that Tocqueville was no racist. It is true that he has a rather low opinion of Islam (Dion 1990, 68; Fredrickson 2000, 114), but he largely explains the behavior of the Kabyle and Arab population in historical and sociological terms. And we must also bear in mind that Tocqueville did not think primarily in terms of a civilizing mission in Algeria (Welch 2003, 242). You will search his works in vain for arguments extolling the blessings to be bestowed on Algeria's Muslim population by France (Dion 1990, 69). And it is precisely this—as we hinted above—that distresses Tocqueville's British correspondents and debating partners. They were shocked by his argument expounding conquest for the sake of national glory, particularly given that Tocqueville quite openly doubts the civilizing effects of (any) imperial policy: "Unlike J. S. Mill . . . who maintained that despotic rule over 'barbarians' was justified only when it was calculated to improve them . . . Tocqueville could admit that he believed the French had barbarized the Algerians rather than benefited them and still argue for expanding French rule" (Pitts 2005, 220).

In the end, Tocqueville's concern was to revitalize France through foreign policy, and this definitely included the acquisition or retention of colonies through force of arms. In America—as Bohlender (2005, 525) rightly argues—Tocqueville had got to know democratic society as a highly expansive way of life, which he assumed could be kept stable only through this constant dynamism. He was compelled to make much the same assumption about France and its democratic structures during the July Monarchy, so that for him (colonial) expansion became *the* antidote to the recurring pathologies of democracy (529). But how to achieve this revitalization and eliminate these pathologies remained far from clear (Pitts 2005, 194). This problem was already present in latent form in the Scottish discourse on virtue. Adam Ferguson called for a militia because he regarded *martial* virtue as a key component of civic life. But how this martial virtue should make itself felt within the framework of the British world empire, which, even as a Scot, he viewed very positively, remained rather hazy. How did the small Scottish militia fit into Great Britain's relatively large maritime military machinery and how can virtue be achieved in such a complex political and military structure? Ferguson provided no answer, probably because he had none to give. Rousseau's position on this was more consistent. He rejected war and thus martial virtues and right from the outset called for small republics. In such manageable political communities, injecting vitality into the political sphere is not a particularly pressing problem because the citizens' close contact with one another through civil society itself guarantees a continuous political dynamism. In large territorial states, meanwhile, this is harder to imagine. So Tocqueville's call for an imperialist approach to injecting vitality and dynamism into French society may be understandable, but he remained very unclear or contradictory with regard to the mechanisms involved. Is it solely the chauvinism and imperial pride of the French masses that is ultimately to ensure the vitality of France and its democratic culture? And if so, how does this chauvinism relate to liberal principles and to freedom in French society and in the colonies?

After all, with respect to freedom in the colonies we must assume that the rights of the peoples crushed by democratic expansionism will play no more than a subordinate role. In the end, warlike colonialism serves to protect the freedom of the citizens of *France* (Dion 1990, 65). This seemed to mark the end of the universalism of the Enlightenment era, which at least ensured a consistent anticolonial critique. In contrast to John Stuart Mill, Tocqueville—in Bohlender's interpretation (2005, 536)—saw very clearly that (colonial) violence is far from alien to democracy; and at least in his posthumously published "Essay on Algeria," he spelled this out with unprecedented consistency and ruthlessness.

So Tocqueville's position on the "Algeria question" is also problematic because of its theoretical inconsistencies—and not just its normative implications. We should not overlook the reasons why Tocqueville ran into such difficulties. As we have underlined, Tocqueville was no classical liberal. There are certainly echoes in his writings of the ancient Roman ideal of virtue, which he regarded as necessary to a lively democracy. Because of this, he felt called to find a means of injecting vitality into the democratic culture of France. Of course, Tocqueville does not call for a citizens' militia in Ferguson's sense. But the associated intentions were certainly not alien to him. This topic largely disappeared from the social theoretical debate in the nineteenth century; there seems to have been a widespread faith that "negative freedom" is enough to preserve liberality and democracy, particularly among liberal thinkers. As a result, most commentators adopted a linear idea of progress with respect to their particular conceptions of peace, and nowhere were hopes of the positive and ultimately peaceful effects of economic and scientific development articulated more strongly than in France. Auguste Comte, the founder of the new science of sociology, shared this optimism, in a stronger form not only than Tocqueville but even than liberals "of like mind" in England, such as John Stuart Mill, in whose work the issue of war remained present, at least under the surface, in light of what he saw as the necessity for colonial civilizing missions. In the work of the French authors to whom we shall turn now, on the other hand, *certain* arguments rooted in the Enlightenment achieved such dominance that war and violence were relegated to an extremely marginal position, which was to have major consequences for the emerging subject of sociology.

■ ■ ■

In view of what we have said about Tocqueville's "*strange* liberalism," it will come as no surprise that other liberals—not least Auguste Comte (1798–1857), who gave sociology its name—put forward arguments different in many ways from their contemporary Tocqueville. In a quite specific way, Auguste Comte codified the classical-liberal thesis of the incompatibility of war and economy, later so widespread within sociology, partly because his writings drew on very different traditions from those of Tocqueville.[11]

Comte's thought was characterized by the search—the desperate search—for social order in an era still marked by the chaos of the French Revolution, the subsequent wars, and Napoleon's rule. "*Bringing the Revolution to an end without having to give up its achievements*—this was the problem that Comte's generation found itself confronted with and that many, along with him, attempted to resolve" (Fetscher 1979, xxi; emphasis in original). We have already described Tocqueville's "imperialist" solution. Comte's solution, the reconciling of "order and progress," had quite different aims in mind but was also deeply intertwined with the topic of war and peace. As Comte states in his early "Plan of the Scientific Work Necessary for the Reorganization of Society" (Plan des travaux scientifiques nécessaires pour réorganiser la société) from 1822, which laid the ground for his subsequent ideas, two key tendencies would shape the present age: "two different kinds of movement . . . : one of disorganization, the other of reorganization" (1998 [1822], 49). He saw it as his task to achieve this work of reorganization with intellectual means, to bring, guided by science, the disparate currents of French society into a harmonious or "truly organic" order (Comte 1973 [1822], 45).[12] Because this could not occur—at least not solely—through a voluntaristic act, Comte had to place his trust in more or less autonomous historical processes that would guarantee this future harmony. He found the intellectual means to this end in certain elements of French Enlightenment philosophy and—of key importance for our purposes—in social theories produced in direct response to the Napoleonic Wars.

Probably no one had more faith in social progress than certain thinkers of the French Enlightenment. While hopes of progress were always very much alive in Scottish moral philosophy generally (not just in the work of Ferguson, but especially that of Adam Smith), these hopes were radically qualified by an awareness of the ever-present contingencies of history. Certain French philosophers, meanwhile, placed considerably more emphasis on progress. The ideas of Turgot and Condorcet were decisive for Comte in this regard (see also Misch 1969, 47ff.). Turgot's (1727–81) influential writings from the mid-eighteenth century have become one of the key points of departure for philosophers of history and historians because for the first time, and in an easily understandable way, they viewed the human race as a homogeneous subject of history (see Rohbeck 1990, 39): "[T]he human race, considered over the period since its origin, appears to the eye of a philosopher as one vast whole, which itself, like each individual, has its infancy and its advancement" (Turgot 1973, 41). On the basis of this idea, the historical process could be described as a coherent one in which we can merely observe differing rates of progress among nations (42). Turgot made it quite clear that the greatest state of advancement was to be found in Europe. In contrast to many other Enlightenment thinkers, he took an extremely dim view of the (alleged) despotism of Asia and especially China (Turgot 1990, 99, 105; Turgot 1973, 47), causing him to devalue other cultures and civilizations. These premises and the assumption of linear progress forced Turgot to correct the negative view of the Middle Ages and especially of medieval Christianity so widespread in the French Enlightenment. In fact, Turgot referred to the liberal effects of the feudal system (Turgot 1990, 106) and produced an interpretation of Christianity suggesting that it had reinforced the natural feelings between people and alleviated the horrors of war (123f., 134; see also Manuel 1962, 40). Only by reinterpreting European history in this way could he establish an uninterrupted historical connection between the ancient and modern worlds. It now became possible to conceive of a "universal history" as the "consideration of the successive advances of the human race, and the elaboration of the causes which have contributed to it" (Turgot 1973, 64). We are looking at the birth of a highly appealing form of philosophy of history, capable of conceiving of progress independent of empirical chronology (Rohbeck 1990, 48).

Condorcet (1743–1794), whom Comte was to refer to time and again, mostly in a positive way (Comte 1875, 570ff.; see also Pickering 1993, 51ff.), built on this foundation a few decades later. In his *Sketch for a Historical Picture of the Progress of the Human Mind* (1795), he too assumes that history has a subject, by positing a parallel between the development of individual abilities and the progress of humanity (Condorcet 1955 [1795], 4). He understands this progress as in principle infinite (ibid.), such that it even seems possible that (individual) death will one day be consigned to history (200f.). Condorcet not only sees many indications that a new stage of civilization has in fact been reached (according to him, politics is already taking its lead from public opinion and philosophy) (127). He is also confident that the unconscious tendencies of history, which bring about progress (such as increasing trade, which prevents wars) (194), can soon be supplemented by conscious processes of control, such that it becomes plausible to imagine an end to the "empire of fate" (fate as the enemy of progress!) (201). The "application of the calculus" (191) will make it possible to steer human or societal affairs, dismantle prejudices, and thus abolish "war as the most dreadful of scourges" (194).

The belief in progress outlined above was not necessarily shaken by the aftereffects of the French Revolution and the devastation caused by the Napoleonic Wars, but the arguments made about it certainly required some reworking. At the very least, in light of the unleashing of revolutionary and national passions, the faith in "calculus" could no longer be upheld in any straightforward way. Once again, there was a need to rely more on the unconscious tendencies or inevitable forces of history if the faith in progress, and especially faith in an ultimately peaceful future, was to be justified.[13] For Comte, a significant role was played here by the writings of Benjamin Constant (1767–1830), who had outlined the contrast between military and industrial societies a few years before Comte's most creative period (on Constant's influence on Comte, see Pickering 1993, 174ff.).

Constant, perhaps the central, though often unappreciated intermediary between the "liberalism" of Montesquieu and that of Tocqueville, had already completed his *Principes de politique* (Principles of Politics) in 1810 (it was to appear in abridged form in 1815) and in it he made a serious effort to grapple with issues of war and peace. The chapter on war ("De la guerre") includes profound reflection on the change in mentality that occurred in the modern age, which indicated that war would soon be no more. Constant begins by praising war, which—if truly a war waged between *peoples* and not just inspired by the wishes of *rulers*—contributed a great deal to the development of human abilities in the past. But Constant believes this is no longer the case. A warlike mood among the general population is a thing of the past, not least because modern mechanized warfare has rid war of any appeal: "The new mode of combat, the changes in weaponry . . . , artillery: these have deprived military life of what used to be most attractive about it. There is no longer a struggle against danger; there is fatality. Courage today is no longer a passion; it is indifference" (Constant 2003 [1810], 278). So nations are no longer belligerent, in part because the damage done by wars has become incalculable and—as experience shows—armed conflicts always lead to internal repression (ibid.). This shift in mentality, according to Constant, is also apparent in the fact that it is no longer possible to legitimize wars merely on the basis of political leaders' thirst for fame. Wars must be justified in new ways, and with great matter-of-factness Constant points to the ever-present danger that the public will be manipulated, which is another reason why he is skeptical about the possibility of ever achieving a truly clear distinction between wars of aggression and defense (287). Constant emerges as a deeply political thinker, whose primary concern is with the negative political effects of wars. In particular, he notes the contradiction between the citizen and the soldier in the great territorial states of the modern age. What may have converged in antiquity is now out of touch with reality. In any case, the ideal of the citizen-soldier seems undesirable to Constant, probably in part because he had always taken a skeptical view of the revolutionary messianism of the French Revolution that was based upon it. Further—as we have underlined—he always sees the danger of internal repression that arises from the presence of a strong army. Simply put, it is near impossible to control armies (288), and this applies particularly if there is conscription. For Constant, not only are conscript armies disadvantageous because the productive (young) male population is taken out of the economy; conscription should also be opposed because it involves the curtailment of individual freedom, which should be resisted from Constant's liberal perspective (289f.). At most, Constant is willing to countenance a voluntary army, as this is not only likely to respect citizens' freedoms but also at least risk of developing into a state within a state (291).

In view of ongoing international tensions, Constant does not, however, dispute the need for an army. It is true that the experience of the European revolutionary wars immediately calls into question the efficiency of voluntary armies. But Constant is not prepared to work on the assumption that such voluntary armies are inefficient, though he clearly has his doubts. If need be—he argues—governments could always fall back on conscription (292). But from a long-term perspective—and this is the crucial point, through which Constant tries to wriggle out of liberal difficulties with standing armies—the question of army structures will eventually become meaningless, *because the key currents of the age will put an end to armed conflicts between nations.*

Constant goes on to develop this argument, conceived in the era of the Napoleonic Wars and thus very surprising, in the chapter "De l'autorité sociale chez les anciens" in particular. He was familiar with the writings of Adam Smith and others through his studies in Scotland, and here he draws attention to the generally peaceful spirit of the new age. But for Constant, who admired Machiavelli and had also got to know that spirit of "civic humanism" that pervaded the writings of Montesquieu and the "Scots" (see Capaldi 2003, xix), the warlike ancient republics ultimately differ from the big modern states because the former combined a great deal of political freedom with negligible individual freedom: "By a remarkable singularity, however, those who offer us antiquity as a model choose by preference exclusively bellicose peoples like the Spartans and the Romans. This is because only these nations lend support to their theoretical viewpoint, only they brought together great political freedom and an almost total absence of individual freedom" (Constant 2003 [1810], 353). Constant, on the other hand, is no longer prepared to pay this price of giving up individual freedom, particularly given that peace—as he states—is inherent in the prevailing Zeitgeist: "Today everything is reckoned in terms of peace" (ibid.). War is a legacy of the past. At most, it is now a means of achieving certain goals, and no longer an end in itself. But even the suitability of war as a means is increasingly in doubt, because it is simply no longer worth the effort (354). As the spirit of the present age is a trading one and the effects of trade are entirely positive, this will eventually lead to a transformation in international relations as well—as Constant argues, referring positively to Adam Smith in particular (356f., 373).

In the treatise "De l'esprit de conquête et de l'usurpation dans leurs rapports avec la civilisation européenne" (The Spirit of Conquest and Usurpation and Their Relation to European Civilization) from 1814, Constant condenses his argument and again makes a highly dichotomous distinction between trade and war: "We have finally reached the age of commerce, an age which must necessarily replace that of war, as the age of war was bound to precede it. War and commerce are only two different means to achieve the same end, that of possessing what is desired. . . . It is clear that the more the commercial tendency prevails, the weaker must the tendency to war become. The sole aim of modern nations is repose, and with repose comfort, and, as source of comfort, industry. War becomes every day a more ineffective means of attaining this aim" (Constant 1988 [1814], 53/54).[14] This established the dichotomy between bellicose and industrial society, which was to have such a decisive impact on nineteenth-century thought.

In fact, this dichotomy between military and industrial society is present in Comte's previously mentioned early text, the "Plan of the Scientific Work Necessary for the Reorganization of Society" (1822) (on the fundamental significance of this text, see Pickering 1993, 222ff.). There are "only two possible goals of activity for a society, however numerous it may be, as for an isolated individual. These are *conquest*, or violent action on the rest of the human race, and *production*, or action on nature to modify it to the advantage of man. Any society which is not clearly organised for one or other of these ends is just a hybrid association devoid of character. The military goal was that of the old system, the industrial goal is that of the new" (Comte 1998 [1822], 66/67; emphasis in original). This dichotomy also finds reflection in the famous Comtean law of the three stages, whose main features are also developed in this text and which were subsequently to remain essentially unchanged (see Scharff 1995). The teleological notion of the necessary historical sequence of a theological-military, metaphysical, and finally—present-day—positive or scientific age, ascribes constitutive significance to different forms of activity (warfare or industrial work). Like Constant, Comte too works on the assumption that in the earliest times, in the theological and then in the transitional metaphysical age, war had functional significance. In times when industrial skills as yet played no role, "society naturally had to take war as the goal of its activity, especially when we think that such a state of things made the means of war easy to come by, at the same time as imposing the law of war by the most energetic incentives that act on man, the need to exercise his faculties and the need to live" (Comte 1998 [1822], 91). But times have changed. Industrial development is now generating different problems. The sciences—most recently "social physics" or "sociology," as it was later to be known—have now entered a phase that might be described as "positive," because in contrast to the metaphysical era the imagination no longer dominates observation, and instead—in sharp contrast—theory building is guided by observation (Comte 1973 [1822], 84).[15]

As Comte argues—and he builds here on the ideas of Condorcet—the time has now come for a scientific analysis of history and society, an analysis, in other words, that is in keeping with the times and that grasps the inherent laws of history and societal development. As he was to state later, in 1844, "Thus the true positive spirit consists above all in *seeing for the sake of foreseeing*; in studying what *is*, in order to infer what *will be*, in accordance with the general dogma that natural laws are invariable" (Comte 1903 [1844], 26; emphasis in original). Like Condorcet, Comte is at pains to eliminate chance from history (Comte 1998 [1822], 95), as this is the only way to comprehend "that civilization is subject to a determined and invariable course" (ibid.). Ultimately, understanding these necessary developments will not only help prevent future violent revolutions, whose harmful impact Comte had experienced (Comte 1973 [1822], 101). Supervision of positive societal formation by the "scholars" ("savants") on the one hand and the "heads of industrial works" ("chefs des travaux industriels") (68) on the other will also put an end to war between states. According to Comte, following Constant, there is a contrast between "military and working life," between the "military and industrial spirit." Though war may have had its positive functions in earlier times, it loses them in the positive age (Comte 1933, 162ff.). The military sphere's loss of function is also evident in a change of mentality, as people are increasingly unwilling to volunteer for military service, and ultimately—as Comte argues with reference to recent American history and drawing on arguments from British political economy—also because the "decline of colonial rule" invalidates all the reasons for war (393). Finally, Comte assumes that the existing armed forces will also be pervaded by the positive spirit and will ultimately function solely to maintain domestic order—in other words as a gendarmerie. However, even this will not become too large, as Comte assumes that violence will disappear within societies as well, particularly given—as he expects—that the leadership role and skills of the new elites will be universally recognized (see also Fuchs-Heinritz 1998, 205, 230). At any rate, with respect to the foreign policy aspects of interest to us here, Comte is consistent: he calls for the freeing of the French colonies and, especially in his later works, proposes that existing states be broken up into smaller entities (230ff.). All of this is clearly intended to help bring about, more quickly or comprehensively, the transition to the positive, peaceful-industrial form of society that is inevitably happening anyway.

At first sight, the ideas on the incompatibility of war and industrial structures put forward by Comte (and ultimately Constant as well) seem to be a mere continuation of certain arguments already set out in Scottish Enlightenment philosophy, particularly by Adam Smith. As we showed in the preceding chapter, in *Wealth of Nations* Smith had also presented a historical-sociological analysis of the link between basic socioeconomic structures and the potential for the existence of specific military institutions. Smith's question was: What forms of army are possible in specific socioeconomic contexts? (see p. 35ff.). In a sense, this was simply a question about the compatibility of *institutions*. So Smith's remarks may be interpreted as a cautious functionalist argument, as he only outlines possible types of military organization but does not really examine whether violence and war per se are incompatible with certain social structures. This functionalist caution is now abandoned in the arguments of Constant and Comte, as they assert that modern industrial society in itself will more or less rule out the possibility of violence and war. This is a far stronger functionalist supposition, which later liberal thinkers often found fascinating and impossible to resist, despite rapidly being confronted with major difficulties and contradictions.

This was soon apparent in the work of the Englishman Herbert Spencer (1820–1903), who also had an outstanding influence on the early theoretical development of sociology. His theory of differentiation was taken up by later theorists of modernization and evolution in the second half of the twentieth century, while time and again the classical figures of American sociology such as Charles H. Cooley and George Herbert Mead, along with their French counterpart Émile Durkheim, drew explicitly on his work, mostly to define their differences from him.

It is quite difficult to determine Spencer's social theoretical position within the debate on war and peace because his later interpreters tended to immediately drag his evolutionary theory into the vehement disputes over Darwinism, Lamarckism, and Social Darwinism. Not only that, but his views changed markedly during his lengthy period of creativity. There is a long tradition within sociology of writers stressing their differences with Spencer while nonetheless, consciously or unconsciously, taking up elements found in some of his works. Furthermore, through his ultraliberal work *The Man "Versus" the State*, Spencer was declared the epitome of the radical libertarian and an ideological stooge of the "robber barons." This may in fact be defensible in the case of this particular text, but not if we include consideration of many of his other works (Francis 2007, 250f.; Taylor 1992, 73). All in all, it is difficult to interpret Spencer's theory in general, and this applies even more to his statements on war and peace.

A fair characterization of Spencer would be to call him a *moderate* evolutionist (Boudon/Bourricaud 1984, 345; for a more antiteleological interpretation of Spencer's work, see Haines 1998). In reality, though he coined the term "survival of the fittest" at an early stage (a term often wrongly attributed to Darwin), he was by no means directly interested in Darwin's key concerns. The main difference between Spencer and Darwin was simply that Spencer was not concerned with the problem of the historical alteration of biological species; he was not convinced that long periods of time were necessary to bring about a significant change among species (Francis 2007, 190). Spencer was interested in the issue of species' environmental adaptation in the here and now and put forward a number of arguments on this subject, some of which were very close to the views of Lamarck.

In light of this it comes as no surprise that by the 1850s, a few years before the publication of Darwin's *The Origin of Species* in 1859, Spencer was developing his evolutionary ideas and applying them immediately to human societies. Drawing on the arguments of Adam Smith and Malthus, he supported the idea of the free play of social forces (see Peel 1971, 138). Spencer assumes a perfect fit between the social organism and the environment as the goal of evolution (Francis 2007, 197), and even in his early writings he makes no distinction between human and nonhuman life. Progress, in any event, is certain. So Spencer deploys an identical descriptive formula to capture both spheres of evolution, the social and the biological: the famous "law of development" from the homogeneous to the heterogeneous, with this process obviously being driven forward by life itself.[16] It should be noted that Spencer's reference to the move "from the homogeneous to the heterogeneous" is quite alien to Darwinian thought. For Darwin,—as J.D.Y. Peel (1971, 142f.) has pointed out—there is no need for the development of ever more complex organisms. But Spencer works on the assumption that such development does indeed occur, clearly drawing on the debate that had been going on at least since the emergence of Scottish Enlightenment philosophy or early political economy with respect to the advancing division of labor. And this was presumably also the reason why Spencer never really abandoned Lamarckian arguments, because to do so would have opened up a gap between biological and sociocultural evolution—which would have conflicted with Spencer's entire theoretical system. The transfer of patterns from one generation to the next, precisely what happens in human culture in other words, would not have fit within his framework without Lamarckian arguments; but the absence of such arguments would have wrecked the notion of the unity of evolution, biological and social, which Spencer made so much of, as well as casting doubt on the notion of a shift from the homogeneous to the heterogeneous (143).

What sounds so simple in the phrase "survival of the fittest" and what Spencer's early writings perhaps suggest is the Social Darwinist notion of perpetual, merciless, predatory competition between individuals on the one hand and between nations on the other. Yet Spencer did not advocate this notion in this form. Again and again, at least in his early and middle work, Spencer balances out individualist-liberal or even libertarian views with references to issues of justice that must also be taken into account (see Francis 2007, 250f.; Taylor 1992, 73). And neither did he assume that this struggle would be "perpetual." His evolutionism was "moderate" or with reservations, in part because it was intertwined with the *dichotomy between the bellicose and industrial social formations* with which we are familiar from the work of Comte.[17] The key point here is that the certainty about progress still observable in the work of Spencer in the mid-nineteenth century, the faith that (social) evolution can be equated with progress, is coming unstuck, as evident, apart from anything else, in this dichotomy.

Spencer is not quite sure how this dichotomy can fit into his evolutionary thinking. As particularly evident in the *Principles of Sociology*, the first part of which was published in 1874, he applies the distinction between bellicose and industrial societies both in the sense of extreme types and in the sense of developmental stages. The second line of argument is better known. But at many points in this work Spencer argues as if, at each developmental stage, societies can move more toward a bellicose or industrial type—dependent on contingent circumstances. "As, during the peopling of the Earth, the struggle for existence among societies, from small hordes up to great nations, has been nearly everywhere going on; it is, as before said, not to be expected that we should readily find examples of the social type appropriate to an exclusively industrial life" (Spencer 1885, 615; see also Haines 1998, 105). Neither is it certain that bellicose societies will disappear completely in the present era, nor can we rule out the possibility that societies existed in prehistoric times in which the warlike spirit was absent. This dimension must be taken into account at all stages of development. Nevertheless, it makes sense to Spencer to work with this dichotomy and affirm that in bellicose societies individualism plays very little role, that the political structures are highly centralized, that questions of status and rank are hugely important and trade is only marginal, and that economic self-sufficiency and autarchy are key characteristics of these bellicose societies. While militant societies are characterized by "compulsory cooperation," in industrial societies "voluntary cooperation" leads to a high degree of individualism and generally egalitarian structures.[18] Among other things, "industrial" social structures are characterized by a relatively pronounced dissociation between military service and citizenship, in other words the armed forces become a kind of profession, decoupled from the status of citizen. And this is linked with the fact that the number of citizens who actively participate in war is fairly small relative to the population as a whole, which in turn makes the high degree of individualism in industrial societies possible in the first place (Spencer 1885, 478ff.). With the advance of industrial society, Spencer therefore expects not only more peaceful but also more democratic structures. In the past, wars have often led to state centralization and thus almost always to restrictions on freedom. So the decline in the number of wars as the number of "industrial" societies increases will also facilitate a major advance in liberalization and democratization.

It is at this point that Spencer's critique of Comte begins. He believes that Comte was unable to see that his own account of the basic structures of industrial societies in the positive age is scarcely compatible with the spirit (which Comte saw as typically French and "militaristic") of anti-individualism, elitism, and collectivism that pervaded his writings (257; see also Boudon/Bourricaud 1984, 349). Spencer's writings do in fact feature an inherent individualism, which sets them apart clearly from Comte's arguments. But—very much in line with his merely typological use of the dichotomy between bellicose and industrial societies—Spencer is not entirely sure whether individualistic features inevitably advance ever further, that is, whether there is a more or less linear developmental path from bellicose to industrial societies. As many of Spencer's interpreters have noted, toward the end of his writing career he becomes ever more skeptical about the ideas of progress he himself had earlier expounded (see, e.g., Francis 2007, 288). A kind of political and social relativism (though still of an evolutionist hue) seems to have made itself felt. In *Principles of Sociology*, Spencer no longer expresses the belief that the ways of life of "civilized" peoples can be straightforwardly transferred to "more primitive" ones and that such transferal can in itself produce a positive outcome (1885, 233). Not only that, but according to Spencer his conviction that the process of evolutionary development and the emergence of true "civilizations" ineluctably promote humanitarianism is a misconception. "Whatever relation exists between moral nature and social type, is not such as to imply that the social man is in all respects emotionally superior to the pre-social man" (239). More important in this context is the fact that Spencer sees disturbing tendencies at work in the highly developed social formations of his own time that seem to undermine all hopes of progress. Prussia and its move toward militarism demonstrated to him (588ff.) that the distinction between militant and industrial societies can only be a typological one and does not point to a linear development. And Spencer does in fact refer repeatedly to the alternation between "militancy" and "industrialism," which seemingly pervades all of human history (429, 568; see also Turner 1984, 28).

It is, however, unclear how this alternation between bellicose and industrial societies in Spencer's theory can in any way be reconciled with his basic evolutionist thesis of development from the "homogeneous to the heterogeneous." If the differentiation of social structures that are increasingly organized in line with the division of labor is truly the hallmark of social change, it remains an open question why militant forms have repeatedly arisen featuring the "compulsory cooperation" that is of course distinguished by *de*differentiated structures. We might conclude that coincidences contribute to this dedifferentiation and thus to the repeated reemergence of militant societies. But as social evolution advances, such coincidences must be ever less likely to occur or the crucial factors leading to militarism must be ever less pronounced. This is because the more radically structures are differentiated, the more difficult it becomes to imagine returning to dedifferentiated forms of social organization in the first place.

Spencer seems to have shared this view. It is true that he refers to the negative example of Prussia in *Principles of Sociology*, warning of the rebarbarization of contemporary European societies. And in view of the ongoing possibility of barbarism and the risk of war, he emphasizes the uncertainty of the future; he even questions the thesis of the unilinear development of humanity and the idea that types of political regime will move closer to one another. But despite all of this, the notion of seemingly objective tendencies toward the development of industrial society appears—quite abruptly—toward the end of the book, which ultimately leads him to reinterpret the typological dichotomy between bellicose and industrial societies as a schema of evolutionary development. So Spencer does assert that in future there will be ever fewer cases of government intervention and thus that political and social structures will become further differentiated. He evaluates the (imperialist) militancy of European nation-states of his time as a (*temporary*) relapse within a fundamentally advancing process of evolution and differentiation: "Citizens will carry still further their resistance to state-dictation; while the tendency to state-dictation will diminish. Though recently, along with reinvigoration of militancy, there have gone extensions of governmental interference, yet this is interpretable as a *temporary wave of reaction*" (Spencer 1885, 660; emphasis added). This should be viewed merely as a relapse because, according to Spencer, war is no longer productive or has been completely overtaken by the productivity of industrial civilization: "Thus, that social evolution which had to be achieved through the conflicts of societies with one another, has already been achieved; and no further benefits are to be looked for" (665). For Spencer: "From war has been gained all that it had to give" (664). This applies to imperialism as well. Though the expansion of the European societies made sense in earlier times and the barbarian peoples were quite rightly "civilized," it is now questionable whether this imperialism, which has always been advanced by military means, can still do justice to the demands of highly differentiated industrial societies, especially given that this imperialism inevitably gives rise to the very militaristic structures that run counter to the industrial type of society (see Turner 2003, 78; Battistelli 1993, 206).

Overall, there is a notably tense relationship between Spencer's functionalist evolutionism and his awareness of the ever-present possibility of a relapse into (warlike) barbarism. As Italian sociologist Fabrizio Battistelli has highlighted, Spencer's naturalistic conception of society's inevitable advancement to ever higher levels not only conflicts with the pacifist and anti-imperialist politics that he openly propagated. It is also unclear why the original driving force of (biological and social) evolution, the conflict between biological organisms or social units, should suddenly have come to a standstill in Spencer's own time toward the end of the nineteenth century, at least in the social sphere, and should tend to promote peace between industrial societies. By taking this stance, Spencer is not only abandoning the still-cherished thesis of the *unity* of evolution; such a stance is really plausible—see Spencer's conviction that war is no longer productive—only if we understand societies as highly rational, coherent actors, which keep their distance from war for reasons of utility. Spencer frames his argument in such a way that the problematic nature of this supposition that society is unified is no longer evident, as societies are now understood as functionally differentiated wholes. But, as a result, the differences between social groups and classes in terms of power and interests are left systematically out of account. What was still present in classical political economy, in the work of Adam Smith, for example, but also that of utilitarians such as Jeremy Bentham and the two Mills, was namely the notion that there are also different classes in highly developed societies, that the "ruling few" have an interest in colonies, that this contributes to the constant risk of war, and that because of this the colonies must be emancipated (at least according to Bentham)—Spencer's argumentational tropes are devoid of all this. Even if it is true that, in contrast to Comte, Spencer used the concept of organism merely as an analogy to social structures, it is clear that he pays little or no attention to conflicts within societies as systematic problems of industrial societies. And this makes it very difficult to ask whether and how, for example, sets of circumstances arise within societies in which (military) force can either become a rational or at least understandable option, or (military) force can be repeatedly deployed, more or less unexpectedly, as the unintended result of actions. So on the basis of theoretical premises, Spencer's functionalism once again reinforces what was in any case already inherent in the liberal tradition of thought and the thesis of the pacifying effects of trade, namely the assumption of the fundamental peacefulness of modern societies (see Battistelli 1989, 28f.).

It was in the writings of Comte and Spencer that *the* classical nineteenth-century liberal conception of peace found its true expression. This was the view held by those who believed they could plausibly lend credence, with sociological and historical arguments, to hopes of worldwide progress—and thus hopes of an end to war—which had formerly often been justified solely in philosophy-of-history terms. In that sense this conception was the very embodiment of bourgeois optimism and the mood that a new era was dawning—a widely held sentiment in European and North American society during the first phase of industrialization.

■ ■ ■

Even within Marxism—the great antagonist of liberalism in the second half of the nineteenth century—this optimism about progress was widely shared. As much as it saw itself as the great opponent of liberalism, Marxism adopted some of its central premises. At the very least, Marx and his supporters shared Enlightenment hopes and therefore expected the emergence of a nonviolent world order following the socialist revolution; as a result, there was simply no discussion of whether there could still be diversity and thus conflict between peoples, religious communities, or other groups following the socialist revolution (see Berki 1971). How such an Enlightenment-style expectation of peace could be entertained in the first place becomes clear in Friedrich Engels's *Anti-Dühring* ("Herr Eugen Dühring's Revolution in Science" from 1878). In a brilliant critique of Dühring's ideas on the crucial importance of war to social change, Engels (1820–95), Marx's closest comrade-in-arms, again sets out explicitly the "fundamentals" of the materialist conception of history, which he and Marx regarded as established by science. Engels was extremely well versed in the literature on war and undoubtedly a good deal more knowledgeable about military history than Marx (see Neumann 1952, esp. 158). Here, step by step, he seeks to demonstrate that all military conflicts and their results are determined by and dependent on the relations of production. So they can never be regarded as the key movers of history. According to Engels, at no point in history has violence been an independent driving force but only ever a means to given—and genuinely decisive—economic ends (1975 [1878], 192). There may be a small number of exceptions, in cases where, under favorable circumstances, economically backward peoples overrun civilizations economically superior to them (219). But this is the exception rather than the rule. In fact: "[A]lways and everywhere it is the economic conditions and the instruments of economic power which help 'force' to victory" (205).

In *Anti-Dühring*, Engels goes so far as to describe the history of war and warfare as fundamentally a history of technological innovation, which must itself be understood as dependent on the relations of production. In this connection he puts forward two arguments intended to prove that, as an expression of the tensions in capitalist societies, militarism is on the point of abolishing itself. First, Engels tells us, the course of the Franco-German war of 1870/71 shows that there is little scope left for further development of the tools of war. War has clearly gone as far as it can *technologically*. Weapons have now "reached . . . a stage of perfection" (204). At the same time—and this is the second *sociological* argument, which must be taken rather more seriously—the development of the military sphere will also come to an end because of the now necessary mass mobilization. In this connection Engels refers to a dialectic of militarism. The introduction of mass armies and universal conscription made necessary by the dynamics of conflict in Europe—the counterpart of or supplement to the extension of suffrage—will be the financial ruin of the existing states, as the costs of the associated armaments explode and become impossible to meet. In addition, as a result of universal conscription, weapons will increasingly end up in the hands of those who have a great interest in toppling the existing capitalist-militarist order, namely the workers (and peasants):

Militarism dominates and is swallowing Europe. But this militarism also bears within itself the seed of its own destruction. Competition among the individual states forces them . . . to resort to universal compulsory military service more and more extensively, thus in the long run making the whole people familiar with the use of arms, and therefore enabling them at a given moment to make their will prevail against the war-lords *in command*. And this moment will arrive as soon as the mass of the people—town and country workers and peasants—*will have* a will. At this point the armies of the princes become transformed into armies of the people; the machine refuses to work, and militarism collapses by the dialectics of its own evolution. (204; emphasis in original; see also Münkler 1992, 63ff.)

So militarism, Engels concludes, will be rent "asunder *from within*" (1975 [1878], 205; emphasis in original).

Engels's interpretation of war in terms of a technological materialism also implies that violence and war must be understood—and, if applicable, legitimized—within the context of the historical process (220). The euphemistic but pithy phrases that Engels uses here exercised a tremendous influence on revolutionary thought and action, particularly in the twentieth century. Deploying Marx's vocabulary, Engels states that (revolutionary) violence is the "midwife of every old society pregnant with a new one" (ibid.). Violence is appropriate or even required if it aids the emergence of a new mode of production. Of course, violence will finally disappear—and here we can see Marxism's liberal inheritance—when there are no longer economic reasons for it, in other words, when communist society has been established. Assuming the lawlike advance of the historical process, Engels is able to provide instructions for action, such that the victims of revolutionary war and revolutionary violence are neglected. This is one of the wellsprings of the fateful tendency, which was to become so typical of Marxist thought, to justify the agony and suffering of the present as a means of bettering the lives of future generations.[19]

Engels does in fact follow the materialist conception of history through to its ultimate conclusion—with major reductionist consequences. However we might assess Eugen Dühring's "contribution" and his emphasis on the role of war in the detail (and Engels's counterarguments are often quite correct), we obstruct the path to adequate historical understanding if we declare certain aspects of reality, such as military factors, to be of merely secondary importance on a basic conceptual level and *per definitionem*. And in fact, while the economic reductionism within Marxism has proved useful in ensuring that our analyses take account of the vested interests of the arms industry, overall it has emerged as out of touch with reality and a hindrance to genuine understanding. Again and again during the past century—always with great difficulty and by mustering every conceivable rhetorical device—Marxists had to reconcile the Soviet Union's foreign policy, which was highly aggressive in practice, with the theoretical postulate of a fundamentally peaceful socialist mode of production. They even had to explain the unthinkable, namely, the war between the socialist states of Vietnam and China in the 1970s. Of course, such "explanations" were far from convincing, and it comes as no surprise that well-informed leftists within Anglo-American sociology, who saw Marxian ideas as quite legitimate, began to think afresh about the independent role of politics and war in history (see Mann 1988a [1977]; Evans/Rueschemeyer/Skocpol 1985; and p. 194ff. below).

References to "Marxism" are, of course, always problematic, when we consider that Marxian theory, before being given its seemingly final codified form by the authorities in Stalin's Soviet Union and in the "fraternal" socialist states, was constantly reinterpreted and thus modified in the debates of the second half of the nineteenth century. By the 1880s at the latest, in view of the progressive improvement in the living standards of sections of the working class, it had become ever more questionable, at least for some "Marxist" intellectuals, whether key tenets of Marxist theory—the labor theory of value and its prognosis that the proletariat would be increasingly impoverished—were in fact tenable. If legitimate doubts could be raised about these core theoretical elements, then it was naturally quite possible to question the likelihood of the revolution that Marx and his supporters expected to occur as well. From this perspective, the integration of the working class into the various nation-states must at least be viewed as a thinkable option. But this led to the insight that—unless one wished to abandon all hopes of a revolution—the revolution was probably still some way off, and that even revolutionary socialists must therefore accommodate themselves to existing conditions for the time being. In an age of competing and highly armed nation-states, this also meant that one had to tackle the question of peace: from the perspective of socialist intellectuals and party leaders, it was very likely to be their own clientele who would be sent to slaughter in any new war (on the political thrust of the German Social Democrats' critique of the armed forces in the German Empire, see Neff 2005). And, in fact, it was not just revisionists but even Engels himself who responded to this problem following Marx's death, going so far as to relativize his hopes of a dialectic of militarism expressed in *Anti-Dühring*. His essay "Can Europe Disarm?" from 1893 is an intelligent attempt, bristling with expert knowledge, to propose detailed measures that might put a stop to the military build-up in Europe.

Right at the start of this text, Engels expresses his fears of total military and economic devastation in Europe, which would shatter all hopes of a socialist revolution, even over the long term (1990 [1893], 372). It is clear from the profound and serious anxieties expressed by the leading socialist intellectual of his time that he is no longer able to believe in the inevitable dialectic of militarism, which he was still expounding in *Anti-Dühring*. Instead, what mattered was to take action in order to preserve the (economic) bases for a socialist revolution, that is, to ensure that these were not destroyed in a European war. So Engels appeals to the major European governments and must therefore fall back—no less than his opponents in the bourgeois camp—on power-political and liberal arguments. In this context, he states that disarmament without revolution is in fact possible. He sees the key to a process of disarmament, which all the European states would have to accept, in the reduction of the terms of service required in the standing armies, because he believed that the longer an army's term of service, the greater its offensive power. He therefore proposes that terms of service be limited and then gradually reduced and—in a peculiar move for a socialist theorist—that the freed-up military personnel be integrated into "civil society," as the noncommissioned officers could help educate children in the schools (380f.).

But it is not this detail that is theoretically significant, but the fact that, in this context, the socialist and internationalist Engels refers to the interests of Germany, to "our" interests (see Münkler 2001, 177). He points out that it is particularly important for Germany to implement this plan to achieve disarmament by reducing terms of service, as this would force France—then Germany's archenemy—into action. Germany would in any case be at an advantage. If France accepts, the risk of war would be massively reduced, especially given that the other European states would most likely follow suit. If France does not accept, Germany could at least be sure of having world opinion on its side (Engels 1990 [1893], 397).

Engels's late writings on war and peace were marked by a pronounced realism. It should also be acknowledged that his writings of the 1890s are pervaded by a spirit of responsibility toward the German but also the European working class, whose sacrifice in a great war he was determined to resist. But, despite this, it is clear that Engels's (and Marx's) thought was characterized—like its liberal counterpart—by significant aporias. And this was bound up, to a significant degree, with social theoretical deficits and biases that the "forefathers" of scientific socialism never truly faced.

Engels was smart enough to realize in his later years that there was little sociological basis for the thesis of the dialectic of militarism that he was still advocating in *Anti-Dühring*. By the 1870s, the idea that the armed masses of workers and peasants would rise up against their governments was plausible only if one ignored nationalism entirely and paid no heed to the fact that the upper echelons of power hierarchies generally had no trouble in "out-maneuvering," in organizational terms, those subject to their rule. Engels did at least revise his original view. But even his works of the 1890s left unresolved how the notion of "our interests" and his appeal to the German government could be reconciled with a consistently internationalist theoretical approach, which both eschews nationalist emotions as aberrations and postulates an objective "course" of history, in which the crucial steps are taken behind the backs of actors.

In view of all this, it is clear that in many respects Marxism (in the shape of Engels's writings) embraced the legacy of liberalism. Marxism shared with Enlightenment and liberalism hopes of an inevitably approaching future peace, though this peace was explained differently *than* in the liberal debate. This was still Engels's position in *Anti-Dühring*. Within the theoretical debate, hopes of "perpetual" peace through an imminent revolution evaporated in the 1890s. From this point at the latest, thinkers within the socialist movement were reliant on a strategy of argumentation and action oriented toward the rules of the existing European state system, making it difficult for them to convincingly set themselves apart from liberals or even power-political realists. This applies in particular to the reformist portion of the socialist movement. The main thrust of Marxist thought was increasingly determined by the various attempts to construct a theory of imperialism, most of which were made around the time of the First World War. Here, the Hitler-Stalin pact of 1939 and the subsequent dispute between Rudolf Hilferding and Walter Ulbricht drew the decisive dividing line. The Social Democrat Hilferding adopted a theory of totalitarianism to explain the alliance between Hitler and Stalin, whereas Ulbricht went so far as to declare British imperialism more dangerous than the Nazis (see Joas 2003, 130f.).

■ ■ ■

If we have looked only at liberal conceptions of peace in the nineteenth century, and if the thinkers mentioned so far discussed war on liberal premises and even socialist theorists relied on liberal figures of thought, it seems natural to ask whether this truly reflects the intellectual developments of the period. Other than the tradition of power-political realism, were there no other approaches that contrasted with the various liberal currents and with socialist conceptions, approaches that offered resistance to the suppression of war, the tendency to divert one's gaze from the historical role of armed violence? In a certain sense this question is rhetorical. At least below the surface, an antiquated bellicism did of course continue to exist in the nineteenth century, a school of thought that saw war as the source of all good things and viewed the idea of a peaceful civilization and the disappearance of martial virtues as concomitant with a general moral decline, an increasing wimpishness and feminization. And in the course of the nineteenth century, this became linked with a biologization of social and political facts that built on Darwin and others and became extremely influential, a biologization that was intended to justify the cutthroat competition between individuals as well as races or ethnic groups. In the shape of Ludwig Gumplowicz (1838–1909) and Gustav Ratzenhofer (1842–1904), there were certainly exemplars of such thinking among the early representatives of German-speaking sociology; they are not part of the discipline's living legacy today. Though there are good normative reasons to be wary of adopting these authors' ideas in any simplistic way, their writings contain important arguments with which we must engage if we wish to understand the role of violence and the significance of war to modernity. (On the issue of a militaristic tradition in sociology, see Joas 2003, 134–62.)

But—from the perspective of our mostly chronological approach—there is no need to advance to the end of the nineteenth century or to the period immediately before the outbreak of the First World War to find such arguments, nor is it necessary to look in the work of those authors who many would prefer to erase from the legacy of sociology because their Social Darwinist arguments now seem embarrassing and unworthy of the subject. Such ideas appear far earlier, and in the work of highly respectable authors, not least among representatives of classical German philosophy.

In this context, however, it should be noted that it would make little sense to interpret these authors as *diametrically opposed* to liberalism in light of their bellicist views. This would be mistaken because certain liberal dogmas—such as the belief in the beneficial effect of competition between individuals and groups—could be interpreted in very different ways, both in a general political sense and with respect to how best to achieve peace. Liberal approaches often took surprising turns.

We might ask, for example, whether Spencer's functionalist thought, his conceptualization of social entities as organisms, might not have led to a very different conclusion from that of an ever more probable and stable peace. In fact, fundamentally different conclusions had already been reached some decades earlier, in post-Kant Germany. Arguments anchored in functionalism, differentiation theory, and evolutionary theory played no real role here, but the metaphor of the organism was nevertheless the starting point for a radical reinterpretation of Enlightenment ideas. In Germany, this intellectual turn and process of reinterpretation are closely linked with the name of G.W.F. Hegel, whose figures of thought were to be crucial to the bellicist and thus essentially "nonliberal" discourse discernible beneath the surface in the nineteenth-century.

Georg Wilhelm Friedrich Hegel (1770–1831) is no longer part of the world of Kant, and not just because he had a different way of looking at conflicts. By reading the works of political economists, he had learned that the development of the market economy inevitably leads to the development of classes and class conflicts, adding a threat from within to the external military threat facing liberal or republican states (Habermas 1997, 121). Hegel (alongside Schelling) was one of the most important critics of the modern theory of natural law. Modern natural law (see p. 17) had been constructed initially on individualist-mechanistic premises. Based on the natural rights of the individual, the form of the legal and political order was explained in terms of its having to comply with the needs and rights of the individual. This made separate "state goals," detached from the goals of individuals, unthinkable. This applies even to the arguments of Thomas Hobbes, which can only be described as an apologia for absolutism, in that even he saw it as the task of the Leviathan to protect citizens' interest in their own survival, which he took to be the ultimate point of departure for social theory.

But the political whole as the overall sum or expression of specific individuals, that mechanistic or static notion, was thrown on the defensive with the onset of romanticism at the latest, when organism metaphors became increasingly popular, metaphors that were ultimately applied to politics and even whole societies (on what follows, see the first-rate account by Mori 1999, 232ff.; see also Taylor 1975, 438). The concept of the "body politic" spread rapidly in the first few decades of the nineteenth century, and it was chiefly qualities such as totality, autonomy, and vital motion that were attributed to such "organisms." The linking of such attributes to this concept of organisms and subsequently to the phenomenon of war was to build up a momentum of its own, which was most clearly apparent in the work of Hegel and which could lead to a speedy departure from the liberal discourse of peace.

As at least one aphorism in Hegel's Jena "Wastebook" (1803–6) reveals, he was deeply ashamed of Germany's political and military passivity, its lack of unity in view of the aggressive policies pursued by Napoleon. The German nation—Hegel complains in the above text—is in fact nonexistent; the Germans are at best "Europe's Quaker nation. They allow everything to be taken from them, the jacket, and in their goodheartedness, lest anyone scowl at them, they hand over the doublet as well. If they receive a slap across the cheek from one quarter, one of the warring powers, they make sure they are lined up to get the other cheek slapped as well" (Hegel 1986 [1803–6], 564). In any case, Hegel refers to the German tendency to shy away from vigorous armed resistance to Napoleon's expansionism as a disgrace, unworthy of a true nation. These private notes by Hegel, unpublished during his lifetime, were anything but fleeting reflections that found no expression in his systematic published writings. In Hegel's case, it is impossible to separate his published writings from his unpublished material (as could be done so straightforwardly and for so long by interpreters of Tocqueville's writings because it was more or less impossible to discern traces of his reflections on Algeria in his "major" works).

This is evident in Hegel's so-called "Verfassungsschrift" from 1800 to 1802. In "The German Constitution," Hegel postulates frankly that it is only in war that the vitality of a state becomes apparent, because it is only in this extreme situation that "the strength of the association between all and the whole," the degree of willingness to sacrifice oneself that the citizen must be ready to demonstrate, is revealed (Hegel 1999a [1800–1802], 7). According to Hegel, the behavior of the different parts of society toward the state as a whole should reflect a "common, free subjection to a supreme political authority" (10). But it is precisely this organic integration of the parts into a large, superordinate whole that is missing in Germany, which is why there is no true state there and that strangely neutral stance toward Napoleon's policies prevails. What is the state? What are the essential components of any state, what are its merely "incidental" ones? Hegel asked himself these questions and his answer is unmistakable. The state is not defined through shared customs or a common religion (20); neither is there a true state even if it exercises comprehensive control over citizens—the state should not be seen merely as a great machine (22ff.). A state exists only if its citizens grasp, of their own accord, the need to identify with it and, crucially, are prepared to engage in collective defense (of the entirety of their property): "For a mass to form a state, it is necessary that it should form a common military force and political authority" (16).

For Hegel, there are good reasons for this focus on the readiness of the state and nation to use violence. For him, perpetual peace is simply inconceivable, because—following Hobbes—he works on the assumption of an ever-present and necessary clash of interests between states. And it is against this background that Hegel interprets international law. The raison d'état of individual states simply cannot be opposed to the law, which means that little importance can be attached to international law. Law can be asserted only through power. Given that, happily, there is no world state, "international law" is invalid or does not exist in reality. All Enlightenment-era conceptions of peace anchored in international law and Kant's cosmopolitanism are dismissed with biting contempt: "If the philanthropic friends of right and morality did have an interest, they might realize that interests, and hence also rights themselves, can come into collision, and that it is foolish to set up a dichotomy between right and the interest of the state (or, to use a morally more repugnant expression, the advantage of the state)" (69/70). And it is this notion of the law's dependence on power that Hegel then calls upon to legitimize violence— violence in aid of the unification of Germany. For Hegel, this violence is a power-political rather than legal or moral philosophical problem, which is why he can call hopefully for the coming of a "conqueror" who will unite all Germans through violence, compelling them "to regard themselves as belonging to Germany" (100). Hegel takes the existence of a German nation, a German people, for granted, a people that might have to be forced to acknowledge itself in order to rescue it from historical "madness": "[F]or madness is simply the complete isolation of the individual from his kind. The German nation may not be capable of intensifying its stubborn insistence on particularity to the degree of madness encountered in the Jewish nation, which is incapable of uniting with others in common social intercourse. Nor may it be able to attain so pernicious a degree of isolation as to murder and be murdered until the state is obliterated. Nevertheless, particularity, prerogative, and precedence are so intensely personal in character that the concept of necessity and insight into its nature are much too weak to have an effect on action itself. Concepts and insight are fraught with such self-distrust that they must be justified by force before people will submit to them" (101).

In his essay on natural law ("On the Scientific Ways of Treating Natural Law, On Its Place in Practical Philosophy, and Its Relation to the Positive Sciences of Right") from 1802/3, Hegel was to sharpen this view still further, producing the kind of reinterpretation of typical modern arguments on natural law mentioned above. He criticizes the usual Enlightenment constructions of natural law inasmuch as their point of departure lies in a fictitious state of nature. According to Hegel, such a construction provides us with a faulty foundation, because the positing of isolated individuals as in Hobbes's thought experiment automatically leads to an initial thesis of random "diversity." This makes it impossible to conceive of all the chance attributes of atomized individuals as any kind of unity: "Now in making this distinction, empiricism in the first place lacks any criterion whatsoever for drawing the boundary between the contingent and the necessary, between what must be retained and what must be left out in the chaos of the state of nature or the abstraction of the human being" (Hegel 1999b [1802/3], 111).

This, so Hegel believes, is the wrong starting point for philosophy, as apparent in the fact that the "empiricism" he refers to entails a highly abridged understanding of freedom. Here the individual is understood merely as a singularity, yet as an isolated entity it must be determined by the external world and thus be dependent on it. But this means that true freedom can only be understood as the abolition, the "nullification of singularity" (137), which leads directly to the notion of an all-embracing whole. With this notion of the People as the "absolute ethical totality" (140), Hegel deploys the metaphor of the organism which, through its peculiar linkage with the phenomenon of war *very generally* (and not only in Germany), was to lead to bellicist arguments. As Hegel immediately makes clear, this ethical totality of the People can only ever assert itself by marking itself off from other totalities, from other peoples. The dignity and function thus ascribed to war takes us clearly away from the Enlightenment thought discussed so far. It can no longer be a matter of conceding the utility of war in the early days of humanity before going on to explain its imminent disappearance because of countervailing social phenomena and forces (be it the spread of republics, be it trade or industry). A very different mode of argument now comes into play. If war now functions to establish identity, then war is a genuine and constant component of the state system. What is more (and Hegel has already used this argument with respect to the unification of Germany), war can now be waged for the sake of identity, with ends and means becoming merged with remarkable rapidity. Is war just a means to the end of establishing and maintaining an ethical totality? Or, because the unique vitality of a people finds expression in it, should war perhaps be understood as an end in itself? Hegel never gave a positive answer to the second question. It was left to authors of later generations to do so.[20] But it can hardly be denied that Hegel paved the way to an affirmative answer.

And Hegel's view of this issue is no different in his far more influential philosophy of law. The *Elements of the Philosophy of Right* was published in 1821, already some years after the passions of the Napoleonic era. Here, in the section on "international law," Hegel again makes it perfectly clear that the Kantian idea of a perpetual peace is utterly implausible because the state of nature between states cannot be eliminated. On the international level there is quite simply no power capable of enforcing the law. At best, there is an assumption that the law "ought" to be obeyed—making peace an invariably precarious state of affairs (§ 333). So disputes between states can be resolved only through war (§ 334), which means that politics must first and foremost promote the state's own survival, its "substantial welfare" (§ 337). But—particularly given that the state embodies the ethical totality—this means "that the welfare of a state has quite a different justification from the welfare of the individual. The immediate existence of the state as the ethical substance, i.e. its right, is directly embodied not in abstract but in concrete existence, and only this concrete existence, rather than any of those many universal thoughts which are held to be moral commandments, can be the principle of its action and behaviour" (ibid.). So morality, Hegel tells us, must not be confused or mixed with politics. As ethical totality, the state's field of activity is beyond any moral claims of the individual.

These remarks by Hegel on international law are the logical consequence of his account of the basic features of state "external sovereignty." Here, Hegel again makes it clear that he views relations between states in analogy to the problem of recognition developed in *Phenomenology of Spirit* (Mori 1999, 230). The state is understood as an individual that can preserve its identity only by setting itself apart from other individuals, in other words from other states (Mori 1989, 68). In *Phenomenology of Spirit*, the problem of recognition between servant and master is described as a life and death struggle (see Kojève 1969, 3–30), and the relationship between states in the state of nature is understood in the same way. But *Phenomenology* on the one hand and the philosophy of law on the other require quite different solutions to the problem of recognition. The struggle for recognition that goes on between servant and master must not, of course, end in the death of either protagonist, as this would render the problem of recognition null and void. Hegel makes much the same argument with respect to international relations, as other states must also continue to exist, so that from this perspective a world state and thus the "death" of all other states is out of the question. As he puts it in § 338, "states reciprocally recognize each other . . . *even in war*—as the condition of rightlessness," such that there is a "*bond*" between states "whereby they retain their validity for each other in their being in and for themselves, so that even in wartime, the determination of war is that of something which ought to come to an end" (emphasis in original). But in *Phenomenology*—and this is the key difference—the way out of, or solution to, the problem of recognition is an emphasis on work, through which the servant can find fulfillment as a human being. On the level of states, such a solution makes no real sense, which is why Hegel is compelled to conceive of the struggle between states as never-ending (and always bound to occur intermittently at the very least), a struggle that forever revolves around the question of identity and that obviously cannot be finally resolved—because this fragile identity can only be strengthened and renewed in battle.

For Hegel independence and differentiation from other states is in fact "the primary freedom and supreme dignity of a nation" (§ 322). It is this differentiation from the external world that constitutes a state's "*own . . . moment*"; it is only involvement with other states (individuals) that brings the substance of the state "[to] existence and . . . consciousness . . . as the . . . absolute power over everything individual and particular, over life, property and the latter's rights" (§ 323; emphasis in original). The ethical moment of war reveals the necessity to sacrifice the individual person in order to preserve the state's independence: the cause of war is not an "absolute evil," it is not a "purely external contingency"; rather, it lays bare the organic core of the state: "The ideality which makes its appearance in war in the shape of a contingent external relationship is the same as the ideality whereby the internal powers of the state are organic moments of the whole. This is apparent in various occurrences in history, as when successful wars have averted internal unrest and consolidated the internal power of the state" (§ 324). It is in the moment of war in particular that citizens must show courage. This is not individual courage but rather the courage to maintain the sovereignty of the state. The citizen should see himself as part of a greater whole, and Hegel put a particular spin on this argument by asserting that the mechanization of warfare, the invention of the "*gun*," is the expression and evidence of the overcoming of *individual* bravery. "The principle of the modern world—*thought* and the *universal*—has given a higher form to valour, in that its expression seems to be more mechanical and not so much the deed of a *particular* person as that of a *member* of a whole. It likewise appears to be directed not against individual persons, but against a hostile whole in general, so that personal courage appears impersonal. This is why the principle of thought has invented the *gun*, and this invention, which did not come about by chance, has turned the purely personal form of valour into a more abstract form" (§ 328; emphasis in original).

In his interpretation of Hegel's writings on war, Massimo Mori states that Hegel stepped up the disparaging of happiness already present in the work of Kant, while his suppression of eudaimonism was ultimately to lead to a radical reevaluation of war. The idea of the sublimity of war seems more prominent here than before (Mori 1999, 237f.), though it is true that even some of the Enlightenment debates on eternal peace provoked a large number of bellicist counterreactions (Kunisch 1999, 70). Nonetheless, Hegel's figures of thought reverse Montesquieu's thesis of the disciplining and pacifying effects of trade. It is not trade that subdues the martial passions. Quite the reverse: only war can "rein in the petty-mindedness of peoples" (Mori 1999, 240), so the promise of a peaceful future cannot be taken seriously. Hegel's trope of recognition through total negation leads—to repeat—almost inevitably to the idea of revitalization through risky, violent undertakings, as the state might seek its truth by consciously jeopardizing its own as yet unthreatened existence. So war as the radical negation of all security may even seem imperative for a state or society as a means of reasserting its true character. In sharp distinction to the Enlightenment, there is no longer any opposition between war and civilization. In fact, war may even express the innermost essence of a civilization. This represents a challenge to the contemporary philosophical revitalization of recognition theory.

■ ■ ■

It would be doing Hegel an injustice to interpret his bellicism merely as ideological justification for slavish obedience of the typically German or Prussian variety, as it is embedded in an argument that emphasizes that war takes people *beyond everyday life* and highlights the *new dimensions of experience* that this makes possible (see also Avineri 1972, 196ff.). As we shall see in a moment, it was by no means only *German* intellectuals of the nineteenth century who were preoccupied by this idea. Certainly, Hegel's remarks on war contain unmistakable ideological excesses. But we should keep in mind that French intellectual history is also full of mythologizing justifications for violence. These range from the ultrareactionary, antiliberal critique of the French Revolution in the work of Joseph de Maistre, which has been interpreted as protofascism (Berlin 1990), through Georges Sorel's reflections on the liberating force of workers' violence in the syndicalist struggle, to Frantz Fanon's comments on the use of force by the colonized to liberate themselves from colonial rule, which inspired panegyrics from Jean-Paul Sartre. In the United States, as the exemplary democratic state, one figure of thought related to Hegel's has taken on considerable force. We are referring to the warlike violence—often invoked in myths as well as practiced in reality—on the "frontier," the border with uncivilized nature and "savage" Indians, a violence that always accompanied the establishment and stabilization of democratic polities (as Tocqueville suspected, see p. 80). The notion of the vitalizing experience of violence was also articulated beyond the frontier context. This is evident, with surprising twists, in the work of William Graham Sumner (1840–1910). His work, which appeared in the late nineteenth and early twentieth centuries, had a considerable influence on the American public and was also important within the emerging discipline of sociology. Sumner's take on this idea is surprising, among others things because, while he endeavored to popularize the ideas of Herbert Spencer in the United States, he came to some very different conclusions about how best to achieve peace.[21]

Sumner's essay "War" from 1903, published just under one hundred years after the works of Hegel discussed here, is interesting chiefly because he takes up certain Spencerian and Hegelian motifs (we shall leave aside the question of whether this was conscious in the latter case), weaving them into an argument with Social Darwinist underpinnings. Sumner was made chair in political economy at Yale University in the early 1870s but, as a former preacher, also felt a great need to make an impact beyond the university. He can probably be described as one of the first American sociologists who explicitly saw himself as such—before the actual professionalization of the discipline in Chicago.

Like Spencer, Sumner attempted to establish the theoretical proximity between sociology and biology. In "Sociology," an essay from 1881, he explained this closeness by pointing out that in both disciplines the struggle against nature is in a sense the foundation of all theorizing: "We have already become familiar, in biology, with the transcendent importance of the fact that life on earth must be maintained by a struggle against nature, and also by a competition with other forms of life. In the latter fact biology and sociology touch. Sociology is a science which deals with one range of phenomena produced by the struggle for existence, while biology deals with another. The forces are the same, acting on different fields and under different conditions" (Sumner 1919b [1881], 173). According to Sumner, the ratio of population to the size and bounty of the earth is one of the key determinants of human life, and sociological theories must be designed with this in mind. Human beings' battle with nature to ensure their subsistence ("the struggle for existence") is, as it were, the natural substrate on which the social body must be built. It is only the construction of the social body that is a conflictual process in the literal sense, as it is initially a matter of ensuring one's control over the earth's bounty *in competition with other people.* So this construction is the result of human beings' struggle over resources, of the "competition of life" (176). According to Sumner, in view of this unavoidable conflict it is clear that the basic principle of the "survival of the fittest" is the fundamental condition of all human life, an eternally valid principle to which human action must necessarily adapt: "The law of the survival of the fittest was not made by man and cannot be abrogated by man. We can only, by interfering with it, produce the survival of the unfittest" (177). And this is the basis of Sumner's radical laissez-faire credo, which rejects all state intervention, such as that intended to eliminate poverty—because it goes against the principles of nature.

It was on these premises that Sumner was to write his essay, "War," which was published posthumously but conceived in 1903. Here he defines war as an *organized* conflict between human beings, which is why it must be considered a relatively late product of humanity's development. As a late historical outcome of the "competition of life," war is a struggle between fairly highly developed societies (Sumner 1919a [1903], 3). As we have seen, Sumner believed that even before the emergence of large human groups, the exclusion of every other individual was a key principle of action within the context of competition between people, a principle aimed at ensuring the maximum of resources for oneself. Cooperation with other individuals and thus the formation of groups takes place only if there is a reasonable expectation that shared effort is more profitable than individual effort (8). What looks here at first sight like a purely utilitarian construction is in reality more complex in character. Sumner ascribes a variety of motives to the human being—not just the pursuit of narrow, selfish interests. According to Sumner, human action is guided by four basic motives: hunger, love, desire for fame, and religious needs. These motives drive the struggle among individuals but also structure the struggle between groups. It is in this context that Sumner introduces his famous distinction between "in-group" and "out-group," claiming that groups and societies—and here we can detect a Hegelian motif—can be kept stable only by setting themselves clearly apart from the external world. Group conflicts, according to Sumner, lead to an enhanced sense of togetherness, while collective identity building occurs via—or may be accelerated by—conflicts and the process of marking one's group off from, or defending it against, another or others: "[E]very other group is to us an 'others-group' or an 'out-group'" (9). He goes on: "We can now see why the sentiments of peace and cooperation inside are complementary to sentiments of hostility outside. It is because any group, in order to be strong against an outside enemy, must be well disciplined, harmonious, and peaceful inside; in other words, because discord inside would cause defeat in battle with another group. . . . It is no paradox at all to say that peace makes war and that war makes peace" (11). "Ethnocentrism," according to Sumner, is the necessary basis of all group formation and thus of human history per se. Ethnocentrism is the emotional bond that prevents potential internal conflicts and clashes of interests and establishes the necessary internal unity of societies amid the never-ending "competition of life" (12).

In this connection, Sumner takes up Spencer's distinction between militant and industrial societies, though without wishing to assert the existence of a historical process leading to a peaceful society as Spencer had done. What is more, he considers this clear distinction between societal types to be misguided, and it was he, rather than overly optimistic liberals hoping for peace, who was to be proved right, at least in historical terms. In any case, for Sumner the will to use violence is present now and always, fed by the four basic human motives, which are crucial to the analysis of the causes of war. So Sumner highlights the irrational factors in human action and draws attention to the emotions that conflicts and wars release. If one accepts this, then according to Sumner there can be no real hopes of a peaceful future: "It is evident that men love war . . ." (29).[22] According to Sumner, the circumstances of the Spanish-American War of 1898 demonstrate that it is pointless to place hopes in human rationality, as philosophy and sociology have always done. It is quite possible, Sumner believes, for human beings to want violence regardless of means-ends calculations: "[W]hen two hundred thousand men in the United States volunteer in a month for a war with Spain which appeals to no sense of wrong against their country, and to no other strong sentiment of human nature, when their lives are by no means monotonous or destitute of interest, and where life offers chances of wealth and prosperity, the pure love of adventure and war must be strong in our population. . . . The presence of such a sentiment in the midst of the most purely industrial state in the world is a wonderful phenomenon. At the same time the social philosophy of the modern civilized world is saturated with humanitarianism and flabby sentimentalism . . . ; by it the reading public is led to suppose that the world is advancing along some line which they call 'progress' towards peace and brotherly love. Nothing could be more mistaken" (29; see also Curtis 1978, 362). In line with this, Sumner does not anticipate peace in the twentieth century but rather—prophetically— "a frightful effusion of blood in revolution and war" (1919a [1903], 30).

What is interesting about Sumner's position is that his Social Darwinist views by no means lead him to a straightforwardly positive evaluation of war. His work does *not* endorse the notion of the will to war, the idea of war as an end in itself or—because it is liberating—as a revitalizing force, as did authors building on Hegel's writings. This is because his Social Darwinist credo is fenced in by a number of other considerations. Sumner does state that one frequently observable effect of wars is the liquefaction of social relations. He asserts that in the past wars undoubtedly drove civilization forward, drawing attention to the "modernizing effect" of the Napoleonic Wars: "The Germans tell of the ruthless and cruel acts of Napoleon in Germany, and all that they say is true; but he did greater service to Germany than any other man who can be mentioned. He tore down the relics of mediaevalism and set the powers of the nation to some extent free from the fetters of tradition; we do not see what else could have done it" (32). We cannot, Sumner thinks, rule out the possibility that wars will have such positive effects in future as well. But he is far too aware of the unintended consequences of social action to truly welcome the waging of wars to achieve specific goals. Wars are always going to break out because of the "competition of life," so they must be accepted as a "natural" occurrence. But—in line with Sumner's laissez-faire credo— they should not be deployed as an instrument, because this simply overestimates the human capacity for control: "A statesman who proposes war as an instrumentality admits his incompetency; a politician who makes use of war as a counter in the game of parties is a criminal" (35).

It is this that explains the "peculiarity" of the anti-imperialist arguments in Sumner's text (see also Marshall 1979, 273f.). It by no means necessarily contradicts his Social Darwinist worldview if he criticizes careless references to "raison d'état" and the Monroe Doctrine as unacceptable attempts to justify the United States' expansionist foreign policy (Sumner 1919a [1903], 36ff.), or if he refers to the great chances of peace in an America relatively insulated from global politics while calling for the integration of Indians and "negroes" into American society (27f.). Quite the reverse: for all his Social Darwinism, Sumner was a convinced anti-imperialist.[23]

As early as the 1890s, Sumner had penned vehement polemics against American imperialism. In the essay "The Fallacy of Territorial Expansion" (dating from 1896), Sumner vigorously disputes that the strength of a state is linked to its territorial extent, which is why it makes no sense for America to seek constantly to acquire new territory. Imperial adventures are best left to others, particularly the British; because of its anti-imperialist origins, the United States is ill-suited to such things. According to Sumner, expansion beyond a certain point, which he does not define more closely, would only produce ever more disadvantages, from higher taxes and a burgeoning machinery of state to restrictions on individual freedom (Sumner 1919c [1896], 292). But it was only with his essay entitled "The Conquest of the United States by Spain" from 1898 that Sumner truly caused a furor. The sarcastic-ironic title presages a text that is concerned with the prehistory and history of the conflict between the United States and Spain in the late nineteenth century, and it is a sophisticated anti-imperialist pamphlet. The Americans, Sumner observes, are conquering Spanish territory. But from a cultural point of view, what is "actually" happening—Sumner tells us—is precisely the opposite. Through their imperialism, the Americans are taking on the very cultural features that had characterized the Spanish colonial power since the late fifteenth century. The United States will become like Spain. Sooner or later it will come to resemble that at once despotic and lethargic power whose death throes over the preceding centuries had been the result of colonial expansion, because this very expansion had always prevented the Spanish rulers from carrying out internal reforms.

Sumner describes it as the great fortune of the United States that it was able to develop in comparative isolation from world events (Sumner 1919d [1898], 332) and thus develop democratic characteristics. But the "pest of glory" (313), the imperialist craving for foreign adventures in order to achieve a dubious expansion of the national territory, is now threatening those very democratic achievements. The militarism that is part and parcel of imperialism—and here Sumner takes up Spencer's distinction between militant and industrial societies (323)—merely encourages plutocracy and thus antidemocratic tendencies that run counter to American political culture. This militarism obstructs awareness of necessary internal reforms, he tells us, referring once again to racism and the failure to integrate the black population, particularly in the southern states (331, 309).

Sumner's fusion of Social Darwinist and strictly anti-imperialist arguments was certainly far from common in the United States. But against the background of American culture and history, especially against the background of Americans' self-interpretation as citizens of a deeply anti-imperialist polity, the emergence of such views among intellectuals and social scientists comes as no real surprise. This mentality was part of the theoretical repertoire of the still young discipline of sociology when the First World War mounted a massive challenge to every theory on war and peace.

The Classical Figures of Sociology
and the Great Seminal Catastrophe
of the Twentieth Century

DESPITE THE INTENSITY of international scientific exchange, at the beginning of the twentieth century the social sciences were strongly influenced by different national traditions. As a discipline, sociology took a particularly wide variety of institutional forms and featured very different theoretical and research programs. The worsening international tensions, ultimately erupting in the First World War, increasingly led to mutual nationalistic stereotyping of the intellectual scene, making it increasingly difficult to refer openly to impulses from other, potentially hostile states. If this was true in a general sense, it applied even more to the discourse on the causes of war and the prospects for peace.

In Germany no one in the bourgeois academic camp of the time was immune to the notion of a powerful, geographically expanding state, including the liberals. Indeed, liberal thinkers in Germany accommodated themselves to imperialist policies with particular ease. This can be explained partly by the close association in German intellectual history between historicism and power-political realism, with the German nation being taken self-evidently as the ultimate basis for all values; the nation's power must be maintained if not enhanced. The Ranke school saw history in terms of action, but this was the action of supra-individual wholes. This is why it focused on the "history of political events based on the principle of the primacy of external policy" (Schnädelbach 1984, 46). This school of historiography was deeply aware of the fact that "the state is based on the principle of power, that its origins are bound up with war and military structures" (Hintze 1925, 546; see below), but this must be understood first and foremost as a corrective to a conception of the state as a purely legal relationship rather than an endorsement of the opposite extreme. The precise relationship between power and law, between historicism and universalism, remained unclear, however. Some exponents of this tradition, often carried away by their enthusiasm in the early days of the new German empire and the wars that preceded its formation, indulged in the pathos of a harsh "realpolitik," linking the popular Social Darwinist clichés of the struggle for survival with a Borussian historical mythology.

This is especially true of Heinrich von Treitschke. Though Treitschke was never representative of the discipline of history in Germany as a whole, similar views were expressed with striking frequency by German scholars. Power-political realism was never as dominant outside Germany—at least in intellectual circles (Joas 2003, 21). This association was not obvious, let alone necessary, on theoretical grounds. But it took hold nonetheless, with consequences for the social sciences and humanities as a whole. This was apparent not least in the school of political economy that rose to prominence in Germany. We have already referred to Friedrich List and his project of developmental nationalism, to be implemented by protectionist means, of the 1830s and 1840s. List had accused classical political economy of not really being *political* economy in the true sense of the term but at most cosmopolitan economy, because it works on the erroneous assumption of a world not divided into nations and states, in other words a homogeneous world. List insisted that, given the developmental disparities in Europe and the world as a whole, economists must pay attention to national differences. In terms of economic *policy*, this means it may be legitimate for a nation to implement protectionist measures (specifically, to introduce protective duties), at least temporarily, in order to safeguard its own industries until such time as they reach the world market standard. So List made the nation, rather than an abstract global economy, the starting point of his analyses and, against all the arguments of the classical political economists, did not shrink from referring to the potential role of wars in fostering development (see List 1885 [1841]; Silberner 1946, 134–71; Etges 1999, 78ff.).

It would surely be wrong to interpret the older and younger German historical school of economics of the second half of the nineteenth century simply as a continuation of List's program, but it does contain similar elements. Roscher, Knies, Schmoller, and Schäffle (on the following, see Silberner 1946, 172ff.) take it for granted that the classical political economists' hopes regarding the civilizing effect of the economy are in vain, and thus that military competition between nation-states will continue. Albert Schäffle's essay "Zur sozialwissenschaftlichen Theorie des Krieges" (On the Social Scientific Theory of War)—clearly inspired by the debates surrounding the International Peace Conference in The Hague in 1899—is particularly interesting in this connection. Schäffle does not dispute that we can expect the incidence of war to diminish at some point, but he sees this merely as the consequence of a stable equilibrium between highly armed nation-states. "[I]t is the peculiar option of full-scale armament rather than the conventional one of disarmament that does most to counter war and promote peace" (Schäffle 1899, 244f.). The idea of disarmament seems to him not only impracticable but totally absurd.[1] So, for all these authors, the point of departure is not the global economy but the German nation-state, and state intervention is of course permitted and sensible if it will benefit this nation-state. The unconditional imperative of free trade seems to them as obsolete as the classical liberal notion that the state should be as small as possible and keep intervention to a minimum. And because they construct their arguments on the premise that armed conflicts will continue to occur within the European state system in future, they discuss the economic pros and cons of wars without prejudice.[2] In any case, they are unable to endorse the British theorists' view that armed conflicts entail *nothing but* disadvantages.[3]

This is the intellectual background to Max Weber's (1864–1920) inaugural lecture at Freiburg on the occasion of his appointment to the chair in political economy (1895) (on what follows, see also the remarks by Hennis 1984; 1988). Here, Weber does not hesitate to describe himself as an adherent of the "German historical school" (Weber 1999 [1895], 131), one who merely radicalizes certain basic assumptions already present in that economic paradigm.

The empirical starting point for Weber's Freiburg address was his observation of the creeping displacement of the ethnic German population of West Prussia and other areas east of the Elbe by Polish peasants. Against the interests of the Junker, Weber calls for the closure of Germany's eastern border to Polish immigrants and an end to the state-subsidized manorial economy in this part of Germany, because the big aristocratic landowners mainly take on cheap *Polish* labor, thus accelerating the displacement of *German* peasants. The Polnicization of Germany's eastern regions must, he demands, be brought to an end; and this is a task for an economic policy designed to maintain or enhance Germany's power.

Weber's stark nationalism may seem surprising, especially against the background of the social theoretical discourse of the eighteenth and nineteenth centuries described in the previous chapters, which of course frequently underlined the pacifying effects of trade and thus tended to ignore the potentially conflictual competition between states. But, in fact, Weber's position is not so unusual. Since List at the latest, many German economists had been convinced that nations inevitably have differing economic interests—and that massive economic conflicts are therefore unavoidable. "There can be no *truce* even in the economic *struggle* for existence; only if one takes the semblance of peace for its reality can one believe that peace and prosperity will emerge for our successors at some time in the distant future" (Weber 1999 [1895], 128; emphasis in original). Weber vehemently rejects "eudaimonist" notions of the future. The Enlightenment faith in progress, Montesquieu's hopes for the benevolent effects of trade, or Smith's (and Ricardo's) firm belief that the economic interests of individuals and collectivities balance out gave way to the seemingly realistic insight that "elbow-room in this earthly [economic] existence" can only be won "through the hard struggle of human beings with each other" (ibid.).

What was clearly apparent in Tocqueville's analyses of Algeria, but was more or less unknown to a broader public, what was generally set out coyly rather than self-confidently in the late writings of John Stuart Mill through a justification of Great Britain's imperial mission dressed up as theory, is now expounded with tremendous vigor in Weber's inaugural lecture, not least because Weber was very clear that "economy" meant *national* economy. He refers to "us economic nationalists" as if it were a matter of course (132). Without further ado, he declares the well-being of the German nation-state the standard of value for economic policy: "The science of political economy is a *political* science. It is a servant of politics, not the day-to-day politics of the individuals and classes who happen to be ruling at a particular time, but the lasting power-political interests of the nation. And for us the *national state* is not, as some people believe, an indeterminate entity raised higher and higher into the clouds in proportion as one clothes its nature in mystical darkness, but the temporal power-organization of the nation, and in this national state the ultimate standard of value for economic policy is 'reason of state'" (130; emphasis in original).

So Weber's "economically" inspired nationalism was not particularly unusual within the scholarly landscape of the time. But the *manner in which* Weber presented the problems in West Prussia in his Freiburg address was something new. First and foremost, according to Wilhelm Hennis, "the scandal" was the "destruction of the harmonious idea that there was a unique economic value, that of 'productivity' or 'profitability.' The economy, and quite naturally more so politics, are the classic domains engulfed with problems, of value *conflicts*. The interest (of the large landowner) in productivity competes with the population issue, the *socio-*

political interest of the state in dislocation. . . . The genuinely impressive feature of the Inaugural Address is the presentation of an evaluative problem which cannot be settled by science, but which could be *clarified* by science" (Hennis 2000a, 146). Weber thus described the difference between fundamental values with unprecedented stridency—a difference that had tended to remain unspoken. The idea that economics must adopt a national perspective was widely shared. But *which specific measures* did this perspective demand within the framework of the German nation-state? Weber now placed this question on the intellectual agenda, a question that could be approached only via decisions about mutually exclusive values. It was this that was disturbing and unusual.

The other unusual aspect was the massive extent to which Weber deployed a Social Darwinist vocabulary, not just the term "struggle" but also "selection," though Weber did cast doubt on the viability of Social Darwinist arguments (in footnotes added for publication).[4] But it is his reference to unavoidable "selection" and the struggle between nations as one of history's central laws of motion, with its Social Darwinist overtones, that now enables him—with seeming consistency—to make aggressive demands for certain economic policy measures intended to help the German nation in this global struggle. He sharpened the tone of this political and intellectual statement in such a way that we may justifiably refer to Weber as one of the key exponents of the "*imperialistic* elements of the national idea" (Mommsen 1984, 53; emphasis added). In fact, it was Weber's inaugural lecture that ushered in the "turn to an impatient imperialism . . . in German public opinion" (Radkau 2009, 128). Looking back over the nineteenth century, Weber laments the imperialist opportunities missed by a German nation that lacked "the simplest *economic* understanding of what it means for Germany's trade in far-off oceans when the German flag waves on the surrounding coasts" (Weber 1999 [1895], 135; emphasis in original). A realistic assessment of not only the economic but also the *political* dimensions would have made Germany's territorial expansion seem far more urgent, if the nation's lack of maturity had permitted such insights. But—Weber at least appears to suggest—it may not be too late for such expansion. Weber clearly had no problems here in accepting the possibility of war: domestic conditions should be subordinated to foreign policy in order to facilitate a powerful "world policy."

If we examine Weber's national and imperialist position here, as particularly evident in his Freiburg inaugural lecture, it is striking that, as one of the great historicists among the classical figures of sociology,

Weber was obviously not seriously attempting to justify the nation as the ultimate source of value. Weber was surely aware that the nation-state is a modern phenomenon and, in any event, not a timeless one, even if he referred to the "elemental psychological foundations" (133) of the nation-state in his inaugural lecture. Yet he never asks the empirically far from ridiculous question of whether this nation-state will continue to exist forevermore. If there can be even the slightest doubt that the nation-state will go on forever, then unlike Weber we should think long and hard before making what may be a temporary historical phenomenon our ultimate normative basis. In some places in his writing, it even seems as though Weber is searching desperately for a way to make the leap into nationalism, in order to get away from the "*chaotic mass* of standards of value, partly eudaemonistic, partly ethical, and often both present together in an ambiguous identification" (131; emphasis in original).[5]

Weber's inaugural lecture at Freiburg does not grapple directly with the questions of war and peace. But his words are highly revealing if we wish to understand why nationalistic sentiment was ratcheted up in Germany in 1914 with such intensity, and why war was endowed with such an excessive ideological charge. Even an analyst such as Weber, otherwise so down-to-earth, was involved in, or even helped shape, the current of nationalism that increasingly made itself felt before the war, a current that played a significant role in ensuring that the shots fired in Sarajevo ultimately led to war.

▪ ▪ ▪

Weber's vehement prewar nationalism is certainly not representative of German sociology as a whole in any simple way; more moderate voices could also be heard. And, of course, nationalism was not a German invention. It also exercised a powerful influence elsewhere, in France for example, where the political camps had diverged radically since the so-called Dreyfus affair and the political Right was espousing an ever more aggressive nationalism. Émile Durkheim (1858–1917), however, the founding father of French sociology, towering above all others, wanted nothing to do with *this* nationalism.[6] The political and sociological views expounded by Durkheim were entirely in accord with the *French* idea of the nation-state; Durkheim produced vehement anti-German pamphlets during the First World War. And yet, beyond the straightforward apologias for war, Durkheim would repeatedly make it clear—and this surely represents a major difference from Max Weber—that there is something more universal and thus more valuable than the Fatherland. "No matter how devoted men may be to their native land, they all today are aware that beyond the forces of national life there are others, in a higher region and not so transitory, for they are unrelated to conditions peculiar to any given political group and are not bound up with its fortunes. . . . As we advance in evolution, we see the ideals men pursue breaking free of the local or ethnic conditions obtaining in a certain region of the world or a certain human group, and rising above all that is particular and so approaching the universal" (Durkheim 1957, 72). These quotations from Durkheim's lectures on the sociology of morality, which he delivered in Bordeaux between 1896 and 1900 and in Paris on several occasions between 1902 and 1915 under the title "General Physics of Law and Morals," in which he also tackles the subject of state and war (see Müller 1991), express precisely what is lacking in Weber's work, namely serious contemplation of the durability and stability of what Weber considered to be the ultimate value: the nation. This no doubt made Durkheim less susceptible to the temptations of nationalism than Weber as world war loomed. But it is not the different attitudes apparent here with which we are concerned, but the question of whether and how "war" found a place within Durkheim's social theories. To answer this question we must consult Durkheim's political sociology. The difficulty here, however, is that Durkheim and the *French sociology* of the time as a whole failed to explicitly formulate a theory of the state and the phenomena directly linked with it.

In comparison to Weber's shrill tone, Durkheim sounds almost defensive. Against the prevailing trend, he tried to combat *exaggerated* nationalism and pick up the thread of an (older) French understanding of the state of a (more) universalist complexion. But it is not just the tone and thrust of his argument that are different. It is also clear that Durkheim lacks the conceptual means to think about the "modern state" sociologically. He defines the state in rather hazy terms, invoking rather than analyzing its tasks and functions. This fit with the French tradition of removing such questions about the state from academic debate and omitting them from the "moral sciences" (Heilbron 1995, 21f.). It is no surprise that in the *Année sociologique*, cofounded by Durkheim, which took on the task of delineating the various branches of the new discipline of sociology, the category of political sociology did not initially appear (Müller 1991, 333).

There is in fact no definition of the state in Durkheim's work.[7] Instead, his point of departure is the individual and particularly the thesis that the state is the agent and guarantor of individual rights—in other words, that the state's key function is to support the liberation of the person from the particularistic ties of "constituent societies" (Durkheim 1957, 57, 62). Durkheim is strongly opposed to any concept of the state that would infringe individuals' fundamental rights or even—as in the work of Hegel—demand a willingness to sacrifice oneself. But, at the same time, he engages ceaselessly with the ideas of Kant and Spencer, whom he criticizes—on differing grounds—for falsely assuming the existence of isolated or selfish individuals. This shows that Durkheim is in search of an individualism capable of resolving the strained relationship between state and individual that had always been viewed as a matter of course by traditional liberalism. Such an individualism can be neither utilitarian nor wholly moral; for him, it consists of a sacralization of the individual, a faith in universal human rights (Durkheim 1973 [1898]; Joas 2008, 133–48). Durkheim believes this individualism to be such a powerful characteristic of the age—he refers to a "cult of the individual"—that the state too must fall in line with it. According to Durkheim, the state will inevitably become a kind of religious institution whose task is to champion this cult of the individual. It is down to the state to "organize the cult, to be the head of it and to ensure its regular working and development" (Durkheim 1957, 70).

From the perspective of power-political realism, Durkheim's thinking may seem touchingly naive. But his idea of the progressive sacralization of the individual proved one of the most important presentiments of the triumphant progress of human rights in the second half of the twentieth century, and key to the sociological analysis of numerous changes in law and morality (Joas 2005).

Politically as well, he was too sensitive to ignore the international tensions and potential conflicts between states or nations. He regarded national defense as a necessity, and saw that this task cannot always be painlessly reconciled with the needs of individuals, such that the state—in the case of conscription for example—must act and make decisions against the immediate interests of individuals. And yet, he believes that this need for national defense will not persist forever. In contrast to the unquestionable empirical fact of the increasing number of *internal* tasks facing the state, its *external* functions would sooner or later die away. On this point, then, he agrees entirely with Comte's and Spencer's ideas on the advance of the industrial form of society and the end of its military counterpart. Yet at the same time he sharply rejects Spencer's utilitarian arguments (and those of classical political economists), according to which the future state of peace will be due solely to the civilizing effect of trade. For Durkheim, it is a *universalist morality* that is primarily responsible for this state. In contrast to his hypernationalist contemporaries, Durkheim did not rule out the possibility that humanity might develop morally to the extent of embracing higher points of reference than family and Fatherland.

But what does that extension of moral universalism ultimately mean for the state and for patriotism? How will one of the "gravest conflicts" of the time, that "between patriotism and world patriotism," be resolved? (Durkheim 1957, 72). Durkheim believes that neither will die out, that the state, as the organ of this universalist morality, will survive and thus that patriotism too will persist, a patriotism that links the individual to a greater and entirely concrete whole, namely a given nation-state. But this patriotism will no longer be true nationalism, but rather—very much in the spirit of this universalist morality—a fusion of "the national [and] human ideal" (74): "As long as there are states, so there will be national pride, and nothing can be more warranted. But societies can have their pride, not in being the greatest or the wealthiest, but in being the most just, the best organized and in possessing the best moral constitution" (75). So Durkheim gives us to understand that he believes in the future transmutation of a narrow-minded particularist nationalism into a magnanimous, cosmopolitan patriotism.

As noble as Durkheim's vision may be and as much credit as he deserves for arguing *against* the prevailing nationalistic trends, his remarks on the state and wars between states throw up numerous problems and must be judged inadequate. First, it is striking that Durkheim, whose interpreters frequently place him close to Rousseau (see, e.g., Lukes 1973, 283ff.), never really discusses one of Rousseau's basic ideas. Most Enlightenment thinkers had of course rejected a world state. Kant, for instance, dismissed the idea of a world republic on the basis that only competition between republics can maintain the dynamism of the historical process and ensure the diversity of civilizations. But Rousseau's argument went further. He questioned whether it is even possible to seriously identify with a polity so large that it defies easy comprehension. He took the view that citizens can be fully involved in their polity—so crucial to a republic—only in small states. So cosmopolitanism is no more than an empty slogan, an expression of the presumptuous claim "to love everyone, only to gain the right to love no one." Even if we regard Rousseau's argument here as overstated, it must be taken seriously.

Against this backdrop, however, Durkheim failed to satisfactorily answer the question of how we are to imagine the values binding people to humanity as a whole—which will help avoid armed conflicts—and how this might be balanced with those values tying them to their own nation. Durkheim's implicit response to Hegel was also unconvincing. Durkheim took his argument that individuals and collectivities gain their identity only by setting themselves apart from one another, through conflict, quite seriously. It is no coincidence that he called for a competition between states, a peaceful one admittedly, an internally focused competition to achieve the "best moral constitution." But this idea was not truly adequate either. This is not because of Durkheim's questionable optimism in an age of nationalism and imperialism. More important is the fact that Durkheim's optimism here runs into difficulties within his own theory. It is true that he calls for a democratic form of society (Durkheim 1957, 84). Yet his plea here is ambivalent in that he fails to provide a formal definition of democracy (in terms of suffrage, for example) while—like many liberals of his time, not least those in France influenced by the "scientific" spirit of Comte—reproaching the people for being unable to think clearly (83). But this means that it is down solely to the state's rulers to bear the enormous burden of guiding and monitoring the peaceful competition between nations to achieve the best moral order. *It is they* who must now attempt to fulfill hopes of an order in which the relations between states are organized rationally and thus without violence. This pulls the rug from under the argument put forward by Kant, who thought peace was in the offing partly on the basis of the self-interest of self-governing nations and who put his faith in this self-interest. Kant's universalist approach to establishing peace differs from that of Durkheim. At least with respect to his time, the latter has more faith in the rationality of the state than that of peoples. To overstate the case slightly, though Durkheim's ideas on human rights as a sacralization of the individual are future directed, in terms of state theory he falls back on an "early Enlightenment" position that Kant had left behind him since the French Revolution, or his text on "Perpetual Peace" at the latest.

To put it in more general terms, the core theoretical problem that scuppered Durkheim's theory of the state was the dual nature of the state. Durkheim believes he can discern a development away from the kind of violent, aggressive state action evident in the external world toward the moral and pacifying actions apparent within the domestic sphere. We are witness, he thinks, to a progressive transformation, away from the permanent state of war that prevails in primitive communities to the permanent law making of modern societies. Theoretically, this seems to rule out a concurrent increase in power *externally and internally*. Durkheim is unable to imagine any regulation of social inequality or any way of guaranteeing individual freedom without the state. The strengthening of the state cannot therefore be viewed as a threat. The events of the subsequent "Great War" were to defy Durkheim's categories. Durkheim's analytical instruments proved helpless in the face of the massive mobilization of the population and close interlinkage of state and society. For some, these developments would serve as a template for the later totalitarian state, the precise opposite of Durkheim's vision.

▪ ▪ ▪ ▪ ▪ ▪

It was in Germany during this period that the search for a social scientific theory of war was to prove more fruitful. Max Weber's theory of the state, developed primarily in his later writings, is vastly superior to Durkheim's. What is more, because of the above-mentioned developments in the disciplines of economics and history, writers in Germany were less inhibited about the topic of war overall, enabling them to produce key studies on the role of war in the past and in the modern age. The most varied parts of Max Weber's substantial oeuvre also feature scattered references to the constitutive role of war in the genesis of modernity, though these were to be less famous and influential than his thesis of the Protestant ethic. In his comparative analyses on the *Economic Ethics of the World Religions*, Weber points to the striking absence of "rational warfare" and competition between states in China and sees this as a handicap for the "development of those types of capitalism *common* to occidental Antiquity, the Middle Ages, and modern times. These were the varieties of booty capitalism, represented by colonial capitalism and by Mediterranean overseas capitalism connected with piracy" (Weber 1964 [1920], 103/4; emphasis in original); in other places, Weber referred to the significance of military discipline to the objectivization of systems of rule (Weber 1978 [1922], 1148ff.); and finally, he discussed in detail the economic foundations of imperialism (913ff.). All of this shows that Weber was alert to the importance of war and the armed forces. He was, of course, aware of the process of state formation in Prussia-Germany, which was advanced mainly by military means, and its consequences. Weber did not, however, study this subject systematically, presumably in part—as interpreters of his work have noted—because his sociology of the state was more typological in orientation and he himself was more interested in the effects of (state) power than in its (bellicose) "sociogenesis" (Breuer 1991, 26f.).

It was thus writers who were intellectually close to Max Weber rather than the man himself who produced systematic analyses of war, with Werner Sombart (1863–1941) being the key figure here. Sombart's 1913 study *Krieg und Kapitalismus* (War and Capitalism) explains the connection between war and capitalism in sharp contrast to the materialist conception of history. His concern is not with how capitalist development generates wars, but instead with whether, to what extent and why capitalism itself is an effect of war. He does not deny the possibility of framing the question in historical materialist terms but merely declares this approach incapable of further enhancing our understanding. Nor does he dispute war's destructive influence on economic activity, particularly of the capitalist variety. In addition to the destruction caused directly by war, he mentions the consequences of breaking off trade relations, excessive taxation, uncertain transport conditions, and national bankruptcy and, above all, the prevention of capital accumulation as a result of duties paid to the warring states. But none of this is the real focus of his theory. It asserts, rather, that state formation and international conflicts from the sixteenth to the eighteenth century facilitated the emergence of capitalism despite all this destruction. He makes his argument here on several different levels. He wishes to show that war has led to the emergence of modern armies and, as he writes, that these "bolster the capitalist system by 1. accumulating capital, 2. shaping mentalities and (above all) 3. creating markets" (Sombart 1913a, 14). Modern armies are effective in shaping mentalities in that for the first time they enforce, on a vast scale, that discipline that we are accustomed to regarding as a basic component of the capitalist spirit and industrial work. Armies were effective in accumulating capital and creating markets because the need to supply them with weapons, uniforms, and provisions led to the development of large production units, because they indirectly boosted mining and metallurgy and rationalized methods of production and business. State organization of the army went hand in hand with the rationalization of the state itself in that the state had to constantly raise funds and provide continuous administration.

Sombart's emphasis on the constitutive role of war in the genesis of capitalism must of course be seen against the background of a more or less open argument with Max Weber over how best to interpret capitalism. In the first edition of *Der moderne Kapitalismus* (Modern Capitalism) from 1902—virtually anticipating Weber's thesis—Sombart briefly discusses the link between "varieties" of Protestantism and capitalism, stating that such a link is quite plausible (Sombart 1902, vol. 1, 380/81). However—as he was subsequently to emphasize repeatedly—it seemed to him too narrow to derive the "capitalist spirit" from these roots, as he was unwilling to view this "spirit" solely as a specific economic *ethic* (see Sombart 1913b, 2). The "capitalist spirit" seemed to him more broadly rooted, which is why Sombart set about drawing up a list of those factors that might have fostered the emergence of modern capitalism in any way. Here he included the *Mätressenwirtschaft* (mistress economy) and luxury consumption of the absolutist age (Sombart 1967 [1912]) as well as foreigners, Jews, and ultimately war. In *Der moderne Kapitalismus*, his later comprehensive magnum opus, which was written between 1903 and 1928 and which ran to six half-volumes, he was to continue his search for the broadest range of causal factors and to defend resolutely the insights he had gained before the First World War. For him, the capitalist and ultimately "Faustian" spirit, characterized by restlessness, the pursuit of power, and boundlessness (1987, vol. I/1, 327), has been fostered to a significant degree by war, while modern armies have provided important impetus to the formulation of this capitalist spirit: "It is with the help of the army that the state, this first finished product of the new spirit, is created" (331). We can, Sombart continues, still discern the background to that "spirit," which is to a significant degree military in nature. This is apparent in contemporary imperialism, which is by no means only economically motivated, but which is nonetheless of considerable significance to the high and late capitalist form of economy in terms of the potential for capital investment and the massive development of arms industries (Sombart 1987, vol. III/1, 67ff.).

As persuasive as Sombart's arguments seem at first sight, they feature significant weaknesses. His assertions about the role of war in the emergence of capitalism were already described as overstatements by Max Weber in his *General Economic History* (1923, 308f.). Had they been warranted, then the vast expenditure on the army "outside the western world . . . in the Mogul Empire and in China" (309) would also have led to capitalist development, and, conversely, the increasing tendency for the state to produce the goods necessary for the country's military needs itself would have curtailed capitalism. During the Second World War, American economic historian John Nef (1950) developed an anti-Sombartian theory of the detrimental effects of armament on economic progress. An extensive debate followed (see Winter 1975). One of its results was the (no doubt correct) insight that Sombart neither relates the constructive and destructive characteristics of war to one another with respect to the genesis of capitalism nor does he make much effort to distinguish the effects of war from other long-term developments. Hence his theory may very well lead to false empirical assessments in individual cases. But this does not render his theory entirely worthless, as it does draw our attention to one way of explaining the genesis and dynamics of capitalism that clearly differs from evolutionist interpretations, Weber's emphasis on the specific features of occidental rationalism, and Marxist explanations.

First, as Max Scheler noted (1955 [1914]; see Lichtblau 1996, 350, n. 121), Sombart's arguments can provide us with powerful insights into the dynamics of capitalism, or at least its early variant. While Max Weber tended to emphasize the dimension of production in emergent capitalism, inasmuch as the Protestant economic ethic encouraged the capital accumulation necessary to production, Sombart supplemented this by quite rightly underlining the role of consumption in the already established new economic system. Sombart had valid reasons for describing the propensity to consume as one of the central drivers of capitalism, and this includes not only the demand for sugar, silk, and porcelain but also the "devouring" of raw materials in and for war.

Second, in a way reminiscent of later studies produced within Anglo-American historical sociology (see chapter 6), Sombart's arguments made it possible to view perhaps not war itself but certainly the lack of a great European empire and the constant armed embroilments between individual states resulting from this lack, as a key dimension within processes of economic centralization and cultural disciplining. Despite the efforts of Charles the Great, Frederick Barbarossa, Napoleon, and Hitler, as John Hall (1987) states, it proved impossible to establish an extensive empire in Europe after the fall of the Roman Empire. The developing competition between states, however, took place within the common cultural arena of the Christian faith. In the absence of strong states or a shared cultural arena, capitalist development would have been obstructed.

■ ■ ■

No less interesting and still relevant to the modern-day debate on war and peace is the work of Otto Hintze (1861–1940) (on Hintze's influence on military history, see Nowosadtko 2002, 113f.). After the completion of Sombart's *Der moderne Kapitalismus*, Hintze devoted two lengthy critical and instructive reviews to it in 1929 (Hintze 1964; 1975c). Of particular interest for our purposes is Hintze's view that while Sombart did attribute to the state and its armed conflicts a specific role in the early constitution of capitalism, he did so in a problematic and one-sided manner. First, with regard to the phase of high capitalism, Sombart did not really take account of the fact that the state created markets and spheres of production in the first place—and does so repeatedly. Sombart was thus seduced by an economistic mode of argument from which he actually wished to distance himself. Second, and this argument is of more importance for our purposes, Sombart showed no real awareness of the fact that the development of capitalism took place within a (European) state system. It is not the interplay of capitalism and the state, but of capitalism and the *system* of states that is theoretically crucial, as it is only in this light that we can grasp the interaction between the domestic activities of the state and recurrent aggression toward the external world.

In contrast to Sombart's assertion—and this is of considerable significance to any interpretation of modern capitalism—the era of early capitalism was not marked by a "boundless expansion" (Hintze 1975c, 432) on the part of the state. At most there was a difficult balance of competition within the international system, resulting in a peculiar and tense relationship between the internal formation of the state and state expansion in Europe. Sombart—according to Hintze's critique—"always conceives the state as being only a closed and isolated system of institutions. He never thinks in terms of a society of states or of a system of states as a whole, with conflicts of interest and wars of rivalry—that is, with what we can call power politics or imperialism" (436). It was this constricted view of the state—and we have already had a hint of this—that ultimately left Sombart incapable of truly grasping the nature of imperialism. Sombart leaves us in no doubt that there is more to imperialism than merely economic motives. Yet for the most part he understands the processes of imperialism solely against the background of a pursuit of colonial acquisitions that must be understood as (somehow) economically rational (448f.), and thus he fails to appreciate the true dynamics of power.

Hintze's 1929 attempt to come to terms with Sombart's work should come as no surprise. At this point in time, Hintze—born just a few years before Max Weber—could look back on an impressive oeuvre, in which the topic of war had always played a key role. Shortly after the turn of the century, Hintze had already produced essays on the connection between war and state formation that are still instructive, but because of the reception history of his work, this fact has gone largely unacknowledged, at least within German sociology. As Joachim Radkau (2005, 833) has recently highlighted once again, Hintze, the "doyen of German administrative history" and certainly one of the most important German historians,[8] was not held in particularly high regard by Max Weber himself. Despite the manifest thematic proximity of their writings, Weber classified Hintze, with far from untypical contempt, as a "lackey of Schmoller." This did not, however, stop Otto Hintze from acting to ensure that Weber's work was widely received during the Weimar Republic, though it was by no means considered beyond criticism at the time. His efforts have gone unacknowledged within German sociology, while not just his name but his ideas as well crop up again and again in Anglo-Saxon sociology, in the work of such distinguished authors as Barrington Moore, Theda Skocpol, Anthony Giddens, Michael Mann, Thomas Ertman, and Philip Gorski.

Hintze's intellectual roots in the traditions of Prussian historiography are clearly apparent; but from the outset he proved open to questions concerning the economy and social movements and developed a strong interest in the emerging sociology, an interest that found expression chiefly after the First World War in his comprehensive engagement with sociological theories. Originally, his great topic was the administrative history of Prussia. But he increasingly branched out to include constitutional and social history on the one hand and international comparisons on the other, such that it is fair to say that he laid the foundations of a historical sociology of the state that probed how it "expressed its power externally and promoted modernization internally" (Kocka 1973, 41).

Hintze's essay "Military Organization and the Organization of the State" from 1906 was and is still central to this topic, and it is a typical example of his argumentational approach.[9] Here, Hintze attempts to demonstrate a close connection between the armed conflicts of early modern Europe and the constitutional development of the emergent states. Using a broad concept of the constitution not limited to constitutional law, Hintze advocates the thesis that in the first instance a national constitution is always a military constitution as well (Hintze 1975b [1906], 181). He does not in principle dispute the Marxist thesis that constitutional developments have been influenced, among other things, by the particular way in which social classes have formed. But this seems to him a partial perspective, because state structures were molded at least as much, if not more, by "conflict between nations" (183). Extending his historical gaze as far back as ancient Rome, Hintze describes how certain defensive structures and types of army exercised a decisive influence on the form of the state. He makes a real effort here to avoid any one-sidedness. He does not merely posit such things as the armed forces or military problems as factors. Hintze is far too prudent for that, and he shows that military problems were directly connected to the organizational problems of power. The organizational capacities of feudal rulers permitted only certain military options, only a certain type of army. Nonetheless, Hintze insists that if we fail to take account of an army's structure, any comparative constitutional history will result in a distortion of historical processes and false conclusions, because—as Marxists have frequently overlooked—it was often military developments that caused processes of social differentiation in the first place.

In concrete terms, Hintze's key thesis—an explosive one for research on processes of democratization—is that because states like Britain could do without a standing army owing to their particularly secure geopolitical status, they avoided the development of strong absolutist structures and thus more easily attained a parliamentary system. The reason for this is that large standing armies, as in Prussia, could all too easily become tools of repression in the hands of monarchs; such armies inevitably went hand in hand with the development of central state administrations, making it all the easier for rulers to turn down the demands of the estates or general population for political participation. According to Hintze, where this was not the case, as in Britain, it was significantly easier for cooperative relations to develop between rulers and ruled, and parliamentarization could gain a foothold more quickly.

Hintze is fairly close to the spirit of the German historical school of economics, according to which economic life develops partly in and through the struggle between nations. But compared with Weber's inaugural lecture at Freiburg, Hintze is too cautious to turn this into an irrefutable principle backed by Social Darwinist concepts. He discusses the liberal conception of peace put forward by Herbert Spencer with remarkable fairness (182), though he ultimately comes to the critical conclusion that Spencer's arguments reflect the "self-satisfied" spirit of a Cobden or Gladstone, who could bask in Great Britain's undisputed (in part economically determined) superpower status. For Hintze, meanwhile, it seems clear that war will continue to play a major rule in the future. In contrast to Spencer (and Comte), he is unable to discern any secular "diminution in the readiness of states for war" 183).

Hintze does not stop there but asks whether the existing constitutional differences, between Prussia-Germany and Britain, for example, will endure, particularly given that through intensified imperial policies—in other words, expansion of its navy—Germany too may now (in the early twentieth century) be tending toward military structures that are bound to have an effect on its constitution. In this connection, Hintze touches only briefly on the link between universal conscription and universal suffrage and asks whether conscription makes it more likely that democracy will take hold (211). He is evidently unable to come up with a clear answer to this. However, it seems to him far more important, or at least easier, to answer a different question, namely whether *imperialism*, the desire to expand into other continents, which has gripped almost all the large European nations, will automatically bring about a convergence of the political systems in Europe. If it is true that it is almost impossible to wage colonial wars with conscripts, that these wars occur far away from the home country and thus on the basis of more or less equal military means for all European states, then such a convergence is quite conceivable, namely a "compromise and *rapprochement* between British and Continental institutions . . . England would be infused with something of the spirit of militarism while the Continent would edge in the direction of a militia and navy" (213).

Hintze's explanatory model is no doubt highly simplistic in places, and his reference to a historically determined militarism in Prussia-Germany and especially to the affinity between militarism and monarchy reads a little like an apologia.[10] His account of developments in Britain is not always convincing (for a critique, see Reinhard 1986 and 1999, 223ff.; Burkhardt 1997, 545ff.). Ultimately Hintze—like so many intellectuals in the then German Empire—is also open to the criticism that he never seriously considered the risk of a massive military confrontation *in Europe*. He did not rule out war, in fact thought it very likely; but apparently believed that this war would occur in the non-European global periphery and would not much affect core Europe.

But we should also note that Hintze's arguments can help challenge common sociological interpretive patterns. They make it clear that, in contrast to the assumptions of both Marxists and rationalization theorists, processes as crucial to modernity as democratization cannot simply be traced back to the necessities of socioeconomic development or an inexorable intellectual and constitutional history. Often, successful democratization is the result of highly contingent processes, such as the belligerent course and outcomes of state formation in Europe. The historical sociology reestablished in the 1970s was to build on this insight (see chapter 6).

■■■

The First World War, which many of the founding figures of sociology lived through and wrote about, was just such a contingent event. At the

same time, it was a crucial crossroads in modern history, an event with
enormous consequences not only for processes of socioeconomic change
but also of huge significance to intellectual history (see Flasch 2000,
260ff. and more recently Kramer 2007), as it set the course for the rise of
fascism and for the social form taken by Marxism. "Mankind survived.
Nevertheless, the great edifice of nineteenth-century civilization crumpled
in the flames of world war, as its pillars collapsed. There is no understanding the Short Twentieth Century without it" (Hobsbawm 1994, 22).
For us today, the inheritors of this chapter of history who ought to have
an easier time understanding it, it is often hard to grasp what went on in
the thinking of intellectuals that enabled them to celebrate war and the
experience of war with such enthusiasm. Many of the texts composed at
the time, particularly by German social scientists, come across now as
unbearably pompous apologia for war, and particularly the waging of
war by Germany. And they were written by individuals who rarely had
the dubious "pleasure" of experiencing war for real on the front line.
Georg Simmel and Max Scheler interpreted the First World War as a
chance to break with the tragic tendencies of modern culture, and believed they could discern in war the deeply moving existential experience
of an ecstatic sense of security within a community—an experience that
liberates us as individuals from all fixed schema, rendering us moldable
again; the obvious response would be to highlight the experience of the
ordinary soldier—the blood, sweat, and tears.

These texts were unquestionably apologetic in character, but it would
be taking the easy way out to disregard them entirely. It may be that these
texts—like those of Hegel and Sumner before them—express a truth that
classical liberalism and the subsequent sociology were simply blind to,
which is why this very liberal sociology proved baffled and helpless in the
face of intellectual and social movements that privileged *mythologies of
violence*. Violence as creativity, battle as an inner experience, the frontline
community as stimulus for a new type of national order—all of this played
a major role in Germany, but by no means just there, and influenced artistic movements as much as the later National Socialist movement. However alien such ideas may have become for us today, they do reflect a
certain dimension of experience.

Even *before* the First World War, in the shape of British "Vorticism"
around Ezra Pound and Wyndham Lewis,[11] Italian futurism around
Filippo Tommaso Marinetti (Sternhell 1994, 28–30), and German ex-
pressionism (Fries 1994, 95–104), there were artistic currents whose representatives tried to break free from a world that they saw as overly

standardized or goal-oriented and thus destructive of freedom (see Mommsen 1994, 115f.; Sieferle 1995, 15). For this artistic avant garde, "violence" seemed a metaphor through which one could escape these constraints, and a war with no discernible enemy or soldiers, a war merely for its own sake and thus devoid of any real meaning, seemed a strange but viable way out of the malaise. Of course, this notion of war and violence had nothing or very little to do with the realities of the subsequent world war. In fact it is doubtful whether the references to war in much of the work of these prewar literati were made with reality in mind. It would surely be wrong to claim that their poems and manifestoes anticipated or expressed a presentiment of war. References to violence and war were no doubt often poetic ciphers rather than attempts at description (Fries 1994, 97f.). And yet their writings articulated an experiential content that could assume a variety of forms. A generation of intellectuals deeply influenced by Nietzsche, Bergson, and Sorel seemed ready and willing to break free from the world as it was, and the mythology of violence produced by the likes of Sorel seemed equally attractive to both Left and Right, though in the age of nationalist movements it is no surprise that these ideas often seemed easier to realize with the help of the nation than an abstract humanity. When it did in fact break out, the war could then be interpreted as the fulfillment of all hopes—however strange this may seem to us today. War was viewed by many, including German intellectuals, as the great chance to gain an identity, an opportunity to enter new dimensions of experience. Not only this, but armed violence could be interpreted as a form of action beyond utility maximization and strict adherence to norms. And we must interpret the war essays of Max Scheler (1874–1928) and Georg Simmel (1858–1917) in this light as well. They are an expression of mythologies of violence that undoubtedly came to play a constitutive role in the reality of violence and war.

Simmel's essays written during the war, his speeches, and other activities (see Joas 2003; Barrelmeyer 1994) do not represent a rupture in his thinking—there are clear points of contact with themes that preoccupied him before the war. But the collection of speeches and writings on war published in 1917 under the title *Der Krieg und die geistigen Entscheidungen* (War and Spiritual Decisions) features novel argumentational turns not apparent in his earlier work. With respect to the prewar era— and here he returns to an "old" topic which he has dealt with often in the past—Simmel refers to a "crisis of culture," to the oppressive sense that "the ends of life are being overrun by its means . . . ; while the objective cultural forms are undergoing an independent growth beholden only to inherent norms. As a result, these cultural forms not only are becoming profoundly alien to subjective culture but are advancing at a rate with which subjective culture cannot possibly keep pace" (Simmel 1999 [1917]: 39). He assesses this experience of alienation as the expression of an overripe, diseased culture and—this is the new element—asks more or less rhetorically whether the outbreak of war might not mark the beginning of the process of recovery (ibid.). Simmel genuinely believes that "in a very direct way" integration into the machinery of war demands "strength and courage, agility and tenacity" (40), enabling those involved to see themselves as parts of a meaningful whole to a greater extent than they could before, such that it would become possible "to alleviate, somehow, the dualism between the individual as end in itself and the individual as part of the whole" (41).

Irrespective of the fact that the manner of this reintegration remained rather nebulous (it is no coincidence that Simmel uses the word "somehow"), right from the outset Simmel insists that the "mental shockwaves felt in Germany" (13) as a result of the war, that ecstatic *Augusterlebnis* (the "spirit of 1914"), will generate a kind of community-building force, that it will at least open up the possibility of definitively resolving the unbearable tensions and insecurities of the prewar era. For Simmel, war "forces those things in Germany that are still viable and fertile to be separated from those that are stuck in the past and have no right to a future: people and institutions, worldviews and concepts of morality. The comfortable placidity of peace may be able to afford space for the stale and internally dead, to unite it, through gradual transitions, with that which is truly alive. This is no longer compatible with the toughness and resolve hammered into our being by the war. The war confronts everyone with a merciless either-or with respect to values and rights and leaves room only for the truly robust and genuine" (21). War, Simmel tells us, entails entirely new dimensions of experience for most people, it is the backdrop to an "absolute situation" (22), which may, not least, give rise to entirely new individual values and social models as well. Simmel is sure that "somehow this war means something different from other wars, that it has what I shall call a mysterious inner dimension, that its external events are rooted in or approach the quite unpredictable but nonetheless certain depths of soul, hope and fate" (29).

Simmel's writings and speeches on war, his hopes that war would trigger the revaluation of all values and the emergence of a new type of human being, may have been disturbing and repugnant to a small number of his followers such as Ernst Bloch and Georg Lukács (see Lichtblau 1996,

399ff.). But in terms of their argumentational objective, they were not exceptional at the time. We may read Max Scheler's (1874–1928) early writings on war in a similar way; again, they should not simply be interpreted as the mystical excesses of chauvinism. In much the same way as Simmel, in his 1916 essay "Der Krieg als Gesamterlebnis" (War as Whole Experience), Scheler states that war is bound up with a community-forging experience, that a "truly shared . . . mode of thought, belief and will" may arise in war, while creative impulses are also set free: "The genius of war widens the world, past and future" (Scheler 1916, 6); like love, which it helps into being through a "rough and harsh" process (16), war is the creator of new "forms of thinking and experience" (8).

There can be no doubt that Scheler's writings on war, conditioned by his sharp rejection of utilitarianism, Darwinism, and other intellectual currents, which he blithely identified with Britain (Hoeres 2004, 249ff.), always entailed an anti-British political impulse. But like Simmel, Scheler was not a true warmonger:[12] he increasingly distanced himself from his early stance on war and largely shied away from attributing positive qualities to war as he had done initially (449ff.). Much the same applies to Siegfried Kracauer's interpretation of the experience of war as the redemptive "liberation of all internal forces" (Kracauer 1915, 422) or at least as their "beneficent marshalling." So it is far from pointless to look for aspects of relevance to social theory in both Simmel's and Scheler's speeches and writings on war. What is particularly instructive in these texts is their authors' sensitivity to the way in which violence and war are intertwined with nonrational or arational modes of action.

If we take this seriously, if we accept this aspect of violence, it rapidly becomes clear why it is a dead end to describe phenomena of violence (and that includes war), which evidently do *not* comply with any instrumental rationality, as "senseless," as a regression from the present level of civilization, or as the release of a "savage" lurking, as it were, behind the mask of civilization—the "beast within." Of course, our aim here is not to dispute that violence may be practiced for instrumentally rational reasons or even out of a sense of moral obligation, and the First World War in particular was a conflict in which it was easier to identify the brutal pursuit of self-interest than any moral impetus. But the armed violence was also fed by experiences and fantasies that have nothing to do with "ends" or "norms." As problematic as their writings are, Sumner and Hegel, Scheler and Simmel at least set us the theoretical exercise of moving beyond an instrumental conception of violence when analyzing violence and wars. Quite often, war generates its own myths, which may in turn lead to violence. Instrumentally rational or normativist approaches to explaining such violence will clearly get us nowhere.

▪ ▪ ▪

War was also a great seducer. As much as the writings of Scheler and Simmel can be interpreted in light of aspects of relevance to social theory, they were first and foremost apologia for war. But such apologias could also be taken much further, descending into out-and-out nationalistic tirades, which even noted social scientists were not immune to (see also Llanque 2000).

If, to quote Julien Benda (1969 [1927]), we can refer to the "treason of the intellectuals," we can study this treason in depth by looking at the conduct of those intellectuals who lived through the war, many of them social scientists. It is almost impossible to believe how quickly intellectuals managed to redefine those intellectual achievements of other countries that had recently been extolled or, conversely, perceived as "bad" qualities of other nations, as soon as it was clear who was on which side. British writers held up czarist Russia as a stronghold of democracy (Stromberg 1982, 187); the music of Wagner, which had been highly regarded, was condemned as sick; and Goethe, Beethoven, and Wagner were declared accomplices of the arms barons in the shape of Krupp (Hynes 1990), just as "Allied" philosophers and sociologists in general sweepingly portrayed German culture as the embodiment of an authoritarian mindset (for an in-depth and comparative analysis, see Joas 2003). So scholars in the Allied nations did not cover themselves in glory in this "war of words" either. But there can be little doubt that it was the *German* professors, with their public appeals, who kicked off this "intellectual" war and went on to escalate it massively. One of the worst agitators in this field was Werner Sombart (on his biography, see Lenger 1994). In light of his 1913 book *Krieg und Kapitalismus* (War and Capitalism), the war might have prompted him to carry out a detailed study of its economic, social, and psychological effects on the countries involved. It might also have provided an opportunity to return once again to the old question posed by the materialist conception of history as to the causes of war, and a chance either to endorse a version of the theory of imperialism or to put forward an alternative conception. But Sombart failed to seize either of these inherent theoretical opportunities. The aim of his book *Händler und Helden* (Merchants and Heroes), published in 1915, is already apparent in its subtitle: *Patriotische Besinnungen* (Patriotic Reflections). He rejects as superficial all interpretations of the war as the product of economic interests or nation-states' pursuit of power; like all major wars, it is about fundamental beliefs, and this war is a deadly battle between Western European civilization and the German soul.

For Sombart, it is Britain, not France, that is the archetype of this Western civilization. He produces a sweeping polemic against utilitarianism and eudaimonism, against individualism and the commercialization of every sphere of life. Very much in the spirit of the critique of utilitarianism so fundamental to sociology, he disputes that we can view societies as aggregates of individuals and actions as the result of the maximization of desires; he declares inadequate both the notion that freedom means the scope for an arbitrary individualism and the reduction of history to the evolution of individualistic social relations. But through the identification of utilitarianism with the British character, what was mostly abstract argument in the work of the classical figures of sociology becomes a nationalistic tirade. It found no favor among those of Sombart's contemporaries who were experts on Britain, though they sympathized with him on a political level (Schwabe 1965, 29): "Often, one can't help but feel that we're fighting against a department store" (Sombart 1915, 46/47). Nonutilitarian currents of British thought are put down to certain thinkers' Irish blood. But the German spirit is resisting the subjugation of the world to this spirit—in a similarly essentialist manner. For Sombart, the war that is raging is Nietzsche's war, a war against utilitarianism and eudaimonism, and in their rejection of and struggle against them, according to Sombart, "those feuding brothers Schopenhauer and Hegel, Fichte and Nietzsche, the Classical and Romantic authors, Potsdam and Weimar, and the old and new Germans were all as one" (55/56). Sombart's portrayal here is not far wrong; but beyond his characterization of a German tradition of critiquing utilitarianism, he tries to identify a positive alternative to the self-interested subject of the British intellectual tradition. Not self-interest, but selflessness, self-squandering (*Selbstverschwendung*), and ecstatic self-advancement (*Selbststeigerung*) are the characteristics of this individual. His virtues are "self-sacrifice, loyalty, guilelessness, respect, bravery, piety and obedience, kindness" (65). The pure form of these virtues is the type of the hero, and "to be German means to be a hero" (64). The war is the result of a heroic worldview and is necessary in order to curb the mercantile spirit.

At this point, as Sombart blithely identifies the nonpolitical cultural patriotism of the classical period of German literature, Nietzsche's emphatically antinationalistic Europeanism, and the (predominantly aesthetically grounded) ideals of personality in general as preliminary steps toward German militarism, his texts become a corruption of historical fact. Sombart had already engaged in hazardous speculation in the psychology of peoples, trying, for example, to trace the capitalist spirit to invariant character traits of the Jews. But at the time he had in a sense immunized himself against criticism by declaring his conscious methodological bias. Now though, capitalism appears unambiguously in his work as the emanation of a mercantile spirit, and this in turn as the expression of a (British) folk personality. He sees the predicament of states as the struggle for survival of these folk personalities as they strive to find full expression. Victory in this struggle belongs to the people who are able to curb the leveling and culture-destroying spirit of commercialism—namely the German people (see also Lenger 1996).[13]

Sombart's attacks, like those of more than a few of his German colleagues, were probably so vehement partly because they were secretly attempting to conceal the fact that this war was very difficult to win, at least in propaganda terms. German war ideology never had a truly universalist aspiration. And, as clearly evident in Sombart's work, it was innately antiliberal: it had a predilection for *preindustrial* values, which stood in marked contrast to the economic and state structures of this Wilhelmine society, which were very modern in themselves (see Kruse 1997, 17f.). All of this made German war ideology rather unattractive to other nations: "While enemy propaganda contained powerful political ideas, Germany lacked an attractive political program that might have made an impression on those who were neutral or opposed the war. It is true that the Germans too had war aims, but these were highly material in nature and ill-suited to winning converts. There was at most a program of sorts for the East, centered on the struggle—so important to socialists—against czarism as the most reactionary force in Europe, along with the freeing of oppressed peoples from the Russian yoke. . . . In comparison with the West, however, there was no sense of mission. Here the Reich was on the defensive ideologically" (Rürup 1984, 15). Britain, France, and the United States had a much easier time formulating their goals, as they could quite convincingly point to the need to combat Prussian militarism (14). This is one of the reasons why writings on war by "Allied" authors come across as far less strident.

This is clearly apparent in the case of Durkheim, who produced two lengthy treatises during the war that were immediately translated into German and were likely used for propaganda purposes. He no doubt also wished to defend himself in these texts against polemics that declared him a friend of Germany, the "Boche with a pasteboard nose" (Lepenies 1988, 78). Nonetheless, in the first text he examines the question of war guilt in a demonstratively unprejudiced tone—*Qui a voulu la guerre? Les Origines de la guerre d'après les documents diplomatiques* (Who Wanted War? The Origin of the War according to Diplomatic Documents) (Durkheim 1915a). In the other, more significant pamphlet entitled "Germany Above All" (Durkheim 1915b), published the same year, he criticizes German policy in the world war as the product of a mentality that found its theoretical expression in the work of Heinrich von Treitschke. The development of an increasingly absolutist state, a cynical stance on international law, the glorification of war as a source of the highest moral virtues, and denunciation of the ideal of "eternal peace" as immoral— Durkheim portrays all of this as an attack on the Enlightenment embedded in German culture. And it is France's mission to oppose this. As evident in letters written during the war, for Durkheim the war does not sound the death knell of the pacifist ideal. Rather, France's victory would enable the triumph of this ideal and put an end to militarism. Durkheim did not live to see the end of the war and the Treaty of Versailles—a stiff test of his conclusions.

Overall, with respect to Durkheim's writings on war, it seems fair to say that—like so many others before and since—he missed the opportunity to develop a theory of war. In light of his theoretical framework, it would have made sense for him to look into the "interplay between symbolic representations of the war, between the unleashing of collective feelings through battle and the necessities of social regulation" (Gephart 1996, 54). But none of that happened. Instead, Durkheim, as Werner Gephart (ibid.) rightly notes, limited himself to identifying the actors who were responsible for the aggressive intellectual climate in Germany and had thus allegedly caused the war.

■ ■ ■

So apologetic sociology texts were common on both sides of the front, though, as we have seen, these could take very different forms in the different national contexts. In defense of sociology, it must be said that some of its representatives proved capable of learning. But it was some time before a certain sobriety and a more realistic view of the war gained ground. Particularly in Germany, the key years were 1916 and 1917, when intellectual stances shifted, not least among leading representatives of the social sciences. In this connection, Kurt Flasch even refers to a "profound shift in ideas": in comparison to his initial writings on war,

Scheler, for example, began to criticize Prussian power politics in increasingly sober fashion (Flasch 2000, 140f.), while authors such as Max Weber, Friedrich Meinecke, Adolf von Harnack, Ernst Troeltsch, Friedrich Naumann, and Hans Delbrück took a leftward turn because the intellectual scene as a whole had shifted to the right, deploying ever more fervent nationalistic rhetoric (279ff.).

These changes are evident, for instance, in the work of Ferdinand Tönnies (1855–1936), such as his highly ambivalent essay "Naturrecht und Völkerrecht" (Natural Law and International Law). Tönnies published one of the seminal works of German sociology in 1887 with his book *Gemeinschaft und Gesellschaft* (Community and Society). Despite its rhetoric of community, which may sound very conservative from a modern-day perspective, he was closer to the Social Democrats. When the war began, he supported it without qualification. He too was caught up in the outpouring of emotion as the nation sensed the dawn of a new era in the early days of the war. Compared with this, a change of mood is evident in his 1916 essay. Tönnies does make some barbed anti-British remarks. He describes conditions between nations as a state of nature in which they may make unrestrained use of all necessary measures and means to achieve their objectives (Tönnies 1916, 581). And he even deploys the idiom of the "storm of war that clears the air" (586). On the whole, though, his line of argument is intended to get the parties to war to look at their war aims more rationally and take a more down-to-earth approach to fighting the war. The nationalistic, belligerent rhetoric deployed by most German intellectuals, which drew sustenance from concepts of masculinity, now seems to him entirely inappropriate; these ideals must be replaced by other, namely scientific ideals: "The true scientific consciousness is just as much, and perhaps even more than the martial sense or military organization, the fruit of the masculine spirit" (585). And he even expresses the hope that limits might be set on war in the future through a "deeper understanding of right, first and foremost that of social life and its laws" (587).

Tönnies's shift in mentality was not spectacular, but it was significant in view of the radicalization of the political Right. The evolution of Max Weber's thinking resembles that of Tönnies in some ways. Before the war, Weber had always strongly attacked the risky foreign policies pursued by Wilhelmine Germany. When the war broke out, he was extremely skeptical about Germany's chances of victory, though he welcomed the war wholeheartedly in late August 1914: "For no matter what the outcome, this war is great and wonderful" (letter to Karl Oldenberg, 28 August

1914, *Max Weber Gesamtausgabe* II, vol. 8, p. 782). During the war itself, he displayed an astonishingly down-to-earth attitude in comparison to other professors. He thought little of the discourse on the "ideas of 1914"; he firmly rejected all plans for annexation, which German intellectuals were especially keen on, and warned passionately against measures that might prompt the United States to enter the war. But even with the future in mind, he was unwilling to renounce the self-confident pursuit of power politics by the German Empire; he saw maintaining the status quo—defending Germany's position as a world power—as simply imperative; for him this was the point of the war (see Mommsen 1984, 190–331).

After the collapse of the empire in the last few weeks of 1918, however, Weber had to recognize that even this goal was no longer achievable and that Germany would have to make do with a more modest role in future. In "Deutschlands künftige Staatsform" (The Future Form of the German State), a series of articles published in the *Frankfurter Zeitung* in November 1918, Weber mostly analyzes the mistakes of the old monarchical regime and welcomes the democratization now inevitable as a result of regime collapse and revolution. Here, Weber raises the specter of German irredentism, should the peace terms imposed by the Allies prove too great a burden for Germany. But in the same context he also makes it clear not only that Germany must abandon all "imperialist dreams" and adhere to a "purely autonomist ideal of nationality" (Weber 1988, 455)— which he had also advocated in the past—but that the country must draw the obvious conclusions regarding its armed forces and armaments and content itself with a system of defensive militia, though this must not render it defenseless (456).

Weber still had the same objectives, but he was level-headed enough to see how little chance there was of realizing them. He did not modify the conception of politics set out in his 1895 inaugural lecture at Freiburg in any essential way. His calls for democratization, which he had already begun to make before the war, must be seen largely against the background of his "ultimate source of value," the power status of the German nation. For him democratization is not a value in itself. This is still evident in 1918 when Weber states: "For many of us, including the present writer, a strictly parliamentary monarchy was and is the technically most adaptable and in that sense strongest form of state, irrespective of the radical social democratization to which we aspire and which will not necessarily be hindered by such a system" (449). Here, Kant's idea of the peaceful character of a republican constitution is transformed into a question about the domestic political prerequisites for an astute foreign policy. His political demands, such as his call for the democratization of the Prussian three-class franchise and the parliamentarization of the imperial executive, were rooted in earlier analyses in which he had investigated the link between the capacity for effective action on the international stage and domestic state structures.

▪ ▪ ▪

American intellectuals were soon drawn into this war, which was at first purely European, as debate commenced over the possibility of the United States entering the war. The "progressive movement" split over this issue, with supporters of the war such as John Dewey and opponents such as Randolph Bourne divided into sharply opposing camps (see Joas 2003 and Schaffer 1991, chs. 8 and 9). In the case of war supporters, the nationalistic overtones were initially fairly moderate compared to the European "war of words." Certainly, Albion Small's "Americans and the World-Crisis" (1917) was a miserable piece of nationalism. The founder of the sociology department at the University of Chicago was not interested in producing a sociological analysis at all but merely in *somehow* establishing a connection between the claim that the German people were simply undemocratic in character and the existence of the Prussian military machine, the glorification of authority within German philosophy, and a typically German, archaic faith in (state) power. And Small was not the only one to let himself be carried away by such invective. One of the pioneers of quantitative empirical social research, Franklin Giddings (1918), published a number of political broadsides against the "metaphysical monster" of the Prussian-German state—the mirror image of Sombart. And the philosophers Josiah Royce and George Santayana also contributed to this highly ideological genre of war publications.

On the whole, though, American intellectual discourse on the war remained within reasonable bounds, which was no doubt due in part to the United States' very late entry to the war in 1917. By studying the upheavals caused by the war, one sociologist and "public intellectual" of the time even managed to come up with macrosociological analytical strategies, which had been neglected utterly by American sociologists. The ideas he formulated were temporarily forgotten, reappearing only after more than thirty years had passed. We are referring to Thorstein Bunde Veblen (1857–1929) and his early form of modernization theory.

Before the war, Veblen had developed a model of evolutionary stages with the aid of certain ideas about action. According to this model, history may be characterized as a series of successive changes from a barbaric to a predatory and finally to a scientific age, the present. In the prewar period, all of this had remained relatively abstract; he deployed it primarily to criticize the excesses of American capitalism, in other words to condemn the "predatory" or irrational elements associated with capitalism, as he did with much popular success in his famous *Theory of the Leisure Class* (1899). But it was only through his reflections on the war that these observations attained the stature of a genuinely useful social scientific theory. In *Imperial Germany and the Industrial Revolution* (1915) and *An Inquiry into the Nature of Peace and the Terms of its Perpetuation* (1917), arguing from a comparative perspective, he advocated the thesis that some countries had cast off their barbaric and predatory remnants more quickly than others and that in terms of modernity the United States and Britain held an overall lead over countries such as Germany, whose roots still lay in the barbaric age, as evident in both past and present in its readiness and enthusiasm for war.

According to Veblen, although economic and technological developments do shape the intellectual structures of a society, there is no clear and direct relationship between the technological structure and societal institutions. Morals, Veblen argues, often lag behind technological dynamics, and furthermore technologies can easily be exported to other societies without necessarily bringing about immediate change in their overall social structure. With the help of this idea, Veblen sets about distinguishing between a political history of the *republican* or *democratic* nations, which runs strictly in parallel with technological developments,[14] and a "non-simultaneous" history of *dynastic* and highly *undemocratic* countries (Germany, Spain, Austria, and Japan) (see Veblen 1964 [1917], 9). In these dynastic states, he argues, though they have reached a sometimes advanced technological level, the national leaders are highly autonomous and politically unaccountable. Their political institutions and morals do not yet reflect the standards of a highly developed scientific and economic structure, so taken as a whole the "degree of their modernity" is still fairly close to a "medieval" level (ibid.). And it is the Germans who are carrying the greatest amount of ballast from the Middle Ages, causing them to opt out, in many respects, of modern political institutions (100).

The crucial point is that Veblen does not explain the different developments occurring in imperial Germany and imperial Japan, on the one hand, and Britain, on the other, with reference to fundamental cultural or sociostructural differences, but simply in light of the head start enjoyed by the British, who have had a dynamic economy since Elizabethan times. The forces of modern industry have not existed long enough in Germany to have brought about the fall of the dynastic state, that despotic organization with its bellicose ambitions (Veblen 1954 [1915], 172f.). In general, though, even in Germany, the system of political-cultural institutions will sooner or later adapt to the industrial changes. Ultimately, with its belligerent policies, imperial Germany is merely a futile reaction against a modern and essentially peaceful civilization (270). Indeed, while the war was still going on, Veblen made the daring suggestion that this world-wide military conflict would lead to a better and more peaceful future because all archaic (political) remnants would be wiped away in all countries—including Germany—as a result of *mechanized* mobilization for war and *industrialized* warfare. *After* this military confrontation, in Germany especially, the aristocratic forms of rule and institutions responsible for this war (and which continued to exist during it) will give way to a rational, peaceful, and democratic institutional structure (1964 [1917], 247; see Biddle/Samuels 1993, 118; on Veblen's war writings as a whole, see Schmidt 2000).

In the two books discussed here, which appeared during the First World War, Veblen anticipated key arguments of later modernization theory, though it is hard to discern his influence on sociology in this regard as he was more of a role model for radical or radically prodemocracy intellectuals than macrosociological theorists. Compared with his earlier works, these two books were distinguished by the fact that—compelled by the events of the war—Veblen now tested his evolutionist constructs in specific areas of empirical research. He applied his assumptions to specific societies—chiefly the United States, Britain, Germany, and occasionally Japan. Though the data used by Veblen seem quite inadequate from a modern-day perspective, his explicitly comparative approach represents genuine progress over his previous studies and other contemporary macrospeculations produced during the first two decades of the twentieth century in the United States. But Veblen's argument also entails a number of highly problematic steps, which are strongly reminiscent of the later debate in modernization theory.

First, he has no hesitation in beginning his comparative discussion with a democratic Western country, which he tacitly presents as the goal of historical development. Here he chooses Britain; strikingly, he almost entirely forgoes analysis of American history. If one asserts, as he does, that it was chiefly Germany's extremely fast industrialization that caused the deficits in the development of its political institutions, it would seem desirable to go beyond discussion of the contrasting case of Britain. Industrialization no doubt was a relatively slow and continuous process in Britain, but American industrialization was probably even more turbulent than in Germany. So his comparative analysis does *not* begin with careful reflection on the historical and sociological foundations of his "own," American society. As a result, Veblen's chosen comparative model almost inevitably led to problematic results and conclusions. *Second*, the assumption that the system of institutions will adapt to economic developments was characteristic of his thinking—virtually by definition, he rules out the possibility of an *enduringly* unbalanced and noncontemporaneous development of societal spheres and sectors, particularly economy and political culture. So the thesis of a close empirical linkage between subsystems—as was to become so characteristic of subsequent functionalism and modernization theory—is already firmly established in Veblen's work. *Third*, Veblen's thinking is marked by concepts of modernization in that he assumes that there is a fundamental rupture between traditional (barbaric/predatory) and modern society. The industrial-mechanistic spirit will eliminate all nonrational elements of society. The idea of an enduring blend or combination of traditional and modern elements does not even arise. *Fourth* and finally, and closely bound up with this, he is in no doubt about the linearity of the historical process. The developmental objective is fixed. There can be only delays and detours, but no fundamentally different paths to modernity, let alone different modernities (plural). In retrospect, these characteristic features of Veblen's theoretical constructs, which he shared with most subsequent modernization theorists, must obviously be viewed as theoretical weaknesses. But this should not obscure the fact that, through his reflections on the war, Veblen produced a model of macrosociological change that might have been used in comparative historical and/or typological studies (see Knöbl 2001, 52ff).

It was a long time before Veblen's macrosociological approach was taken up again in the United States. For various reasons, until the early 1950s macrosociology generally struggled to gain a foothold, with micro- and mesosociological forms of analysis clearly predominating. It was only after the Second World War that modernization theory again dared take the plunge into macrosociology, unconsciously picking up the thread of some of Veblen's key ideas (see Knöbl 2001). But at least one other major figure in American sociology and contemporary of Veblen—George

Herbert Mead (1863–1931)—recognized the potential of Veblen's mode of analysis. He responded to it in 1918 with a long and favorable critique of *An Inquiry into the Nature of Peace and the Terms of Its Perpetuation*, though he criticized Veblen's rigid social psychological categories and the fact that his economistic and functionalist approach tended to pass all too easily over those cultural and social movements that stressed solidarity and that have the potential to promote peaceful relations between people, and between states (Mead 1918, 759f.).

So in contrast to Veblen, in his own reflections on war and peace Mead is unwilling to put his faith only in the quasi-automatic effects of economic-technological trends, focusing instead on the capacity for action and organization, as human beings must in principle be capable of universalizing feelings of solidarity, that is, extending them to humanity as a whole, thus bringing about peace. Mead believed there were solid grounds for hope in this regard. Even the feeling of national belonging— as Mead argues in close if probably unconscious proximity to Durkheim's lectures on the sociology of morality—tends to entail universalist elements, moral values with the inherent potential to exercise an impact beyond one's own national group: "It is a consciousness that comes with the feel of the greater values that belong to more complete community life" (761). And in fact Mead sees such tendencies at work in Germany as well; feelings of solidarity found expression there before the war in the exemplary German social security legislation, which Veblen is far too quick to dismiss. And this solidarity that may be observed in Germany, Mead suggests, does not have to be restricted to the *German* people and thus remain particularistic, but gives us reason to hope that we may eventually see a global peace that *binds nations together*.

Mead's criticisms of Veblen were no doubt justified. But they cannot conceal the fact that, like most other American sociologists of the time, he lacked a decent theory of the state that might allow him to make meaningful statements about the link between war and modern society. Mead's real interest lay in the question of what alternative there might be to a social integration achieved through the friend-enemy schema. His hopes lay with forms of open, discursive problem solving at the national and international level. With this in mind, after the war he produced sociological texts on the potential for "international-mindedness." Here he questions whether William James's idea of "useful labor" (1929, 388) is realistic, putting his faith instead in the comprehensive institutionalization of open discussion on the national and international level. For him, this was the only way to avoid charged notions of the Enemy (for an in-depth look at Mead during the First World War, see Joas 1985, 23ff.; on Dewey's views, see Westbrook 1991).

▪ ▪ ▪

One of the most important social theoretical debates during the prewar era—on the links between capitalism and imperialism—was greatly intensified by the war. It quickly became clear that authors' interpretations of imperialism could be as different as their political views, as is only too apparent in the particularly famous interpretations of Vladimir I. Lenin (1870–1924) and Joseph A. Schumpeter (1883–1950).

Lenin's wholly economic interpretation of imperialism, produced in the middle of the war, was based on the preparatory work done by the English liberal J. A. Hobson and subsequent Marxist interpretive efforts by Rudolf Hilferding and others. They had either, like Hobson, put the imperialist endeavors of the European-American powers down to workers' underconsumption, imposed by big business, and the resulting presence of surplus capital that had to be invested in colonies, or, like Hilferding, pointed to the fall in the rate of profit in the home countries, which also led inevitably to state-backed commercial expansion into the colonies. Lenin wrote *Imperialism: The Highest Stage of Capitalism* in 1916, but it was another four years before it was translated from the Russian into other languages. Here he develops his version of this theory with great rigidity and determined radicalism, basing himself on the *Marxist* premise of the primacy of the economy. He attempts to show empirically that over time economic crises develop into political ones. These have ultimately culminated, or were bound to culminate, in countless peripheral military conflicts and finally in a "great war," because now the world is divided up between the major powers and no other viable alternative remains. Imperialism is the final stage of capitalism, and the functional requirements of big business that are part and parcel of imperialism lead to catastrophic conflict. Because of the imminent revolution, however, this will also usher in the establishment of a global socialist society.

Lenin's ideas were captivating in their elegance but suffered from the significant disadvantage of putting imperialism down to purely *economic* factors and disregarding other aspects. He completely ignored the fact that colonial rivalry at the time was almost never truly the result of economic factors and the colonies rarely generated a profit. There were factors of power politics and national prestige at play that found no place in Lenin's theory. After all, it was not the actual colonial rivals of France and Britain that were fighting each other in the war. Instead, Germany, still relatively insignificant in terms of its colonial possessions, was fighting a coalition of several large colonial powers. Lenin's theory also failed to explain why the trading links between the wartime enemies—Britain and Germany for instance—had been fairly close before the war. But for many people who were unwilling to side with any of the protagonists in this conflict, his book seemed a revelation, prompting their conversion to Marxism. Meanwhile, in view of the theoretical problems, the "bourgeois" camp adopted other strategies to explain imperialism, including Joseph Schumpeter in "The Sociology of Imperialism," published immediately after the war in 1919.

Interestingly—as Raymond Aron (1958, 20) was probably the first to notice—there is a certain similarity between Veblen's theory and Schumpeter's theory of imperialism, and it is anything but coincidental. Austrian-born economist Schumpeter (1883–1950), who later taught in the United States—one generation younger than Max Weber—cannot be counted a member of the German historical school of economics (for his biography, see Swedberg 1991). Schumpeter's early economic magnum opus *The Theory of Economic Development* from 1912 is basically at home in the neoclassical camp, though he was to make major criticisms of it, at least in his early creative period (see Röpke/Stiller 2005). The way he sets out his arguments reflects this. He no longer refers to the economic struggle between nations, or to a *national* economic policy and its national imperatives. Instead, Schumpeter's analyses emphasized the internal functional mechanisms and developmental dynamics of a global economy that he viewed in essentially abstract terms (beyond specific historical-political institutions). So it was not *national* economics that he was engaged in—as Friedrich List would no doubt have criticized him for and as Sombart did in 1928 in *Der moderne Kapitalismus*.[15] Both before and after the "Great War," Schumpeter's theories painted a highly optimistic picture of economic processes (Osterhammel 1987, 116). He believed that the functional requirements of the economy were always fundamentally the same; these requirements must be met—irrespective of the particular political system, though with differing means—and have commensurate consequences for society.

This is evident in the previously mentioned "Sociology of Imperialism." Here, in much the same way as Veblen, Schumpeter defines contemporary imperialism as "the objectless disposition on the part of a state to unlimited forcible expansion" (1951 [1919], 7). This definition is a legitimate attempt to combat the enormous extension in the meaning of the term "imperialism" within debates among socialist theorists (see Schröder 1973, 38). As apparent in his historical analyses, Schumpeter's definition can be applied only to a relatively small number of eras and countries. The notion of an "objectless disposition" is intended to prevent the branding of every act of foreign policy, usually motivated by economic factors of some kind, as imperialist. Schumpeter considers this conceptual or theoretical strategy misguided and tries to understand imperialism in a very narrow sense as a kind of culturally conditioned disposition for expansion, expansion that is both violent and, in principle, endless. Such an approach to the phenomenon of imperialism is promising as it enables us not only to distinguish between different imperialisms (plural—see the original German title of Schumpeter's essay) but also to take account of the particular dynamics of political processes and their cultural preconditions.

But Schumpeter squanders the potential of his essay. Referring to the rational "social habitus" of capitalist modernity (Schumpeter 1951 [1919], 87), he immediately consigns this phantasm of endless violent expansion to the past, declaring it irrelevant to the present. This allows him to describe imperialism too as an atavism. In the age of capitalism, he believes, there is nothing left to sustain imperialism; it is merely a holdover from absolutism that manifests itself in certain social structures and in the psychology of individuals. With his "proof" of the pacifist character of capitalism, Schumpeter smoothly picks up the thread of liberal arguments and theories of the kind developed by Montesquieu as well as Bentham and Mill. He explains the threat of war in the present as the result of occasional political irrationalities and resulting upheavals, specifically in light of export monopolism, though these are *not*—as socialists thought—a *necessary* result of capitalist development. Accordingly, general *free* trade will facilitate peaceful relations between capitalist states, and—from a global standpoint—an entirely realistic vision of the future. Schumpeter does not go into the specific features of high-tech warfare, though it would have made sense to do so given his emphasis on the importance to economic progress of technological innovation.

Important though Aron's emphasis on the similarity between Veblen's and Schumpeter's approach may be, it must not cause us to elide the differences between the two. Veblen's theory contains elements critical of a capitalist market economy, which Schumpeter's approach does not. But Veblen and Schumpeter both fail to grasp the nature of modern nationalism or patriotism when they conceive of it merely as a dynastic or feudal remnant (Veblen 1964 [1917], 31ff.; Schumpeter 1951 [1919], 125). Their optimism about the prospects for peace is due not least to a more or less unspoken attachment to the legacy of liberalism or classical political economy respectively, which were only too willing to believe in the rationalizing and pacifying effects of economic processes. Schumpeter especially is also open to the criticism that his notion of the atavistic character of imperialism (and of war in modern societies) was based on a highly partial interpretation of imperialist policies. As liberal theorist of imperialism John A. Hobson had already done at the beginning of the twentieth century, Schumpeter quite straightforwardly equates imperial policies with mercantilist-style protectionism, leading to the dubious inverted argument that, virtually by definition, free trade itself is anti-imperialist.

But as Bernard Semmel (1970) has shown and as we pointed out in the preceding chapter, this is simply wrong, because imperial ambitions could be linked with arguments in favor of free trade. Schumpeter had built his arguments about the prospects for peace on a thesis of historical discontinuity, according to which the mercantilist imperialism and colonialism of the eighteenth century had been superseded by an intrinsically peaceful and anti-imperialist free trade in the early nineteenth century. This free trade had been sidelined only temporarily after 1880 as a result of a protectionist backlash, which had led to the world war and had been triggered by the remnants of "feudalism" in modern societies. When all of these remnants had finally been eliminated—those who endorsed this view hoped—there would now be nothing to stand in the way of a peaceful and anti-imperialist age.

Of course, this reconstruction is open to attack. It is certainly not the case that, for example, free-trade discourse in mid-nineteenth-century Britain was entirely anti-imperialist. British free-trade theorists were in no doubt that it was one of the benefits of open markets that they allowed Britain, the "workshop of the world," to make use of free trade in order to preserve or even extend its status as a world power. One could go a step further and argue—in purely economic terms (see chapter 3, p. 69ff.)—that the free-trade-based empire was necessary in order to maintain the vitality of emergent industrialism. So there could be absolutely no question of a rupture between mercantilism and the free-trade system that might be demonstrated with reference to imperialism, as Friedrich List and others had quite clearly seen. Schumpeter's view was thus a distortion of the historical facts that allowed the peaceful and harmonious vision of history characteristic of classical liberalism to be maintained—a vision of history still capable of seducing people into an exoticized view of war and persuading them that it was unworthy of more in-depth analysis.

▪ ▪ ▪

Led astray by reductionist theories, disconnected from reality, incapable of analyzing the social reality of war or indeed quite prepared to risk their academic reputation to produce war propaganda and construct hackneyed visions of the Enemy—this would be a fair description of many social scientists across the world during the First World War. Even when social science publications were not directly propagandistic, even when analyses appeared that cast light on certain aspects of the war (theories of imperialism helped elucidate the causes of war, for instance), and even when thinkers such as Veblen made use of the broader perspective enabled by the war to further develop impressive theoretical constructs, one obvious topic was avoided or overlooked to a striking degree. We are referring to the immediate consequences of war and the social changes that the "Great War" brought in its wake. Hardly any contemporary social scientists examined this topic, which would have formed a genuine bridge to the experiences of contemporaries on the front line and at home.[16] But there is one notable exception: Emil Lederer (1882–1939). Lederer was born in Bohemia and went to Heidelberg in 1910. In 1911 he became editorial assistant, and later chief editor, of the *Archiv für Sozialwissenschaft und Sozialpolitik*, edited among others by Max Weber and Werner Sombart. He completed his postdoctoral thesis in economics at the University of Heidelberg in 1912. Strongly influenced by Schumpeter, Lederer was appointed professor in economics in Heidelberg in 1922. Finally, in 1931, he succeeded Werner Sombart at the University of Berlin before being forced to flee to the United States to escape the Nazis (for details of his biography, see Speier 1979 and Krohn 1995; on his work, see Salomon 1940 and Marschak et al. 1941; on Lederer's contributions to the sociology of the state and war, see the recent work by Huebner 2008).

Remarkably, in the early days of the First World War, Lederer already made a thoughtful attempt to record how collective actors were behaving under the influence of the war. This was reflected in his important essay "On the Sociology of World War" from 1915. Here, his aim was to get to grips analytically with those features of the war that surprised everyone, including social scientists and military experts. His intention was to maintain "cool objectivity" and "adopt a standpoint outside of the war even in its midst." In view of the vast nexus of factors that had led to the war, he took one sentence to divest the responsibility issue of its preeminent status. Against all pompous assertions as to the meaning of the war, he reserved the right to doubt its meaning; indeed, he saw it as the duty of the sociologist and historian to view the war as potentially "meaningless" and not derivable from cultural or socioeconomic principles. Lederer tries to do what the vast majority of social scientific writers on the war failed to, namely reflect on the conditions of possibility for the war's specific features. While most authors addressed people's experience of community at the outbreak of war and their experience of life on the front only to generalize about this experience, Lederer attempts to trace it back to the specific conditions of war in the context of universal conscription (2006 [1915], 244f.).

Just as Lederer reflects on this experience and takes account of similarities in the countries involved in the war, he takes much the same approach to the way in which the machinery of war has acquired a technological momentum of its own, and the seeming paradox of a state increasingly dependent on its society yet increasingly flexing its muscles within the world at large. Here again he underlines those things the parties to war have in common and the increasing independence of organizational forms from the cultures of the specific countries. While the majority of social scientists contributed to the production of self-justifying nationalist ideologies, Lederer observes the structural homogeneity of the feuding ideologies. Modern nationalism does not bring out nations' unique cultural characteristics, but makes them similar, as does the competition between states in the military sphere; nationalism becomes no more than the ideology of the power-hungry state.

Lederer means these realities to be understood as historical and contingent rather than deterministic. And again it is in light of the dual impact of the abstract power-focused state and community experience that Lederer explains the conduct of intellectuals. On the one hand, the modern power-focused state has such a suggestive effect on people's minds that, beyond all official propaganda, intellectual currents tend to move in the desired direction of their own accord. On the other hand, the large number of war ideologies in one and the same country, the "veritable cacophony of divergent idealizing judgements about the war" (266), clearly have no consequences for the events of the war. "[T]he only measurable dimensions of this war are different states' levels of organization" (ibid.). But these autonomous events are of course always subjectively experienced and interpreted. Those who welcome the suspension of social differentiation within the community experience induced by the power-focused state have abandoned "the struggle for individual rights and for rights of society against the state" (267). But it is this struggle that Lederer wants to take up once again, or continue. According to his hugely state-focused analysis, the route to a different modernity is certainly not reached via the euphoria of the war experience.

Lederer sees two other possibilities. The first lies in an economy "oriented to the collective interest" (ibid.), though not if this entails state domination of society in the sense of state socialism, but only if, through a radically changed economic mentality, greater justice instead of greater affluence becomes the central theme of economic life. Lederer considers this break with trends toward increasing state power domestically and internationally desirable but utopian.

He sees a second possibility as more realistic, namely that "states around the world ally with one another in such a way that dynamic conflictual tendencies are denied freedom of movement" (ibid.). He does not elaborate on how we might construct such an order. But perhaps we may interpret his idea in the sense of a linkage of states through multilevel networks, a post-Hobbesian system of states, to borrow Philippe Schmitter's term (1991). In any event, Lederer showed that even under the highly charged conditions of total war it is possible to engage in sober reflection upon it. But Lederer was not just a lonely voice in the wilderness (of the war). Even after the war his exemplary analyses made little impact.

The period immediately preceding the First World War saw the first attempts to analyze more closely the relationship between war and modern society, in significant part because of specific disciplinary circumstances in the different nations. Increasingly, in Germany, many of those close to the historical school of economics at last attempted to make a serious study of the role of war in processes of social change, key examples being Max Weber, Werner Sombart, and Otto Hintze. Paradoxically, the impact of the First World War itself did not ultimately promote this new social theoretical sensitivity. Quite the opposite. On all sides, but particularly in Germany, the "Great War" brought intense emotion, raging chauvinism, and mystical bellicism, especially among those who, as social scientists, ought to have dealt with it in a more level-headed and professional way. So the intellectual terrain won before the war in tackling the problem of war was lost again during it, as was apparent after 1918. The dream of a nonviolent modernity that gripped many nineteenth-century sociologists and social theorists had merely been briefly interrupted. The dreaming went on after the war, and, as we shall see, only a few scholars here and there ever managed to give the various disciplines a brief reminder of the reality of war.

Sociology and Social Theory from the End of the First World War to the 1970s

THE "GREAT WAR," this rupture with the civilization of the nineteenth century, surely might have prompted profound sociological analyses of war and peace. But such expectations were to be disappointed. It is true that the war brought in its wake a dramatic upheaval in the cultural landscape; prewar culture lost its credibility, particularly in the defeated countries or in those worst affected by the war. The Enlightenment faith in progress was eroded, while liberalism as a political movement *with mass appeal* disappeared in almost all European countries. From now on, numerous analyses were published expressing a pessimistic view of civilization. In the 1920s, while some of the relevant authors were American social scientists (see Knöbl 2001), many more of them were European. But there was clearly a large gulf between a general cultural pessimism and increasing skepticism about the realism of Enlightenment ideals on the one hand and precise sociological studies of the phenomenon of war on the other. Such studies continued to be few and far between. In fact, far fewer sociological texts on war appeared than in the pre-1914 period, in sharp contrast, incidentally, to works of fiction. From 1925 on, a number of novels that were seen as attempts to come to terms with the war appeared. In comparison to fiction, sociology remained largely silent, and we must scour the broader field of social theory to find new approaches worth mentioning for the period between the end of the First World War and the beginning of the Second, especially any that satisfy modern-day scientific criteria. But even if we extend our search in this way, we will find that the amount of material varies according to the national context, not least because the relevant disciplines developed very differently in different countries.

■ ■ ■

After 1918, French sociology proceeded along the channels laid down by Durkheim, for which close cooperation with anthropology was always a distinguishing feature—an approach still associated with the name of Marcel Mauss. This approach certainly included an interest in the phenomenon of war. But it was difficult to analyze the connection between war and modern society within its framework, as had analyses produced in the eighteenth and nineteenth centuries. So it was not until the 1930s that innovative studies of war appeared. At the center of these efforts lay the Collège de Sociologie, which was founded in Paris in 1936 and survived for just three years. The Collège, a loose-knit grouping initiated by Georges Bataille (1897–1962), Roger Caillois (1913–77), and Michel Leiris (1901–90), aimed to foster a sociology that would investigate the forces observable in modern society that bind people together, particularly the energies released in collective experiences and effervescences, energies expressed in rituals, festivals, and games (Moebius 2006, 13). This was an ambitious scientific agenda, particularly given that such a sociology "saw itself not as a sociological specialism, such as the sociology of religion, but as the general sociological investigation of 'communitizing movements'" (135/36). The aims of this program for a sacred sociology, as it was called, were not solely scientific in nature. Grounded in a critique of contemporary civilization, those close to the Collège also wished to promote the revitalization of society through such collective effervescences. This reflected a normative and political aspiration drawn from numerous sources, one that proved equally suited to the pursuit of artistic goals and the struggle against fascism.

Roger Caillois (1913–78) was the key driving force behind analyses of war within the Collège.[1] Born in Reims, Caillois, like Leiris a student of Marcel Mauss, joined the surrealists at an early stage. The title of his crucial essay, "War and the Sacred" (1980 [1939]), already indicates the thrust of his arguments, which were anchored in anthropology and above all the sociology of religion, arguments that he fleshed out in subsequent writings, particularly his book *Bellone ou la pente de la guerre* (1963). Caillois attempts to establish a link, a peculiar one at first sight, between elements of Durkheim's sociology of religion and Ernst Jünger's text on the "Kampf als inneres Erlebnis" (Battle as Inner Experience). His arguments here are initially embedded in general reflections on the nature of the sacred and of religion in "primitive societies." According to him, sacred objects give rise to horror and reverence, leading to a more or less sharp separation between the profane and these sacred objects. This separation sets in motion a specific social dynamic because people constantly attempt to overcome it. A festival, for example, Caillois believes, connects participants to the sacred because the orgiastic character of the festival, the process of losing oneself, the nocturnal frenzy, and so on convey a sense of horror, of the forbidden—in other words, the sacred—and thus intimate a return to a time before this separation had occurred. "In fact, the festival is presented as a reenactment of the first days of the universe, the *Urzeit*, the eminently creative era that saw all objects, creatures, and institutions become fixed in their traditional and definitive form" (1963, 103; emphasis in original). But the evolution of societies eliminates the stirring character of the festival, which loses its wildness, and this may, Caillois suspects, be functionally necessary for societies whose structures become ever more complex as this process of evolution unfolds. Festivals lose their power or are substituted by other things, and Caillois points out that, with the rise of states, recurrent periods of festival may be replaced by alternating phases of war and peace (127). War, according to Caillois's thesis, is in a sense a substitute for the festival, and therefore armed violence is another way of approaching the sacred. Just as the festival rips people out of their familiar world, from their private and family lives, armed violence also transports them into a kind of transcendental frenzy. Caillois's speculations are certainly very daring, but his analyses clearly show that we may profitably view war and the armed forces from a defamiliarizing anthropological or sociology-of-religion perspective. Is not the military uniform a mechanism through which individuals give up their personalities, symbolic of their perfect slotting into society? Is not violence in modern wars of such monstrous proportions that it is difficult even to grasp it rationally or understand it normatively? Is violence not underpinned by a kind of delight in destruction, which must perhaps even be understood as the true essence of war? Does war not often entail a revitalizing power, as Hegel believed—a figure, incidentally, who played an important role for the Collège (Moebius 2006, 213)? Here Caillois is trying to capture those experiences of the soldier in battle that defy comprehension from an instrumentally rational or normative standpoint and conceptualize them theoretically through the category of the extraordinary. In the spirit of Durkheim's study of tribal religion, characteristic features of war—such as its waste through destruction, or license to commit acts of violence—are interpreted as a modern form of collective unfettering, enabling counterintuitive insights into the "functionality" of war.

Caillois was by no means blind to the fact that festivals unite, whereas wars often aggravate the differences both within and between societies (Caillois 1980 [1939], 178). He cannot be accused of abandoning conceptual nuances in order to suggestively evoke simplistic analogies (e.g., between the war and festival). However, it ultimately remains unclear in Caillois's work whether (and if so, to what extent) First World War battles of mass annihilation bear any resemblance to war in comparatively "simple," albeit state-based societies[2]—in other words, whether and to what extent insights gleaned from ethnological materials can be applied to modern societies.[3] Furthermore, for all the fascination that Caillois's texts exercised and continue to exercise, there is often a thin dividing line in his work between harnessing these insights gleaned from a sociology of the sacred and a hazardous turn toward a "sacred sociology" (Hollier 1987; Joas 2008, 51–64) that carried out sectarian group experiments and encouraged people to live out violent fantasies, these being celebrated as a route out of the ruptures of modernity, as a form of liberation leading to true personal sovereignty. This was undoubtedly reflected in Caillois's self-image as intellectual aristocrat (Moebius 2006, 365f.). Nonetheless, Caillois's arguments are just as important as the thinking of Sumner and Hegel: the writings of all three authors can serve as a corrective to the *instrumentally rational* interpretations of violence and war that dominated both "liberal" and "Marxist" sociology.

The Collège de Sociologie was a collection of fairly idiosyncratic individuals; they were certainly not representative of the French academic sociology of the time. But they set new trends within a social scientific milieu in which there was little interest in tackling the topic of war.[4] These intellectuals did not, however, get to the point of exploring the link between war and *modern* society in a truly *systematic* way.

■ ■ ■

In Germany, after the end of the First World War, historians such as Hintze, economists like Sombart, and sociologists such as Lederer continued their scholarly studies of the links between war and modern society; but it is fair to say that after the death of Max Weber the German social sciences failed to maintain the once-high standard of macrosociological reflection. Though a new generation of scholars with significant theoretical potential emerged (such as Karl Mannheim or the authors of the early Frankfurt school), the sociology of the Weimar Republic era was afflicted by acute crisis, a predicament then aggravated by National Socialist rule and the forced emigration of many intellectuals during this period. The question of whether Weimar sociology as a whole in fact saw the start of something new and sustainable (and that there was therefore no crisis)— a new beginning that was all too quickly nipped in the bud by Nazism— can be left to one side here. All that matters for our purposes is that between 1918 and 1933 the problem of war and peace never really became an important topic of scholarship. War in general or the world war that had just ended failed to inspire sociology or the other disciplines in the social sciences and humanities in any appreciable way. The few authors who were exceptions to this rule linked the topic of war directly with that of the German state, which was either rejected on political grounds or credited with little stability following the end of the Reich. It was in this context that the first major analyses to at least touch on the topic of war appeared in the mid-1920s.

Friedrich Meinecke's *Machiavellism: The Doctrine of Raison d'État and Its Place in Modern History* (originally 1924), for example, was an attempt to interpret the modern state against the background of the experiences of the First World War. The historian Meinecke (1862–1954), who accepted the departure of the monarchy and nailed his colors to the Weimar constitution as a "republican by reason," interpreted the history of the modern state essentially as one of conflict between empiricism and rationalism, between the actual state with its often brutal power politics on the one hand and the reason-based state of the kind envisaged by Enlightenment thinkers on the other. According to Meinecke, the control of state power politics from below imagined in the Enlightenment did not occur; even worse, the triumph of the Enlightenment in the wake of the French Revolution had in fact unleashed armed violence on an unprecedented scale, because in modern democracies power politics and raison d'état could develop a virtually inexorable momentum (Meinecke 1957 [1924], 347). Tremendous forces were mobilized in the wake of conscription, introduced in the painful aftermath of 1789, forces that thwarted Kant's hopes of peace. As a result of the republicanization of political life, of the nation-state itself, war had become a "daemonic force which scorned the rein of *raison d'état* and threw its rider in the abyss" (422). Through its interplay with an ever-advancing military technology, the French Revolution ultimately destabilized the European state system, such that the relative tranquillity of earlier times was now a thing of the past: "The very restrictedness of the power-resources had been the means of salvation to European humanity and ultimately even to the State itself, and had constantly warded off the hypertrophy of power" (418). The new age was structured quite differently, as evident in the world war that had just ended. The raison d'état that had applied hitherto could no longer be the principle underlying the (European) political order. The new will to annihilate the enemy expressed in the world war had destroyed the essence of European political life, "that group of free and independent states, which at the same time felt themselves to be one large family, and amongst which the balance of power was always eventually restored" (423/24). As a result, Europe had lost its world historical role.

Meinecke's own reference to the near-inexorable momentum of a spiral of violence triggered by processes of democratization and nationalization leaves him at something of a loss. In his view, we cannot rid ourselves of raison d'état, power politics, and Machiavellianism; so the crucial thing is to guard against any idolization of the state and to reshape the state in such a way that it accords with moral law (429). This is good Enlightenment thinking, but fails to take account of the very thing that Meinecke himself had described shortly before as leading to the collapse of the European state system, namely the nationalization of the masses, which "scorned the rein of *raison d'état.*" Meinecke does not really pay theoretical attention to societies' internal dynamics, which have an effect on international politics and are thus crucial to the question of war and peace. He is left with no more than vague hopes of the emergence of a "European sense of community" and of a genuine league of nations not dominated by a single power (431)—unlike the contemporary League of Nations founded in Geneva. How such a "genuine" league of nations should be established and, above all, how it should achieve stability against the background of the near-inexorable dynamics of violence he describes remains unclear. But Meinecke suggests that the sophisticated arguments for an eternal peaceful alliance between nations so common in the Enlightenment era would probably be thwarted by reality now. Even building on these arguments no longer seems a promising approach to Meinecke, whose basic stance is one of barely concealed resignation or at least bafflement.

Alfred Weber (1868–1958), who had occupied a chair in national economics in Heidelberg since 1907 and—along with his brother Max—played a central role in the establishment of sociology in Germany, published *Die Krise des modernen Staatsgedankens in Europa* (The Crisis of the Modern Idea of the State in Europe) in 1925, just one year after Meinecke, a book with similar ambitions to Meinecke's in aspiring to explain the contemporary age. But in contrast to Meinecke, Alfred Weber refers not just to a crisis of the European state *system* but to a crisis of the state itself, and—again unlike Meinecke—is particularly interested in the sociopolitical "foundation" of the contemporary state and the processes of change occurring within it. Weber concludes that the early modern state was originally closely entwined with capitalism, though in such a way that the state's leading role was never in question. This applied not only to the mercantilist state but also and in particular to the liberal state as it developed in the nineteenth century. But this liberal state had been transformed in the 1880s—with incalculable consequences for the politics of peace, as comparative analysis lays bare. While the liberal state was still a "peaceful entity" (A. Weber 1925, 73) in the sense that it embodied an autonomous rationality that made it possible to coolly calculate the preconditions for the state's continued existence, this subsequently changed radically. With the end of the liberal era, the state had in a sense been subdued by capitalism. Capitalist interests had penetrated the state, as a result of which it had got out of control (74). This was one of the key reasons why the armed forces had gained such autonomy and a militant "neo-imperialism" (102) had arisen that ultimately caused the world war. A "pervasive sickness" (75) leading to disastrous conflicts had gripped the state, but by no means just in Germany, and Weber tries to apportion blame for the war evenly among the European nations.

But this is as far as Alfred Weber's sociological reflections on state and war go; they remain on a relatively abstract level, as a result of which—in much the same way as in Meinecke's work—his ideas on how to achieve a peaceful order are also rather vague. Weber doubts that it will be possible to establish a European equilibrium on the same basis as before. Harshly criticizing the League of Nations, he calls for the European countries to regulate their affairs themselves (154) and for a kind of European federation in which Britain, France, Germany and Italy would play a central role (165). But it remains unclear how such a federation could be realized in view of his earlier comments on the overpowering of the state by capitalist-militarist interests. As with Meinecke, Alfred Weber fails almost entirely to link his normative perspective back to his sociological analyses.

With hindsight we must surely regard this failure to make such a link, to mediate between empirical analysis and normative stance, as a shortcoming. Nonetheless, it should be acknowledged that both Meinecke and Alfred Weber—both of whom supported the Weimar constitution—made a serious effort to produce analyses that were clearly linked to empirical reality and understood war as a normative problem requiring resolution. This could by no means be taken for granted in Germany at the time. Writers on the far right of the political spectrum often failed entirely to ground their analyses empirically or attempted simply to elide the gulf between norm and reality that was clearly visible in the work of Meinecke and Alfred Weber. This was done in very different ways and the intellectual level was generally low. But there were exceptions, and two authors are still of interest here, Hans Freyer (1887–1969) and above all Carl Schmitt (1888–1985).

Hans Freyer's *Der Staat* (The State) appeared in 1925, the same year that Freyer took up the first chair in sociology at the University of Leipzig, thus laying the basis for the later so-called Leipzig school of sociology. This school produced scholars such as Helmut Schelsky who were to play a significant role in the discipline in the later West Germany. Freyer is often placed within the spectrum of the "conservative revolution" (see, e.g., Breuer 1993). In a neo-Hegelian tone, he takes the elevation of the state to an extreme in this book. In contrast to Meinecke and Alfred Weber, right from the outset Freyer has no interest in the history of the modern state or the different forms of statehood in modernity. Instead, he outlines an ideal state whose innermost core is revealed in war. Deploying language with mystical overtones, Freyer, whose roots lay in the youth movement of the later Wilhelmine empire and was close to the philosophy of life (*Lebensphilosophie*) while he worked on his postdoctoral thesis under Georg Simmel (see Sieferle 1995, 164ff.), sees in the state the telos of cultural development: "The goal of spirit is the state. . . . The state . . . is spirit at its final destination, it is culture as the most complete realization of its purpose; it is the most conclusive form and most objective manifestation of destiny imaginable in the here below" (Freyer 1925, 20). But this state is by no means an abstract entity. Rather, Freyer believes, it is the expression of a naturally ordered, unequal community whose members all submit to a hero or leader: "A form of human life that is based on the law of the community reaches its apogee in the hero. The community is represented by the hero, who is able to capture the spirit of faith within the bounds of his great soul. The community is held together by a hero who towers above it" (62). In his view, the state is not only the expression of a community based on unity of blood (see also Breuer 1993, 91); it is also the creator of this community, and here the leader must play his historical role. Only through the "political act does the state weld a living form of human life, with all its productive powers, into the unity of the people, and the wealth of forms into the unity of the realm" (Freyer 1925, 98).

Freyer leaves us in no doubt about what he means by "act," first and foremost. The task of statesmen is to "give the realm its place within space, its duration in time, its power among the powers, and its reality in the real world" (148); this goal is to be achieved primarily through war, which stands to reason given that Freyer sees politics as a battle. Politics thinks in terms of "victory and defeat," so it "always reckons with war"

(142). Freyer thus elevates war to the status of normative benchmark. Taking up and extending Hegel's bellicist arguments, Freyer asserts that the essence of the people is expressed in absolute war—that it is only through war that the people can truly find itself: "Those wars to the death that put the state to the ultimate test not only tend to demonstrate to friend and foe the intensity of the state's vitality in a practical sense; they also reveal to our understanding the state's structural character. Never again can the object of our concern, namely the state, be presented by historical reality itself in such a pure form as during this time of the greatest demands and greatest achievements" (141). Freyer does not think in terms of a crisis of the state; rather, he has his sights set on a *new* state, and he reinterprets the horrors of war, including the world war, as an opportunity for the emergence of a new *Führer* state in which the conflicts and diverging opinions of bourgeois society no longer have any place. The invigorating role of (armed) violence should be used to build a new, truly organic state "community," though we are left wondering how the positive and community-*creating* experience of (armed) violence relates, in concrete terms, to the notion of the *blood*-based unity of this community, to which Freyer himself repeatedly refers.

While few modern-day readers are likely to get much out of Freyer's writings, by now no more than testimony to the fascination exercised by blood-and-soil rhetoric and bellicism within Germany, even among sociologists, the same cannot be said of the work of Carl Schmitt. Schmitt rejects the label "bellicist" as applied to his work, and with some justification. For him, in contrast to Freyer, while war is the origin of the political sphere, it is not necessarily an end in itself. And although anti-Semitic invective is by no means absent from Schmitt's work, he largely kept his distance from the language of blood-and-soil deployed by Freyer. He specialized mainly in polemical, often cynical, and sometimes very one-sided conceptual and historical analyses that prepared the ground for National Socialism in a quite different way from in the case of Freyer. But the undoubted argumentational brilliance displayed by Schmitt, an expert in constitutional law, makes him a figure with whom we must get to grips *even today*, particularly if we are examining war and peace from a social theory perspective, and not just if we stand on the political right.

By the mid-1920s, Schmitt had already coupled his characteristic conception of the political with reflections that led directly to analyses of the European state system and thus to the question of war and peace. This is particularly clear in Schmitt's essay *The Concept of the Political* from 1927 (Schmitt 2007a/1994a [1927]), in which he sweeps aside pluralistic theories of the state and democracy and declares the question, "Who decides?" the central political and constitutional problem. Schmitt immediately equates this question of decisions with that of the identification of friend and enemy. Pluralist and liberal conceptions of the state and democracy, according to Schmitt, shirk the question of "which social entity ... decides the extreme case *and* determines the decisive friend-and-enemy grouping" (Schmitt 2007a [1927], 43; emphasis added). But, in fact, the distinction between friend and enemy is the very core of the political, and the sovereign is that individual who can enforce this distinction. *How* and on the basis of which considerations this distinction between friend and enemy occurs is of no further concern to Schmitt and he leaves this to the workings of highly contingent circumstances and contexts. So all that matters is *that* a decision is made as to who is the enemy (see Hofmann 2002, 159). Schmitt is advocating a view of the state in which the unity of the state is guaranteed by these clear distinctions between friend and enemy—in other words, by the exclusion of those that are declared enemies. Political identity is possible only through identification of the enemy, according to Schmitt, who, incidentally, makes peculiar reference to Emil Lederer's masterly essay "On the Sociology of World War," though the thrust of this work was quite different from what Schmitt suggests here (Schmitt 2007a [1927], 45, n. 19).[5]

For Schmitt, this conception of the political by no means applies only to the field of domestic politics; he leaves us in no doubt that it also applies to international politics.[6] The state, according to Schmitt, defines the right to wage war. To the state "as an essentially political entity belongs the *jus belli*, i.e., the real possibility of deciding in a concrete situation upon the enemy and the ability to fight him with the power emanating from the entity. As long as a politically united people is prepared to fight for its existence, independence and freedom on the basis of a decision emanating from the political entity, this specifically political question has primacy over the technical means by which the battle will be waged, the nature of the army's organization, and what the prospects are for winning the war" (45/46). Schmitt's existential conception of war as expressed here is based on the assumption of the inevitability and inescapability of the political. But Schmitt does not necessarily want war as Freyer seems to and therefore does not endow it with an elevated normative status. And, in fact, Schmitt wishes to steer clear of normative statements in general. So he merely concludes that war requires no justification and in any case cannot be justified. It is a form of self-assertion against "a real enemy" (49) that closes off all normative questions from the outset.[7] The existential struggle with the enemy is neither just nor unjust, it "is," which is why for Schmitt a "discriminatory concept of war" is not only meaningless but detrimental and leads inevitably to an uncontrolled escalation of violence. Schmitt justifies this at first glance counterintuitive assertion by stating that the notion of just and unjust enemies, the conclusion that by waging a war a state has violated universal norms of justice that apply to the whole of humanity, criminalizes this state and can only lead us to conclude that this state and its (criminal) leaders must be destroyed. This would make the deployment of every conceivable means virtually imperative for *both* parties to war, as an honorable defeat would be simply unacceptable on these premises: through strict application of a discriminatory concept of war, Schmitt concludes, existential war of the kind that had prevailed so far within the European state system would turn into a wave of genuine wars of annihilation.

Schmitt makes it clear that he wishes to avoid such outcomes. In any case, in his view there is no such thing as a norm of justice with a claim to universal validity, and that includes any that might relate to wars. At most, universal norms are a cover for specific power interests, which is why in reality wars in the name of humanity—to enforce universal norms or rights, for example—do not and cannot exist. For Schmitt, the notion of war in the name of humanity is just propaganda intended to conceal national ambitions, nothing more. Schmitt's critique of universalist ideologies here follows almost logically from his definition of the political sphere. The identification of friend and enemy leads automatically to the pluralism of states. A political entity simply cannot be universal; there can be no world state, because the identity of the state arises solely by identifying other states as enemies (see Hofmann 2002, 103). Humanity, according to Schmitt, is not a political concept (1994a [1927], 80ff.), so that references to the supposed interests of humanity or the claim that we need a world state are at best irrelevant and at worst deliberately misleading.

Inevitably, Schmitt's critique of universalism is also aimed at the Enlightenment project of a federal community of nations, first realized (however imperfectly) after 1918 in the so-called League of Nations. His rejection of all such projects is not solely due to a German nationalistic perspective but has much deeper roots: as we have just seen, any trace of a political approach with the merest hint of universalism seems suspect to him. Ultimately, from Schmitt's perspective, any league of nations would entail the risk outlined above of aggravating armed conflicts, because the discrepancy between universalism and federalism cannot be eliminated: the norms that supposedly express the solidarity of the league's individual member states would continue to collide with their actual conduct. And it is this fact that immediately throws up the question of who gets to decide about the violations committed by individual member states and how they are to be assessed. But, according to Schmitt, this inevitably brings us back to the debate on just and unjust wars, in other words the discriminatory concept of war, which inevitably leads to an escalation of violence. Warring protagonists branded as lawbreakers and to some extent enemies of humanity would have no other choice than to opt for total war in order to avoid physical and moral annihilation by the enemy. Simply because of its structure, the League of Nations necessarily becomes a means of legitimizing a total war intended to destroy completely the criminalized enemy—a war that, in contrast to earlier times, no longer recognizes any neutral positions in conflicts, as no one can evade the (violent) punishment of a criminalized state (Schmitt 1999 [1938], 41f.). Yet Schmitt deliberately kept quiet about the fact that the First World War itself was virtually a total war and that Adolf Hitler, whose rule he had tried to justify in his writings, was now gearing up for a far more "total" war on the basis of a deeply particularist ideology.

But Schmitt's evidently profound resentment toward what he saw as an amalgam of Versailles, Geneva, and Weimar, and the National Socialist vision of the international political order that he developed in response, should not cause us to reject his thinking too quickly, particularly given that similar arguments can be found in the work of Western democrats such as George Kennan (see Waltz 1959, 113). In fact, a dispute between universalists and traditionalists occurred within the American debate on peace prospects and international law between the two world wars, and some of the arguments put forward here resemble those of Carl Schmitt (see Krakau 1967). Once again, in attempting to outlaw the use of violence, the universalists, in an internally consistent way, came up with new justifications for the use of violence in order to enforce the prohibition on violence. This argumentational dilemma and the small step from universal moral responsibility to a crusading political mentality have been key characteristics of American liberal thinking on peace and American foreign policy itself. President Wilson's policies and their intellectual background, for example, were referred to as an "imperialism of good intentions." The danger of allowing one's own side unlimited scope for definition and rashly deploying violent forms of intervention in order to bring about liberal orders—through mechanisms intended to ensure the peaceful resolution of international conflicts—should be regarded as the dark side of the republican conception of peace.

In any event, Schmitt leaves us in no doubt that Germany can have no interest in the postwar status quo, and that the contemporary European system must be viewed as one that subjugates Germany, a state of affairs that is worse than war because Germany's "right and honor" are being violated (Schmitt 2000 [1925], 294). For Schmitt, Germany's subjugation, made permanent by the League of Nations, is in substantial part an effect of modern imperialism, namely American imperialism. *First*, Schmitt believes, the Geneva conception of a league of nations is merely an appendage to the American Monroe Doctrine. This doctrine preceded the League of Nations not only temporally but also in a logical and objective sense: while the United States gave the League, which it initiated but did not ultimately join, a seemingly universalist structure, at the same time it implanted particularist interests in this structure, namely the Monroe Doctrine. As a result, the United States of America could block off any European influence in the Western Hemisphere, while at the same time retaining every means of applying pressure to Europe. The United States was both present and absent in Geneva: "Eighteen American states [most of which are dependent on the United States], a third of the membership of the League, now take part in decisions on all European or Asian affairs[. B]ut the American Monroe Doctrine, whose primacy is . . . recognized in Article 21 of the Covenant of the League of Nations, has precedence over the League Covenant and prevents the interference of the Geneva League in American affairs" (Schmitt 2011 [1932], 40). *Second*, Schmitt is hugely critical of Schumpeter's broadly accepted theory of imperialism, which simply denies the political character of the economy (184). The emerging economic dominance of the United States in the world economy is by no means due solely to economic dynamics but was secured by a whole series of international agreements. The specific form of imperialism may be different from what it was in the nineteenth century. Yet nonetheless, American imperialism is merely the continuation of a form of power deployed by the British in the nineteenth century. And Germany must defend itself against this political and economic imperialism of the United States, Schmitt asserts, as he lays the ground intellectually for the expansionist policies of the National Socialists.

Schmitt's call for Germany to defend itself against American imperialism cannot be understood as a normative appeal. Instead, his argument is anthropological in character, and here he relies heavily on Hobbesian ideas. He shares Hobbes's pessimistic interpretation of human nature (Schmitt 1996 [1938], 36), and like him he takes the view that what exists between states is merely a more or less unregulated state of nature

(Schmitt 1994b [1928], 122). The lively "combat of elementary forces" between states (Schmitt 1996 [1938], 49) can only find expression under pre- or extralegal conditions, a state of affairs that can only apparently be overcome—whether through a league of nations or an imperialism posing as mere economics.

This, however, compels him to sketch out new notions of international political order. If European international law has become invalid (not least because of the rise of the United States as a world power and the open enforcement of a discriminatory concept of war that was part and parcel of the Versailles Treaty), we are left with the question of what might replace Europe's traditional system of international law beyond what he views as the hypocritical universalist ideas underpinning the League of Nations. So it comes as little surprise that Schmitt makes use of a National Socialist vocabulary and expresses National Socialist ideas in 1939. For Schmitt, at the beginning of the Second World War, the "Reich"—as a geopolitical order that he consciously views as an alternative to the Anglo-American universalism of the League of Nations—seems the only conceivable system that promises new global political stability while not undermining that conception of the political sphere that arises from the inevitability of the struggle between states: "As soon as . . . large regional spheres of interest are recognized under international law with a prohibition on outside intervention, and the concept of the empire gains traction, it becomes possible to imagine the coexistence of clearly defined regions in a sensibly divided-up world, and the principle of non-intervention can have its ordering effect within a new international law" (Schmitt 1994c [1939], 344). In Schmitt's view, however, this stability existing between such regional spheres can only ever be temporary, as it will never be possible to eliminate the Hobbesian state of nature between states (or major powers within their spheres of influence).

After 1945, Schmitt could no longer propagate the theory of political order developed in 1939; but this did not induce a shift in the basic structures of his thinking. Instead, in such works as *The Nomos of the Earth in the Jus Publicum Europaeum* (2003a [1950]) and *Theory of the Partisan: Intermediate Commentary on the Concept of the Political* (2007b [1963]), Schmitt builds on, develops, and adds nuance to his old arguments. He now focuses on interpreting the historical genesis and specific features of the traditional European system of international law, asking what its end might mean for the present and what might happen in the future. In this connection, Schmitt again underlines that the European state system and traditional international law laid the foundations for a political order *based on Europe*, which could become established precisely by excluding other parts of the world. Schmitt's thesis, which is still worth considering, is that, with European expansion and the incipient division of the world by the major European powers, the discourse of international law began to embrace the notion of a world with global lines of demarcation (Schmitt 2003a [1950], 88, translation modified, HJ/WK) from the fifteenth century at the latest, a mode of thought that separated the European sphere of power and law from its non-European counterpart. Beyond the so-called amity lines, beyond the sphere in which the "memory of a common unity in Christian Europe" held sway (94), a state of lawless freedom was assumed to exist:

> This freedom meant that the line set aside an area where force could be used freely and ruthlessly. It was understood, however, that only Christian-European princes and peoples could share in the land-appropriations of the New World and be parties to such treaties. But the commonality of Christian princes and nations contained neither a common, concrete, and legitimating arbitrational authority, nor any principle of distribution other than the law of the stronger and, ultimately, of effective occupation. . . . This was a tremendous *exoneration* of the internal European problematic. The significance in international law of the famous and notorious expression "beyond the line" lies precisely in this exoneration. (ibid.; emphasis in original)

So the establishment of a fighting zone beyond Europe's borders was in a sense the precondition for limiting war in Europe (97).

Here again, in analogy to his friend-enemy distinctions, Schmitt thinks in terms of exclusion: it was the exclusion of non-European territories that laid the foundation for a European identity. However, according to Schmitt, in order to consolidate this plural identity consisting of a great variety of states, constitutional and international law had to develop essentially as follows. The emergence of the modern state, with the three key attributes of centralized law making, domestic territorial unity, and the overcoming of confessional civil war (128f.), gave rise to a political form that made it possible for jurists to understand it in analogy to a person. The personification and personalization of the state as "magnus homo"—and this was crucial to the issue of war and peace—enabled the legalization of relations between states, with the same law of *jus ad bellum* applying to all those states adhering to this legal framework. The idea of the *justus hostis*, the just enemy, went hand in hand with this right from the start; because he has the right to wage war, this enemy should not be criminalized. It was precisely this, Schmitt believes, that paved the way for the rationalization and humanization of war, with pure war between states, war as duel, being the end product of the development of international law in Europe. The issue of just war, in other words the discriminatory concept of war, had been successfully suppressed—the indispensable precondition for limiting war in Schmitt's view. As he was to write elsewhere, it is "extraordinary . . . an incredibly human accomplishment, that men disclaimed a discrimination and denigration of the enemy" (Schmitt 2007b [1963], 90).

For Schmitt, it was this limitation of war that was the result and achievement of European international law. But as he repeatedly underlines, this limitation did not function so well solely because of the discipline of the European states, but also because international law created a Europe-centric geopolitical order, which was stable precisely because it excluded other regions of the world and the Europeans created for themselves a more or less lawless sphere of action in these regions. Europe's geopolitical structure as established through international law, Schmitt thought, "made possible a continental law of European sovereigns against the background of the immense open spaces of a particular type of freedom" (Schmitt 2003a [1950], 148).

This is also Schmitt's point of departure for explaining the decline or end of this European international law and the geopolitical order established by it. For Schmitt, *first*, the independence of the Anglo-American and Latin American countries and concomitant emergence of a "Western hemisphere" is the beginning of the end for the old Europe-centric geopolitical order, as this equalized colonial and European territories in legal terms such that the identity of Europe, attained through exclusion, could no longer be maintained (220). *Second*, Schmitt draws a parallel between the development of a world economy that was clearly up and running around 1900 and the rise of universalist thought (234), a type of thought that conflicted with the principles of traditional international law in that greater emphasis was again placed on the propagation of universal standards of justice, including with respect to war. The notion of the just war, in other words the discriminatory concept of war, which was for long successfully suppressed, now reappears—not least in the form of an American universalist interventionism, which was the intellectual basis for the League of Nations (so hated by Schmitt) and later the UN. *Third* and finally—as Schmitt asserted in 1950 in his final, highly topical argument—the discriminatory concept of war, by now widely accepted and ultimately undermining traditional international law ever further, was also backed up by the monstrous impact of nuclear weapons; for Schmitt, the use of such terrible weapons against anything other than an "unjust enemy" would be unthinkable—and in the early days of the Cold War their deployment was both envisaged and planned for. The enemy, according to Schmitt, *must* necessarily be an unjust one, because otherwise there would be no way of justifying the use of such weapons (321). This finally pulled the rug from under European international law and ultimately the state as "bearer of the most astonishing of all monopolies, namely the monopoly of political decision-making, this showpiece of European form and occidental rationalism" (Schmitt 1991, 10).

It is no coincidence that in the period after the Second World War Schmitt begins to take a particular interest in the figure of the partisan, whom he finds fascinating because he has always operated outside of international law. The partisan embodies "true enmity," so for Schmitt he represents the political figure par excellence. As an irregular combatant without uniform, the partisan, who according to Schmitt is distinguished by irregularity of battle, high mobility, political engagement, and closeness to nature (Schmitt 2007b [1963], 20), has always been an alien element for European international law. Yet the Spanish partisans of the early nineteenth century—and they are probably the epitome of such fighters in Schmitt's eyes—were the first to take up the struggle against Napoleon and thus restore the seriousness of war (88), in contrast to the disgraceful stance of the German governments of the time, which generally hesitated over whether to go to war and resist aggression and constantly put off such decisions, ultimately proving themselves to be unpolitical. As long as European international law still functioned, the partisan of this period—and he found his German equivalent in 1813 in the wars of liberation—was in any event the exception. Now however, Schmitt indicates, this figure seems to be increasingly significant. In view of new revolutionary ideologies, the image of the partisan has changed—he has become more offensive and no longer necessarily close to nature. But in a world in which traditional European international law has collapsed and—in view of the global political deadlock between the rival atomic powers—a "normal" war between states, now waged on a different basis, scarcely seems possible, he is more than ever the embodiment of the political actor. He has taken the decision to engage in battle through his will to define the enemy. In Schmitt's somehow nostalgic view, the partisan is both an anachronistic and admirable manifestation of the political.

Though conventional war is finished, casting a veil over the heart of the political, there is still the partisan. From time to time at least, the partisan breathes new life into the political realm, awakening its timeless power, namely the will to choose one's enemy (see Münkler 1992, 121f.).

Looking back on Schmitt's analyses, it seems fair to say that the brilliance of his arguments is often due to major conceptual biases and theoretical inadequacies. The very definition of the political through the friend-enemy distinction causes Schmitt to work toward a completely uniform and homogeneous notion of state and society from the outset. For him, genuine state authority represents the political unity of the people, such that he simply nips the question of the (graduated and empirical) legitimacy of the state in the bud. The state either is—or is not. There is nothing in between. As commentators have noted (Hofmann 2002, 15), this not only abolishes the gulf between is and ought but makes it impossible from the outset to examine empirically the particular relationship that exists between state and social forces, because the "true" state both creates and embodies social unity. All of this has repercussions for Schmitt's understanding of war. Questions concerning, for example, the connection between capitalism and war, the interplay of war-promoting and war-inhibiting forces, and the consequences of wars, of the kind still common in the social theories formulated under the German Empire, become almost impossible to pose in this way. Of course, Schmitt discusses such things as the imperialism (of the United States), which presents itself as mere economics. But at the same time the interpretive foil of the political sphere, which he always regarded as crucial, prevents him from considering economic and cultural phenomena in their own right and with regard to their possible repercussions for the political sphere. Ultimately, Schmitt is indulging in a political reductionism to which all other manifestations of the social must submit conceptually and theoretically.

This also molds his assessment of intellectual currents and positions, whose capacity to inhibit wars was still considered worthy of discussion in the classical phase of sociology at least. We are not, of course, required to share the optimism of a Durkheim or Mead with respect to the universalization of values, in other words their profoundly humanistic vision of purely peaceful competition between nations based on this process. But neither must we accept Schmitt's brute and virtually unfounded dismissal of the impact of norms and values as such. Because of his radical view of contingency, Schmitt himself is unable to answer the eminently sociological question of what brings about specific friend-enemy distinctions in the first place; so it is quite plausible to take values seriously into account when analyzing the causes of war and peace. Nor is it empirically proved that universalism is primarily responsible for the dissolution of traditional European international law and the concomitant brutalization of war. It is not just that wars of annihilation have also been waged in the name of particular values. Even more important in this connection is the fact that right from the start the raison d'état that developed along with European international law proved largely incapable of limiting the desire for territorial expansion—regardless of universalist "ideologies." Attempts to keep raison d'état within ethical bounds—as already noted by Meinecke—had always failed. In this sense Schmitt's depiction of the European geopolitical order as stable glosses over the reality (Hofmann 2002, 204). Though Schmitt has good reason to emphasize that the European geopolitical order established by European international law has gained its specific form through the exclusion of other parts of the world, it is also true that he makes no effort to relate the intra-European stability attained as a result of exclusion to the normative costs of this exclusion. Despite his seemingly strict antinormativist pose, Schmitt's position is ultimately based on highly particularist values and ignores all the extra-European consequences and costs of European stability. From Schmitt's perspective, the "benefit" to extra-European regions made possible by the collapse of the *jus publicum europaeum*, the emerging possibility that they might be included within a larger global framework on an equal basis, is of no further interest.

So as brilliantly as Schmitt develops his arguments, he abandons many of the insights gained in the eighteenth and nineteenth centuries. He did not, for instance, produce an analysis of the connection between war and modern society based on the classics of sociology. In the period between 1918 and 1945, useful analyses of this kind were generally to be found in other national contexts (on the few exceptions in Germany, see Kehr 1970 [1930]), not least in the United States, where large portions of the German social sciences' macrosociological legacy ended up as a result of forced emigration from 1933 on. The German social sciences, which in many ways still played a leading role during the establishment of the discipline at the turn of the twentieth century and which—see Sombart and Hintze—had also produced important studies on the topic of war, were either destroyed or at least subject to major restrictions as a result of Hitler's rule. Many high-ranking social scientists chose or were forced to emigrate, and it was mostly the less intellectually significant figures who offered their services, often quite consciously, to the National Socialist racial program, producing racist studies of use to *Volkstumspolitik*—policies rooted in the ideology of the *Volk*. This meant that new developments in social theory increasingly occurred elsewhere—particularly in the United States, though even here there were very few intensive and systematic studies of *war and peace*. The liberal legacy prevented this from happening, especially in the United States, and once again it was intellectual loners who took an interest in the topic of war.

■ ■ ■

The Berlin-born Hans Speier (1905–90) was just such a loner. Under the Weimar Republic, in the shape of studies published much later as *German White-Collar Workers and the Rise of Hitler* (1986 [1933]), he wrote one of the classic works of political sociology and sociostructural analysis; he brought his macrosociological skills, gained among other things through practice of a Weberian mode of analysis, with him to his new home, to which he had fled from the National Socialists. As an expert in the study of public opinion, Speier was immediately absorbed into the machinery of the American government to investigate German propaganda methods when America entered the war in 1941 (see, e.g., Speier 1948). But he had already engaged intensively with the topic of war before that date; as he himself put it (Speier 1989a, 13), he was the first social scientist in the United States to hold lectures on the sociology of war before the Second World War. He was in fact particularly well equipped for this task, having been assistant to Emil Lederer in Heidelberg, who, as we have seen, produced one of the few substantial sociological studies of the First World War. Speier became his colleague once again in the 1930s, this time at the university-in-exile, the graduate faculty of the New School for Social Research in New York City.

Speier was never in any doubt that Hitler spelled war. As early as 1936, in the essay "Militarism in the Eighteenth Century," he attempted to produce a typology of modern militarism after 1789, which he tried to differentiate from the bellicose culture of feudalism and from the militarism of the absolutist era. According to Speier, we are dealing with an extreme form of militarism "when the distribution of power and esteem assumes the form of centralization of control, an attendant state monopoly of raising, controlling, and equipping armies, and a universality of military mores" (Speier 1989b [1936], 70). No significant connections between modern militarism and feudalism can be found on the basis of this definition, and only a few between modern militarism and absolutism (71). According to Speier we should not, however, make too much of this absolutist legacy—the key features here being a tendency toward centralization, bureaucratization, and state control of the economy—as a clear division between military and nonmilitary activities was constitutive of the absolutist system of rule, a division that is no longer to be found in this form in modern militarism. Furthermore, for Speier, absolutist militarism was always counteracted by the antiheroism of European Enlightenment thinkers and their often critical view of the armed forces (84), so that mitigating factors undoubtedly played a role here. Speier also notes that industry made its arrival in European societies following the end of absolutism. This, he claims, must have engendered the devaluation of heroic-bellicose virtues (86), as liberal currents of thought had of course always claimed (see chapters 2 and 3).

Yet militarism has *not* disappeared as a result of industrialization, which throws up the question of what sustains it under these new conditions. Here Speier is faced with a question to which he was to find no satisfactory answer. In 1943, in "Ludendorff: The German Concept of Total War," he interpreted the militarism of the German Empire as a "class militarism on a half-feudal basis" (Speier 1989c [1943], 99), though this is rather unconvincing given that he had tended to downplay the feudal roots of modern militarism in his 1936 essay. Speier is compelled to remain on the level of description, describing the militarism of Ludendorff and his concept of "total war" and the related concepts deployed by the National Socialists as a specific reaction to the experiences of the First World War, though without managing to produce a plausible account of the militarism that had led to that war.

But despite these conceptual and theoretical difficulties, Speier continues to study the topic of war, and in some cases his analyses are very much in line with those of Emil Lederer (1979 [1920]) on "Die ökonomische Umschichtung im Krieg" (Economic Fluctuations in War). In "Class Structure and 'Total War'" (1939), Speier analyzes "total war" and predicts a trend toward ever larger firms, a change in labor relations, a lessening of social inequality, and changes in the structure of capitalism as a result of increased control of property, before going on in 1940 to examine typologically different forms of warfare and battle in the essay "The Social Types of War." Heavily influenced by his reading of Clausewitz, Speier distinguishes between absolute war, instrumental war, and the antagonistic battle. For Clausewitz, absolute war was still a kind of ideal type, which he believed would never be waged so unconditionally in reality. For Speier, born later, it was almost inevitably a real type, because "unrestricted and unregulated war" intended to wipe out and destroy the enemy completely (Speier 1940, 445)—to quote his definition of absolute war—had become a reality in the age of insane ideologies.[8] Speier's types may also be read as a critique of the dangerous tendency to endow war with a special status, a tendency found in the work of some of the authors dealt with here. As Speier makes only too plain, references to the playful and extraquotidian elements of battle (as Caillois had made) make sense only if we relate them to a specific form of conflict, namely the antagonistic battle (451). For Speier, to try to describe absolute war through these categories is completely misguided and out of touch with the reality of modern war.

■ ■ ■

With respect to their broad historical and macrosociological arguments, Speier's analyses were something of an exception in the 1930s and early 1940s. Speier saw his intensive engagement with war and militarism as—in today's terms—"political sociology." He viewed the study of wars as a means of gaining key insights into the division of power and power dynamics in modern societies. At the time, similar ambitions were present in the work of just one other American scholar, a political scientist who had also been grappling with new war-related forms of power since the 1930s, namely Harold D. Lasswell (1902–78). His essay "The Garrison State," which he published in the *American Journal of Sociology* in 1940 (see also Berghahn 1981, 43ff.), has become quite famous. In much the same way as Speier, Lasswell, one of the few American social scientists to make use of psychoanalysis to explain clearly irrational mass and political behavior, emphasized the tremendous social and economic upheavals that twentieth-century wars had caused and would continue to cause. Going beyond Speier, he warned that in future the war efforts of differentiated modern societies would require two things if they were to be successful: psychological manipulation and the brutal, sometimes terroristic disciplining of citizens (Lasswell 1940, 458ff.). Lasswell feared that in every warring state democratic rights would be dismantled sooner or later, that the people would soon be entirely at the mercy of the "specialists on violence." Although he did not consider the rise of such war-induced "garrison states" inevitable, he thought it at least possible—and not just in the totalitarian societies of Germany, Russia, and Japan, but, with much piquancy, in the United States as well. Though some of his ideas seem overdrawn from a modern-day perspective and his pessimism about the future excessive, and while it is particularly irritating that he made such a close connection between the (possible) developmental characteristics of the United States and those of the totalitarian regimes (see Friedberg 2000), Lasswell's arguments are still of considerable significance. For the first time, a prominent American social scientist was reflecting systematically on the social, economic, and political consequences of international conflicts in the age of total war. Lasswell's ideas opened up a new understanding of military conflicts: even more than Speier, he no longer viewed war as an isolated event, as a mere interruption of civilizational progress, but as the hallmark of an entire era that was capable of setting the course for the rise of quite different social and political worlds. This, of course, included a good deal of cultural and civilizational critique, yet, in contrast to so many other authors, this did not cause Lasswell to eschew serious empirical study of social change.

▪ ▪ ▪

As we have underlined, even in the United States few authors were as ambitious as Speier and Lasswell. Scholarly interest in armed violence did pick up there in the 1930s because of the growing threat of a new war. But this interest went unchanneled by a theory of social change, a shortcoming of the American social sciences as a whole at the time (Knöbl 2001, 39–154). The spectrum of studies produced thus ranged from a general critique of civilization that included consideration of war to detailed studies of war-related phenomena that paid little heed to theory.

In the United States, the cultural and civilizational critique concerned with the new phenomenon of totalitarianism was grouped mainly around the *Review of Politics*, founded in 1939, a journal to which a large number of European immigrants contributed.[9] Economic historian John U. Nef (1899–1988) was one of those close to the journal who took a fairly persistent interest in war (see, e.g., Nef 1943), but his historically oriented texts failed to reach great theoretical depth. The studies in history and political science by German immigrant Alfred Vagts (1892–1986) (*A History of Militarism*, 1937; see Berghahn 1981, 38ff.) and by political scientist Quincy Wright (1890–1970) (*A Study of War*, 1942) were certainly more significant, though here again issues in social theory tended to stay in the background.

"Cultural critique without much theory"—this description also applies to Pitirim Sorokin (1889–1968), former private secretary to Russian prime minister Kerenski in the period following the February Revolution of 1917. After being exiled by the Bolsheviks, he eventually ended up in the United States in 1923 and obtained a post at Harvard, where he became the dominant figure in the sociology department before the Parsons era. He had published a number of studies on war while still in Russia (see Ionin/Cernych 1989, 137ff.), was fascinated by the subject throughout his life, and devoted important passages to it in his magnum opus *Social and Cultural Dynamics: A Study of Change in Major Systems of Art, Truth, Ethics, Law, and Social Relationships*, published between 1937 and 1941 (but see also Sorokin 1943/44 and 1945). Because he lacked the Enlightenment optimism about progress, because he had a generally cyclical view of history and saw his own time as materialistic and thus degenerate and believed it would come to an end in the near future, he was able to devote particular attention to the negative aspects of history—including wars. He did not however develop a refined theoretical perspective. His main thesis was that historical study of the course and frequency of wars offers few grounds for the Enlightenment faith in progress—but also few grounds for any equally problematic emphasis on decline: "As in the data presented there is nothing to support the claim of disappearance of war in the past, so is there nothing to support the claim, in spite of the exceptionally high figures for the twentieth century, that there has been (or will be) any steady trend toward increase of war: no, the curve just fluctuates, and that is all" (Sorokin 1937, 361/62). Sorokin essentially provides a wealth of data on wars, which show among other things that since the twelfth century the number of casualties in (European) wars has increased significantly faster than the numerical strength of armies and that, since then, the structures of wars have changed in many other important ways as well.

The United States' entry into the Second World War attracted the attention of many other leading American social scientists. Even the nucleus of sociology in the United States, the so-called Chicago school of sociology, which had seen its center of gravity as lying within micro- and meso-sociology since the time of Park, Mead, and Thomas and had largely failed to develop much interest in international conflicts, now wished, or was compelled, to make a contribution.

Not all of the work that flowed from this is of the highest caliber. Robert E. Park's (1864–1944) "The Social Function of War: Observations and Notes," a late essay from 1940, is generally disappointing and rather vague. Other authors of the Chicago school, meanwhile, produced interesting analyses, the main figures here being Everett Hughes and Louis Wirth. Hughes's (1897–1983) essay from 1942, "The Impact of War on American Institutions," which was anchored in democratic theory, considers the effects of war on the structure of American institutions and value system. Chiefly against the background of the debate on America's core values kicked off during the war, Hughes discusses the question of whether the institutional system typical of the United States, often based on the voluntary principle and established by private benefactors, can survive in view of massive economic changes, and especially the state intervention that was on the increase as a result of the war. "Our minds and the economy of our emotions will undoubtedly have to become adjusted to less apparent freedom than we have become accustomed to" (Hughes 1942, 402). Hughes's essay provides surprising insights into the shift in Americans' willingness to participate against the background of war-related changes.

Louis Wirth (1897–1952), originally from Germany, rose to prominence mainly on the back of his studies of the Jewish ghetto in differing national contexts (*The Ghetto*, 1928) and general reflections in urban sociology ("Urbanism as a Way of Life," 1938); as a student at the University of Chicago, he had helped spearhead the movement opposing America's entry in the war between 1916 and 1919 (Boyer 2004). During the Second World War he wrote a number of sociological commentaries on the war and joined the debate on Hobbesian "power-political realism" in his essay entitled "International Tensions as Objects of Social Investigation," though this appeared only in 1948 and was written with the incipient "Cold War" in mind. His reflections attempt to clarify the concept of "international tension." Here Wirth exposes the hollowness of this term; he stresses the need to differentiate between the rulers and ruled of two rival nations, and shows that seemingly immutable state interests may change, that they are often redefined in such a way as to aggravate or alleviate conflict, and that these tensions—against the assumptions of power-political "realists"—rarely follow a rational and thus predictable pattern. Wirth is a Kantian in that he believes that the majority's judgment is sounder in a free country and the rulers have fewer opportunities to drive the masses into a war through the construction of scapegoats (1948, 49). But he is enough of a skeptic to know that a democratic form of government will not take hold in a short span of time and that evil, the will to commit wicked acts, will not simply disappear among peoples and rulers: "The widely held faith, especially among scholars and educators, that lack of understanding between peoples lies at the root of international conflict, is not always justified. Correlatively, the almost universal belief that better understanding would prevent the development of tensions or ease those that exist, may also be questioned" (52). In situations in which governments, as in Nazi Germany, desire power and have evil intentions, such understanding takes us no further; in such cases, as we might interpret Wirth, violent resistance is the only remaining option. Overall, through his nuanced arguments and his reflections on the concept of interests and the meaning of the term international "tensions," Wirth often shows himself to be more realistic than most power-political "realists"—a surprising feat for someone who rarely argued on the level of international relations over the course of his life's work (for a review of Wirth's sociology, though from a different perspective than interests us here, see Vortkamp 2003).

▪ ▪ ▪

As interesting as the works of Hughes and Wirth are, they are not representative of the processes of change that now set in within the American social sciences. The social sciences' involvement in the war was related mainly to the fact that the relevant disciplines, which were now rather better established than in the period between 1914 and 1918, provided significant empirical knowledge and were thus of potential use to the war effort. Conversely, this also injected into these disciplines an interest in war-related issues, providing major stimulus to research on wars, their causes and consequences. In sociology, this stimulus immediately led to the development of the subdiscipline of "military sociology." As it was simply a fact that American sociology had the tools to produce knowledge of use to administration of the war effort, it makes sense that those sociologists working for the American armed forces underwent increasing professionalization within the discipline as well—not least because of their ever-greater and subsequently near-exclusive focus on the armed forces. For the most part, this was no longer a political sociology in the sense of Speier or Lasswell, featuring multiple points of contact with social theory, but rather a highly specialized organizational sociology that had few repercussions for the development of the discipline as such. This resulted in a problematic division of labor between a subdiscipline of military sociology entrusted with the analysis of the armed forces and a general sociology that paid almost no attention to violence and war. This would have been of little import had military sociology developed a substantial and stable interest in issues of social theory of its own accord. But this did not happen. As the field became ever more specialized and divided into ever more subdivisions—as also occurred in other subdisciplines—it no longer paid attention to the discipline's theoretically ambitious questions, and studies worth mentioning from a social theory standpoint are few and far between within the field of military sociology (for recent surveys of military sociology and its history, see Kernic 2001; Heins/Warburg 2004; and Leonhard/Werkner 2005).

The American Soldier, a study produced under the direction of Samuel A. Stouffer (1900–1960), was the first major empirical work in military sociology in the United States. Social theoretical ambitions are very much in evidence here. Based on data collected within the American army itself, this four-volume work from 1949 produced important findings on class-specific behavior; the adaptability and morale of ordinary soldiers and officers; the significance of group processes to the functioning of the units; and the soldiers' immediate experience of battle. The passages on "combat experience," specifically on coping with fear in battle, not only provide—for the first time within the discipline of sociology—an empirically grounded insight into the enormous psychological stresses to which soldiers are exposed in battle. Stouffer's analyses also form a very interesting contrast to those of Roger Caillois, which were more philosophical and speculative in intent and which built on the literary accounts of battle produced by Ernst Jünger. Neither Stouffer himself nor other sociologists, however, analyzed in more depth soldiers' profound emotional experiences in battle that emerge so clearly in *The American Soldier*. There was an obvious opportunity here to use these extreme behaviors and experiences to reconsider traditional models of action, to ask, for example, what we can learn about "normal" action from action in extreme situations, how crucial security is to coping smoothly with everyday actions, for instance. None of this happened; the trend toward the "sealing off" of military sociology was already evident at a fairly early stage.

Much the same can be said of "Cohesion and Disintegration in the Wehrmacht in World War II" by Edward A. Shils (1910–95) and Morris Janowitz (1919–88), another famous work in military sociology. On the basis of interviews with German prisoners of war, they brought out the importance of group processes to the *morale of the troops* in Hitler's army and demonstrated—contrary to expectations—that a robust Nazi worldview or nationalistic belief in Germany played a comparatively minor role in comparison. In recent times critics have raised objections to their ideas. The explanatory power of the "primary group," of which Shils and Janowitz made so much, they assert, has been overestimated. This is simply because, given the huge losses suffered by the *Wehrmacht*, especially on the eastern front, these groups never existed for very long, and the idealization of the group by the soldiers themselves was undoubtedly ideological to some degree (see Bartov 1991, esp. 29ff.). Yet Shils and Janowitz still deserve credit for being the first to highlight the great importance of informal structures in such a strongly hierarchical and formalized social formation as an army. Their study not only laid the foundations for primary group research as a whole, of the kind that was to become so influential within American sociology in the 1950s, but also stimulated the study of informal behavior patterns within organizational sociology. The analyses produced by Shils and Janowitz were not really harnessed to advance social theory; but both authors, here and in subsequent publications, at least attempted not to decouple those issues of special interest to military sociology from more general ones.

▪ ▪ ▪

Studies in the sociology of the armed forces and war that appeared after 1945, at least those with social theoretical aspirations, came predominantly from the United States, and there were good reasons for this. These lay both in the history of the discipline and in the history of the world itself. In the United States the discipline underwent an uninterrupted process of establishment and development, while the wars and crises that had afflicted Europe prevented this from happening there in the same way. For the first time, American sociology took on a clear leadership role within international sociology, which also meant that social theoretical analyses of war—when they appeared, which was rare enough—were developed chiefly in America. The sociologies of other democratic countries could not keep up, either because—as in France—the preconditions for the development of the subject were for a long time simply absent as a result of the German occupation and the political upheavals caused by the war or because—as in the United Kingdom—sociology was weakly institutionalized and still required disciplinary development. In the case of Germany, at least West Germany, a difficult new beginning had to be made following the forced migration of many intellectuals and the Nazis' appropriation of sociology; unsurprisingly, German sociology often took its lead from its already highly professionalized American counterpart.

So sociology's geographic center of gravity shifted as a result of the war. Nonetheless, it is fair to say that the topic of war continued to be marginalized within the discipline. As mentioned above, in the shape of a fairly strong military sociology, a sociological subdiscipline had become established in the United States since the 1940s that grappled intensively with the institution of the "armed forces." But otherwise sociological and social theoretical studies of war remained thin on the ground. This was reinforced by the hegemonic position attained by modernization theory

184 • Chapter 5

within macrosociology since the 1950s, as its Enlightenment assumptions resulted, from the outset, in a distorted view of violent phenomena. Beneath the surface, the "dream of a non-violent modernity" was having its effect. Researchers studied isolated societies, interpreting developments and processes within them as wholly endogenous. They paid no attention to war. Given the terrible violent events that had taken place just a few years or decades before, events in which the American nation and especially the European countries were embroiled, this can only be described as a spectacular case of the suppression of war. The ever-present risk of nuclear annihilation arising from the arms race between the United States and USSR was also largely ignored. Only a very small number of theoretically minded sociologists made any effort to exploit the insights gained within military sociology, let alone continue the military-related "political sociology" of a Hans Speier or Harold D. Lasswell. Again, those who did so were the exceptions. Raymond Aron (1905–83) stands out here— one of the few non-American sociologists who enjoyed great *international* prestige in the 1950s and 1960s (see Hall 1981, 157–96).

Aron, the leading French sociologist of the early postwar period and the key "bourgeois" rival of the left-wing intellectuals around Jean Paul Sartre, was influenced more by German than French intellectual traditions. In any case, he was not rooted in the Durkheimian tradition. He had lived and worked in Germany from 1930 to 1933 and took his lead from Max Weber's conceptualization of the state, with a particular interest in conflicts and international disputes. After France's occupation by German troops, Aron went to Great Britain, where he published articles in support of de Gaulle's struggle against Germany. After liberation in 1944, he immediately returned to France, where again he initially worked mainly as a journalist, before being appointed chair in sociology at the Sorbonne in 1955 (see Aron 1990).

Aron's wide interests ranged from the history of sociology to empirical analyses of industrial society (see also Aron 1958); a few years earlier, in 1951, he had produced one of the first major analyses of the Cold War, combining both political science and sociology, in the shape of *The Century of Total War* (Les Guerres en chaîne). This topic was to preoccupy him over the next few decades. Aron takes a clear political stand here, calling for Europe to arm itself in order to ward off the (military) threat emanating from the Soviet Union. This first required good relations between France and Germany (Aron 1954 [1951], 314). Aron shows himself to be a "power-political realist" in this study. He acknowledges that the world political situation with regard to nuclear weapons has rung in

a new age of international relations, referring to "the recession of national states, the rise of the continent-states" (165). But, he believes, this
changes nothing about the fact that conflicts determine world politics,
and these must be subjected to rational reflection, particularly with respect to the USSR's desire for power and expansion. Idealistic notions of
politics are of no use in the present situation; and, of course, they also
came to grief in the 1930s when confronted with Hitler's Germany. The
mistakes made then must not be repeated, which is why Aron turns to the
topic of Europe's warring past again and again.

In this connection, Aron makes it clear that the imperialism of the
nineteenth and early twentieth century was by no means economically
determined, that in fact the key factor was the pursuit of power. Political
will was the real driving force behind imperialism: "It will not be denied
that capitalism tends to incorporate underdeveloped territories into its
system. Nor is it to be denied that colonial conquest may be regarded as
a function of economic expansion. But whatever the plausibility of such
a view, two questions remain to be answered: Were the African colonial
empires founded in accordance with this pattern? Were the European
wars a consequence of these quarrels for the division of the planet? The
facts, if invoked without bias, answer these two questions negatively"
(58/59). What applied then with respect to power politics, Aron believes,
still applies now, especially against the background of the Soviet desire
for expansion: Western European politics must take this into account and
must not cherish false hopes. The state of nature described by Hobbes,
Aron suggests, may no longer pertain between states, but it still exists
between the blocs that have now been established. The old rules of power
politics continue to apply in the Cold War (169ff.).

In 1962 Aron turned out a monumental work running to many hun-
dreds of pages. The title itself reveals the author's tremendous ambitions:
Peace and War: A Theory of International Relations (1962; Paix et guerre
entre les nations). Here, Aron aspired to provide nothing less than a general analysis of international power relations and lay the foundations for
a sociology of the nuclear age. But with his unique conceptual apparatus,
he not only examined—as the secondary title might imply—those aspects
of relations between states of relevance to foreign policy; in fact, he aimed
to formulate a *general theory of power* by systematically examining the
interconnection between domestic and international conditions as well.
As Aron declares in this book, once again in Hobbesian fashion, any
theory of international relations must assume the risk of wars, which
then requires us to take account of the means to be deployed in them.[10]

This also applies to international relations in the nuclear age. Aron does all he can to enter into the world of ideas characteristic of military strategists in the age of nuclear war, the theory of deterrence and mutually assured nuclear destruction, which he discusses almost in the manner of game theory, in a matter-of-fact and unemotional style, asking what "chance" there still is of a nuclear war despite the seemingly unsurpassable irrationality of such an event. He sees the waging of nuclear war as implausible but not inconceivable. So even in the age of nuclear weapons war is a tool of politics, at least as a threat.

In 1976, Aron produced another big book on war or on a theorist of war, *Clausewitz: Philosopher of War* (1983; Penser la guerre, Clausewitz), which once again clearly expresses Aron's understanding of politics, state, and war. Aron claims here that his power-political realism is entirely compatible with Clausewitzian principles: even in the age of nuclear arms, strategy remains within the Clausewitzian framework (Aron 1983, 309). Borrowing from Clausewitz, Aron describes politics as the "intelligence of the personified state" (399) and accepts with some qualifications Anatol Rapoport's description of him as a "neo-Clausewitzian" (315). Aron is well aware that the nature of statehood has changed since the time of Hobbes and Clausewitz, that transnational processes are now occurring on a far greater scale. Yet he still maintains the notion of the state's unity (398). The nation-state has by no means become obsolete, despite the existence of supranational military blocs. In this sense, Aron believes, the instrumental rationality associated with the state, raison d'état, continues to be the guiding principle of international relations. The world's political leaders should take account of this. Aron believes that there are good prospects of such rational action on the part of the world's rulers. The very existence of nuclear weapons will make crusades for peace (or democracy) impossible, likely marking the beginning of the end for the Wilsonian illusion of pacification and democratization, which Aron believes to have been of no benefit (412f.). For Aron, abandoning the illusion of a world without weapons seems a prerequisite for any halfway effective curtailment of war, a form of violence that—he leaves us in no doubt—will continue to exist in future.

▪ ▪ ▪

We want to briefly mention another important non-American sociologist who produced writings of great importance to the analysis of war in the 1950s. Polish-British Weberian and conflict theorist Stanislav Andreski (1919–2007) did more to study historical changes in the form taken by war than Aron, and particularly shed light on the shift in the population's involvement in armed conflicts. As a Polish officer in the Second World War he himself had been taken prisoner by the Soviets, fled to Great Britain, and then fought the Germans on the British side. From a comparative historical perspective, his book *Military Organization and Society* from 1954 examines the question of the link between war and warfare on the one hand and social inequality on the other. It is clear to Andreski that war is a significant factor in the stratification of societies. But wars by no means produce uniform effects on inequality; the different forms of warfare make sure of that: "[T]he intensification of warfare may make it necessary to enlist the support of the masses by granting them various privileges, in which case a substantial leveling may take place. The necessity of such a course will depend mainly on whether mass armies are, in view of the state of tactics and armament, more or less efficient than professional armies" (Andreski 1968 [1954], 29). So wars have both reduced and increased social inequality, and no clear-cut relationships emerge here. But Andreski does not stop at this preliminary finding, instead going on to examine which kinds of warfare lead to which specific outcomes in which societies. Here he discovers the importance of what he calls the "Military Participation Ratio," which is dependent on the "proportion of militarily utilized individuals in the total population" (33). For Andreski, mass wars have a different stratifying effect from the cabinet wars in the age of European absolutism, while total wars of the kind that became typical of the twentieth century in Europe have different effects from limited or small-scale armed conflicts. And this, Andreski believes, must be subjected to systematic study if we want to investigate the nature and transformation of social inequality, an issue of such importance to sociology, while also remembering that war is a far from rare occurrence in world history. Even today, Andreski's empirically sensitive studies could be of great importance to the study of processes of stratification, democratization, and centralization in regions of endemic armed conflicts. But this potential has so far gone untapped.

■ ■ ■

As the nuclear age dawned, American sociology produced Aron's key antagonist within the sociology of war in the shape of C. Wright Mills (1916–62). Whereas Aron entered into the conceptual world of the armed forces, C. Wright Mills pointedly did not, and for programmatic reasons. He was unable to believe that the means of mass destruction were politically controllable. Mills had risen to prominence within American sociol-

188 ■ Chapter 5

ogy through his translations of Max Weber's work and above all through important studies on the analysis of social structure (*White Collar*, 1951). But he also played a major role in the broader public sphere as a staunchly left-wing intellectual and was to become one of the heroes of the so-called "New Left" after his early death. Mills consciously refused to adopt the perspective of the military strategists, a refusal based mainly on his view of the power structures of American society. His work was informed by an analysis of his age in which the nation-state's institutions of violence played a central role. In most other writings in this genre, in contrast, the armed forces played (and play) no role. It was just this suppression of the existence of the state's institutions of violence in which Mills was unwilling to partake, which is why his book *The Power Elite* (1956),[11] which caused a major stir, took a particularly close look at the armed forces.

Mills's innovative thesis, which was anything but self-evident within sociology at the time, is that elites in contemporary American society are undergoing a fundamental shift, one that is not only changing the position of the armed forces within this society but has turned the basically antimilitaristic culture of the United States on its head. Mills shows that the United States was originally founded as a nonmilitary, if not antimilitary polity; the state, after all, emerged from a revolution against the British and their mercenaries (Mills 1956, 175). Though the first presidents of the United States of America were often generals, the U.S. Constitution expresses distrust of the armed forces (176). What is more, in the entire nineteenth century the military elites (not least because of the stationing of the armed forces on the Western frontier) never really succeeded in linking up with the other social and political elites (ibid.).[12] During this period the armed forces thus had to forgo political power almost entirely. The civilians retained control, and this was possible because in a United States that faced few external threats, the armed forces had never managed to truly convince society of its importance. And in connection with this, it was all the easier for a military code of honor to be formulated and accepted that enshrined the renunciation of politics: "This renunciation has gone quite far: it has been incorporated in the military code of honor. Inside their often trim bureaucracy, where everything seems under neat control, army officers have felt that 'politics' is a dirty, uncertain, and ungentlemanly kind of game" (174).

But according to Mills it is precisely this that has changed dramatically in the twentieth century, because of a number of crucial factors. First, Mills points to the failure of civilian politicians; increasingly, they have turned to the armed forces in search of expertise to advance their global political ambitions, allowing these armed forces to get their foot in the door of power for the first time. This military knowledge is also increasingly in demand as a result of the development of military technology, scarcely comprehensible by laypeople, and this has resulted in the politicization of the armed forces (199/200), which have now defined quite specific political tasks for themselves. Even worse, a worldview has begun to take hold within American politics in which military criteria are increasingly decisive. This has happened in part because America's massive military build-up in the Second World War led to the merging of economic monopoly and military bureaucracy, making it all the easier to bring the military view of the world into politics—with incalculable consequences, according to Mills. A military-industrial complex and a "military definition of reality" predominate so utterly within contemporary American society (185) that much of the American elite can now see domestic politics only from a foreign policy perspective, viewing the former as "ways of retaining power at home in order to exert abroad the power of the national establishment" (186); war or military options now seem the only remaining means of achieving their aims. All in all, this means that American capitalism has developed into a "permanent war economy" because of this shift in the character of the elite (215), which shows the liberal idea of a Herbert Spencer to be quite untrue: "[T]he classic liberal expectation of men like Herbert Spencer has proved quite mistaken. What the main drift of the twentieth century has revealed is that as the economy has become concentrated and incorporated into great hierarchies, the military has become enlarged and decisive to the shape of the entire economic structure" (215).

Mills explored this "military definition of reality" in another book that was at least as much political pamphlet as scholarly study (Hess 1995, 151) and that bore the sensational and apocalyptic title *The Causes of World War Three* (1958). Mills deals mainly with the politics of deterrence here, which had also been Aron's key concern. But his objective is quite different. For him, in the age of the nuclear deterrent, the insanity of the military mindset, one that is no longer influenced or curbed by any civilian or political considerations, is quite plain. In the United States (Mills's primary point of reference, though he has no wish to play down or justify the totalitarian regime of the USSR), a largely depoliticized public has lost all control over events; according to him, as the USSR and United States compete in an insane arms race, the power over life and death is in the hands of a bureaucratic power apparatus consisting of military chiefs and a small number of politicians. What this small, powerful grouping views as the rational balancing out of potential threats, Mills sees as nothing more than a "military metaphysics" that is entirely divorced from reality. This grouping is incapable of thinking in anything other than military terms, with consequences that are far from rational and therefore risk triggering a new world war, which would be the final such war: "Just now, the chance of a deliberately planned war is perhaps not as great as is the 'accidental' precipitation of war. But the prime conditions of the 'accident' are not themselves accidental; they are planned and deliberate. The war mechanism of U.S. men and machines is all set up and triggered to go. It stands opposite a similar mechanism of Soviet design and maintenance. The first cause of World War Three is, obviously, the existence of these bureaucratic and lethal machineries. Without them there could be no war" (Mills 1959 [1958]), 52).

Mills's text on the "causes of the Third World War," which again sold very well, was in significant part a moral or ethical manifesto. Against a foreign policy that was accepted without question and, in an age of nuclear weapons, was in fact often guided by game theory, he wished to put forward a different model of politics, and especially to reinject morality into (international) politics (Hess 1995, 150). Inevitably, this sometimes led him to take his polemics too far, overstating, for example, the autonomy of military institutions and their influence (Domhoff 2006, 548; Wolfe 1999, 93ff.). Nonetheless, with plenty of help from Weberian categories, Mills managed to break through the "orthodox consensus" (Atkinson 1971) at a fairly early stage in the history of American sociology, a consensus that painted an overly harmonious picture of American society, while forgetting not only the nuclear threat but also, often, the violent conflicts of the time. Despite all the overstatements, his focus on how changes in elite structures in the United States had led to the rise of the armed forces remains one of the few approaches within the field of social theory to take (potential) war seriously.

▪ ▪ ▪

With his political sociology in the tradition of Speier or Lasswell, Mills was a lonely figure in the 1950s. But a new interest in military matters was fueled by another source. We are referring to the problematic processes of development in the Third World, which had failed to comply with theoretical models. Development policies guided by modernization theory were initially formulated on the assumption that military institutions would play no significant role in developmental processes. But this proved a fatal mistake: in most regions of what was later called the Third World, hopes of rapid democratization went unfulfilled and even the "civilizing" of politics failed to occur. Instead it was the armed forces that often took center stage as they increasingly shaped the destinies of the underdeveloped countries. This forced revisions of modernization theory and threw up new questions.

British political scientist Samuel E. Finer (1915–93) was the key figure to explore issues of military rule in the Third World. In the early 1960s—within a modernization theory framework—he examined at least aspects of this topic in depth. His study *The Man on Horseback* (1962) was prompted by the observation that in the "new" states and nations that emerged after 1945 the armed forces often levered out the civilian governments and took power themselves through coups. Finer concluded that we must treat military coups as the rule rather than the exception. But this requires us to analyze which (infrequently occurring) conditions facilitate or have facilitated the civilian (rather than military) control and leadership of the national polity so typical in the history of Western countries. Ultimately, as a hierarchically organized, cohesive organization often endowed with great prestige and the capacity to use force, at first sight the armed forces seem always and everywhere predestined to take over the political leadership roles in a society as well. So why have military governments appeared far less often in the West than in the so-called "new" states and nations?

Finer's explanation for the regionally variable frequency of military interventions in civil affairs was based essentially on the rather nebulous modernization theory concept of "political culture." He claimed that the political cultures of Great Britain and the United States, which are most developed from a comparative international perspective, made and still make a military putsch least likely to occur, whereas the generally undemocratic political cultures of the Third World countries have failed (and will continue to fail) to prevent intervention by the armed forces. Although this explanation seems rather unconvincing and even slightly tautological, Finer at least managed to provide a historical overview that reveals the factors and conditions that made the military putsch—an extremely unusual and almost unthinkable occurrence within the European state system before 1789—possible in the first place. "Contemporary military intervention is the fruit of the five factors which emerged from the paroxysm of the French revolution, between 1789 and 1810: the doctrine of nationality, the doctrine of popular sovereignty, the insurgence of popular armies, the professionalization of the armed forces, and, finally, the emancipation of imperial dependencies" (Finer 1962, 219/20). Only the idea of nationality and popular sovereignty, Finer tells us, made it possible for military leaders, in the name of the people, to replace the civilian authorities in order to save the nation. Because of its stable democratic political culture, however, this has rarely been the case in the West, in contrast to the developing countries, where military leaders' desire for power, supported by an emotionally charged nationalism, has gone unchecked by civilian norms.

As important as Finer's arguments were, it is telling that they did not inspire further reflections, precisely because of their modernization theory premises. Neither Finer nor other authors close to modernization theory investigated the "normal" activity of the armed forces or of military leaders, namely waging war. This is particularly striking given that a comparative study of warfare in the Third World and, for example, Europe could have shed light on specific developments in different regions. But no such studies appeared: war and macrosocial violence were anything but a major topic of social scientific analysis in the 1950s and 1960s (on the highly specialized debate on civilian-military relations in the Third World, see Berghahn 1981, 67–84).

It is fair to say that modernization theory was particularly neglectful of the topic of violence. Like perhaps no other theoretical school of sociology, other than its great rival of Marxism, it clung to the Enlightenment faith in progress; within this framework, it assumed the meaningfulness and continuity of the historical process. For this reason alone it was scarcely capable of appreciating the historical and sociological significance of war and violence. But it would be unfair to limit such criticisms to modernization theory. It had no monopoly on progressive optimism (see Tiryakian 1999, 474ff.), as apparent in the fact that analyses of the armed forces that were highly critical of modernization theory were also unwilling to draw the requisite theoretical conclusions. The liberal legacy of sociology, whose roots lay in the eighteenth and nineteenth centuries, made its presence felt beyond modernization theory.

In his landmark book *The Military in the Political Development of New Nations* from 1964 (which in a sense provided an alternative to Finer's study), sociologist Morris Janowitz, who was theoretically indebted to the Chicago school and did much to develop its legacy (see chapter 5), also did without the modernization theory concept of "political culture." He explained the significantly greater frequency of intervention by non-Western armies in civilian affairs with reference to quite different factors—namely, the very different class structures in Europe and the "Third World," historically determined differences in the social position of the armed forces, and completely different methods of military recruitment. At least in this study, however, he too thought it unnecessary to make a detailed analysis of the armed forces' characteristic activities, the use of force or waging of wars. Sociology as a whole, with few exceptions, had adopted a linear understanding of history that smoothed out ruptures and caesuras and maintained a firm faith in progress, so that wars and violence seemed no more than disturbances; as such, there was clearly no need to grant them analytical priority (see Joas 2003). Janowitz, however, with a background in military sociology but never narrowly limited to it,[13] did tackle the question of war and its consequences more directly. He was especially concerned with the link between war and democracy, which had also been a key concern for Andreski. To what extent, he asked, have military conflicts and institutions opened up opportunities for political participation and helped extend civil rights? And what are the preconditions that ensured that in some countries the armed forces were democratically embedded and thus "tamed" but not in others? His essay "Military Institutions and Citizenship in Western Societies" (1976) provided an answer to this question and made it clear just how much we must view civil rights and their development in the age of nation-states against the background of military institutions. Janowitz's ideas did not go uncontested (see Berg 2000; Berg 1994 is the partially overlapping English version), but, in much the same way as Andreski's arguments, they continue to be the starting point for any theoretically substantial discussion of democratization.

The period following the Second World War has left modern-day sociology a quite meager intellectual legacy in terms of the politics of peace and understanding of war. Until the 1970s, far too few sociologists and social scientists seriously attempted to get to grips with the topic of "war," a topic of such universal importance. The question for us now is whether, and if so how, this has changed in recent times.

After Modernization Theory

HISTORICAL SOCIOLOGY AND THE BELLICOSE
CONSTITUTION OF WESTERN MODERNITY

IT IS FAIRLY EASY to unearth analyses of armed violence of relevance to
social theory produced between the 1970s and today—easier, at least,
than for the period between 1945 and 1970. And a new theoretical movement was in fact beginning to make its presence felt, particularly within
sections of American and British sociology, its leading exponents no longer prepared to accept the prevailing neglect of war. This newfound interest in "war" grew out of a complex theoretical mix. Though political elements and current affairs no doubt played a role here, in the main this
interest was clearly due to internal theoretical developments.

Within American sociology, the turn to "war" was directly connected
with the debate on modernization theory. This paradigm, which dominated the social sciences in the 1950s and 1960s, had not only forecast
simplistically that the "underdeveloped countries" would come to resemble the United States and Western Europe both structurally and culturally: that they would become Westernized. What is more, modernization
theorists' historical picture of their *own* (Western) societies was also
rather simple. Concepts such as industrialization, nation building, and
democratization, conceived as subprocesses of modernization, provided
an interpretive foil against which the history of the United States or Western Europe could be concisely sketched out; this generally resulted in a
highly linear schema of development devoid of major ruptures or contingencies (Knöbl 2001, 155–218). The linearity of this schema was due in
significant part to the functionalist assumption that social subsystems are
closely and irrevocably interdependent. According to this assumption,
once such things as economic modernization (industrialization) had
begun, it was only a matter of time before other societal spheres would
take on compatible (modern) forms, such as democratic political structures. According to this interpretation, the history of Western societies

since the late eighteenth and early nineteenth centuries was already mapped out at quite an early stage, just as now—in the 1950s and 1960s—the history of the (still) underdeveloped countries was viewed as predetermined: as soon as they had "taken off" economically, they would necessarily develop into modern and democratic nation-states. In light of the premise of closely enmeshed subsystems, deviations from the linear model of development could only ever be viewed as temporary—and ultimately insignificant.

As we have emphasized, this evolutionist picture of history, on which (functionalist) modernization theory was usually based, was broadly accepted in the 1950s and 1960s. But there was no lack of critics. One important strand of this critique that helped ensure that war, so disruptive to the notion of historical linearity, eventually gained in importance for social theory, was associated with the name of Max Weber. In the main, it was American authors inspired by Weber who opposed the simplistic historical constructions of modernization theory. They understood that social processes are generally conflictual in nature, that we can by no means always assume that the relations between social subsystems and processes will be harmonious, and that the concepts of power and coercion are crucial to any sociologist wishing to explain unexpected twists and turns in the historical process. Thus, conflict theory was born (see Joas/Knöbl 2009, 174ff.), a school of thought that borrowed from Georg Simmel, but whose most influential strand was Weberian in orientation, with Reinhard Bendix and his students being the key figures here. Bendix (1916–91), who was educated at the University of Chicago but then taught at Berkeley for many decades, certainly drew on modernization theory in his historical-sociological analyses. Right from the start, however, he strove to counter the assumptions of linearity and interdependence or equilibrium so typical of modernization theory. He did so partly because of his great skepticism about the structural-functionalism underpinning this theory. In line with this, he countered functionalism with an alternative theoretical apparatus, which was to lead to quite different conclusions. This was particularly apparent with respect to the core concepts of political sociology. While functionalists and "orthodox" modernization theorists used the term "political system" as a matter of course and thus implied the existence of—somehow smoothly unfolding—political processes and appropriate states of equilibrium between the political system and its neighboring systems, Bendix insisted from the outset that politics is more than just a process of fine-tuning. According to him, power and domination and thus the use or at least threat of violence have always played a central role in politics. As Bendix made unmistakably clear in one of his early studies (*Work and Authority in Industry*, 1956), the logic of bureaucracy and domination in particular cannot simply be subordinated to or derived from socioeconomic logic, so we must accept that the political sphere obeys its own laws. Bendix concluded that because of the tensions between social subsystems and particularly the creative and destructive potential of power, an overly linear view of history will always lead us astray. This then led him to suspect what he later strove to demonstrate so impressively (e.g., in *Kings or People*, 1978), namely that within the process of modernization, states or societies by no means all take the same path; instead, traditions—particularly traditions of domination—induce quite different developments.

Bendix's students built on this and—like Randall Collins (1986), who developed his own theory of conflict—advanced or radicalized Bendix's ideas on historical macrosociology. In the late 1960s and early 1970s, developing Bendix's ideas seemed like a valuable endeavor for political reasons as well. For members of the so-called New Left, it was increasingly clear that it was near-impossible to get to grips with hierarchical relations and violence through the key structural-functionalist concept of the "political system." It was difficult to capture the civil rights, students', women's, and anti–Vietnam War movements with the functionalist notion of system, let alone the war that was raging in Southeast Asia. There was a need to find different concepts better suited to analyzing the conflictual aspects of American society and world politics—and the concept of the state, with its European and particularly German overtones, now began to play a greater role in the United States. War thus became a key focus of analysis as well, though initially from a historical perspective for the most part. Norbert Elias's *The Civilizing Process* (1978 [1939]), which was written in the interwar period but received only much later owing to the prevailing circumstances, also exercised a covert effect in this context. On a broad historical foundation, Elias argued that a monopoly on violence increasingly develops within states, and he linked this suggestively with the increasing affective control on the part of individuals to which this allegedly gives rise. If we read these ideas as asserting a linear decrease in manifest violence, Elias too appears to be a modernization theorist. If, on the other hand, we read them as a theory of how the conditions pertaining within and between states impact on mentalities, then Elias's work—especially his later output—is an important source of inspiration for a historical and comparative sociology.

Within American sociology in the 1970s, the theoretical reorientation toward history, state, and war is particularly apparent in the writings of two authors whose work continues to occupy a preeminent position in the field of historical sociology—Charles Tilly and Theda Skocpol. At an early point in his oeuvre Tilly (1929–2008) examined social movements in Britain and France, particularly in the eighteenth and nineteenth centuries, and in the 1960s and 1970s he became one of the leading scholars of protest. His studies had made him aware that it is quite often the state or state building processes that sparked off social protests in the first place. It was taxes to finance wars, food crises caused by wars, and the like that inspired protest. So "riots," the formation of protest movements, and—in however rudimentary a fashion—the formation of classes were not simply "intrasocietal" phenomena and processes but often the contingent outcome of international embroilments, not least wars. Tilly became increasingly interested in the—evidently so momentous—violent pursuit of international power politics. This was apparent, at the very latest, when he joined a comparative historical research project, actually inspired by modernization theory, and published the volume *The Formation of National States in Western Europe* in 1975. This book, enduringly colored by Tilly's opening and concluding chapters ("Reflections on the History of European State-Making" and "Western State-Making and Theories of Political Transformation"), painted a picture of the historical process in Europe since the seventeenth century quite different from that generally emerging from studies rooted in modernization theory.

Tilly did not refer to a coherent developmental process leading, as it were, to *a specific* goal. Instead, he emphasized the comparatively wide range of different routes to European modernity. According to Tilly, these routes were determined in significant part by the geopolitical position of the various states and the differing armed embroilments associated with this. The process of state building in Europe depicted in this book by no means follows a logic that might be conveyed by the functionalist term "political development," which both plays down historical reality and implies linearity (Tilly 1975b, 21). State building in Europe involved a great deal of violence as military rivalry gave rise to a peculiar, intensifying economic-military dynamic: "After all, taxation was the chief means by which the builders of states in the sixteenth century and later supported their expanding armies, which were in turn their principal instrument in establishing control of their frontiers, pushing them out, defending them against external incursions, and assuring their own priority in the use of force within those frontiers. . . . So turned the tight circle connecting state-making, military institutions and the extraction of scarce resources from a reluctant population" (23/24). Neither can there be any question of describing the process of state formation primarily in terms of the extension of rights. This too is a teleological supposition, which seems plausible only if we arbitrarily fix the late eighteenth century as the starting point and the second half of the twentieth century as the final destination of political development. If, however, we abandon such questionable temporal assumptions, it becomes clear that in many ways state building in earlier phases of history was a brutal process that stripped various sections of the population of their rights, and that even the nineteenth and twentieth centuries by no means saw the *continuous* extension of political and social rights: "The European national revolution of the last few centuries did not so much expand political rights as concentrate them in the state and reduce their investment in other sorts of government" (37). So according to Tilly we should not forget the (bloody) costs of the centralization of power in the context of nation-state formation when analyzing the genesis of European modernity. The notion of the breakthrough and expansion of democracy, frequently inspired by modernization theory, is far too one-dimensional to even begin to convey the historical reality of state formation in Europe. According to Tilly, what we must do is analyze armed conflicts *between* states in Europe if we wish to understand the dynamics *within* specific societies. A circumscribed perspective focused on the individual society is of no use here, which is why Tilly recommends German historian Otto Hintze as one of the few authors whose work might help us understand the link between the violent international dimension of state formation in Europe on the one hand and internal constitutional developments on the other (Tilly 1975c, 626).

This volume, edited by Tilly, opened up a new field of research. For some historically minded sociologists, the concept of the state, and with it armed violence and its consequences, now took center stage; this was due in large part to the almost simultaneous appearance of a sensational dissertation by a young sociologist from Harvard, a text that backed up and extended Tilly's arguments. We are referring to Theda Skocpol (b. 1946) and her first book, published in 1979, *States and Social Revolutions: A Comparative Analysis of France, Russia, and China*, undoubtedly one of the most influential sociological texts of the second half of the twentieth century. Even more than in the case of Tilly, it is quite apparent from reading Skocpol that the ambitious project of placing state and war at the center of social theory has a whole slew of impediments to overcome. This project, after all, faced criticisms not only from modernization theorists but also from Marxist authors, who still very much set the tone of theoretical debates in the 1970s and 1980s.

The crucial fact here is that Skocpol was a student of Barrington Moore, who had produced a brilliant early alternative to modernization theory with his famous book *Social Origins of Dictatorship and Democracy*, published in 1966. Moore, the committed left-winger, who utilized a Marxian analytical toolkit but drew also on Max Weber, spurned the modernization theorists' thesis of unilinearity and referred instead to differing paths to modernity that reflected differing solutions to the class issue, particularly in rural areas. This is already apparent in the book's subtitle: *Lord and Peasant in the Making of the Modern World*. His critical student felt that Moore had still not gone far enough in moving away from modernization theory, that he remained overly attached to the "society-centered" perspective that dominated both sociology and Marxism. As a result, according to Skocpol, in much the same way as the Marxists and modernization theorists whom he assailed, Moore failed to bring out the autonomous role of the state and violent *inter*national conflicts and their genuinely society-changing consequences (a point already explored in Skocpol 1973). We must at the very least supplement Moore's class-based perspective, Skocpol states, by paying greater theoretical attention to the state and the violence it produces, through an approach that eschews Marxian traditions of thought. Though Marxians too had fiercely debated the state since the late 1960s and 1970s, they always interpreted it essentially as an instrument of the ruling classes for maintaining the status quo. As a result, they failed to take the state seriously enough, believing they had already "seen through" its functionality with respect to class structures. The state was always a mere epiphenomenon resting on class structures. As a result, entire libraries of Marxian literature on the state arose, but always on the premise that its structures and actions can ultimately be deduced from class relations.

It was with this kind of perspective that Skocpol now wished to break, and her stance toward both modernization theory and Marxism was explicitly informed by the work of Otto Hintze (see p. 129ff.). There is a certain irony in a staunchly left-wing author borrowing theoretically from Hintze, the official Hohenzollern historiographer; but there were solid reasons for this, in that Skocpol was able to use Hintze to achieve her goal of shedding light on the *inter*national dimension of social change. It would certainly have been possible to exploit Max Weber's work as well in order to capture this dimension. But this was a far from obvious move, given the state of the debate at the time: in the United States in particular, an interpretation of Weber championed by Talcott Parsons continued to make itself felt, and in this context (due to whatever misunderstandings) Weber was viewed as a key source for modernization theory. Hintze's work made it possible to take a clear stand against both Marxism and modernization theory. As Skocpol made clear in the theoretical chapters of her study, Hintze's texts are so helpful partly because they enable us to understand the autonomy of the state. As Skocpol, following Hintze, argues, precisely because of its embeddedness within an international state system, the state can develop its own logic of action, a logic that gives it potential autonomy and freedom vis-à-vis social classes. And this is also why the state may be viewed as a relatively homogeneous organization capable of taking action, as a quasi actor: "The state properly conceived . . . is a set of administrative, policing, and military organizations headed, and more or less well coordinated by, an executive authority. Any state first and fundamentally extracts resources from society and deploys these to create and support coercive and administrative organizations. . . . [These] administrative and coercive organizations are the basis of state power" (Skocpol 1979, 29). This theoretical conception of the state and its autonomous actions was so important to Skocpol because it was the only means of solving a key explanatory problem in her study *States and Social Revolutions*, namely the surprising outbreak of revolutions in agrarian-based bureaucratic empires that appeared quite stable at first sight. Skocpol's key thesis was that the social revolutions so important to the history of the modern world, the French Revolution of 1789, the Russian revolutions of 1905 and 1917, and the "long" Chinese Revolution from 1911 until Mao Zedong's assumption of power succeeded only because dynamics internal *and* external to these societies came together in a particular way.

It was defeat in war and foreign policy "disasters," Skocpol argued, that caused these empires to collapse. As they strove to modernize, the prerevolutionary regimes ultimately became incapable of taking effective action to compensate for military defeats or back up their claimed international standing, which is what sparked off these crises or revolutions. So it was wars and international embroilments that made it possible for the relevant classes to successfully mobilize the masses and finally seize power.

Prerevolutionary France, Russia, and China all had well-established imperial states with proven capacities to protect their own hegemony and that of the dominant classes against revolts from below. Before social revolutions could occur, the administrative and military power of these states had to break down. When this happened in France 1789, Russia 1917, and China 1911, it was not because of deliberate activities to that end, either on the part of avowed revolutionaries or on the part of politically powerful groups within the Old Regimes. Rather revolutionary political crises, culminating in administrative and military breakdowns, emerged because the imperial state became caught in cross-pressures between intensified military competition or intrusions from abroad and constraints imposed on monarchical responses by the existing agrarian class structures and political institutions. The old-regime states were prone to such revolutionary crises because their existing structures made it impossible for them to meet the particular international military exigencies that each had to face in the modern era. (285)

Here (and this is where she marks herself off from traditional Marxian approaches), Skocpol was careful to emphasize that prerevolutionary armed conflicts themselves were *not* due directly to economic interests: "The international states system as a transnational structure of military competition was not originally created by capitalism. Throughout modern world history, it represents an analytically autonomous level of transnational reality—interdependent in its structure and dynamics with world capitalism, but not reducible to it" (22).

Skocpol's arguments caused a stir for a number of reasons. Her attempt to construct an emphatically antivoluntarist theory of revolution was subject to both enthusiastic praise and severe criticism, as was her concept of the autonomy of the state (borrowed from Otto Hintze). Even more crucially, Skocpol painted a picture of modernity quite unfamiliar to sociologists. Regardless of the fact that her study made no claims to universal validity (as she herself underlined, her conclusions on the causes of revolutions applied only to agrarian-bureaucratic empires lying far in the past), the new interpretive framework that she was pointing toward was bound to be of immediate interest to anyone concerned with processes of macrosocial change. Because if Skocpol was right that these three great social revolutions were dependent on the occurrence of armed conflicts, then the standard narratives of the inevitable victory of modern structures lost much of their plausibility (in the case of France, the narrative of the inexorable breakthrough of a democracy-bringing bourgeoisie, a narrative deployed by both modernization theorists and Marxists; in the case of Russia and China, the Marxist notion of the inevitable victory of a revolutionary urban or rural proletariat). If these revolutions, which did so much to shape modernity, were in fact caused to a significant extent by largely unpredictable political decisions to wage war, in any case by decisions that cannot be traced back to economic processes, then the history of modernity must also be narrated in a quite new way. In this case, many bourgeois-democratic or socialist "achievements" may not be the inevitable outcome of an essentially linear historical process but the result of contingent circumstances. This suddenly puts a different shine on European modernity, as Europe's extremely bloody history must now be seen in connection with its celebrated democratic advances. On this view, democracy is not an inevitable evolutionary breakthrough, but rather an institutional "coincidence" that we must trace back to extremely violent circumstances, and we should probably be far more cautious about assuming its continued existence in future than many authors have tended to be.

Tilly and Skocpol kicked off the debate on state and war within American historical sociology with empirical studies. The arguments put forward here may have been plausible, but it was clear that they would prevail against modernization theory and Marxism only if they led to a convincing research program. Such a program was in fact developed quite rapidly, and it had four key characteristics: (1) the state was understood through the prism of organizational sociology as a coherent quasi actor; (2) state actors (whether princes, heads of state, chancellors, etc.) were conceptualized as individuals acting in instrumentally rational ways, which often went hand in hand with a perspective similar to the theory of rational action, though the scholars involved did not always concede or even realize this; (3) the relationship between "state constitution and military constitution" brought into play by Hintze was discussed; and, in connection with this, (4) as emphasis was placed on the autonomy of the state, war was made *the* key object of research. This opened up a complex of themes that had played no major role since the time of Max Weber, Werner Sombart, and Otto Hintze. Within this framework scholars could tackle afresh issues in the sociology of taxation regarding the financing of wars, the formation of social classes as conditioned by wars, and the emergence of different types of political regime (see Knöbl 2008, 49ff.).

A research program on this theoretical foundation (the label "state-centered approach" was to take hold to describe it) was then propagated in a self-confident and proactive way within the fields of macrosociology and historical sociology in the mid-1980s, as exemplified by the multiauthored *Bringing the State Back In*, coedited and with an introduction by Skocpol. Charles Tilly's chapter carries the provocative title "War Making and State Making as Organized Crime." Here Tilly spelled out with much radicalism—far more than any of the other contributors to this 1985 publication—the connection between political modernity and war, as logically derived from the assumption of instrumentally rational state actors within a violence-ridden milieu. Because it is particularly easy to legitimize the raising of taxes to ensure that a country can cope with crises and bring wars to a victorious conclusion, Tilly assumed that rulers are keen on such wars and crises and thus behave no differently from criminal gangs of extortionists: "Since governments themselves commonly simulate, stimulate, or even fabricate threats of external war and since the repressive and extractive activities of governments often constitute the largest current threats to the livelihoods of their own citizens, many governments operate in essentially the same way as racketeers" (Tilly 1985, 171). Of course, as Tilly himself was aware, this was overstating things. But his aim was to make it clear that war inevitably involves a direct connection with capital accumulation and resource extraction through taxes, in other words that central intrasocietal processes of change were directly connected with the military activities of the state: the belligerent rulers needed access to credit-providing capitalists and/or taxable subjects, which in turn fostered their interest in a flourishing economy. According to Tilly, state formation in Europe occurred in such disparate ways not because the princes and rulers had different intentions and projects, but because the business of war was more difficult to run in some regions of Europe than others. State formation was dependent on the capital accumulation needed to wage war. In areas in which taxes could be siphoned off without much difficulty, for example, because easily taxable trade was booming, it was possible to construct a state apparatus far less centralized and repressive than in regions with a generally self-sufficient population. This process resulted in the establishment of the European system of nation-states, which no one had intended to create, but whose structure, with all its centralized and less centralized states, was crucially influenced by this interplay of "war making, extraction, and capital accumulation" (172).

Tilly went on to examine the issues touched on here in greater depth, and in his ambitious book *Coercion, Capital, and European States, AD 990–1990* (1990) he asserted the existence of three trajectories of state formation in Europe. These were determined by the various ways in which governments could levy taxes in different regions. Into the nineteenth century, trajectories of state formation described as "coercion-intensive" (Prussia and Russia), "capital-intensive" (early modern city-states) and "capitalized-coercion" (France and Britain) brought in their wake very different forms of state development and, in connection with this, quite different prospects of democratization (Tilly 1990, 30). So as Tilly brings out once again, the emergence or breakthrough of parliamentary regimes depended not so much on any kind of cultural preconditions but rather—far more concretely—on trajectories of resource extraction and thus state construction that were feasible or infeasible in the past.

All of this underwent further development within American historical sociology. Others did not always go as far as Tilly in assuming actors' instrumental rationality. But Tilly's and Skocpol's exemplary analyses brought in their wake a number of comparative studies, mostly focused on Europe, which underlined the link between the levying of taxes and war on the one hand and political stability or the development of differing forms of regime on the other. In this context, it was the "military revolution" that became the key focus of interest, a term that had been coined within British historiography in the 1950s and had been subject to intense debate since the 1970s (for an overview, see Parker 1988 and Rogers 1995). This refers to an advance in military technology in Europe between 1500 and 1700 that resulted in a massive increase in the size of armies. For scholars influenced by Skocpol and Tilly, this was of immediate interest, because the costs of such military developments could be met only through extraction of ever higher taxes by the state. The question arose as to whether this military revolution influenced the development of the state and whether it was perhaps this that set the course for later regime types (whether parliamentary or absolutist in nature). Brian M. Downing (*The Military Revolution and Political Change: Origins of Democracy and Autocracy in Early Modern Europe*, 1992) produced a major comparative study on this subject, claiming that specific forms of the financing of the military revolution or particular geopolitical conditions (such as Britain's island status) induced corresponding political developments at an early stage. This was very much in line with the arguments of Otto Hintze, and Thomas Ertman expressed the same kind of thinking in another comparative study (*Birth of the Leviathan: Building*

States and Regimes in Medieval and Early Modern Europe, 1997). Here he attempted to show that such things as the origins of parliamentary forms of government must in some cases be placed earlier than the beginning of the military revolution; yet military factors were nonetheless decisive, particularly the *timing* of the military embroilments of the various territories. The funds needed for armaments varied according to the era, and the number of trained administrative personnel differed in different places (we might think here of the fact that universities emerged at different times in different parts of Europe). As a result, *the way in which* the machinery of state developed, whether it became generally centralized-authoritarian or parliamentary-consensual in character, often depended on the contingent convergence of the most varied processes. As a result, influenced by the theoretical framework established by Tilly and Skocpol, American sociologists in particular made intensive studies of the roots of democracy *in Europe*, some of which lay far in the past; in line with the premises of this approach, however, they generally put the form of democracy down not to cultural conditions but to military-political ones.

Very few scholars went on to systematically examine other eras and regions beyond Europe with respect to the role of war. One exception here was Theda Skocpol herself, who included consideration of Asia right from the outset in her *States and Social Revolutions*. Her 1992 book on the history of the American welfare state (*Protecting Soldiers and Mothers: The Political Origins of Social Policy in the United States*) made the United States the object of analysis and dared to approach an era none too distant from the present, focusing on the late nineteenth and early twentieth century. In this book, Skocpol argued that it was primarily the consequences of the American Civil War that laid the ground for the specific features of the later American welfare state, and its contemporary "backwardness" when compared with its Western and Northern European counterparts. It was "Benefits for Veterans," which expanded enormously after 1865 and covered an ever larger number of people, that represented the first, though quite peculiar beginnings of the American welfare state. The Republican Party in particular used the veterans' pensions as a means of patronage in order to win votes. The benefits paid were substantial, even in comparison with Europe. But according to Skocpol, this pension system, established as outlined above, was *not* a European-style insurance scheme, but at best "an unabashed system of national public care, not for all Americans in similar work or life circumstances, but for the deserving core of a special generation. No matter how materially needy, the morally undeserving or less deserving were not the nation's responsibility" (Skocpol 1992, 151). On this basis—Skocpol tells us, couching her arguments in terms of path dependency—it was difficult to advance to a policy oriented toward more universalist standards of welfare provision, as in Europe. It was the Civil War and its aftereffects that ultimately prompted the American state to pursue social policies that inevitably had little in common with the principles and measures typical of Western and Northern European welfare systems.

To repeat, then, the American historical sociology described above focused primarily on the connection between war and resource extraction and the consequent extension of political and social rights. With the exception of Skocpol, the relevant authors tended to concentrate their attention on Europe, which led to a number of difficulties. First, it remained unclear whether *all* the key characteristics of the modern state can really be derived from specific constellations of *state and military* factors. Tilly's narrative, based on rational choice premises, assumed that the growing accumulation of power by formerly small political units had led via war to comparatively large and homogeneous nation-states. It throws up the question of why other world regions did not develop in a similar way. Why is it only in Europe that the modern state took shape through the mechanism of "war making, extraction and capital accumulation" emphasized by Tilly? Is not the desire for virtually endless accumulation of power and thus for war itself in need of explanation? Were there not also cultural reasons for the enduring readiness to pursue military expansion beyond Europe? Must we not explain the quite different structure of political institutions in other parts of the world or in other historical eras at least partly with reference to cultural influences? (See the criticisms in Wittrock 2001, 61.)

Even if one accepts Tilly's premise that state actors act on the basis of rational choice within a conflict-ridden environment, and even if one suppresses critical questions as to the relevance of cultural traditions, it is still unclear just *where* in history the fiscal-military dynamics described by Tilly can be observed. In Europe, certainly, but did this also apply to other regions of the world? In his essay "War Making and State Making as Organized Crime," mentioned earlier, Tilly himself gave some indication of how we might answer this question, alluding to the fact that most of the developing countries that became independent after 1945 have a quite different history of state emergence and formation behind them and probably also ahead of them than the European states. In many places, the fiscal-military mechanism was quite unable to take hold: after decolonization, the "societies" of Asia and Africa were mostly "provided with" a state or had one imposed upon them, with their borders generally being guaranteed from outside after 1945, by the superpowers or the UN. So after 1945 the state-military competition observable in early modern Europe did not apply in these places, and according to Tilly this inevitably had consequences for the relationship between state and civil society on the one hand and the form of the state on the other. And this made Tilly skeptical about the prospects for democratization in the Third World. Because of their genesis, the military organizations that now existed there occupied a virtually unassailable position of power of a kind that never pertained within the European process of state formation in previous centuries. "To the extent that outside states guarantee their boundaries, the managers of these military organizations exercise extraordinary power within them. The advantages of military power became enormous, the incentives to seize power over the state as a whole by means of that advantage very strong. Despite the great place that war making occupied in the making of European states, the old national states of Europe almost never experienced the great disproportion between military organization and all other forms of organization that seems the fate of client states throughout the contemporary world" (Tilly 1985, 186).

We return to the point addressed here by Tilly in our discussion of "failed states" in the next chapter. But of more importance in this context is the critical insight that it is difficult to capture state formation outside of Europe—not just after 1945, but already in the nineteenth century—using Tilly's conceptual toolkit. In Latin America, both the state and war had a quite different meaning from that assumed by Tilly and those authors influenced by him with their Europe-centered framework. Their analyses always worked on the assumption of clear power structures and equally clear conflicts, in light of which rational actors set the fiscal-military cycle in motion, which then led—unintentionally—to the development of rational state structures. But such conditions did not pertain everywhere, as clearly shown in recent times by a historical sociology focused on Latin America. In the initial stages of Latin American independence in the early nineteenth century, wars were fairly frequent, so here too we should be able to observe the emergence of the mechanism of state formation emphasized so consistently by Tilly. Yet the form taken by warfare in Latin America was very different from that in Europe—with all the resulting consequences. In this connection, Miguel Angel Centeno refers to the significance of differing forms of war: whereas numerous European wars were fought with total commitment and thus led to an increase in state authority as resources were ruthlessly extracted from the civilian population, to the centralization of political power and weakening of regional identities, to increased emotional attachment to state institutions on the part of the population, and to the final transformation of subjects into citizens (Centeno 2002, 22), the Latin American wars of the nineteenth century were more limited conflicts, brutal as they were. As a result, resources were mobilized far less systematically, so stronger state structures did *not* develop after independence. "The armed effort was small enough so as to not require the militarization of society throughout the continent" (26). Because of this, in Latin America the state never attained full tax sovereignty nor could it even come close to enforcing the monopoly on violence to which it formally laid claim. Various hostile groups mounted a constant challenge to the legitimacy of central government, including by force of arms (Waldmann 2002, 23ff.). As a result, civil society in Latin America was and remains profoundly pervaded by violence, and even civil war is an ever-present threat (see also Knöbl 2006a).

Overall, these findings on the special features of the comparatively early process of state formation in Latin America did not refute Tilly's arguments or the state-centered approach as such (on postcolonial state formation in Africa, see Herbst 2000, 97ff.). But they do at least highlight the fact that any theory that seeks to explain the connection between state formation and war must pay heed to the particular forms and types of military conflict if it is to reach meaningful conclusions. Despite this qualification, it is fair to say that the research program that emerged in the United States facilitated new insights. These cast doubt on the plausibility of the conventional historical narratives found within Marxian approaches and modernization theory by bringing out the crucial role played by armed violence in the construction of modernity (see also the recent contribution by Spreen 2008).

▪ ▪ ▪

British sociology saw quite similar developments at around the same time. Here too historical sociology was flourishing. But in Britain the theoretical framework used to analyze war and military force was more ambitious and had a greater contemporary focus than in the United States, with the debate being shaped by three authors in particular: Michael Mann, Anthony Giddens, and Martin Shaw.

It is no easy task to assess Michael Mann's (b. 1942) contribution to social theories of war and military force. This is essentially because Mann, who has been working on a multivolume world history of power since the 1980s (*The Sources of Social Power*, 1986 and 1993), has developed a conceptual toolkit through which he attempts to capture systematically the ways in which war has shaped the development of modern societies. Because of this project's terrific scope, Mann's run through world history includes numerous theoretical references to the issue of war, which we are unable to review here in detail. What is clear, however, is that Mann is one of the few authors who pulls no punches in ascribing to the military sphere a constitutive role in the ordering of the social. Mann's position here is informed by his vigorous critique of the idea, commonly held by sociologists, that "society" is the discipline's central concept. Mann shows that sociology has rashly identified the sphere of the nation-state with that of society. It has equated the coherence and internal homogeneity of the modern nation-state with "society" as such, despite the fact that pre-modern social orders were constituted quite differently and did *not* exhibit such coherence. To ignore this, Mann tells us, is to obstruct our capacity for sociological understanding, particularly the insight that in different eras of human history war played an important but also highly variable role, and that war was one of the key driving forces behind the coherence and unity of the modern nation-state.

Because of this, right from the outset Mann broke with the concept of society; instead, the central theme of his analyses is the way in which order is created by four different power networks. According to him, it makes sense to examine empirically the extent to which ideological, economic, political, *and* military networks have interlocked in the most diverse periods of world history, thus establishing social order. The specific power networks did not always have the same capacity or spatial range. In some eras economic networks were more extensive than ideological ones, in some parts of the world military networks were more significant and stable than political ones, and so on. Mann ultimately turns all of this into an empirical question, making him receptive to historical variability in the formation of social order rather than hastily projecting a particular form of order (such as the nation-state) onto other eras and regions. It is this that puts him in a position to tackle our key concern of the role of war in processes of social change in a far more systematic fashion than has happened in sociology in general, and within historical sociology in particular.

First, Mann is able to show that war and military resources played a huge role in the establishment of empires even in the millennia before the birth of Christ and that military power networks were anything but derivative phenomena. Military forces often possessed considerable autonomy of action, administered large territories, and thus created the preconditions for the spread and stabilization of other power networks, such as economic ones. The military pacification of a territory could increase the security of economic transactions. Military power helped build an economic-political infrastructure (the introduction of currencies, the codification of law, and the establishment of an administrative system based on literacy) and thus helped establish an enduring order. It is no doubt the case that military resources and thus war itself were in turn dependent on certain economic preconditions. But Mann reminds us that economically backward territories were often in a position to overrun "more advanced" empires, which should encourage us to take the autonomy and independent influence of military power networks seriously. So his thesis is that neither the logic of action exhibited by the armed forces nor that of politics can be explained by the mode of production. This, of course, is a decisive rejection of both the economic determinism that plays such a dominant role for Marxists and the evolutionist ideas common among those close to modernization theory, according to which historical processes are best understood as mere culturally molded processes of differentiation. According to Mann, war and violence and their role in establishing order cannot be understood with the conceptual tools of these approaches (see Mann 1988a).

Second, with the aid of the power networks model, Mann is able to show that the path to *European modernity* from the end of the Roman Empire was in fact extremely bellicose. Borrowing from the ideas of Tilly and Skocpol—but even more forcefully than them—he spells out just how much, for example, British public finances were shaped by war. According to his analysis, most of the English or British state's revenues were "devoted" to war in the period between 1130 and 1815, which again underlines that the history of key institutions of European modernity cannot be written without taking account of macroviolence. The implicit upshot of Mann's analyses is that the Weberian notion of rationalization and of the modern state as a rational institution, while not wrong, all too easily tempts us to underestimate how closely this rationality is bound up with various forms of armed violence (Mann 1988b).[1]

Third, and in connection with this, Mann shows that it is simply impossible to understand the formation of classes without factoring in a process of state formation backed by force of arms. According to him, classes have not existed throughout history, as Marxism assumes when it conceives of history as consisting of class struggles. In fact, conflicts between classes arose only as part of a reaction to state centralism and taxation. Since the end of the Middle Ages in Europe, it was as a result of state intervention, the recruitment of soldiers, and levying of taxes that those affected organized themselves, that they found a common addressee, and that their actions were directed toward a *common* goal. According to Mann's thesis, this process of class formation would not simply have occurred autonomously from below. It could develop only through this dialectic between state intervention and the "response" to it. This dialectic made itself felt within the bourgeoisie, later among the workers, and finally among the peasantry as well, which explains among other things why the formation of these classes differed so greatly in different countries. According to Mann, the differences in class formation were not due primarily to specific sociostructural or economic factors but to the particular circumstances in which a particular state—acting within an international state system in Europe—coped with armed conflicts and siphoned off the resources needed to do so from the population. So the struggle for civil, political, and social rights was often a response to state intervention, with war being the crucial background variable. The rights of citizens in Europe did not simply spring from economic conditions, prompting Mann (and Skocpol too) to underline that any history of democracy in Europe must take account of war (see Mann 1993): it was the diversity of Europe and the armed conflicts to which it gave rise that touched off a political dynamic within individual societies through which democratic demands could be formulated and—where circumstances were favorable—enforced.

Fourth, and finally—as Mann insisted in several essays published in the 1990s—current political developments should not prompt us to abandon the thesis of the independence of military power networks. Because we must assume that power networks are intertwined, we must always be open to the possibility of side effects that cannot be controlled and are potentially violent in character. Mann therefore warns against interpreting the current peaceful process of European unification as the beginning of the end of history. According to Mann, the great hopes that many members of the public as well as a good number of social scientists place in Europe and the EU should not tempt us to lapse back into a teleological view of history: we cannot entirely rule out the possibility that Europe may once again see violent conflicts, if, for example, it is struck by economic crisis; nor should we make Europe the benchmark for the world. The European Community or Union arose in a way that was exceptional in many respects. Under the American nuclear umbrella and as a result of the United States' preeminent influence in the 1950s and 1960s, conflicts between Western European states were rendered impossible from the outset. The beginnings of a supranational entity could begin to take shape in a manner virtually without parallel elsewhere. So we should be aware of this European exceptionalism, rather than rushing to interpret the peacefulness of European unification as a preliminary step toward the emergence of an equally peaceful world society, as this would again blind us to the actual diversity of social change processes; we cannot rule out the possibility that these will entail military conflicts, precisely because different power networks are entwined in complex ways (see Mann 1998).

Mann has not yet completed his "world history of power." He is yet to produce an overall interpretation of the twentieth century. He has however explored elements of this history, particularly its violent aspects, in his books, which can be read as groundwork for the overall interpretation to come. A book on European fascism (*Fascists*, 2004) and especially one on ethnic cleansing (*The Dark Side of Democracy: Explaining Ethnic Cleansing*, 2005) spelled out once again how necessary it is to take account of the embeddedness of modernity and, not least, of democracy, in military processes. According to the thesis elaborated by Mann in his comparative study of 2005, the background to ethnic cleansing, as a typically modern phenomenon, is the nation-state and thus, for the most part, the notion of an organic, cohesive, and ultimately homogeneous or "pure" nation. But such notions explain little in themselves. It is in fact very concrete factors that trigger attempts to realize these ideas and phantasms and thus lead to large-scale atrocities. As Mann tries to show, ethnic cleansing tends to occur in unstable international contexts or in association with wars. It begins when internal and international conflicts become intertwined, when constructs of the enemy within the international sphere are transferred to domestic politics. This is what gives ethnic cleansing its internal momentum, which defies any mode of analysis that merely takes account of actors' rationality. The dynamic side effects and tensions within the institutional complex of a modern nation-state embedded in an international system are frequently terrible, but—as Mann repeatedly underlines—*not* alien to that system or contrary to modernity. Those who close their minds to this insight will always be surprised by such violent phenomena and can interpret them only as temporary deviations from the process of modernization, which essentially proceeds without friction or violence—and this is to misunderstand them.

In the mid-1980s, Anthony Giddens too produced a book located to some extent within the same discursive context as Michael Mann's work, and he made the role of war in emerging modernity the center of analytical attention. Giddens (b. 1938) published *The Constitution of Society*, his theoretical magnum opus, in 1984. While this (primarily action theoretical) study naturally contained numerous reflections on social order, the macrosociological consequences of the arguments presented here went largely unelaborated. Giddens attempted to remedy this shortcoming a year later in *The Nation-State and Violence: Volume Two of A Contemporary Critique of Historical Materialism*, an essentially historical study of modern nation-states' susceptibility to violence. Giddens, who argued from a historical perspective like few other grand theorists of the 1970s and 1980s, used a theoretical framework similar to that of Michael Mann. He drew particular attention to the process of power accumulation, which has proceeded discontinuously throughout human history; passing through a number of stages, this process ultimately triggered the emergence of clearly defined national entities during the era of European absolutism at the latest, entities that Giddens calls "power containers." Largely as a result of military and technological developments, truly homogeneous territories took shape for the first time that were consistently structured by political power. Self-contained entities with clearly recognizable boundaries arose, and their form was further perfected in the emerging nation-state system of the nineteenth and twentieth centuries—with a degree of control and comprehensive surveillance that was quite unprecedented. Starting from the thesis of "power containers" that became established over time, Giddens now presented an analysis of the contemporary era in which war played a decisive role. According to Giddens, the internal pacification of society brought about by the process of modernization, the disciplining of the population, and its effective integration into the nation-state—facilitated by the granting of political and social rights—did indeed result in an astonishing degree of pacification *within* societies. But it is just this that allowed the use of force on a massive scale beyond their boundaries. According to Giddens, once the state had been established, its resources of violence could be removed from the interior of society and deployed in all the more unbridled fashion in wars between societies: "[M]y theme will be that the correlate of the internally pacified state—class relationships that rest upon a mixture of 'dull economic compulsion' and supervisory techniques of labour management— is the professionalized army" (Giddens 1985, 160). So there are good reasons why total war was waged in the era of internally quite homogeneous nation-states. For Giddens, this international violence within the constitution of modernity is so important that alongside capitalism, industrialism, and internal surveillance, he views the potentially violent international state system as a key structural feature of modernity. We can produce a persuasive analysis of modernity only if we examine the interplay of the four structural features mentioned above, if we grasp that these features are consistently associated with massive conflicts, not least armed conflicts. And in contrast to the theories expounded by liberal theorists of the nineteenth century and modernization theorists of the twentieth, we cannot self-evidently assume that a particular complex (such as capitalism or industrialism) simply neutralizes the potentially conflictual character of another (such as the state system). In fact, Giddens tells us, it is always possible for these systems to reinforce one another and produce unintended side effects, which should make us skeptical about excessive hopes of peace and any attempt to exclude war from social theory.

But Anthony Giddens himself went no further in systematically analyzing the bellicose features of modernity. After 1990, his books dealt mainly with the modern subject or modern identities and increasingly lost sight of macrosociological realities. Giddens certainly continued to examine such realities, but in the form of quite optimistic theories of globalization, which are essentially impossible to square with the key assertions found in his more substantial contributions from the 1980s. Giddens's transformation from a historical sociologist informed by conflict theory to optimistic essayist analyzing the contemporary world cannot be explained on internal theoretical grounds.

But not all British social scientists who had grappled with the topics of war since the 1970s moved on to lofty debates on identity and globalization. With great tenacity and consistency, Martin Shaw (b. 1947) has explored various aspects of war, a topic that has long preoccupied him, his particular foci being the role of the armed forces in contemporary Western societies and the connection between war and other forms of macroviolence. In the early 1990s, in *Post-Military Society*, Shaw tried to get to grips with the question of how, on a basic conceptual level, we might even begin to grasp modern Western states' ability and willingness to wage war, especially that of the United States and Britain. It is after all striking that while the superpower of the United States still wages wars (as did Britain in the Falklands War), the traditional meaning of the term "militarism" no longer seems to apply so straightforwardly to these societies. Shaw thus calls for a distinction between "militarism" and "militarization" on the one hand and the desire to wage war on the other. According to Shaw, militarism, defined as the "influence of military organization and values on social structure" (Shaw 1991, 11), and militarization, as the permeation of the social structure by military values, do not necessarily go hand in hand with actual readiness for war. Largely unmilitarized societies, on the other hand, may well want war. Shaw lends plausibility to this distinction, which seems slightly peculiar at first sight, by referring to processes that occurred in Britain and the United States in the 1980s and early 1990s. Conscription had long since been abolished, so it was no longer so easy to identify any massive military influence on society. In other *Western* societies too, the influence of the armed forces on the social structure seems to be diminishing—at least in comparison with the nineteenth and first half of the twentieth century. The close linkage that Morris Janowitz claimed existed between citizenship and military service (see the previous chapter) is becoming unimportant because increasingly professionalized armies are now emerging. This is why we can refer to the incipient demilitarization of society *in the West*, as classical militarism is becoming less significant there. "Classical militarism could be seen as the product of the mix of statism, labour-extensive mass production, and mechanized warfare, which has increasingly been surpassed in the West, is now challenged in the East, but remains powerful in the South" (93). But this does not mean that Western societies no longer go to war. In this connection, Shaw rejects all hopes of peace found in evolutionist thought or modernization theory. Wars will continue to take place, but those fought by Western states will no longer incorporate the entire population. Instead, these states will deploy highly specialized, comparatively small armies, which can minimize losses in their own ranks because of their vast technological superiority compared with their opponents, usually from the non-Western world. So the term "post-military society" as used by Shaw is *not* meant to imply the emergence of a peaceful world, but to draw attention to a transformation in the character of warfare particularly evident in Western societies. From a social theory perspective, analyzing this transformation is crucial, because these limited wars throw up questions about the democratic control of military intervention; at any rate, such wars stimulate different social dynamics from those during the era when war entailed the mass mobilization of entire populations.

More than ten years later, well after the end of the Cold War, the fall of the Berlin Wall, and the end of Soviet communism, Shaw produced a new work on war and modernity in the shape of *War and Genocide: Organized Killing in Modern Society*. Its key thesis matched that found in his 1991 book; according to Shaw, the concept of "post-military society" continues to be meaningful. Wars waged by Western societies can still be described in the same way as in 1991, and we may refer to them as "risk-transfer wars" (Shaw 2003, 238) in that when Western countries deploy military forces they do all they can to minimize their own losses and transfer risk to "indigenous" allies as far as possible (see also Heins/ Warburg 2004, 121ff.). What is new—and here there are similarities with Michael Mann's *The Dark Side of Democracy: Explaining Ethnic Cleansing*—is that Shaw asks whether, in view of the form of contemporary conflicts, we can uphold the traditional distinction between war and other forms of macroviolence; we must also examine whether the intertwining of war with other forms of violence was not far closer, even in the past, than has generally been conceded. With regard to these questions, Shaw takes a clear stand, provocatively associating war with genocide and revolutionary violence. According to him, revolution and genocide are often better understood as variants on or phases of war, because in the past both revolutionary and genocidal dynamics were all too frequently directly bound up with war (Shaw 2003, 27ff.). This does not mean that we must abandon the conceptual distinction between war, genocide, and revolution. But we must take seriously the insights provided by a historical sociology with a sensitivity to war, because it has shown that it is far from easy to separate the dynamics internal and external to a society; that internal opponents are all too easily identified with external ones; and that war quite often results in revolutionary civil wars—and the killing of internal dissidents. Shaw's analyses at least provide an opportunity to consider these questions in greater depth, even if the finer points of his arguments may not be completely convincing. He is no doubt correct that genocidal processes rarely follow a preset instrumentally rational logic but gain their horrifying dynamism within a broader framework of conflict (37). But if this is so, then it is all the more vital to analyze the intertwining and interdependence of differing processual logics and their unforeseeable results (on the specific logic of violence, see the interesting reflections of Waldmann 2007, 147ff.).

After the East-West Conflict

DEMOCRATIZATION, STATE COLLAPSE,
AND EMPIRE BUILDING

OUR REMARKS on developments in Anglo-American historical sociology and its emphasis on war might seem to imply that the social sciences no longer suppress the topic. Sociology in particular might seem at last to have overcome the intellectual barriers blocking its way. But such an interpretation of historical-sociological debates since the 1970s would be precipitate and misleading. We must bear in mind that it was only in the United States and Britain that sociologists tackled the topic of war. Historical sociology was not destined to enjoy similar success in other countries—a surprising state of affairs considering the great interest in historical processes shown by the founding fathers of the discipline, Émile Durkheim and Max Weber. Theoretical and historical analyses of war remained few and far between. The topic of war did make it onto the social scientific agenda in association with the lively debate on a "democratic peace" in the late 1980s and 1990s; that on "failed states" and "new wars" in the 1990s; and the debates from around 2000 concerning the American imperium. Yet German and French sociologists were conspicuous by their absence, despite the fact that the debate that we will be describing here would certainly have benefited from a grounding in sociological argument. The three debates mentioned above were dominated by monocausal or monothematic approaches to the topic of war. By "monothematic," we mean those social scientific analyses of the contemporary world and of social change—often quite popular among the general public—that reduce complex realities to a single characteristic (for a critique, see Joas 2012, 106–128).

Debates on the "democratic peace" went on chiefly within the subdiscipline of "international relations." We must turn briefly here to the vexed relationship between this discipline and sociology. American scholars left their mark on both disciplines after the Second World War, to such an extent that international relations was even referred to as an *"American social science"* (Rengger 2000, 12; emphasis added). And after 1945 both subjects featured quasi-hegemonic theoretical currents that developed at the same time, though (and this was *not* necessarily bound up with the two subjects' disparate epistemological interests) they started from entirely different premises: while structural functionalism was dominant within sociology from around 1940 until the mid-1960s, it was the so-called realism associated with scholars such as Hans Morgenthau and Kenneth Waltz that held sway within international relations theory. Structural functionalism and realism declined in importance from the mid-1960s, before enjoying at least short-term renaissances in the late 1970s in the shape of neofunctionalism in sociology and neorealism in international relations (on this periodization of "international relations," see McSweeney 1999, 25).

There is no need to undertake explicit comparative studies of structural functionalism as the then dominant sociological approach and realism as its counterpart within international relations in order to grasp what a different understanding of theory we are dealing with here. Even if realists, and some structural functionalists, based themselves on Max Weber, the "realist" Max Weber was almost *exclusively* the Weber of the Freiburg inaugural address (Smith 1986, 26ff.). In line with this, realists understood (and continue to understand) the international system in Hobbesian style as an anarchic one; because states can never be sure of their rivals' intentions, they struggle for security and attempt to assert their sovereignty through their armed forces and the potential threat that these entail. This applies *regardless of the nature of a given political regime*, which realists make no attempt to analyze in order to explain international dynamics. Having established the existence of such anarchy, it follows that there can essentially be no trust between states, that the anarchical system is inevitably a "self-help system," one in which states only ever pursue and must pursue their own strategic interests—because any kind of international cooperation is improbable and a rare occurrence at best (see, e.g., Mearsheimer 1998b, 334ff.).

Obviously, such a theory was of little use to Talcott Parsons or functionalists close to him. The disregarding of normative aspects in the analysis of international relations, so typical of realism, was inevitably alien to Parsonian thought and to most other schools of sociological theory. Further, from Parsons's perspective there was probably little to be gleaned from the field of international relations anyway, because its realistic accounts of the international system captured the reality of the Cold War very well, with the United States and the Soviet Union, along with their allies, constantly anticipating each other's moves in attempts to enhance its own power (on the connection between the Cold War and the rise of realism, see Onuf 1998, 227). In light of this, it is understandable that in the 1950s many sociologists failed to systematically examine these issues or saw them as a field of no relevance to sociology.[1]

Conflict theory—formulated in explicit opposition to Parsons's theoretical constructions—might seem predestined to have formed a bridge between sociology and international relations. Yet Lewis Coser and others showed only negligible interest in this endeavor. His work does include references to his collaboration with peace researcher Johan Galtung. But he made no concerted effort to explore the field, nor did he truly engage with realist theories (see Coser's remarks on his collaboration with Galtung in Coser 1967, 6). We might surely have expected Ralf Dahrendorf to have greater affinities with the subject of international relations, then dominated by the realists. He more than anyone tried to advance the conflict theory perspective as an independent approach (see Dahrendorf 1968, 139/40), so it would have been quite conceivable to forge links with realist positions. This could not happen, however, because Dahrendorf's conflict model of society was tailored exclusively to the social organization of domination, whereas the sphere of international politics, though it may not be entirely devoid of law, is surely without clear hierarchical order. Dahrendorf took the same view when he conceded that extending his conflict theory into the field of international relations was desirable but problematic (Dahrendorf 1972, 16 and 34). So even Dahrendorf failed to penetrate the field of international relations. Among leading sociologists, only Raymond Aron was intensively involved in debates on foreign affairs, but he remained an isolated figure in this respect (see chapter 5). The 1950s were thus characterized by a nonrelationship between the two disciplines, and this was not to change fundamentally in the 1960s and early 1970s, when realism and structural functionalism slowly lost influence. Essentially, this nonrelationship persists to this day, despite the "sociological turn" proclaimed by some international relations scholars and Randall Collins's development of conflict theory.

But back to the debate on the "democratic peace." The focus here was exclusively on democratization, which was examined for its significance to the capacity for peace, the entire debate being underpinned by the vision of peace developed by Kant in 1795. As we showed in detail in chapter 2, in "Perpetual Peace" Kant had argued that war itself has its own inherent driving force, one that ultimately leads to peace. He backed up this thesis with an argument about the conditions of mobilization. This posits that all states tend toward the organizational form of the *republic*. This is said to be the only way to ensure that a regime enjoys widespread legitimacy, thus creating the conditions necessary for states to hold their own militarily in an era when wars between nations were starting to occur. Through its selective function, then, war itself brings about an increase in the number of republics, as nonrepublics are ultimately handicapped on the international stage. According to Kant, however, once large numbers of republics exist over the long term, changes inevitably occur in international relations. Republics are controlled by the people, who are unlikely to have any interest in throwing themselves needlessly into aggressive international adventures—as they themselves would have to pay the blood price.

These, then, were the Kantian arguments that were to play an important role in the debate that was now taking off. Kant—and it is important to emphasize this—did not assert that republics are essentially more peacefully inclined than other regimes. Their peaceful character relates only to *other republican states*, which Kant explained through a basically cultural argument: because conflicts are resolved peacefully within republics, their peaceful culture carries over to their external relations. As the number of republics increases, a zone of peace, of increasing international cooperation and mutual trust, will gradually emerge. This opens up the prospect of a worldwide confederation, an alliance in which it is no longer violence but legal rules that order relations among states.

Since the end of the nineteenth century, the period when the social sciences began to emerge, there had been no serious discussion of Kant's ideas on how to achieve peace. As we have seen in the preceding chapters, power-political realism, liberalism, and modernization theory, which were based on assumptions quite different from those of Kant, were far more prominent. It was only in the early 1980s that this changed, with global political developments and new political circumstances playing a crucial role in the resumption of the debate on Kant's ideas. The immediate trigger for this debate, at least the academic variant, was the great two-part essay by Michael Doyle from 1983 entitled "Kant, Liberal Legacies, and Foreign Affairs" (see also Doyle 1986). This breathed new life into the debate with its key thesis, derived from Kant, "that there exists a significant predisposition against warfare between liberal states" (Doyle 1983, 213).

It is no mystery why this idea of Kant's, which had lain dormant for so long and was revived by Doyle, was embraced so eagerly in the late 1980s. Doyle's essay coincided with the rise of Gorbachev and the end of the Cold War. The notion of a "democratic peace" would surely have been viewed with suspicion as mere ideology at the height of the Cold War.[2] Now, though, within the context of the "Third Wave of Democratization" identified by Samuel Huntington (1996) and others, the optimistic vision of a democratic and thus peaceful international system no longer seemed so outlandish. The political instrumentalization of this idea began immediately. It appealed to Margaret Thatcher and members of the George H. W. Bush administration as well as to left-leaning peace researchers (Ray 1997, 50), all of whom wished to extend the global reach of democracy—though often for very different reasons. In addition, Kant's popularized ideas drew so much attention partly because they were associated with a substantive thesis that clearly ran counter to the still influential realistic currents within the discipline of international relations. Ultimately, what Kant's revivers (like Doyle) are saying is that states' internal conditions (may) decisively influence international relations, that the international system will not inevitably remain anarchic forevermore, and thus that, in principle, an enduringly peaceful order is possible. So it is no surprise that it was (power-political) realists who helped make this debate on the "democratic peace" particularly lively with their attacks on the "Kantians."

From the very beginning, however, the debate suffered from the fact that Kant's ideas were discussed from a curiously ahistorical perspective. First, they were immediately operationalized and reformulated to produce a quantitative research design usable by social scientists. There is of course nothing wrong with this in itself, but because the variables must remain constant, the terms "war" and "democracy" were stripped of all historical context. Both changes in democratic structures and changes in the form taken by war were ignored. Further, Kant's revivers all too rarely took heed of the debate about Kant around 1800, within German philosophy for example, which had already cast doubt on the viability of his ideas (see p. 58ff.). So the rich array of arguments on offer fell victim to a process of operationalization within the social sciences, though—as we shall see—the results of this process were not particularly convincing. Ultimately, the debate was also "ahistorical" in a figurative sense, as the debaters largely ignored the findings on war produced by Anglo-American historical sociology. As evident in studies by Tilly, Mann, and others, scholars working in this field had shown in detail that political-military processes inevitably produce side effects that defy notions of rational control. On this view, the (democratic) political process obeys no clear logic; instead—to use Michael Mann's language—it interacts with other power networks in an often-chaotic way. From such a perspective, it would be counterintuitive to imagine that one particular model of regime alone would lead to specific outcomes; in this case, that democracy alone were to lead to peace.[3] But it is just this insight, emanating from historical sociology, that the "Kantians" ignored in the debate that we now outline.

Surprisingly, the participants in this highly contentious debate did reach a consensus on certain points. Notably, most of them agreed with the thesis that democracies are *not* fundamentally more peace loving than other types of political system (Morgan/Campbell 1991, 188). This was already inherent in Kant's work, as he merely referred to the peacefulness of republics *among themselves*. Within the context of the revival of Kant's ideas, Michael Doyle endorsed this cautious view in his above-mentioned essay. Further, Doyle (1983, 323ff.) underlined how quickly in the past democracies had turned pure conflicts of interest into ideological crusades, which often made their foreign policies extremely violent. So with respect to democracies Doyle showed himself anything but a naive optimist about peace. In fact his interpretation of the relationship between democratic and nondemocratic states had a highly pessimistic slant; he argued that, because of a crusading mentality, democracies *may* even go beyond the imperatives of realpolitik (though this is not inevitable). So Doyle and most of the supporters[4] of the thesis of a "democratic peace" did *not* endorse the so-called *monadic* theory of peace, which states that democracies are fundamentally more peaceful. They were in agreement with the realists in this respect. In contrast to the realists, however, supporters of the "democratic peace" thesis advocated and continue to advocate the *dyadic* and originally Kantian version, which refers to the *relationship between democracies or republics*.[5]

But the debate on this enduringly contentious dyadic thesis immediately threw up fundamental methodological and definitional issues; it proved extremely difficult to develop relevant research projects, while the problems of operationalization proved almost insurmountable. If scholars wished to examine, for example, the period between 1800 and the present in order to test this thesis, then they had to analyze reciprocal relations among all states that have existed since then, in other words they had to ask between which states, in any given calendar year, war was waged. They then had to filter out relations between *democratic* states and clarify whether and in how many years they were at war. This procedure resulted in large data sets, but these were not very helpful in at least two respects.

First, it remained unclear what exactly the term "democracy" meant. Which states were democratic in the nineteenth century, where was there universal male suffrage, let alone votes for women? Against the thesis that democratic states do not wage wars against one another, realists cited the British-American war of 1812 or that between the United States and Mexico from 1846 to 48, to which advocates of the "democratic peace" thesis responded that given its electoral law at the time, Britain especially was not a democracy, and neither was Mexico—and perhaps not even the United States, given discrimination against African Americans. So none of these cases can be deployed to falsify the thesis. These skirmishes did not, of course, advance the debate. Advocates of the "democratic peace" thesis defended it by applying ever stricter definitional criteria to the term "democracy"; all this achieved was to massively reduce the number of democracies, as there were virtually none to be found outside of Europe and North America until well into the twentieth century, and because of exclusionary structures democratic mechanisms never came fully to fruition even in the Western context. This raised the question of how convincing, and above all how universally applicable, the thesis of a "democratic peace" really was.

Second, the definition of "war" also represented a practically insurmountable obstacle. At what point do we consider states to be at war? Does war begin at 100 deaths, 500, 1,000? These sound like cynical questions, but they must be posed, precisely because specific definitions of war frame in advance how we deploy specific data and lead to the exclusion of other data, which has resulted in peculiar classifications that clearly distort the results of investigations. Just one example. If we define war as an event involving at least 100 deaths, then both Brazil and the Soviet Union were "normal" participants in the Second World War, and both China and Ethiopia were full-fledged combatants in the Korean War.[6] Clearly, we are going to come up with some very questionable findings if we proceed on this basis.

The conclusions drawn about these methodological problems by different authors varied enormously. Of the advocates of the "democratic peace," eventually just a few still claimed that democracies have *never* fought against each other. Such an assertion would have been simple, elegant, and easy to falsify and would therefore have great explanatory potential, but as the criteria for falsification remained hotly disputed, it seemed to make sense to drop the *absolute* version of the thesis (Russett 1995, 169). What happened was that every time the realists put forward a counterexample to challenge the absolute version, its advocates tried to exclude the countries involved from the definition of democracy or disputed that a war had in fact taken place. In order to avoid such fruitless discussions, exponents of the "democratic peace" increasingly embraced the toned-down idea that democracies *rarely or markedly less often* wage wars against one another than other regimes. They no longer wished to entirely rule out, in principle, the possibility of wars between democracies.

Another trend within the debate saw both sides increasingly turning away from quantitative methods toward case studies. It had proved impossible to resolve the dispute between realists and exponents of a "democratic peace" by processing large amounts of data, so the focus subsequently shifted to critical case studies, in other words examination of democratic countries that had become involved in a war or just managed to avoid one. Detailed analyses seemed all the more necessary because it had never been entirely clear what exactly the causal mechanisms are through which democracies (supposedly) regulate their conflicts peacefully. Of course, as we have mentioned, Kant put forward several arguments to explain republics' peaceful character vis-à-vis other republics: a structural one, namely the control exercised by a population unwilling to go to war and the resulting constraints on rulers' actions; and a cultural one, namely the nonviolent culture of negotiation within and between republics. But, and this is the question with which the debaters were increasingly concerned, which of these is decisive? It did not take realists and most supporters of the "democratic peace" thesis long to agree that the structural argument is ultimately unconvincing, as it is overly captive to the naive Enlightenment faith in the goodness of the "common people" and idealizes the functioning of democracies. The structural argument assumes a quasi-autonomous process of public opinion-forming, unswayed by rulers' propaganda and just as dubiously contrasts a peace-loving majority with a belligerent elite (Gates/Knutsen/Moses 1996, 4; Owen 1998, 149ff.); further, the structural argument includes the untested assertion that the majority of citizens is greatly interested in foreign affairs and is therefore motivated, and able, to impose its will whenever there is a threat of war; and finally, the implication here is that autocrats rule with autonomy and without taking into account their country's elites. Yet this is anything but self-evident: "checks and balances," though not democratic in character, are also to be found in dictatorships. Such regimes also tend to feature highly complex decision-making structures.

It is true that there are no free elections in dictatorships; but data on the temporal connection between democratic elections and war provide no clear conclusions, so it would be wrong to ascribe to the institution of democratic elections a significant influence on decisions to go to war (Morgan/Campbell 1991, 190ff.; Layne 1998, 183f.; Gowa 1999, 20ff.). Overall, then, the structural explanation of the democratic peace proved quite unconvincing.

Among "Kantians," this inevitably enhanced the strategic importance of the cultural argument, and it was this that they subsequently focused on (Chan 1997, 74ff.; Maoz/Russett 1993, 636). This already seemed apposite in light of the empirical observation that merely formal democratic institutions have little influence on the willingness to wage war. There is evidence to suggest that democratizing states, democracies undergoing a process of consolidation, are in fact more belligerent than other countries,[7] and that while democracies have increased in number since the 1970s, the frequency of armed conflicts has not decreased or has in fact increased (Maoz 1997, 194). So it was only logical if the debaters were increasingly preoccupied with political culture.

If one argues, in much the same way as Kant, that republics or democracies feature a culture based on nonviolent conflict resolution, one that seeks compromises within the domestic political sphere, in other words a culture in which the prevailing atmosphere is one of "live and let live" (Maoz/Russett 1993, 625), and that this culture may be carried over into relations between states, then it is far from clear why in the past democracies have taken quick and aggressive action against authoritarian regimes or have at least threatened violence against other democratic states (see Daase 2004). The nonviolent culture of negotiation clearly played no decisive role in these cases (Elman 1997, 14; Russett 1993, 31). So the cultural argument in defense of the thesis of a "democratic peace" emerges as quite problematic. We can escape such difficulties only if, *first*, rather than declaring the "objective" state of democracy or liberalism in two regimes the cause of their peaceful conduct toward one another, we instead examine their *perception* of one another as liberal or democratic, and/or, *second*, distinguish between *liberalism and democracy*, because not all democracies are truly liberal. Both these argumentational strategies were in fact pursued by exponents of the democratic peace thesis.

The *first* strategy emphasized processes of mutual *perception* between liberal or democratic regimes, which was believed to explain a proclivity for peace—because the openness of the political process[8] or *mutually* assumed existence of a culture of negotiation creates trust, preventing hasty recourse to armed violence (Maoz/Russett 1993, 625). The crucial quality of democratic states, then, is not their "peaceful disposition" but their capacity to generate trust (Huntley 1996, 58), which then—in an encounter between two democratic states—prevents violent conflict. The *second* though not exclusive strategy was to distinguish quite sharply *between democracy and liberalism* to counter the above-mentioned criticism that democratic states do in fact act aggressively toward other states. This strategy was most clearly evident in the work of John Owen. In a number of studies (Owen 1997; 1998),[9] he not only combined the structural and cultural argument, emphasizing the aspect of mutual perception in the latter case, but also distinguished sharply between a liberal political culture and democratic procedures. According to Owen, liberal culture is characterized above all by an emphasis on individual autonomy, the value of self-government, and tolerance, which is bound up with a tendency to avoid violence. Of course, these qualities are not found in every democracy, which is why there are cases—examples may be found in ancient Greece as well as the medieval Italian city-states—in which democracies or republics do in fact wage war on one another. On this view, then, it is not democracy as such that is the key variable, but the potential for democratic control plus a genuinely *liberal* political culture.[10]

The argumentational strategies described here undoubtedly rendered the thesis of a "democratic peace" more tenable than approaches that rely entirely on the structural argument. At the same time, however, the introduction of the element of perception undermined the theory, as politics clearly entails ceaseless processes of redefinition, and power-political rivals can very quickly be labeled as illiberal or undemocratic while useful allies are declared flawless democrats. Critics could point out, for example, that according to the theory of democratic peace America should never have entered into the First World War, because before 1914 most Americans perceived the German Empire as a democracy and this began to change only as relations deteriorated, with Germany's authoritarian traits receiving increasing emphasis (Collins 1995; Oren 1995).

Moreover, the culturalist arguments put forward by Owen and others had the serious consequence of implicitly dashing Kantian hopes of perpetual peace. It is possible to imagine that formally democratic institutions will spread across the world within the context of the above-mentioned "third wave," but it is scarcely possible to imagine that (Western) liberal culture will also do so. What this plausible skepticism does is to radically limit the theory's scope of application both spatially and temporally. It can be tested only within the Western world—and only in the post-1945 era. This is a problem in part because within this spatiotemporal context these states had, and have still, many other features in common alongside liberal values, features that might explain the long postwar peace. Is it not conceivable that the exceptional affluence in the European-American world after the Second World War influenced both the prospects of developing a liberal culture and the propensity for war, because—as the utilitarian argument we encountered earlier would have it—in this geographic context there was very little to be gained and everything to lose from the waging of international wars (see Mueller 1988)? Power-political realists in turn might argue with some justification that the peace that prevailed after 1945 was merely a result of the Cold War, as wars were prevented solely because of the bipolar distribution of power on the European continent, the military parity between the Soviet Union and the United States, and the existence of nuclear weapons (Mearsheimer 1998a, 4f.; Cohen 1994, 220; Gowa 1999, 3 and 113). But other quite different explanatory approaches are quite plausible here too. Is it not just as conceivable that because of numerous experiences of violence in the twentieth century, most Europeans now have an ingrained aversion to organized violence, in other words that contingent learning processes have taken place, which may be linked only very indirectly to liberal values? And finally, to adopt another quite different argument, could we not simply reverse the direction of causality in Owen's explanatory schema, according to which liberal culture determines peace? Could we not argue with Otto Hintze—admittedly in modified form—that it is peace that makes stable democracies possible in the first place, in other words, that the advocates of the "democratic peace" thesis have wrongly declared the dependent variable independent? It would then make more sense to analyze the geopolitical, international, and military preconditions for democratization than to investigate the consequences of democracy or liberal culture on the international system (Thompson 1996). There are unlikely to be any clear and straightforward answers. But these very questions have increasingly problematized the theory of a "democratic peace," which as recently as the early 1990s was still being described as providing the only law in the discipline of international relations ("there are no wars between democracies"). Even the attempt to distinguish between democracy and liberalism and to make a liberal culture *the* decisive determinant of peace ultimately makes no difference in this respect.

So if we sum up the course of the debate between the "Kantians" and their opponents, most of whom were power-political realists, it is clear that they were unable to reach any uncontentious conclusions. Plainly, though, the high political and normative expectations originally bound up with Kant's (or Doyle's) thesis remained unfulfilled.[11] As the debate showed, we cannot expect even the global advance of democracy to lead to entirely new international constellations with commensurate consequences for processes of social change. In this respect, then, the realists' attacks on the theory of a "democratic peace" were highly successful. Further, scholars had to seriously consider whether or not this theory—irrespective of the scope of application one ascribes to it—has now become irrelevant, because most wars are no longer waged between sovereign states, whether democratic or not, and warfare has changed utterly (Rengger 2000, 118ff.). We shall have more to say on this in a moment.

But this should not lead us to conclude that power-political realism has proved the superior theory and that we ought simply to accept its premises. The reverse is true: the "sociological turn" propagated within the discipline of international relations since the 1980s has brought out the problematic nature of key realist assumptions and shown that many aspects of realist theory remain unclear. The anarchy of the international system assumed by realists, for example, is not something objectively given but is dependent on interpretation by states. To cite a famous essay title, "Anarchy is what states make of it" (Wendt 1992). In line with this, the preferences of states within a state system can never simply be derived through a process of deduction. This represents a problem for realism in that it is unwilling and unable to make statements about how preferences with respect to foreign policy arise *within* states in the first place—quite apart from the problematic fact that realism treats states as coherent actors, while leaving transnational forces out of account (Jervis 1988, 324ff.). All of these are genuinely *sociological* questions and problems, which the debate on a "democratic peace" touched on but never systematically discussed.

Though this debate bore meager fruit, it did at least reveal that whether war breaks out or peace prevails is not determined solely by a Hobbesian state system, democratic procedures within a state, or a liberal culture. The specific interplay of institutions within states is probably just as significant (Czempiel 1992, 261f.). In other words, we must ask whether there are other, more important factors determining the particular form taken by foreign policy than the type of political system regarded in isolation. We must pay at least as much attention to the relationship between military and civil institutions (Elman 1997, 38f.) as to complex and historically variable interactions between political, military, and economic actors. If we concede this, we are compelled once again to confront questions that had already been posed by Anglo-American historical sociologists, concerning, for example, the institutional capacity to exercise control over foreign policy and changes in this capacity, as well as changes in the character of war. If it is no longer big wars between states that dominate conflicts across the world, do we not have to conceive of the connection between war and democracy in a quite different way as well? Might we not raise the—provocative but far from implausible—prospect that a free press has by no means led modern-day democracies to become less violent but merely to avoid big wars, instead privileging the smaller but equally dirty methods of covert operations and limited conflict (Cohen 1994, 218; Rengger 2000, 120)? What methods of control might be applied to such operations and interventions (Müller 2004, 41)? With respect to these questions the position of the "postmodern" armed forces is naturally of much interest, as is the contemporary Europe-wide shift away from conscription armies to professional ones, along with the concomitant shift in the armed forces' responsibilities (Shaw 1991; Dandeker 1994). Again, none of these questions is easy to answer. But it is these questions—and not so much the abstract issue of whether democracies wage war on one another—that we must address if we wish to gain a clearer view of the dynamics of contemporary global conflicts.

■ ■ ■

The problem of changes in the armed forces' role has recently attracted a lot of attention, though only by a rather circuitous route, including the theoretically constricted social scientific debate on so-called failed states. While the discussion of democracy and peace suffered from a narrow, monothematic focus on types of political system, another kind of one-sidedness was evident in the study of privatization, marketization, and "capitalist penetration."

The debate on "failed states" or state decline began at a point when the modernization theorists' optimism about the development of the so-called Third World countries was gradually evaporating (see also Hein 2005, 6ff., and Erdmann 2003, 278). By the 1970s at the latest, it had become clear to most development experts that many (though *not* all) of the states that had gained independence after 1945 were afflicted by a depressing degree of economic stagnation. Regardless of which specific causes the relevant experts believed they could identify to explain this (and there were of course plenty of candidates for such "decisive" factors depending on their theoretical persuasion), they did at least agree that economic success is crucially linked with stable legal and governmental structures. This prompted more detailed study of governmental and political processes in the impoverished regions of the world (processes that were considered problematic) and examination of what distinguished these areas from Western Europe and its history or from the comparatively successful developmental path of non-Western societies in parts of Asia.

As early as 1982, in a well-regarded essay entitled "Why Africa's Weak States Persist" Robert H. Jackson and Carl G. Rosberg had laid key foundations for the debate that soon commenced on processes of state collapse; they highlighted the curious paradox that most states in what they refer to as "Black Africa," in other words the continent south of the Sahara, have managed to retain their legal status despite pervasive violence and despite numerous rebellions and uprisings. Clearly, the weakness of the state in this region has not led to its downfall. However weak they may be, these states continue to exist, mainly because they are recognized by the international community. On this view, it is bodies such as the UN and the Organization of African Unity that guarantee the survival of these "states," though they quite obviously lack every characteristic of functioning statehood (such as a monopoly on violence, well-organized administrative system, and governable state territory). According to Jackson and Rosberg, as a result of this external guarantee of a state's existence, the process of state formation here will be quite different from that in Europe and will not, therefore, lead to stable conditions. In Europe, the *institutional* process of state formation beginning in the early modern period, in other words the creation of efficient state institutions, preceded its *legal* counterpart; in terms of their institutional structure, the European states emerged *before* a legally regulated state system. This meant that, because they lacked legal protection, weak and dysfunctional states simply went under. In Africa, during and after the period of decolonization, this was turned on its head. When the African states were established, there already existed a highly developed international law and, in the shape of the United Nations, a global community which, at least in legal terms, protected all its members—in other words, all those states that had joined the organization. As a result, states were and are kept alive because of the preserving effect of international law, despite them rarely achieving any sort of stable institutional structure or losing whatever stability they may have possessed.

This discussion, which initially focused on Africa and a few other regions, subsequently became more theoretically ambitious. In the 1990s

Canadian political scientist Kalevi J. Holsti (b. 1935) published *The State, War, and the State of War* (1996), a benchmark work in that it went much further in systematizing the connection between war and the forms of statehood than had Jackson and Rosberg. This direct focus on violence and war seemed imperative partly because, after the fall of the Soviet Union and thus the end of a comparatively stable bipolar world order, the impression grew that violent conflicts were on the increase. Holsti (1996, 82) argued that only in those parts of the world in which there are strong states—in other words, states capable of demonstrating authority and demanding loyalty on the basis of functioning institutions—is there any prospect of peaceful conditions in the first place. If such stable statehood is lacking, this immediately calls into doubt the affiliation of regions or sections of the population to the political community; and it is only a matter of time before secessionist movements take off and the state begins to disintegrate. "The conditions of weak states . . . almost guarantee armed conflict . . ." (136). In this connection, Holsti also pointed out that most of the wars fought after 1945 were not really fueled from outside, not even during the Cold War, when the two superpowers played a seemingly decisive role. In fact, their causes were to be found internal to societies, which again points to the importance of functioning states.

As states grew increasingly weak or collapsed in certain regions of the world, basic political science concepts were no longer seen as universally valid. Scholars noted, for instance, that the notion of "sovereignty" found in constitutional and international law is little more than a bad joke with respect to these crumbling states, as their power centers hardly ever manage to enforce laws throughout the *entire* state territory, raise taxes and thus develop the country's infrastructure, and so on. So Trutz von Trotha (b. 1946), who—exceptionally among German sociologists—has dealt in depth with this topic, refers merely to "parasovereignty," because in certain parts of the world a cohesive and essentially "sovereign" actor that controls the police and armed forces has been replaced by "a horizontal system of competing regional and local security-providing regimes" (see von Trotha 2005, 33; see also von Trotha 2000). In view of this lack of state authority, von Trotha believes, small or sometimes large groups tend to arm themselves and become embroiled in an often long and terrible war with enormous costs for the civilian population, if it is still possible to distinguish between soldiers and civilians in the first place. It is therefore no surprise that this seemingly omnipresent violence has often been central to the definition of so-called failed states: "*Failed* states are tense, deeply conflicted, dangerous, and contested bitterly by warring factions.

In most failed states, government troops battle armed revolts led by one or more rivals. Occasionally, the official authorities in a failed state face two or more insurgencies, varieties of civil unrest, different degrees of communal discontent, and a plethora of dissent directed at the state and at groups within the state" (Rotberg 2004, 5; emphasis in original).[12]

So to a certain extent the collapse of state order seems to bring in its wake the Hobbesian state of nature, raising the question, of much relevance to social theory, as to which patterns and dynamics a given violent event entails. How can we explain large-scale and, above all, enduring violence, and can it be captured with the traditional concept of war? It was German ethnologist and sociologist Georg Elwert (1947–2005) who suggested a new theoretical approach to the problem of violence with the concept of the "market in violence" (Elwert 1997). The assertion contained within this concept was that the existence of "spaces open to violence," in which there is no (longer a) state monopoly on violence, may lead to a spiral of violence propelled by economic motives. Precisely because, in an economy already damaged by violence, theft and robbery are the only activities that promise any return, both individual and collective actors are in a position to deploy violence rationally and make it a permanent feature.

This idea of *markets* in violence, based largely on rational choice premises, gained much plausibility in part because, at around the same time, French economists in particular produced analyses of civil war that demonstrated, among other things, that in many regions of the world armed conflicts are kept alive by humanitarian intervention (Jean/Rufin 1999). These civil wars, it is claimed, have lasted so long only because they have been fueled from outside by remittances from so-called diaspora communities or by international humanitarian aid projects; this has enabled the warring parties to avail themselves of vital resources on an ongoing basis. It is this that has perpetuated war.[13] At the same time, these open economies of war are claimed to have crucially influenced the structures of violence, so that guerrillas, for example, have increasingly endeavored to control ports, airports, and other places of transhipment through which (humanitarian) supplies flow. Once this has occurred, the following constellation ensues. The political and thus economic support of the masses becomes superfluous; the resources vital to waging war can be requisitioned without mass support, resulting in an essentially endless spiral of violence. Political goals are mostly pushed into the background, and war becomes a business, beyond all political considerations.

From the early 1990s at the latest, the debate on "failed states" went hand in hand with discussion of shifts in the nature of statehood as such, shifts that seemed in evidence even in "robust" Western nation-states. The discourse of globalization that began at this point inevitably had to deal with the phenomenon of the nation-state, its spread and future. Quite incompatible views emerged in this context. While some referred to the disappearance or retreat of the state (Strange 1996; Albrow 1998), others saw merely a change of form but otherwise emphasized that the nation-state should continue to take center stage in social scientific analyses of the contemporary world (Weiss 1999; Mann 1997; Fligstein 2001; Holsti 2004). Regardless of the extreme positions put forward by this or that scholar, however, it became clear that we require a typology that reflects the historical and geographic variability of modern states, while being careful not to endorse the notion that every deviation from the European state model of the 1950s and 1960s suggests the decline of the state. It was in this context that scholars began to question whether the relationship between state and market has not changed fundamentally, with direct consequences for state structures. Philip Bobbitt (b. 1948) argued along these lines when he made the striking suggestion that we should characterize the present-day form of the state—emerging after the age of the classical nation-state—as the "market state," which has by no means become impotent, but which does operate in line with different principles from those in the past. These "market states" have to struggle, for example, with the contradiction that while they have centralized ever more decision-making processes and drawn in powers from formerly unsupervised fields, they have also lost authority, to "institutions, including deregulated corporations, which are in but not of the State, NGOs . . . , which are in but not of the market, and clandestine military networks and terrorist groups, which set up proto-markets in security and function as proto-states at war" (Bobbitt 2002, 234). This peculiar interpenetration of state and market-like processes captured so well by Bobbitt, this emergence of hybrid structures, has in fact been much in evidence since the 1990s, particularly in the realm of state-sanctioned violence (see also Hibou 1998). In this context, commentators also referred to a new "preventative security order" characterized among other things by a very different discourse of security, especially with regard to the growth of the private security industry (von Trotha 2003a, 56). A major private market in security has emerged in the Western nation-states, featuring not only private police forces but now even private *military* contractors. This was

interpreted as a sign of how much even military force, once the key hallmark of state power, is now subject to a process of marketization; here,
continental Europe appears to be set on a path already well trodden in
North America as well as Britain.

Although every state in Europe, with the exception of Britain, had
conscription before the end of the Cold War, it has subsequently become
the exception, and now exists in only a few Western European countries—even Germany recently abolished it (Haltiner 1998; Jehn/Selden
2002). In this region (as occurred earlier in North America), conscription
armies seem to have outlived their usefulness and are increasingly being
replaced by professional ones. It is certainly true that pure conscription-
based armies rarely existed even in the age of the classical nation-state, as
a substantial portion of military personnel were always professional soldiers. Nonetheless, it is quite clear that the decision by many states to
forgo conscription has introduced a further process of marketization at
the core of state activity. The personnel of state power is no longer "con-
scripted" as a matter of course. It is the pressure of the market that regu-
lates what staff (now including women; see Enloe 2000) the state has at
its disposal in the military sphere. The classical triad of civil obligations—
liability for tax, compulsory education, and conscription (for male citizens)—has thus collapsed; citizens are still forced to register with the tax
authorities and attend school, but not to sign up. This move away from
mass armies and the turn to much smaller professionalized forces also
has side effects with respect to the marketization of violence.

What is clear is that the large-scale downsizing of mass armies in the
highly developed industrial societies has set free a considerable military
potential now accessible via the market. This applies not only to (surplus)
weapons but also to military personnel, large numbers of whom have
sought and continue to seek new employment opportunities (Leander
2002). Unemployed former military personnel formed the basis for the
rise of the "privatized military industry," that is, the numerical proliferation of private military companies (often referred to as PMCs), which
now enjoy a massive turnover (Avant 2004, 154; on this complex, see
also the multiauthored volume by Jäger/Kümmel 2007). Of course, the
rise of PMCs is not due solely to the sudden increase in available personnel. What happened is that this supply of personnel met with social contexts well suited to those hybrid fusions of state and private structures
touched on earlier. The creation of private military companies—even if
only in terms of the outsourcing of certain support services for the various national armed forces—was in line with the general tendency to-

ward privatization in a wide array of societal spheres. This shift was further accelerated by the fact that, especially in the highly industrialized states of the West, warfare has become ever more complex. It is now almost impossible to wage war without support from civilian specialists, as evident in the military action by the United States (and its allies) in Iraq, where a considerable amount of military "input" came from private firms.

There is no great appetite for the state regulation and supervision of these PMCs, and this is due in part to the significant benefits that accrue to those Western states that hire *private* military forces. Though cost-related arguments probably hold little water, as the outsourcing of logistical services is not financially beneficial (Avant 2004, 155), it is beyond dispute that in combat situations that may cost lives the use of private firms shields the hiring states from questions about the legitimacy of a given war. The civilian casualties caused by these private firms are not ascribed to the hiring state, and dead staff members are not fallen soldiers requiring public remembrance. So certain military sociologists are probably right to suspect that both the shift away from conscription and the increasing privatization and marketization of military violence enable Western states to wage (potentially more vigorous) wars, in whatever parts of the world, and usher in a renaissance in military violence as a more or less normal instrument of policy (Kernic 2004, 81).

This marketization of the military sphere not only has political consequences in the highly industrialized, mainly Western societies themselves and deadly consequences in those places, such as Iraq and Afghanistan, in which Western states were and are waging war. In fact these PMCs play a significant role in many Third World countries, though Western countries may be neither able nor willing to impose control in these cases. Here, a market in private military services that emerged in the West encounters the "markets in violence," described by Elwert, in Africa, Asia, Latin America, but also Europe (see the former Yugoslavia, Ehrke 2003).

As the territory of many—mostly Third World—countries fragments, there is a growing tendency among various local actors to employ PMCs, most of which are based in the highly developed industrial societies, to achieve short-term military superiority; the key question here is of course which of the parties (local warlords, regional powers, or the "servants" of what remains of the state machinery) can pay most, or pay anything at all (Lock 2003, 101; Ruf 2003: 81; see also Bendrath 1999). We are probably on safe ground in assuming that the proliferation of these PMCs further intensifies the spiral of violence. The very use of such private military

236 • Chapter 7

firms is likely to further delegitimize whatever state structures may still exist and lead to the progressive fragmentation of actual relations of domination, making the establishment of a state monopoly on violence an ever-more distant prospect (Leander 2005, 617). This is the case not least because PMCs operate in a market segment that obeys its own logic (of violence), a logic that does *not* culminate in an end to violence: in markets in violence, demand often creates its own supply. The more violence is perpetrated, the greater the demand for (protective) violence—as Charles Tilly (see p. 203) has claimed. This means that the providers of violence—and that includes the PMCs—have an interest in creating threatening scenarios that make a strong public impact. In the form of military consultant firms, they themselves are often crucially involved in the evaluation of threats (Leander 2005, 612ff.).

So all of this seems to suggest that the shift in the form of the Western nation-state is interacting in significant ways with state collapse in non-Western countries and may lead to forms of macroviolence that cannot be captured with a purely state-centered logic. The marketization of armed violence, the end of its embedding in state structures, may confirm the view suggested by Elwert that war or civil war has taken on market-like forms and can best be understood in light of the instrumentally rational action orientations of key actors. Elwert, however, also cautiously suggests that such economies of violence can exist over the long term only if the violence is underpinned by secondary motives (ideologies, etc.). So Elwert is quite aware of the *theoretical* question of whether—as he suggests in his essay's subtitle ("Observations on the Instrumental Rationality of Violence")—we can in fact analyze violence *solely* from instrumentally rational perspectives. And this point was to play a central role in the debate on so-called new wars.

It was Israeli military historian Martin van Creveld (b. 1946) who opened up this debate in 1991 with the spectacular thesis contained in his *The Transformation of War*. According to him, the conventional notion of war as a violent dispute between states, decided through large-scale battles, is long-since obsolete. Since the end of the Second World War at the latest, such wars—as he argues—have become far less important; they have been superseded by so-called LICs (low intensity conflicts), in which mainly nonstate groups attempt to challenge a state opponent enjoying far superior weaponry through a wide array of different strategies (ranging from guerrilla warfare to terrorism). Van Creveld also asserted that even during decolonization it was near impossible for the colonial powers' regular armed forces to win such LICs, which are every bit as terrible as "traditional" wars, and that this is still the case today—and indeed for all states: for those of the First and Second Worlds, but especially for those of the Third World. Because LICs offer such good prospects to the "weak," this form of conflict will shape world politics in the future as well; this means that a mentality informed by Clausewitz that puts its faith in the distinction between state, army, and people will be largely meaningless. Now and in the future, van Creveld concludes, wars will no longer be waged mainly between states, so the distinction between soldiers and civilians is no longer clear and will increasingly be ignored by the parties to war. The constant increase in the number of civilian casualties in the wars of the twentieth century tells its own grim story in this respect.

The debate kicked off by van Creveld quickly subdivided along various lines, with attempts being made to further systematize his arguments and also to produce a synthesis that connects the regional problem of "failed states" and the violence endemic to them with the new foreign policy and military challenges faced by Western states. The term "new wars" appeared, a term made known to a broad public in significant part by the contributions of political scientists Mary Kaldor in Britain and Herfried Münkler (b. 1951) in Germany. Kaldor (b. 1946) linked the typology of old versus new wars directly with phenomena of globalization, painting a fairly gloomy picture of global political developments as a whole. The "new wars," which according to Kaldor are distinguished by the new forms of criminal financing described above and by a comparatively low level of intensity, exhibit no clear "geo-political or ideological goals" (1999, 6), but this does not mean they are entirely unpolitical. Rather, these new wars must be interpreted as a reaction to exclusion from a comparatively affluent world; it is against this exclusion that a "politics of particularist identities" (ibid.) is mobilized, a politics that results in those forms of violence exhibiting the hallmarks of "new wars" mentioned above. In contrast to those who refer to markets in violence, Kaldor, who formulated her analysis mainly with a view to the conflict in Bosnia (which she has interpreted as a prototypical conflict of the globalized world), does not go so far as to emphasize only the instrumental rationality of the parties to violence. Kaldor at least grants the combatants—as victims of globalization, as it were—the political motive of a counterreaction to globalization, however diffuse a form this may take.

The desire for synthesis is also clearly evident in the work of Herfried Münkler. Münkler, however, presents more systematic arguments than

Kaldor because he is unusually aware of the history of thinking about war, prompting him to strive for conceptual clarity (1992; 2002). From a comparative historical perspective, his book *The New Wars* provides a typology of the most recent forms of warfare, including detailed accounts of the distinction between classical guerrilla warfare and terrorism and the problem of military intervention by Western democracies in troubled regions. Münkler's thesis is that "new wars" have three key characteristics: the denationalization or privatization, asymmetrization, and autonomization of armed violence (Münkler 2005, 3f.). "New wars" must be seen as directly connected with processes of state collapse that give "private" actors unprecedented scope for action; these wars rarely feature well-matched opponents, so that there is no longer any real possibility of symmetrical battles between armies, and attacks on the civilian population or massacres predominate; and, finally, the violence perpetrated in these "new wars" is no longer embedded within a military framework but has taken on a life of its own.

Hostile to evolutionist assumptions and rationalization theory, Münkler takes the view that, in contrast to the conflicts that took place in pre- and early modern Europe, the "new wars," waged mostly in the Third World, are not state-building wars. While war brought positive economic effects in its wake in Europe, because infrastructure had to be rationalized in order to wage it, this does not apply to "new wars." Here conflicts are waged with comparatively low-cost weapons, and funding usually comes from outside. So rather than the economy being developed in order to wage war, the economy itself takes on a violent character—as Münkler pointedly asserts: "In the new wars . . . force becomes the dominant element in exchange relations themselves—either by being bought in order to produce certain results, or because the exchange of equivalents is overlaid or completely replaced with extortion and open threats of violence. Whereas classical inter-state wars are no longer worthwhile, because they cost more than they yield for each of the participants, the new wars are highly lucrative for many of the participants, because in the short term the force used in them yields more than it costs—and the long-term costs are borne by others" (77).

Finally, Münkler underlines that the term "civil war" can no longer be meaningfully applied to "new wars" because the aim here is no longer to gain power within the state in order to implement political projects of one kind or another (23). Because they are embedded in "shadow globalization," in an essentially criminal war economy, in a sense these "new wars" wage themselves; they are no longer instruments of policy (33/34), as Münkler attempts to bring out while moving well away from the political interpretation of these "new wars" (underlining exclusion from the globalized world) at least hinted at in Kaldor's work.

Overall, with their accounts of "new wars," both Münkler and Kaldor advocate the thesis of an epochal military and political rupture. The "Westphalian system" founded in the seventeenth century, they believe, was based on the territorial state and the assumption of symmetry between actors within the international state system. This symmetry no longer exists in this form—and neither does the system of war that formerly applied. "New wars" now predominate.

But this claim of an epochal shift is open to criticism. Stathis N. Kalyvas (2001), for example, has pointed out that it is wrong to draw such a sharp distinction between "old" and "new" wars. If, for instance, accounts of "new wars" allude to systematic looting, we should not necessarily conclude that they are motivated solely by economics. So-called warlords are often motivated by a fusion of economic *and* state-building motives, as in every process of state formation in history. Without knowing how subsequent history was to unfold, modern-day analysts of thirteenth-century Europe would probably come to the conclusion that the ruling cliques were nothing but "robber barons" devoid of political ambitions—warlords, in other words. Yet in many cases, though this came to light only much later, their actions were highly successful. Their zones of influence did sometimes give rise to states, so it may be rather precipitate to deny warlords in the contemporary Third World all political ambition or impact from the outset.[14] Conversely, the strong emphasis on economic motives in analyses of these allegedly "new wars" risks romanticizing "old wars" and civil wars. No one, after all, would seriously dispute that looting has always been a feature of combat, even in the civil wars that occurred during decolonization in the 1950s and 1960s. Further, even the ideological element of these "old" civil wars could be quite marginal: often, networks existing between various groups, such as those based on kinship, were more important in the formation of war coalitions than ideology or politics, which often made an impact only as a result of superpower intervention (Kalyvas 2001, 107; see also Brzoska 2004 and Chojnacki 2004).

What is more, the state formation in Europe advanced by force of arms had its own peculiarities, which simply did not apply elsewhere (especially in the nineteenth century), revealing a Eurocentric aspect to the notion of "new wars." The wars that occurred in the context of the Latin American independence movement did *not* have the same state-building effects as in Europe. Further, even in the so-called age of nation-states, symmetrical wars between states tended to be the exception. In the nineteenth century, the rule was in fact "low-intensity conflicts," at least if we break away from a perspective focused purely on Central Europe: "[T]here is no obvious correlation between the degree of a state's development and the deadliness of its warfare. Much of the killing in this period arose from low-intensity conflicts that were ongoing, undecided, periodically genocidal, had recurring edges of terrorism and may be thought of as local wars" (Geyer/Bright 1996, 624). So many of the key features of "new wars" already apply to the nineteenth century, which should make us cautious about embracing assertive theories of epochal rupture.

Finally, we must ask whether the broader theoretical structure that generally frames analyses of "new wars" is truly persuasive, and whether its exponents have fleshed it out in a convincing way. In Kaldor's work for example the idea is that the losers from globalization generate a "politics of identity" that then leads to the escalation of violence described as "new wars." But claims of a "reaction to" are rather imprecise and almost always apply in one way or another, particularly given that the concept of globalization is so broad and nebulous that every conceivable process of change may be subsumed under it; "reaction to" seems to be more of an "ad-hoc argument" than a genuine explanation. Even Münkler, whose theoretical aspirations are greater than Kaldor's, largely fails to explain how exactly his ideas on "new wars" relate to the classical social theories discussed in this book—to liberal, Marxist, and Kantian ideas on the prospects for peace. Münkler makes the occasional critical reference to these views, but he remains too much of a Clausewitzian to systematically examine the social embedding of wars. But this might be just what we need in order to ground the debate on "new wars." How else can we assess the adequacy of the notion of "markets in violence" (which leans heavily on the rational choice perspective) than by discussing the extent to which the processes of economization emphasized in theories of modernization and globalization affect other forms of action (namely acts of violence)? How plausible is the claim made by some protagonists of the "new wars" thesis that these conflicts now revolve solely around economic utility maximization rather than ideological concerns? And how would such a stance relate to the references in Kaldor, but also in the work of Münkler himself, to the religious and ethnic causes of "new wars," which can hardly be traced back to economic structures or utility-maximizing individual or collective behavior? It remains unclear whether the concept of "new wars" really has much to offer those wishing to advance social theoretical debates.[15]

▪ ▪ ▪

The 1980s and 1990s—as we have seen—saw the advance of very different concepts of war and peace. Whereas the macrolevel process of democratization stood center stage in the debate on a "democratic peace," a process that many, following Immanuel Kant, hoped would directly contribute to establishing peace, the discussion of "failed states" and "new wars" was quite different. Here too a macroprocess often mentioned by sociologists was central, namely the progressive economization of the world. A key question was therefore to what extent the traditional structure and modus operandi of Western states are being changed by processes of marketization and deregulation and to what extent the privatization of military violence corresponds with the markets in violence found in the Third and Fourth Worlds. In contrast to the so-called Kantians' diagnosis in the debate on a democratic peace, the analysis here was generally pessimistic: the capitalist penetration of the world threatens to enduringly undermine political stability and encourage conflictual processes. It is no surprise that from the late 1990s on, partly in response to the attempts at theorization described above, another macroprocess moved to the center of attention, namely the hegemonic penetration of social relations across the world. It is the debate on the American empire that preoccupies many authors, though there are plenty of links here with the topic of "failed states."[16]

It was already apparent during the Clinton administration that the United States no longer acted on a multilateral basis; instead, it pursued a foreign policy that clearly prioritizes American interests, increasingly claiming the right to intervene all over the world. This was combined with an unwillingness to accept any restrictions on its own actions. What was still being sold with rhetorical aplomb and thus to some extent camouflaged under Clinton later became increasingly obvious—at least since the arrival of George W. Bush and the aftermath of 9/11 and the Iraq War (see the excellent account by Menzel 2004, 93–151). In any case, such policies could no longer be straightforwardly interpreted in terms of the classical power politics of the nation-state; the economic and military significance of the United States was far too great for that. Here unilateralism could only mean that we are dealing with either a new hegemony or an American Empire.

The debate reached fever pitch as leading thinkers vied over the concept of "empire," with very different theoretical and political motives coming into play; the question of the link between war and imperium was discussed with corresponding antagonism. One of the critics of American foreign policy was French historian and political scientist Emmanuel Todd (b. 1951), whose *After the Empire: The Breakdown of the American Order* (2003; *Après l'empire. Essai sur la décomposition du système américain*, 2002) was provocative even in its title. Todd asked himself why, within the international community, the United States was behaving in such a destabilizing way, why it was so recklessly pursuing a unilateral policy disturbing to most other states. The answer he came up with was to some extent psychological. According to Todd, American elites are (rightly) afraid that America will be marginalized, and this is why they are acting so irrationally in the foreign policy sphere. American power now rests on shaky foundations. The American economy has long since lost its world-beating status and is dependent on massive inflows of foreign capital, which will inevitably have political consequences. This (already apparent) loss of political power, he says, is currently being papered over by a "theatre of dramatized militarism" (Todd 2003 [2002], 21) as the United States rushes around the world intervening militarily in one place after another, but this can no longer stabilize American power. This is reinforced by the fact that, because of an often very one-sided foreign policy, in any event one not conceived in line with universalist criteria, the United States has squandered much of its credit in the world over the past few decades: "Two types of 'imperial' resources are especially lacking in the American case. First, its power to constrain militarily and economically is insufficient for maintaining the current levels of exploitation of the planet; and second, its ideological universalism is in decline and does not allow it, as before, to treat individuals and whole peoples equally as the leading guarantor of their peace and prosperity" (77). This is precisely why—Todd concludes—the American empire has not led to a stable and peaceful world.

Michael Mann's analysis *Incoherent Empire* (2003) is not fundamentally different from Todd's, though he argues in a more systematic way. Mann already sees imperial tendencies in American foreign policy under Clinton, but in his view it was the election of George W. Bush, the increasing political influence of the Christian Right, and finally September 11,

2001, that prompted a decisive turn toward imperialism (2003, 8f.). From a comparative historical perspective, he asks whether the imperial strategy adopted by the United States, which he himself firmly rejects for normative reasons, has any real chance of success. Mann thinks not, because imperial policies can no longer be pursued as in the eighteenth or nineteenth century owing to a completely different global political situation. Though the United States clearly occupies a hegemonic position simply because of its enormous military expenditure (which makes up 40 percent of all such spending worldwide), its actual manpower resources are comparatively small. With just 5 percent of troops worldwide, American power can be maintained only through a network of military bases strewn, or in fact carefully positioned, across the world. The Americans are certainly making a huge effort to build up such a network, but it is clear that this will not result in the pacification of large areas. This—according to Mann—is the key difference from British imperialism in the eighteenth and nineteenth century. In this era, it was quite possible to pacify territories by recruiting indigenous troops and through the British method of "indirect rule." This is now unthinkable because nationalism has become a global phenomenon; there can be no question of America openly intervening in other countries as the British did so self-evidently and unproblematically. Because of this nationalism "local allies" are in short supply (27ff.), so the preconditions for imperial policies are worse than they were before the First World War. Even entirely new weapons systems and America's vast military superiority over all other powers cannot fill this gap. Mann therefore believes that the imperial policies of the United States will in fact have paradoxical effects, provoking increased resistance in other countries and further strengthening international terrorism, ultimately achieving the exact opposite of what the "new imperialists" originally had in mind—weakening, not strengthening, the United States' global political status.

It is no surprise that within the debate on the American imperium some intellectuals have openly defended the policies of the Bush administration or called for a more openly imperial approach. Examples include economist Deepak Lal, who was born in India but teaches in Los Angeles, and British historian Niall Ferguson. Lal (b. 1940) simply reverses the premises of dominant ideas on the structure and functioning of the modern state system, claiming that such a system was a historical exception and imperial rule has been the norm in world politics since time immemorial (Lal 2004, xiv). He then links this claim with the thesis that imperia have always been the guarantors of prosperity and peace. So there is no need to mourn the end of the Westphalian system. Instead, according to Lal, the aim should be to push the United States toward a self-confident imperial policy. "The order provided by empires has been essential for the working of the benign processes of globalization, which promote prosperity. Globalization is not a new phenomenon and has always been associated in the past with empires. This book argues that not since the fall of the Roman Empire has there been a potential imperial power like the U.S. today" (xix). Because the collapse of imperial rule threatens peace and prosperity, the United States must pursue a resolute imperial strategy and policies similar to those of Britain in the late eighteenth and nineteenth centuries. On this view, the task of the American Empire would be to maintain peace in order to facilitate free trade. Only through such a liberal imperialism, though one that must not attack the worldview, morality, or lifestyles of other cultures, would there be any prospect of global prosperity. "If the purpose of the present Pax, as it was for the British in the nineteenth century, is to promote and maintain a liberal international economic order (LIEO), the relevant liberties are civil and economic. Political liberty, as we shall see, may be desirable for all sorts of reasons, but to put it above domestic order can damage the LIEO by setting up that feared clash of civilizations. The purpose of the American imperium, in my view, should be as it was for the British in the nineteenth century, to promote that globalization which leads to modernity. The ensuing prosperity will do much more to fend off threats to peace than attempts to thrust Western cultural mores and values down recalcitrant throats. What the new imperialists need to remember, I will argue, is that the modernization they rightly seek in the world does not need and may in fact be hindered by attempts to promote Westernization" (65/66). To put it in a nutshell, what Lal is propagating is a free-trade imperialism on the British model without the missionary components so typical of the Bush administration, with its rhetoric of democratization and human rights. The global prosperity that this would engender—Lal argues, drawing openly on modernization theory—would minimize ideological and religious conflicts and thus stabilize the United States' imperial power status over the long term.

Niall Ferguson's work contains a similar romanticization of the imperial past (*Colossus*, 2004). Ferguson (b. 1964) is in no doubt that an American imperium already exists:

It goes without saying that it is a liberal democracy and market economy, though its polity has some illiberal characteristics and its economy a surprisingly high level of state intervention. . . . It is primarily concerned with its own security and maintaining international communications and, secondarily, with securing access to raw materials (principally, though not exclusively, oil). It is also in the business of providing a limited number of public goods: peace, by intervening against some bellicose regimes and in some civil wars; freedom of the seas and skies for trade; and a distinctive form of "conversion" usually called Americanization, which is carried out less by old-style Christian missionaries than by the exporters of American consumer goods and entertainment. (Ferguson 2004, 13)

He therefore calls for the United States, which still cultivates an anti-imperial self-image because of its revolutionary history and its struggle for independence from Britain in the eighteenth century, to self-confidently embrace its imperial status in the world. There is a dire need for a liberal imperium, because "many parts of the world would benefit from a period of American rule" (2). Such an imperialism would also be a good thing because—and here comes the direct link with the debate on "failed states"—only intervention by the United States can prevent state collapse in many parts of the world. "Might it not be that for *some* countries some form of imperial governance, meaning a partial or complete suspension of their national sovereignty, might be better than full independence, not just for a few months or years but for decades? Paradoxically, might the only hope for such countries ever to become successful sovereign states (especially if we regard democracy as a key criterion of success) be a period of political dependence and limited power for their representative institutions?" (170; emphasis in original). In much the same way as Lal, Ferguson points out that decolonization, particularly after 1945, ultimately did the independent states little good. Within the context of struggles for independence, imperialism was wrongly identified as the cause of the problems of the non-Western world. In fact, many of the problems only really set in once colonial rule had come to an end, ranging from growing poverty to never-ending armed conflicts (see 173). Only an "effective liberal empire" (301), a role only the United States is currently capable of playing, can put an end to this state of discord and achieve global political stability, though only if the political elites in Washington take on this task.

What is so irritating about these defenses of America's imperial aspirations is the reference to the British Empire, which functions as a role model for both Lal and Ferguson. The remarkable thing here is not so much the romantic, idealized view of that empire, one a good number of the peoples colonized by the British would have disagreed with. What is really odd is that Britain is defined so straightforwardly as an imperium in the first place. The obvious question here is when exactly the British Empire was ever unchallenged. In the late eighteenth century, when it lost its American colonies? In the early nineteenth century, when it had to fend off Napoleon? In the second half of the nineteenth century, when new rivals were soon to appear in the shape of Germany and the United States? If we try to answer these questions seriously, then doubts immediately arise as to whether the British Empire was ever really an imperium. It is true—as Michael Mann and others underline—that Britain's power was substantial in the nineteenth century; the British were very good at playing other nations off against one another. Yet it would be false to state that Britain was truly hegemonic during this period, let alone a genuine imperium (Mann 2003, 264). The country was too dependent on the cooperation or acquiescence of other major powers. But even if we disregard all of this and assume the existence of a British imperium, it is surprising that neither Lal nor Ferguson put forward any real arguments to explain how this empire could collapse so quickly and why it was unable even to prevent the carnage of the First World War. Those who recommend the construction of a new imperium, this time an American one, would be convincing only if they could show that an implosion of imperial power can be ruled out *in future*, that there would be no serious attempts to take up arms against the imperial power, and that the imperial peace will in fact be more stable than anything that could be achieved through conventional foreign policy within a more or less egalitarian system of states. But Lal and Ferguson can do none of this, leaving their arguments looking quite unconvincing.

German scholar Herfried Münkler has tried to follow a middle course between severe criticism of American imperialism and apologia à la Lal and Ferguson. Münkler leaves us in no doubt that, apart from anything else, we must understand the debate on empires as a reaction to the increasing number of "failed states," the multiple problems afflicting the United Nations when it comes to taking action and coordinating its actions, and the terrorist attacks of September 2001: "As discussion resumed on the political-economic model of empire, it soon became clear that it promised precisely what the UN-centred international community and the network of metropolises were incapable of delivering: namely, a decisive push into areas without a state, in order at least to prevent genocide and massacres, and to protect the fragile lines of communication among the world's great economic centres. The first of these tasks now traded under the name of humanitarian military intervention, the second under that of the war on terror" (Münkler 2007, 148).

As ever, in his comparative historical analysis of imperia, Münkler is concerned with conceptual clarification, with differentiating precisely, for example, between hegemonic and imperial political entities. Further, in contrast to Lal und Ferguson, he is not content merely to assess the role of the United States politically. *Empires: The Logic of World Domination from Ancient Rome to the United States* (2007) is also a theoretically ambitious attempt to work out a theory of imperial power, inasmuch as he systematically examines its preconditions and consequences. Münkler underlines that imperia, as a result of their own ideological claims (he refers here to the self-sacralization of imperial power; Münkler 2007, 85), often subject their own political decision makers to peculiar constraints. Because of this ideological content, imperial projects have self-disciplining effects that often make it difficult to change course or to place limits on imperial policies. The United States in particular may face increasing problems because of the contradiction between imperial reason and an imperial mission rooted in American history (the aspiration to democratize; insistence on the worldwide enforcement of human rights, etc.):

> In order to hold its subglobal world, an astute imperial policy should keep out of the problems of the global world and protect itself from them by drawing 'imperial boundaries with the barbarians'; what happened outside would then concern the empire only if it posed a threat to its own security. To a large extent, the policy of long-lasting empires—the Chinese and the Roman, in particular—was geared to such a perspective. But it is scarcely an option in the age of democracy and media saturation: it would continually contradict the imperial mission of the United States, and without such a projection of moral purpose the US empire would lose much of its strength. To put it plainly, it may be that the American empire will founder not on external enemies but on the moral overload associated with its mission, because this makes it impossible to maintain the required indifference to the external world. (154)

What is more, because of the constant "booty pressure," *democratic* imperia all too readily lose sight of imperial reason: under democratic conditions, it is difficult to communicate the need for military intervention, particularly if there is no clear benefit to the imperium's citizens. But the strategic considerations on which imperial policies are based do not equate to such straightforward cost-benefit calculations, which is why this too may cause problems in the United States with respect to a rational imperial strategy (157).

Overall, though, Münkler considers it quite possible for the United States to pursue an imperial policy, in part because it has achieved a certain unassailability as a result of its superior weapons technology (118). But his assessment that the "classical forms of guerrilla warfare lost much of their capacity to raise the costs of imperial *domination*" (ibid.; emphasis added) is problematic, at least if we take the concept of power seriously. Münkler is probably right that guerrillas and warlords will not pose any immediate threat to the imperial power of the United States; and it is also true that because of their hopelessly inferior technology, when guerrillas and warlords take up arms these days they are more likely to destroy their own societies than vanquish the United States (131f.). But stealth bombers and cruise missiles are ill-suited to establishing power over a territory, let alone securing such power over the long term, thus achieving "pacification." An imperium that only ever demonstrates its power now and then through the use or threat of force is different in structure from one that literally *dominates*. It is likely to divest itself of all sources of legitimacy very quickly if it is unable to ensure a stable peace—quite apart from the important question of whether an imperium that has almost no prospect of achieving an imperial peace, and must therefore constantly intervene militarily, can be financed over the long term. Münkler (rightly) places great emphasis on the connection between state collapse and self-perpetuating violence on the one hand and the debate on the American empire on the other. In light of this, we cannot plausibly be optimistic about the future prospects of such an imperium, one that fails to guarantee peace. So it is doubtful that we can evade the wealth of social theories on war and peace elaborated in the preceding chapters by placing our hopes in a world pervaded by the power of a new imperium.

The debates on a new imperium and on the wars waged by imperia, as we have seen, were often centrally concerned with analyzing the contemporary world. Within the context of these intellectual debates, however, very different and primarily historical topics, such as "colonial wars," again received much attention. The key questions here were whether and, if so, how colonial wars differ from other military conflicts; whether colonial wars in Africa and Asia in the nineteenth century were discrete events or, given the oppression of the indigenous population, a more or less permanent state of affairs (Wesseling 1997, 4f.); and whether the experience of colonial violence served as a horrifying inspiration for the war waged in Europe and associated policy of extermination in the second third of the twentieth century—a point raised sixty years ago by Hannah Arendt[17] in her *Origins of Totalitarianism* (1973 [1951]). To begin with this last aspect, most researchers seem to be cautiously skeptical about Arendt's thesis, as colonial wars were neither "total wars" nor always genocidal. So the effects of colonial wars on European societies should not be exaggerated, though the impact of colonialism as such on colonizing societies (let alone areas under imperial rule) can scarcely be overstated. But since it is very difficult to verify Arendt's thesis, not least for methodological reasons, the first question, on the characteristics of "colonial wars," seems more important when it comes to the relationship between social theory and war. We are however immediately confronted with the problem that the term "colonial wars" is often applied to very different types of conflict: those between states (see the Spanish-American War at the end of the nineteenth century) are just as often referred to as "colonial wars," as are wars of liberation (see the American War of Independence in the 1770s and 1780s) or typical wars of conquest, such as those waged by Europeans in Africa in the second half of the nineteenth century (Wesseling 1997).

When it comes to recent research, it is these wars of colonial conquest that have attracted particular interest, inasmuch as they were waged "not merely to defeat the opponents but also to annex their territory and to subject their population" (Wesseling 1997, 4). In contrast to war in the European theater (and here we are reminded of the ideas of Carl Schmitt, see p. 170ff.), colonial wars of conquest, though not waged as 'total wars' in the sense of mobilizing the entire population of the imperial nations, were unlimited with respect to their goal. This was the total subjection of a population and its territory. "In 'normal' wars in European history, the war aims were generally limited. The peace conditions often included territorial provisions, but normally they concerned only a portion of the territory. In colonial wars, in contrast, war aims were absolute. Colonial conquerors came to stay. Their aim was the permanent and total subjection of the population, or, in other words, the establishment of a lasting peace" (Wesseling 1997, 5). One of the key reasons for these unlimited goals, and this is another characteristic of colonial wars of conquest, was that the imperial powers claimed for themselves the status of superior civilization and regarded the subjugated population or the people they aimed to subjugate as inferior, generally with racist rationales (Klein/

Schumacher 2006, 11). In view of this "colonial situation" (Balandier 1951), it comes as no surprise that despite the apparently enduring stability of imperial rule in many parts of the world, there was a need to use force if the non-European peoples were to remain in a state of subjugation: violent police operations, punitive expeditions, and indeed massacres were part of the everyday reality of imperial rule. German sociologist Trutz von Trotha goes so far as to assert that the massacre was absolutely central to the development of colonial rule: because it lacked all legitimacy, this was the only way to ensure that no one was left in any doubt about the Europeans' superiority. The massacre was no accident but rather a constitutive component of colonial rule—and this applies even to those territories that were viewed as unproblematic and peaceful from the vantage point of the European metropolis (see von Trotha 1994, esp. p. 42ff; von Trotha 1999).

In this sense, it is by no means outlandish to assert not only that colonial wars of conquest had unlimited aims but that it was seldom possible to clearly distinguish such conflicts from peace (Walter 2006, 23). From the conquerors' perspective, there was a constant need to engage in violent "pacification," though whether colonial warfare turned genocidal very much depended on the external circumstances, such as various racist prejudices or the presence of aggressive white settlers (Steinmetz 2003; von Trotha 2003b; Kreienbaum 2010). Military tactics alone could create a setting ripe for genocide: because of the asymmetrical nature of warfare, the imperial forces often had great difficulty distinguishing clearly between combatants and noncombatants, such that the latter could all too easily become targets. But to repeat, genocide was not the norm, so it was not inevitable. There were other ideas on how to oppress people and other means of doing so, and these were implemented quite systematically, with the "establishment of camps, the use of barbed wire to seal off large areas of the front, weapons and food blockades, resettlement of the indigenous population, the destruction of fields and livestock and finally aerochemical warfare" (Brogini Künzi 2006, 274; Schumacher 2006, 112; Malinowski 2009) being tried individually or together to control rebellious populations. These means were still being deployed in the Vietnam War, as exemplified by the "Strategic Hamlet Program" (see, e.g., Bergerud 1991, 50ff.).

With almost complete decolonization after 1945 (see Rothermund 1998), the colonial war of conquest became a thing of the past. However, and this takes us back once again to the debates on how to interpret the contemporary world, it is becoming ever clearer that, in terms of its effects, the colonial era is far from being over and done with, and that this insight has consequences for the analysis of modern-day wars. If we cite aspects of the influential though not uncontested interpretation of imperialism put forward by Ronald Robinson (see esp. 1977 and 1986),[18] according to which Great Britain's free-trade imperialism was in fact the norm, and thus military interventions and occupation of territories were generally the exception in the classical age of imperialism (according to Robinson, such occupations were required primarily in cases where the imperial power could not rely on the collaboration of the indigenous elites), the parallels with the contemporary world become obvious. The similarities here are not necessarily linked with the fact that there was a need for military intervention in, or occupation of, non-Western regions of the world in order to "open them up" for free trade, as in China in the nineteenth century. These similarities have instead to do with the fact that nowadays, even if they no longer see themselves as imperial powers, economically and militarily potent nation-states can and will exert their influence wherever their economic and strategic-military interests are at stake—and this includes military intervention. We should not expect a continuous period of war or peace, but one in which war will flare up again and again, at least sporadically. In this sense, then, the difference between the classical age of imperialism described by Robinson and the contemporary era is not so great after all: recurring "small" and "new" wars, military interventions, and peace missions exhibit at least some characteristics whose similarities with the seemingly distant past are only too apparent. Free trade in itself—as the history of social theorizing on war from Montesquieu through Friedrich List to Ronald Robinson teaches us—no more guarantees peace than does globalization: both entail their own specific potential for conflict and thus the risk of war.[19]

Conclusion

NONE OF THE DEBATES on peace-engendering structures and processes that have taken place since the 1980s in social theory have produced convincing results. The thesis of the "democratic peace" has proved essentially unviable, at least with respect to the so-called Kantians' initial claim of global validity for their statements. The discussion of "failed states" and "new wars" has focused largely on processes of state decline or marketization but has done little to place these processes within a broader theoretical framework. Finally, the arguments put forward by theorists of an American imperium, which entail antithetical positions, have failed to show that this attempt to spread American power throughout the world will in fact succeed and bring about peace. As different as these approaches are, what they have in common is that they are monothematic or monocausal. It is always *one particular* macrosocial process that has guided the analysis of wars and their possible cessation.

If we look back over the history of social theorizing about war and peace as we have presented it here, this monothematic approach seems quite incredible. The basic structures of most modern-day theoretical models have already been thoroughly thought through and discussed in the past, and it almost always proved impossible to sustain the arguments in their original simplicity and elegance. So it seems reasonable to conclude that greater awareness of social theoretical debates of the past ought to induce a healthy skepticism about the efficacy of supposedly new ideas on how best to achieve peace and new theories of war. It also seems fair to conclude that it might be fruitful to abandon the monothematic approach entirely and put our efforts into synthetic concepts instead. The most ambitious attempt to come up with such a synthesizing conception of peace, which is having an increasing impact worldwide, is in our opinion that of Dieter Senghaas (b. 1940). We would like to conclude with a brief look at his work, as this is an effective way of recapitulating the findings discussed in the preceding chapters.

Senghaas is a student of Ralf Dahrendorf. The latter's studies of stratification in consolidated nation-states prompted him to examine the stratification of the international system. Since the late 1960s he has been one of the outstanding figures both in the field of foreign and development policy and in peace studies in the German-speaking world and beyond. In his studies on the history of development published in the 1970s, he advanced the reception of dependency theory approaches in Germany, though without entirely committing himself or submitting to a rigid theoretical system (see Senghaas 2000). By the early 1990s and following the collapse of the Soviet Union, he began a root-and-branch revision of his early views, clearly taking account of modernization theory, though integrating it into a concept of peace that synthesized a whole range of approaches. He referred to this conception as the "civilizational hexagon" (see, e.g., Senghaas 1994, 26; 2007, 15ff.). The claim here is that a lasting peace is associated with six key conditions: first and most importantly the deprivatization of violence and thus the establishment of a genuine monopoly of violence, the development of the rule of law, the binding together of citizens and concomitant affective control in Norbert Elias's sense, the efficacy of democratic principles, the presence of social justice, and finally the existence of a constructive political culture of conflict resolution. All these factors and principles must, Senghaas tells us, be taken into account if we wish to achieve lasting peace. Forms of "regression" cannot, however, be ruled out, making it a never-ending task to uphold and extend the principles contained within the civilizational hexagon (Senghaas 2007, 25).

Senghaas is aware that his concept of peace is anchored in the European experience. But he is convinced that the principles it expresses can also be universalized, not least because his civilizational hexagon is specifically intended to provide a nonreductionist analysis of war and peace: "Thinking in terms of the civilizational hexagon essentially means thinking configuratively rather than monothematically or in terms of an atrophied theory. Monothematic or atrophied thinking on the civilizational project of internal peace concentrates on *one* of the six points of the hexagon in order to shed light on it to positive or critical ends (including fundamental criticisms)" (Senghaas 1994, 27; see also Senghaas 2007, 25–29). His multidimensional approach, meanwhile, has the capacity to circumvent or respond constructively to the justified criticisms made of every monothematic conception of peace developed in the history of social theory.

The civilizational hexagon, as Senghaas sees it, is the precondition for the development of peaceful conditions *within* states. But this does not yet amount to the civilizing of *international* politics. For this, according to Senghaas, there are further prerequisites. First, individual states must be protected from violence in order to minimize the Hobbesian security dilemma that is always present within the system of states. Second, freedom within states must be protected, despite the difficulty of reconciling this with the principle of nonintervention on the international level. Third, people must be protected from poverty and hunger and, fourth, from chauvinism and nationalism—in other words, cultural diversity must be protected (see Senghaas 2010).

Senghaas links in his conception liberal-utilitarian and Kantian ideas, insights from power-political realism, and institutionalist ideas from the field of international relations. He does not discuss foreign policy in isolation from domestic politics. The specifics of his conception are certainly open to debate: we might place more or less emphasis on this or that process or principle within the civilizational hexagon than does Senghaas. Some might wish to develop, and for good reasons, a heptagon or octagon; and more than a few will find themselves unable to endorse the optimism by which Senghaas sometimes gets carried away. But this is of secondary importance in the present context. The key point is that in many respects Senghaas's mode of analysis learns the lessons of past debates on war and peace in exemplary fashion, lessons that few need to take to heart as much as social theorists. We are thinking *first* of the insight that neither processes of democratization nor the expansion of trade alone is capable of ensuring a stable peace, but that there are elements at play within both trade and democracy that *may* have a pacifying effect. So it is of little benefit to develop theories of war and peace by referring to just one of the macroprocesses often cited by sociologists. Rationalization, individualization, secularization, differentiation, and so on would no doubt suffer the same fate as democratization and economization: individually, none of them can explain the capacity for peace displayed by states or the international system of states. So any approach that considers one of these processes in isolation is unlikely to get us anywhere; apart from anything else, historical sociology has brought out like no other subdiscipline in the social sciences the unpredictable entanglement and contingent interaction between the widest range of societal subprocesses, which may, among others things, give rise to violence. So if we want to develop a theory of war and peace, the crucial requirement is to systematically examine the interplay of various social macroprocesses. This is the most important theoretical finding of our examination of this problem in the history of social theory. We aim to challenge sweeping references to "modernity" and "modernization." The macroprocesses identified here should not be understood as supposed subprocesses of modernization that are normally closely entwined. These processes should instead be seen as relatively autonomous ones that we must analyze separately but between which there are empirical relationships of causality. Only by taking this approach can we examine just how mutually dependent they are, their varying temporal structures, the tensions between them, and their specific potential for integration—without functionalist presuppositions. This is why the present work is characterized by a latent polemic against functionalist thought—a species of thought not restricted to texts that label themselves "functionalist."

Like the leading representatives of recent historical sociology in Great Britain and the United States, we are skeptical about theories such as those of progressive functional differentiation, rationalization, and modernization. Like them we target historically specific economic, social, and political processes. In contrast to them, even such outstanding sociologists as Charles Tilly and Michael Mann, however, we do not believe that the action theories inherent in such historically sensitive analyses can or should be rooted in models of rational action. This book, therefore, also often criticizes the assumptions of these models. It may seem paradoxical to those who see military action as the prototype of strategic action, but we wish to show that examination of military action is in fact a particularly good way to demonstrate how poorly such a narrow theory of action does justice to social reality.

Second, what we learn from both the history of social theory and Senghaas's hexagon is that the path to peace is a stony one, that it is at the very least far from definite that we shall see the emergence of a better, peaceful world. This is true not only because, owing to their mutual interaction, societal subprocesses have unforeseeable and at times disastrous side effects, but also because violence can be a source of fascination and war may be precipitated for its own sake, as thinkers from Hegel to Sumner have spelled out. Those who forget this aspect, those who believe that social macroprocesses (from democratization to economic integration) are crucial to resolving the problem of peace, that they will "fix" everything, are setting themselves up for unpleasant surprises. Analyses of war and peace, therefore, are always partly reliant on action theories that sound out the spectrum of potential action rather than rush to embrace premises likely to induce false hopes about the pacification of international relations.

Third and finally, the history of social theorizing on war and peace teaches us to insist on terminological precision. Senghaas, for example, links domestic and international analysis without precipitately abandoning established conceptual distinctions. In these days of the "war on terror," this seems more vital than ever. This so-called war entails few of the characteristics traditionally associated with the term. Serious attempts, beginning at the latest with Rousseau (see chapter 2), to achieve definitional precision, seem to have been abandoned with this phrase. We risk relapsing to the stance of Hobbes, whose concept of war covered both mere anarchy and wars between states, ultimately making it quite fuzzy. The arbitrary extension of the meaning of terms—war and civil war, violence and genocide—has never proved beneficial in the social sciences. To talk of "civil war" in "our" cities was just as much a dead end as references to "structural violence." And this seems likely to hold true if we add the "war on terror" to the "war on poverty" and "war on drugs." Such rhetoric does more to obscure our ideas than to deliver new insights. But does this not mean that we are denying what is new about certain phenomena? By taking such a stance, have we ourselves succumbed to the "suppression of war" within the social sciences and social theory that we wish to highlight? Only time will tell.

NOTES

Preface

1. Here we would like to express our gratitude to Nathalia Zlobinska and Arne Dreßler for procuring texts and for valuable comments and suggestions on the manuscript as well as Patrick Wöhrle and Daniel Stinsky for preparing the index.

Chapter 2

1. It was Hobbes's theoretical conception that was of most interest to those engaged in the philosophical and sociological discussion on war and peace, even if they consciously opposed it. There is no need to belabor the point that the classical figures of sociology—from Tönnies (1896) to Parsons (1937)—engaged repeatedly with Hobbes's ideas. But cf. the key role played by Hobbes in chapter 2 of our book *Social Theory* (2009 [2004], 27–32).

2. On the distinction between several variants of the possible modernization of European thought and European politics in this period, see the brilliant book by Toulmin (1990).

3. Hobbes was probably the first thinker to consciously introduce the "state of nature" as a thought experiment and to coin the term, though similar intellectual elements had already appeared in the work of Grotius. The "state of nature" became a key notion for all subsequent theories of law, regardless of whether it was conceived as a merely hypothetical condition or as one rooted in reality (Tuck 1999, 135).

4. In fact Hobbes's implicit assumption of an anarchic state of affairs between states was and is a poor reflection of the reality of international politics. As Hedley Bull (1977, 47ff.) has brought out, the relations between states were not and are not as (legally) unregulated as Hobbes suggested, and it was and is always inadequate to judge the actions of politicians concerned with international affairs *solely* in light of efforts to maintain state power or security.

5. Representatives of the so-called Cambridge school have demonstrated this above all in the field of "intellectual history." For a survey of the Cambridge school, see Hellmuth/von Ehrenstein 2001. It is important to grasp that the positions put forward by the Cambridge School have not gone uncontested. There continues to be major conflict, though it has become less intense in recent times, between historians such as Skinner or Pocock, who underline the outstanding

importance in early modern Europe of a discourse of virtue informed by ancient templates, and those who point instead to the centrality of a transformed discourse of natural law (for a brief overview, see Geuna 2002, 178ff.). The most easily accessible text on the significance of the ancient discourse of virtue is by Skinner (1998), who refers to the "neo-Roman understanding of civil liberty."

6. The idea of the civilizing and war-preventing effect of (international) trade can be found prior to Montesquieu. Such ideas extend further back, to at least the early seventeenth century, when French monk Eméric Crucé (1590–1640) introduced them to the contemporary debate on how best to establish peace (see Howard 1977, 19f.). But *The Spirit of Laws* was hugely influential. Twenty-two new editions had appeared just two years after its first publication, and translations were immediately begun into almost every European language, so that it seems quite legitimate to view Montesquieu's work as the starting point for a liberal conception of peace.

7. It is also notable what a wealth of arguments Montesquieu musters to spell out the dangers of imperial endeavors. Only the power of the British, based on supremacy at sea, could combine freedom and imperium (Böhlke 2005; Montesquieu 2005 [1733/34]).

8. For a brief but precise overview of the economic, political, and religious backgrounds to the Scottish Enlightenment, see Emerson 2003. For a highly innovative interpretation of the Scottish Enlightenment, particularly from the perspective of discontinuities between the Calvinist tradition and new experiences, see Camic 1983.

9. While Millar engaged intensively with the topic of war, his statements on the revolutionary wars of the 1790s, which were informed by his great sympathy for the French revolutionaries, tended to revolve around current affairs rather than systematic issues (see esp. his *Letters of Crito, on the Causes, Objects, and Consequences, of the Present War*, 1796). His remarks on war, militias, and standing armies in *The Origin of the Distinction of Ranks* (1793; originally 1771) borrow heavily from passages in *Wealth of Nations*, which is unsurprising given that Millar was a student of Smith (see Millar 1793, 212ff.).

10. Armitage was one of the first to point out that issues of imperial power played a role in the debate on the virtuous republic. But he merely hints that the gradual ousting of ancient political ideals was not due only to the penetration of capitalist market relations, through which Hobbesian or property-based individualist notions of freedom increasingly rose to prominence. Rather, according to what we might call Armitage's "world historical" argument, the almost total cessation of the tradition of "civic humanism" was probably due to world political and therefore contingent circumstances rather than an internal British or European developmental logic. Even Britain's merely "*maritime* empire" entailed the very difficulties that the ideals of "civic humanism" wished to highlight. With his emphasis on these imperial influences, Armitage, who published this text in an anthology coedited by Quentin Skinner, differs from the dominant vision of the

Cambridge school but is also in alignment with it in underlining the contingency of intellectual processes, as does Skinner in particular.

11. Jennifer Pitts points out that the awareness of the unintended effects of human action, so marked in *Scottish* Enlightenment philosophy, had significant consequences for the conceptualization of human history: "Smith did not regard Europe's development as the result of a uniquely progressive culture. Rather, he believed, on the one hand, that the transition from hunting to commercial societies was natural and presumptively universal, and on the other that the fact Europe had advanced farthest was accidental and fortuitous. Moreover, on Smith's view Europe's history was in many respects not a model of pure natural development at all" (Pitts 2005, 32). For Smith, such things as the extension of political participation in the Roman empire, the abolition of slavery and bondage, and the decline of the Catholic Church in Europe (processes and phenomena that he assessed positively with respect to their peaceful effects) were not historical necessities but the unintended consequences of actions, leading to the further insight that commercial and civil society in Europe by no means gave this continent the right to expedite progress in other places (32f.). "Moreover, Smith reminds us, to live under a good system is not necessarily to understand how it evolved, or even exactly how it works: even if Europeans benefited from a fortunate set of circumstances to produce relatively free and effective governments, they might not be in a position to export those institutions" (33).

12. "Among the more remarkable features of such writings [of the Enlightenment] . . . is that an increasingly acute awareness of the *irreducible plurality and partial incommensurability* of social forms, moral values, and political institutions engendered a historically uncommon, inclusive moral *universalism*" (Muthu 2003, 282; emphasis in original).

13. On the significance of the militia issue to the discourse of virtue or the "neo-Roman understanding of liberty," see Skinner 1998, 73f.

14. When originally published in 1752, this essay bore the title "Of Luxury," but was renamed in 1760 and is known today under the title in the text.

15. In the next clause, however, Hume makes it clear that this luxury must remain within reasonable bounds if it is to have a positive effect.

16. Elsewhere he states, "Peace and unanimity are commonly considered as the principal foundations of public felicity; yet the rivalship of separate communities, and the agitations of a free people, are the principles of political life, and the school of men" (Ferguson 2006, 73).

17. With his arguments for a militia, Ferguson could draw not only on ancient traditions but also on Scottish nationalist thought in the period immediately before the parliamentary union between England and Scotland (1707). Andrew Fletcher's "A Discourse of Government with relation to Militias" (1997 [1698]) caused a furor within the heated discursive landscape of the time. In a fairly systematic way, this treatise develops the idea of the standing (mercenary) army as a threat to freedom and highlights the unique military and constitutional develop-

ment of the British Isles ("And 'tis as evident, that standing forces are the fittest instruments to make a tyrant"; Fletcher 1997 [1698], 18/19). In an instructive essay, Matthias Bohlender has advocated the thesis that Ferguson transformed Fletcher's constitutional focus into a general sociomoral issue. But this contrast between Fletcher and Ferguson with respect to their arguments on the militia is probably too sharp, and Bohlender seems to be going too far in asserting that Ferguson's insistence on the institution of the militia implies the "birth of society" out of the "practices of war" (see Bohlender 1999, 25).

18. On this nexus, see also Robertson 1985, 200–232.

19. "War is . . . a species of procedure by which one nation endeavours to enforce its rights at the expense of another nation. It is the only method to which recourse can be had, when no other method of obtaining satisfaction can be found by complainants, who have no arbitrator between them sufficiently strong, absolutely to take from them all hope of resistance" (Bentham 1843b, 538/39).

20. "It is . . . the quantity of capital which determines the quantity of trade, and not the extent of the market, as has been generally believed. Open a new market,—the quantity of trade will not, unless by some accidental circumstance, be increased: shut up an old market,—the quantity of trade will not be diminished, unless by accident, and only for a moment" (Bentham 1843c, 54).

21. "The monopoly, indeed, raises the rate of mercantile profit and thereby augments somewhat the gain of our merchants. But as it obstructs the natural increase of capital, it tends rather to diminish than increase the sum total of the revenue which the inhabitants of the country derive from the profits of stock" (Smith 2007, 396; on Smith's stance on colonialism, see the persuasive account by Pitts 2005, esp. 53ff.).

22. "In this respect, the study of anti-imperialist political thought shows quite clearly that the idea of an Enlightenment project that celebrated universal values at the expense of cultural difference has obscured what was, in fact, a genuine and contentious struggle among eighteenth-century thinkers about how to conceptualize humanity, cultural difference, and the political relationships among European and non-European peoples" (Muthu 2003, 264; see also Richter 1997).

23. For an excellent collection of studies on "civilizing missions," see Barth/Osterhammel (2005).

24. The most user-friendly compilation of the relevant texts (though in abridged form) is Hoffmann/Fidler (eds.), *Rousseau on International Relations* (1991a).

25. Rousseau underlines that wars always have negative repercussions for the sociopolitical structure of the countries waging them (1997a; see also Hoffmann 1963, 323). It should be noted here that Rousseau, influenced strongly, like Montesquieu and Ferguson, by the ancient (republican) ideal of the citizen, was never willing to defend martial virtues: "That the art of war is pernicious seems indeed to be one of Rousseau's most settled convictions" (Hassner 1997, 212).

26. It is, however, doubtful that Rousseau can consistently maintain this separation between state and population. Particularly in the case of wars between

"well-governed" republics, in which the general will "rules," the distinction between state and population would be done away with. In this case one would in fact legitimately annihilate the enemy population in order to win the war. The humanization of war to which Rousseau aspires would no longer be possible in the case of warring republics: "But this means that the citizens' patriotic identification with the state, as demanded by Rousseau, makes virtually every single citizen a combatant almost by definition. As a result, the distinction between innocent citizens, who according to the laws of war must remain unharmed, and the defenders of the fatherland, who it is quite legal to kill, threatens to break down" (Asbach 2002, 255). Asbach underlines that this problem was acknowledged by Rousseau himself in *Émile*, where he states that wars between republican states are more awful than those between monarchies—precisely because of the citizens' strong patriotic identification (ibid.).

27. Here again it is apparent that Rousseau placed his hopes not in international law but in deterrence between republics (with a basically defensive orientation), which is why representatives of power-political realism within the theory of international relations are quite able to cite Rousseau (for a critical analysis, see Williams 1989).

28. "It is apparent . . . what should be thought of those supposed Cosmopolites who, justifying their love of the fatherland by means of their love of the human race, boast of loving everyone in order to have the right to love no one" (Rousseau 1994, 81).

29. Voltaire, like Kant later on, presumably knew nothing of the major differences between Saint-Pierre and Rousseau, straightforwardly identifying Saint-Pierre's conception of how to attain peace with that of Rousseau because the second part of the "Projet pour rendre la paix perpétuelle en Europe," and thus Rousseau's own position, was published at a later date.

30. On Voltaire's assessment of Saint-Pierre's writings, which was by no means always negative, see Perkins (1960).

31. In what follows, we rely in particular on Hassner's 1961 essay, which is still well worth reading and a rich source of ideas.

32. It is worth mentioning in this context that it was by grappling with the Abbé's plan for peace that both Rousseau and Kant "shifted away from their initial emphasis on reforming international (legal) conditions and began to underline the crucial importance of changing the internal structures of society and political rule" (Asbach 2002, 303).

33. This is probably also the reason why power-political realists have repeatedly attempted to interpret Kant in such a way as to make him fit their own theoretical frameworks (see Waltz 1962; for an overview of such interpretive efforts, see Hurrell 1990).

34. At one point in the *Critique of Judgement* (2007 [1790]) it emerges that Kant does not in fact want peace at any price. In a kind of existential interpretation of war, as expressed far more sharply later by Hegel, Kant writes: "War itself,

provided it is conducted with order and a sacred respect for the rights of civilians, has something sublime about it, and gives nations that carry it on in such a manner a stamp of mind only the more sublime the more numerous the dangers to which they are exposed, and which they are able to meet with fortitude. On the other hand, a prolonged peace favours the predominance of a mere *commercial spirit*, and with it a debasing self-interest, cowardice, and weakness, and tends to degrade the character of the people" (93; emphasis in original).

35. Kant's rejection of the customary idea of a balance of power is unequivocal: "For a permanent universal peace by means of a so-called European balance of power is a pure illusion, like Swift's story of the house which the builder had constructed in such perfect harmony with all the laws of equilibrium that it collapsed as soon as a sparrow alighted on it" (1991c [1793], 92).

36. Volker Gerhardt (1995, 17ff.) points out that Kant's shift away from the thesis of the productive effects of war is closely bound up with his interpretation of the French Revolution. "But with the internal development of state structures, the world historical events in Paris being a case in point, securing freedom and equality has itself become an *explicit institutional* goal of politics. So there is no longer any need for an automatic mechanism rooted in nature" (23; emphasis in original).

37. In reality, in other words in the thought of individual liberal philosophers, economists, and sociologists, the utilitarian and "democratic-universalist" conceptions have not always been kept clearly apart. Nonetheless, it makes sense to refer to them as separate conceptions, as each gives rise to quite different prognoses and evaluations.

38. It should be noted here that Kant's reference to the republic by no means implied a desire to overthrow monarchies. His aim was the constitutionalization and legalization of monarchical power. But Gerhardt (1995, 90) points out that "republics" in the Kantian sense can certainly be equated with "constitutionally based parliamentary democracies." And this allows us to refer to a "democratic-universalist" conception of peace with respect to Kant and his successors.

39. While Kant speaks of a worldwide "federation of free states," a "federation of peoples" in "Perpetual Peace" (1991d [1795], 102f.), in the "Metaphysics of Morals" he refers to a "permanent congress of states," though it is unlikely to include all states, which is why he then adds that "perpetual peace, the ultimate end of all international right, is an idea incapable of realisation" (1991e [1797], 171; see also Hurrell 1990, 193). It is these passages that made it quite possible to interpret Kant as a thinker close to power-political realism (again, see Waltz 1962, 339f.).

40. Pierre Hassner (1961, 670) is right to state that in his writings of the 1780s and 1790s Kant had in fact raised the long-standing and very broad debate on peace to a completely new level, to that of the philosophy of history and—we might add—that of political sociology.

41. In contrast to the other two authors, Friedrich Gentz (1764–1832), writing

in 1800, doubts that there can ever be perpetual peace; thinking along the same lines as power-political realists, he believed that war between states is the price that must be paid for leaving the state of nature: "We must view wars between states as conduits in which the build-up of human hostility—which would cause devastation and obstruct all legal relations, even among individuals, if left to its own devices—is concentrated at certain points and is, as it were, expelled into certain channels. For all its horrors, war is the guarantee of the only legal framework possible among human beings, and as paradoxical as it may sound, it is undeniably true: without war there would be no peace on Earth" (Gentz 1989 [1800], 389; see also Dülffer 1990, 56ff.).

42. Carl Schmitt has provided the most compelling analysis of this problem with his remarks on the "discriminatory concept of war." In his opinion, the universalist proscription of war that this concept entails empowers certain parties to conflict to take action against the real or supposed aggressor in the name of humanity. In this way, a conflict between two orders becomes a conflict between order and disorder, between preservers and disturbers of order. The turn towards the "discriminatory concept of war" (2003b [1938] meant not only that one's enemy was no longer viewed as legitimate but also that one need no longer harbor any moral scruples toward the enemy. As a result, the potential for limiting conflict was lost. Wars returned to the status of crusades, their aim no longer victory but the total destruction of the other side in this "global civil war." Hence, Schmitt tells us, whether intentionally or not, attempts to institutionalize the republican-liberal conception of peace resulted in the ideological downgrading of the enemy, which itself represented a danger to peace (see chapter 5). This assertion, which lacks solid empirical corroboration, was intended to justify a Europe united under the Nazis. But indisputable democrats have frequently expressed similar concerns as well, as evident, for example, in the debate between universalists and traditionalists in the United States between the world wars with respect to international law (see Krakau 1967).

43. Paine's work also exhibits the intertwining of "utilitarian" and "democratic-universalist" motifs: in the fifth chapter of part two of *The Rights of Man* Paine delivers a stirring plea for the peace-promoting effects of trade: "In all my publications, where the matter would admit, I have been an advocate for commerce, because I am a friend to its effects. It is a pacific system, operating to cordialize mankind, by rendering nations, as well as individuals, useful to each other. . . . If commerce were permitted to act to the universal extent it is capable, it would extirpate the system of war, and produce a revolution in the uncivilized state of governments" (Paine 1992 [1791/92], 172).

44. The question of whether citizens' democratic participation, the rule of law within a country, or the interlinking of states through trade relations increases the probability of a peaceful foreign policy is in fact open to empirical verification, which is one of the reasons why it is still of contemporary interest. The results of the many studies on this topic are contentious in the detail. All in all, though, they

by no means leave liberal conceptions of peace looking groundless, and point quite unanimously to the existence of a kind of special peace between the liberal states. In the 1990s a furious debate flared up among social scientists over Kant's idea of a "democratic peace," something we shall be looking at in more detail in chapter 7.

45. We should mention at this point that alongside the critique of Kant's conception of peace expounded by Fichte, Görres, and Schlegel, which we might classify as a radicalization of republican ideas, it was also possible to argue on the basis of a quite different position, one espoused by the likes of Novalis. In *Christianity, or Europe*, Novalis cast doubt on the likelihood that "the secular powers can put themselves in equilibrium" (1844 [1799], 26), a comment aimed at more than just the representatives of power-political realism. He also went beyond this, attacking all constructions of world peace in a general sense, including the Kantian variant, as he took the view that war "will [never] cease until the palm-branch be taken up, which a spiritual power alone can offer us. . . . Religion alone can again awake all Europe; she alone can give security to the people; can invest Christendom with higher glory, and visibly reinstate her on earth in her ancient peace-making office" (27). Novalis's hopes stand in stark contrast to one of the most commonly espoused viewpoints of the eighteenth century. Rousseau for one—though he was scarcely interested in the *reform* of Christianity—could find nothing at all in the Christianity of his time of value to the politics of peace. With a view to the power politics of the day, Rousseau had argued in his essay on Poland that the Christian powers and states in particular were anything but trustworthy, and could not be less suited to stable alliances (1997c [1772], 257).

46. According to the influential interpretation of Clausewitz expounded by Raymond Aron (1983, 231), the author belonged "to the eighteenth, and not to the nineteenth, century," which is why it seems justified to us to deal with him here in the context of the *Enlightenment* debate on war and peace.

47. "[W]ar is an act of violence pushed to its utmost bounds; as one side dictates the law to the other, there arises a sort of reciprocal action, which logically must lead to an extreme. This is the *first reciprocal action*, and the *first extreme* with which we meet" (Clausewitz 1968, 29; emphasis in original).

48. "As long as the enemy is not defeated, he may defeat me; then I shall be no longer my own master; he will dictate the law to me as I did to him. This is the *second reciprocal action, and leads to a second extreme*" (Clausewitz 1968, 30; emphasis in original).

49. "If we desire to defeat the enemy, we must proportion our efforts to his powers of resistance. This is expressed by the product of two factors which cannot be separated, namely, *the sum of available means and the strength of the will*. . . . But the adversary does the same; therefore, there is a new mutual enhancement, which, in pure conception, must create a fresh effort towards an extreme. This is the *third case of reciprocal action*, and a *third extreme* with which we meet" (Clausewitz 1968, 30; emphasis in original).

Chapter 3

1. Sankar Muthu underlines that these differences between the thought of the eighteenth and nineteenth centuries may have reflected disparate political sensitivities. As eighteenth-century thinkers, Kant, Diderot, and Herder (as well as Enlightenment thinkers in other nations) were deeply critical of the European countries, "for they viewed them as violent, absolutist, war-seeking, aggressive, and corrupt" (Muthu 2003, 280). But in the nineteenth century—Muthu argues—the social and economic changes triggered by the French Revolution had led to a change in mentality: "The myriad social and political changes that the French Revolution ushered in eventually seemed to yield a political sensibility among many nineteenth-century European political thinkers that made them far more sanguine about the achievements of 'European civilization' than their eighteenth-century forebears. They were thus more amenable to the view that Europe had genuinely advanced beyond the non-European world and, hence, they were more open to the idea that it should forcibly lead non-European peoples toward a higher form of political rule, economic rationality, and social development" (280). And this even applied to the social *critics* of the nineteenth century—not least Marx.

2. Albert O. Hirschman's (1986, 117ff.) influential argument must be mentioned in this connection. He claims that the thesis of "doux commerce" so common in the eighteenth century was pushed into the background chiefly because of the negative social consequences of industrialization. While there is no doubt much to be said for this assertion, we should also be clear—and we return to this point in the next chapter in our analysis of Max Weber's inaugural lecture at Freiburg—that the positive effects attributed to trade also began to appear increasingly implausible because of the growing number of apparent trade conflicts and the rivalry between nations associated with them.

3. On the debate over whether the world order envisaged by European international law was bifurcated from the outset (one version for the civilized nations and one for the uncivilized regions, where a quite different order prevailed, or at least where European standards did not apply), see Keene 2002. Keene's intention here is to critique by getting at concealed truths, but other authors made the same point with self-assurance and no normative scruples. The best-known example is probably the view expressed by Carl Schmitt. In 1950, in *Nomos of the Earth*, he referred self-evidently to the fact that the Jus Publicum Europaeum, with its "limitation of war," only worked because it was restricted to Europe, while beyond the "amity lines," namely in the non-European world, unrestricted violence could prevail: "[T]he essential presupposition and foundation of this spatial order and its concept of balance lay in the fact that from the seventeenth to the nineteenth century the great European powers could expand virtually unhindered across the world in colonies outside Europe" (Schmitt 2003a [1950], 161, translation corrected). The limitation of war did not apply to colonial wars (309). On the

ambivalence of the concept of civilization in the history of "international law," see Mazower 2006.

4. So the idea of free trade was not one that might be interpreted in isolation from *power-political* considerations. The sharp rupture between mercantilist and (their own) free-trade ideas, which the representatives of political economy repeatedly asserted, was not so sharp after all, given that the free traders also tried to increase the nation's power, though the means—determined by a novel understanding of economic processes—were different (see Etges 1999, 34).

5. List himself had been in the United States and was crucially influenced by his stay there. On the "American School of Political Economy," which produced polemics against free trade from the 1840s, see Etges 1999, 191–99; see also Earle 1952.

6. Boesche 1987; for an interpretation of Tocqueville that places him close to "civic humanism," see Smith 1985.

7. "The best part of the nation shuns the military profession because that profession is not honoured, and the profession is not honoured because the best part of the nation has ceased to follow it. . . . Moreover, as among democratic nations . . . the wealthiest, the best educated, and the most able men seldom adopt the military profession, the army, taken collectively, eventually forms a small nation by itself, where the mind is less enlarged, and habits are more rude than in the nation at large. Now, this small uncivilized nation has arms in its possession, and alone knows how to use them" (Tocqueville 2007 [1835/40], 565).

8. This applies even to the great monograph on Tocqueville by Sheldon S. Wolin (2001); German scholar Michael Hereth (1986, 145ff.) takes a different approach and deserves credit for making Tocqueville's writings on Algeria a central topic in his interpretation of Tocqueville's oeuvre. Among recent publications in Germany, Harald Bluhm (2006) and Matthias Bohlender (2005) in particular have drawn attention to the significance of the "Algeria question" to Tocqueville's thought.

9. For Tocqueville, anyone who has been in Africa knows that "unfortunately Muslim society and Christian society do not have a single tie, that they form two bodies that are juxtaposed but completely separate. They know that this state of things seems to become more so every day, and that nothing can be done against it. The Arab element is becoming more and more isolated, and little by little it is dissolving. The Muslim population always seems to be shrinking, while the Christian population is always growing. The fusion of these two populations is a chimera that people dream of only when they have not been to these places" (Tocqueville 2001c [1841], 111).

10. "As soon as it is admitted that the whites and the emancipated blacks are placed upon the same territory in the situation of two alien communities, it will readily be understood that there are but two alternatives for the future; the negroes and the whites must either wholly part or wholly mingle. I have already expressed the conviction which I entertain as to the latter event. I do not imagine

that the white and the black races will ever live in any country upon an equal footing. But I believe the difficulty to be still greater in the United States than elsewhere" (Tocqueville 2007 [1835/40], 301).

11. It should be noted that Comte's thought also influenced the views of other "social theorists of war and peace" already dealt with in this chapter. John Stuart Mill, who greatly admired Comte's early writings, contacted him after publication of his famous magnum opus *Cours de philosophie positive*, written between 1830 and 1842 and published in 1843 (for an introductory survey, see Pickering 1997).

12. As Mary Pickering (1993, 37) highlights, even in his earliest essays Comte expressed the view that a correct interpretation of history was the key to appropriate action, making historical reconstruction the basis of his sociology, the new science of social consensus.

13. This is also what Pickering has in mind when she states that Condorcet's thought differed from that of Comte mainly in the sense that the former had a good deal more faith in the possibility of *conscious and active* control of the future (Pickering 1993, 153).

14. Constant's "The Spirit of Conquest" is also an attempt to come to terms with Napoleon's policy of conquest. The anticolonial pathos of the Enlightenment, which was to be lost in the work of Tocqueville, is still in evidence here (Pitts 2005, 173ff.).

15. The concept of the "positive" means the "real as opposed to imaginary." It refers to the contrast between the "useful and unprofitable," that between "certainty and indecision," and between the "precise [and] vague" (Comte 1903 [1844], 66ff.).

16. Few could match William James's parody of this supposed law: "Evolution is a change from a non-howish, untalkaboutable, all-alikeness to a somehow-ish and in general talkaboutable not-all-alikeness by continuous stick-to-gether-ations and something-elsifications" (James in Myers 1986, 43).

17. It is often pointed out in the secondary literature that the dichotomy between bellicose and industrial society was deeply anchored in Enlightenment-era traditions of British-American radicalism. This sharp dichotomy was based on that between government and society, as expressed so pointedly by Thomas Paine right at the start of his pamphlet *Common Sense* from 1776: "Society is produced by our wants, and government by our wickedness" (Paine 1976 [1776], 65; on these roots, see Peel 1971, 58, Taylor 1992, 173). So M. W. Taylor (1992) is right to underline that the individualist ideas so fundamental to Herbert Spencer's work can be understood as a kind of (conservative) transformation of English radicalism in light of their embedding in an evolutionist theory and their specific political expression.

18. The distinction between the social structures of industrial and militant societies is, however, rather unconvincing. As J.D.Y. Peel (1971, 209ff.) and others have always rightly emphasized, those who present this dichotomy in this way

replace differences in rank (militant type) with functional roles (industrial type), without going on to ask whether these functionally differentiated roles involve significant power differentials—which would cast great doubt on the typical view that industrial societies are distinguished by an egalitarian structure.

19. Incidentally, Marx deploys a similar argumentational device in his treatment of colonialism. As is well known, Marx constructed his stage model of history in a highly Eurocentric manner and then struggled to fit non-European economic structures into what he had claimed to be the necessary succession of modes of production (on the following, see Avineri 1968). It is no coincidence that he then coined and adopted the term "Asiatic mode of production," which was defined purely in geographic terms. He defined this mode of production in terms of the lack of private property while conceptualizing it in a peculiarly ahistorical way. This left it unclear how it could change at all—and here lie the roots of his arguments on the colonial question. If Marx postulated the worldwide victory of socialism while at the same time assuming that the necessary precursor of socialism is developed capitalism, then he could only conclude that the colonization of "Asiatic" regions is the prerequisite for speeding up their history and a *sine qua non* for any conceivable transition to socialism. As Avineri (1968, 12) puts it: "Just as the horrors of industrialization are dialectically necessary for the triumph of communism, so the horrors of colonialism are dialectically necessary for the world revolution of the proletariat since without them the countries of Asia (and presumably also Africa) will not be able to emancipate themselves from their stagnant backwardness." So Marx was quite aware of Britain's crimes in India and identified them as such, but was at the same time uninterested in, or even opposed, the Indian revolts of the late 1850s. The crimes of colonialism and the violence they implied might well be terrible. But for Marx—his self-confidence due to his supposed knowledge of the historical process—they are merely a necessary step on the path toward a future socialist society in Asia as elsewhere.

20. See the remarks on Hans Freyer in this volume (p. 163). This is not to dispute that contemporaries of Hegel wished to take this step to a certain extent. Fichte and Clausewitz—at least during certain phases of their work—had an existential conception of war and called for the removal of all limits on war. On Fichte, see Münkler 1999.

21. This explains why a number of interpreters regard application of the label "Social Darwinist" to Sumner as problematic at the very least (see Bannister 1987, 88).

22. Even pacifists were not blind to the obvious appeal of war and violence. In 1910, not long before the outbreak of the First World War and contemporaneously with Sumner, the highly sensitive William James (1842–1910) tried to find a morally acceptable alternative to war, which he greatly feared, in order to avoid it. James highlights the timeless fascination of war, which pacifism—so far—has been unable to counter, robbing it of its persuasive force: "Showing war's irra-

tionality and horror is of no effect on him [modern man]. The horrors make the fascination. War is the *strong life; it is life in extremis*" (James 1971 [1910], 350; emphasis in original). So James is keen to channel emotions hitherto centered on war in a new direction, to set in motion a kind of *civil* disciplining and self-disciplining of the population with respect to peace, a *humanistic-democratic* mobilization of society, intended to arouse the same kind of enthusiasm as the noise of battle in the age of imperialism. In institutional terms, compulsory service to the community seems to him an appropriate means of achieving such goals. Numerous practical schemes have undoubtedly been implemented in response to this idea, but it is quite unable to resolve the problem of war in analytical and normative terms. In any event, this text is central to understanding the significance of heroism in a nonmilitary sense to the philosophy of American pragmatism (see Cotkin 1994).

23. And in general it is by no means the case that all Social Darwinists were militarists and imperialists. Some of them believed that war eliminated the biologically superior and was a source of degeneration, as demonstrated by Pitirim Sorokin (1928) (see Joas 2003, 146ff.).

Chapter 4

1. Schäffle had in fact tackled the subject of war in some detail before the turn of the century in his multivolume magnum opus *Bau und Leben des socialen Körpers* (Construction and Life of the Social Body) from 1878. Passages in the second volume, some of them detailed, show that he had long since begun to formulate the views he articulated around 1900 (see Schäffle 1878, 250ff.).

2. In line with this, Schäffle takes issue with the idea that armament is unproductive, an idea he believes to have originated in Britain (1878, 233ff.).

3. Again, we underline that the methods of the historical school of economics did not *inevitably* lead to these nationalistic conclusions. The historical school also had adherents outside of Germany, who came to quite different conclusions (see Silberner 1946, 193f.).

4. That Weber cannot really be described as a "Social Darwinist" is apparent in the fact that he does not positively assess, or pay attention solely to, the results of the struggle for survival among "species" in his inaugural lecture. With his appeal for economic policy measures, he wishes to stop the "selection" taking place to the disadvantage of the German population in West Prussia and prevent the victory of the "less economically developed nationality" (Weber 1999, 126; Beetham 1974, 43; see also Radkau 2009, 132).

5. Since the 1980s, Wilhelm Hennis has advanced a highly original and in many ways persuasive interpretation of Weber's work, asserting that Weber was interested primarily in the anthropological-characterological issue of the quality of humanity and that his view of the German nation was derived from this.

For Weber, according to Hennis (2000b, 75f.), the nation-state did represent an important value, but not the ideal of the nation-state as such, but only the formative consequences of this "life order" on human beings. This is not the right place to investigate the veritable interpretive industry that has grown up around Weber's oeuvre. We merely note that there should be no doubt that the idea of the nation state played a major role in his work, even if it was in second place in Weber's scale of values. (On these issues, see esp. the recent work by Radkau 2005 [abridged English version 2009] and the related review essay by Joas 2007).

6. Durkheim's reserve toward this nationalism was presumably bound up in part with the fact that the frequent blending of nationalist and anti-Semitic sentiment, also found in France, must have been deeply repugnant to him as a secular Jew.

7. This does not mean that Durkheim does entirely without definitions. But his efforts here ("[T]he state is a special organ whose responsibility is to work out certain representations which hold good for the collectivity. These representations are distinguished from the other collective representations by their higher degree of consciousness and reflection," Durkheim 1957, 50) can scarcely be regarded as a guide to the construction of theoretical tools for analyzing the state.

8. Hintze's impact on the school of German history known as "historical social science" is surely beyond dispute. It is from this grouping, namely from Jürgen Kocka, that we have the most accurate appreciation of Hintze as the "most methodologically advanced, if not in fact . . . the most important German historian of the late German empire and inter-war period" (Kocka 1973, 41). For other important interpretations of Hintze's life's work, see Oestreich 1964, Gilbert 1975, Gerhard 1970, Büsch/Erbe 1983, and Hübinger 1988.

9. For a similar argument, see also the essay "The Formation of States and Constitutional Development" written four years earlier.

10. It is in Hintze's writings on war, in which he straightforwardly and uncritically defends Germany's geopolitically determined militarism (see Hintze 1914) that this apologetic tendency is most clearly apparent.

11. See the first few sentences of a manifesto in the journal *Blast* from June 1914—surely written without reference to the war that broke out so soon afterward: "1. Beyond Action and Reaction we would establish ourselves. 2. We start from opposite statements of a chosen world. Set up violent structure of adolescent clearness between two extremes. 3. We discharge ourselves on both sides. 4. We fight first on one side, then on the other, but always for the same cause, which is neither side or both sides and ours. 5. Mercenaries were always the best troops. 6. We are Primitive Mercenaries in the Modern World. 7. Our *cause* is No-Man's" (quoted in Hynes 1990, 9).

12. Hermann Lübbe expressed the relatively moderate stance of Simmel and Scheler in the following terms. In the work of Simmel, war is "mediatized with a view to the existential, rather than existence with a view to war. This is why the

national emphasis of his discourse seems toned down and the solidarity with the Fatherland which this emphasis expresses less immediate" (Lübbe 1963, 220/21). Simmel's "celebration of war as freeing us to attain existential authenticity," Lübbe states, "has [found] its psychological-anthropological counterpart in Max Scheler's philosophy of war" (ibid.).

13. Hermann Lübbe (1963, 212) commented on Sombart's *Händler und Helden* in the following apposite terms: "Beyond their laughable aspects, his ideas seem more bizarre than dangerous. If his ideas could stand up to allegedly scientific examination, one wonders what other views might also be presented as validated by science."

14. "The modern state is variously described by Veblen as democratic, peaceable, cosmopolitan, individualist, and characterized by representative government and a propensity to insubordination (which he juxtaposes to servility). The modern state is guided both domestically and, especially, internationally by the rule of 'live-and-let-live.' Its institutions are free and popular. It has features of democratic equity and noninterference, self-help and local autonomy" (Biddle/Samuels 1993, 104).

15. In *Der moderne Kapitalismus*, Sombart draws a sharp contrast between a mostly British-style social economics, on the one hand, and national economics (*Volkswirtschaftslehre* or *Nationalökonomie*), based ultimately on mercantilist ideas, on the other (Sombart 1987, vol. II/2: 913ff.).

16. Again, the exception here was Max Weber, who repeatedly investigated the probable sociostructural and political consequences of the war in his wartime writings on (contemporary) politics.

Chapter 5

1. Georges Bataille, incidentally, also tackles the relationship between the sacred and war in his writings, but considers the analogies between war and transgression drawn by Caillois (see below) implausible.

2. It should however be noted that theoretical elements of Caillois's approach were applied by historians, with much success, to the experiences of soldiers in the First World War. See the brilliant study by Leed 1979.

3. Bataille (1989, 65f.), for example, had little time for the notion that war and religious experience are closely related. In his view, the emergence of military discipline and order left no space for the originally spectacular and potentially transgressive battle; as a result, instrumentally rational considerations had made greater inroads into warfare.

4. In his analyses of fascism and the concept of sovereignty, generally of a very dark hue, Bataille (1997, 28ff., 70) too tried to establish to what extent the armed forces and armed violence have shaped the political and religious thought of modernity.

5. For a critique of Schmitt's "political existentialism," which we will not repeat here, see Joas (2003, 152–57, and Großheim 1999; of the contemporary literature, see Kuhn 1933, Marcuse 1968 [1934], and Strauss 2007 [1932].

6. In his 1932 text *Der Begriff des Politischen*, Schmitt was to state that, while it is true that the friend-enemy distinction entails the idea of the life-and-death struggle, the concept of the enemy does not necessarily imply personal hatred (Schmitt 2007a [1927/32], 28). This point is important, as it has consequences for Schmitt's view of how "traditional" European international law operates.

7. What commentators have described with respect to Schmitt's arguments on domestic politics, namely that his ultimate aim is to eliminate value rationality as such through the motif of the state of emergency, conceived solely in decisionist terms (Hofmann 2002, 68), also applies to his arguments on international politics: every attempt to initiate a normative discussion is nipped in the bud through reference to the existential character of war.

8. Though Speier always underlined that his typological distinctions are never to be taken literally (1940, 453), he must have been secretly aware that in the era of totalitarian ideologies reality was catching up all too quickly with conceptual imagination in the case of absolute war.

9. See, for example, the essay by N. N. Alexeiev, which was fairly representative of the journal, "Modern Culture and the New European War" (1940).

10. However, as Aron was later to state self-critically in his memoirs (1990, 303ff.), in *Peace and War* he underestimated the transnational dimension (e.g., economic processes, ideologies, religions) while relying too heavily in his analysis on the fiction of rational actors; in other words, he failed to pay adequate attention to diplomats' dependency on the ruling political and social classes and the irrationalities that enter into international politics as a result.

11. "The book caused a firestorm in academic and political circles, leading to innumerable reviews in scholarly journals and the popular press, most of them negative" (Domhoff 2006, 547).

12. Mills, however, does not forget to underline that "violence as a means and even as a value is just a little bit ambiguous in American life and culture": in the nineteenth century, it mostly emanated from the people, because at this time military force was "decentralized in state militia almost to a feudal point" (Mills 1956, 177/78).

13. This was reflected in the journal *Armed Forces and Society*, whose foundation in 1976 he was largely responsible for; the title itself indicates that the aim was to move away from any narrowly conceived version of military sociology.

Chapter 6

1. For a critique of Mann's interpretation of the British public finances, see Braddick 2000, 12ff.

Chapter 7

1. This does not mean that Parsons never addressed the issue of international tensions. At the end of his book *The System of Modern Societies* (1971), he states: "Certainly, the history of modern societal systems" has been "one of frequent, if not continual, warfare," but he does not consider this "incompatible with what seems a secular trend toward reduction of violence both internally and internationally" (Parsons 1971, 141). Genov 1989 provides an overview of his contributions on this topic. Nonetheless, Parsons too fits the picture of widespread suppression of war, which is remarkable given his involvement in American postwar planning for Germany and Japan.

2. In terms of quantitative research on war, there were in fact a number of major studies, such as those by R. J. Rummel (see his *Understanding Conflict and War*, 1975–81), which contain similar ideas; at the time, however, in view of their lack of practical relevance, they could be safely ignored—no one, after all, believed that the Soviet empire was going to implode. For a brief survey, see Rummel 1983.

3. Representatives of historical sociology were mostly skeptical about the ideas put forward by Kant or Doyle. This was partly because—as indicated above—the former often based their own analyses on rational choice premises, so their view of international relations was generally informed by power-political realism. But it was also bound up with their skepticism about the tendency to view the democratic political system in isolation, a tendency typical of the debate on a democratic peace, which often drew on quantitative social research.

4. Exceptions include the above-mentioned Rummel and Ray 1997, 59.

5. Another point of agreement is that the debate on a "democratic peace" has confirmed Kant's thesis of the political and military strength of democracies— a thesis vehemently disputed by Samuel Huntington (1967 [1957]) and others. Liberal democracies are said to have a substantial capacity to defend themselves; despite the fact that they are often attacked because of their attractive system of values (and the resulting magnetism so threatening to authoritarian states), such systems have proved amazingly robust (Lake 1992). At the very least, on this view, the defensive capacity of popular regimes in the past proved great enough that there is little need to worry about democracies' survival (van Evera 1998, 70; see also Reiter/Stam 2002, 10–83).

6. These examples are from Chan 1997, 70.

7. On the thesis of the belligerence of *new* democracies, see Mansfield/Snyder 1998.

8. "Maximizing information is of particular importance in the creation of security regimes, where the risks of error and deception can be catastrophic. . . . Transparency allows a democratic dyad to embrace concessions at a much lower risk of the other side defecting, because of the public nature of the process in-

volved in reversing policies. Thus, states sharing an open political system develop high levels of mutual formal and informal communication which, in turn, lowers the cost of forming a regime. . . . Openness allows the transgovernmental networks of democratic dyads to share information on their respective domestic conditions, thus facilitating transnational logrolling of support for regime" (Solingen 1996, 82).

9. Weart (1998, 21) presents similar arguments, stating that the key to explaining peace lies in the political culture of governmental decision makers.

10. The debate has certainly gone through some peculiar twists and turns. Initially, the supporters of the thesis of a "democratic peace" thought that their position placed them securely within the framework of Kant's arguments. Over time, however, it became clear that a closer reading of Kant would have helped avoid some of the debate's dead ends. In the 1980s and early 1990s, some scholars still argued that when Kant spoke of republics' great capacity for peace he actually meant democracies. But others gradually began to reflect on why Kant referred quite explicitly to republics and *not* to democracies (Gates/Knutsen/Moses 1996, 6; see also Chan 1997, 64).

11. Jürgen Habermas has provided us with some interesting studies over the past few years, in which he applies to the field of international relations his general attempt to transform Kant's work in light of communication theory. These studies are mainly normative in orientation, though they do not preclude an "empirical accommodation," in other words identification of favorable conditions for the realization of a normative ideal (see esp. Habermas 2008). His theory of communication as a whole, and especially the studies highlighted here, have made a major impact on the theory of international relations (see Niesen/Herborth 2007).

12. Generally, the implication here is that violence is a result of state collapse. From an empirical perspective, however, it is probably equally plausible to assume that, in many regions of the world, the state building that began after decolonization has itself contributed substantially to violent processes and their inexorable momentum.

13. This prompted Edward Luttwak's (1999) undoubtedly cynical call to allow such wars to play themselves out without humanitarian aid or constant peace efforts from outside. This, he suggested, is ultimately the only way to break the vicious circle of violence.

14. Peter Waldmann is one of the few sociologists in Germany to engage seriously with the topic of violence *within* states on the basis of his own empirical studies; he too doubts that instrumentally rational interpretations of violence are of much use in analyzing conflicts in many parts of the world (2003, 14ff., 146). In his studies, Waldmann has always quite rightly placed great emphasis on the complex interactions characteristic of civil war (see, e.g., Waldmann 1999). In his studies of Latin America, he has also brought out how, as a result of the particular form taken by state building, violence may also be interpreted as a component

of social order—as in the case of Colombia (see Waldmann 2003, 136–65; Waldmann 2007). If this is correct, then the notion of "new wars" and its implicit thesis of an epochal rupture is untenable.

15. For a more fruitful approach to the interplay of religious and political-economic circumstances, see Kippenberg 2011.

16. The debate on empires must of course be seen in connection with postcolonial debates among historians and historical sociologists, who among other things have asked to what extent colonies and colonialism have impacted on the colonizing countries or empires, ultimately on a structural level (see Cooper 2005; Steinmetz 2005; Calhoun/Cooper/Moore 2006).

17. "When the European mob discovered what a 'lovely virtue' a white skin could be in Africa, when the English conqueror in India became an administrator who no longer believed in the universal validity of law, but was convinced of his own innate capacity to rule and dominate . . . , the stage seemed to be set for all possible horrors. Lying under anybody's nose were many of the elements which gathered together could create a totalitarian government on the basis of racism. 'Administrative massacres' were proposed by Indian bureaucrats while African officials declared that 'no ethical considerations such as the rights of man will be allowed to stand in the way' of white rule" (Arendt 1973, 221).

18. Robinson's interpretation requires modification because he views imperialism primarily as a means of capital valorization, leading him to deny other motives for imperial projects (for a critique, see Bayly 1989, 9f.).

19. At the end of the George W. Bush presidency, the mood in the United States had in any case changed utterly. The confident sense—as the only remaining superpower—of being the center of a new imperium has given way to serious economic and political anxieties about the future. The main anxiety is that America stands helpless in the face of an epochal shift in power toward Asia, and may also fall behind Europe. So far, it is unclear what strategic conclusions will be reached in light of such reassessments. It is just as unclear where the debate on peace will now go—how it will respond to the challenge of new global political upheavals.

BIBLIOGRAPHY

Albrow, Martin (1998), *Abschied vom Nationalstaat. Staat und Gesellschaft im Globalen Zeitalter*. Frankfurt/M.: Suhrkamp.

Alexeiev, N. N. (1940), Modern Culture and the New European War, in: *Review of Politics* 2, 1: 21–33.

Allan, David (2006), *Adam Ferguson*. Edinburgh: Edinburgh UP.

Andreski, Stanislav (1968 [1954]), *Military Organization and Society*. 2nd expanded edition. Berkeley/Los Angeles: University of California Press.

Arendt, Hannah (1973 [1951]), *The Origins of Totalitarianism*. New edition with added prefaces. New York: Harvest.

Armitage, David (2002), Empire and Liberty: A Republican Dilemma, in: Martin van Gelderen/Quentin Skinner (eds.), *Republicanism: A Shared European Heritage*. Cambridge: Cambridge UP, 29–46.

Aron, Raymond (1954 [1951]), *The Century of Total War* [Les Guerres en chaîne]. London: Verschoyle.

——— (1958), *War and Industrial Society* [La Société industrielle et la guerre]. London: Oxford UP.

——— (1962), *Peace and War: A Theory of International Relations* [Paix et guerre entre les nations]. London: Weidenfeld & Nicolson.

——— (1965 [1961]), *Main Currents in Sociological Thought. 1: Montesquieu, Comte, Marx, Tocqueville, the Sociologists and the Revolution of 1848* [Les Grandes Doctrines de sociologie historique]. New York: Basic.

——— (1983 [1976]), *Clausewitz: Philosopher of War* [Penser la guerre, Clausewitz]. London: Routledge.

——— (1990 [1983]), *Memoirs: Fifty Years of Political Thought* [Mémoires]. New York: Holmes & Meier.

Asbach, Olaf (2002), *Die Zähmung der Leviathane. Die Idee einer Rechtsordnung zwischen Staaten bei Abbé de Saint-Pierre und Jean-Jacques Rousseau*. Berlin: Akademie Verlag.

Atkinson, Dick (1971), *Orthodox Consensus and Radical Alternative. A Study in Sociological Theory*. London: Heinemann.

Avant, Deborah (2004), The Privatization of Security and Change in the Control of Force, in: *International Studies Perspectives* 5, 2: 153–57.

Avineri, Shlomo (1968), Introduction, in: Avineri (ed.), *Karl Marx on Colonialism and Modernization: His Despatches and Other Writings on China, India, Mexico, the Middle East and North America*. New York: Doubleday, 1–28.

—— (1972), *Hegel's Theory of the Modern State*. Cambridge: Cambridge UP.

Balandier, Georges (1951), La Situation coloniale: Approche théorique, in: *Cahiers internationaux de sociologie* 11: 44–79.

Bannister, Robert C. (1987), *Sociology and Scientism: The American Quest for Objectivity, 1880–1940*. Chapel Hill: University of North Carolina Press.

Barrelmeyer, Uwe (1994), Der Krieg, die Kultur und die Soziologie. Georg Simmel und die deutschen Soziologen im Ersten Weltkrieg, in: *Sociologia Internationalis* 32, 1/2: 163–90.

Barth, Boris/Jürgen Osterhammel (2005), *Zivilisierungsmissionen. Imperiale Weltverbesserung seit dem 18. Jahrhundert*. Konstanz: UVK.

Bartov, Omer (1991), *Hitler's Army: Soldiers, Nazis and War in the Third Reich*. Oxford: Oxford UP.

Bataille, Georges (1989), *Theory of Religion* [Théorie de la religion]. New York: Zone.

—— (1997 [1933]), The Psychological Structure of Fascism [La Structure psychologique du fascisme], in: Fred Botting/Scott Wilson (eds.), *The Bataille Reader*. Oxford: Blackwell, 122–46.

Batscha, Zwi/Hans Medick (1986), Einleitung, in: Adam Ferguson, *Versuch über die Geschichte der bürgerlichen Gesellschaft*. Herausgegeben und eingeleitet von Zwi Batscha und Hans Medick. Frankfurt/M.: Suhrkamp, 7–91.

Batscha, Zwi/Richard Saage (eds.) (1979), *Friedensutopien—Kant, Fichte, Schlegel, Görres*. Frankfurt/M.: Suhrkamp.

Battistelli, Fabrizio (1989), Zwischen bürgerlicher Gesellschaft und Natur. Das britische soziologische Denken von der Schottischen Schule zu Herbert Spencer, in: Hans Joas/Helmut Steiner (eds.), *Machtpolitischer Realismus und pazifistische Utopie. Krieg und Frieden in der Geschichte der Sozialwissenschaften*. Frankfurt/M.: Suhrkamp, 18–48.

—— (1993), War and Militarism in the Thought of Herbert Spencer: With an Unpublished Letter on the Anglo-Boer War, in: *International Journal of Comparative Sociology* 34, 3/4: 192–209.

Bayly, C. A. (1989), *Imperial Meridian: The British Empire and the World, 1780–1830*. London: Longman.

Beetham, David (1974), *Max Weber and the Theory of Modern Politics*. London: Allen and Unwin.

Benda, Julien (1969 [1927]), *The Treason of the Intellectuals* [Trahison des clercs]. New York: Norton.

Bendix, Reinhard (1974 [1956]), *Work and Authority in Industry: Ideologies of Management in the Course of Industrialization*. Berkeley: University of California Press.

—— (1978), *Kings or People: Power and the Mandate to Rule*. Berkeley: University of California Press.

Bendrath, Ralf (1999), Söldnerfirmen in Afrika—Neue politische Vergesellschaftungsformen jenseits des modernen Staates, in: Wolfgang R. Vogt (ed.), *Frie-*

denskultur statt Kulturkampf. Strategien kultureller Zivilisierung und nach-haltiger Friedensstiftung. Baden-Baden: Nomos Verlagsgesellschaft, 251–88.

Bentham, Jeremy (1843a [1782]), Essay on the Influence of Time and Place in Matters of Legislation, in: John Bowring (ed.), *The Works of Jeremy Bentham.* Vol. 2. Edinburgh: William Tait, 169–94.

——— (1843b [1786–89]), Principles of International Law, in: John Bowring (ed.), *The Works of Jeremy Bentham.* Vol. 2. Edinburgh: William Tait, 537–60.

——— (1843c [1793]), A Manual of Political Economy, in: John Bowring (ed.), *The Works of Jeremy Bentham.* Vol. 3. Edinburgh: William Tait, 31–84.

——— (1843d [1786–89]), Emancipate Your Colonies!, in: John Bowring (ed.), *The Works of Jeremy Bentham.* Vol. 4. Edinburgh: William Tait, 407–18.

Berg, Manfred (1994), Soldiers and Citizens: War and Voting Rights in American History, in: David K. Adams and Cornelis A. van Minnen (eds.), *Reflections on American Exceptionalism,* Keele: Ryburn, 188–225.

——— (2000), Soldaten und Bürger: Zum Zusammenhang von Krieg und Wahlrecht in der amerikanischen Geschichte, in: Wolfgang Knöbl/Gunnar Schmidt (eds.), *Die Gegenwart des Krieges. Staatliche Gewalt in der Moderne,* Frankfurt/M.: Fischer TB, 147–73.

Bergerud, Eric M. (1991), *The Dynamics of Defeat: The Vietnam War in Hau Nghia Province.* Boulder, CO: Westview Press.

Berghahn, Volker R. (1981), *Militarism: The History of an International Debate.* Leamington: Berg.

Berki, R. N. (1971), On Marxian Thought and the Problem of International Relations, in: *World Politics* 24, 1: 80–105.

Berlin, Isaiah (1990), Joseph de Maistre and the Origins of Fascism, in: Berlin, *The Crooked Timber of Humanity: Chapters in the History of Ideas.* London: John Murray, 91–174.

——— (2001), Montesquieu, in: Berlin, *Against the Current: Essays in the History of Ideas.* Princeton, NJ: Princeton UP, 130–61.

Berry, Christopher J. (1997), *Social Theory of the Scottish Enlightenment.* Edinburgh: Edinburgh UP.

Biddle, Jeff/Warren J. Samuels (1993), Thorstein Veblen on War and Peace, in: Warren J. Samuels/Jeff Biddle/Thomas W. Patchak-Schuster (eds.), *Economic Thought and Discourse in the 20th Century.* Aldershot: Edward Elgar, 87–158.

Bluhm, Harald (2006), Einleitung: Tocqueville—der klassische Analytiker der modernen Demokratie, in: Bluhm (ed.), *Alexis de Tocqueville. Kleine politische Schriften.* Berlin: Akademie Verlag, 11–47.

Bobbitt, Philip (2002), *The Shield of Achilles: War, Peace, and the Course of History.* New York: Alfred A. Knopf.

Boesche, Roger (1987), *The Strange Liberalism of Alexis de Tocqueville.* Ithaca, NY: Cornell UP.

Bohlender, Matthias (1999), Die Poetik der Schlacht und die Prosa des Krieges. Nationalverteidigung und Bürgermiliz im moralphilosophischen Diskurs der schottischen Aufklärung, in: Johannes Kunisch/Herfried Münkler (eds.), *Die Wiedergeburt des Krieges aus dem Geist der Revolution. Studien zum bellizistischen Diskurs des ausgehenden 18. und beginnenden 19. Jahrhunderts*. Berlin: Dunker & Humblot, 17–41.

——— (2005), Demokratie und Imperium. Tocqueville in Amerika und Algerien, in: *Berliner Journal für Soziologie* 15, 4: 523–40.

Böhlke, Effi (2005), Montesquieus *Betrachtungen über die universale Monarchie in Europa*. Eine Einführung, in: *Montesquieu. Franzose—Europäer—Weltbürger*. Herausgegeben im Auftrag der Berlin-Brandenburgischen Akademie der Wissenschaften von Effi Böhlke und Etienne François. Berlin: Akademie Verlag, 219–24.

Boudon, Raymond/François Bourricaud (1984), Herbert Spencer ou l'oublié, in: *Revue Française de Sociologie* 25, 3: 343–51.

Boyer, John W. (2004), Judson's War and Hutchins's Peace: The University of Chicago and War in the Twentieth Century, in: *University of Chicago Record* 38, 2: 2–14.

Braddick, Michael J. (2000), *State Formation in Early Modern England, c. 1550–1700*. Cambridge: Cambridge UP.

Breuer, Stefan (1991), *Max Webers Herrschaftssoziologie*. Frankfurt/M./New York: Campus.

——— (1993), *Anatomie der konservativen Revolution*. Darmstadt: Wissenschaftliche Buchgesellschaft.

Brogini Künzi, Giulia (2006), Der Wunsch nach einem blitzschnellen und sauberen Krieg: Die italienische Armee in Ostafrika (1935/36), in: Thoralf Klein/Frank Schumacher (eds.), *Kolonialkriege. Militärische Gewalt im Zeichen des Imperialismus*. Hamburg: Hamburger Edition, 272–90.

Brown, Michael E./Owen R. Coté/Sean M. Lynn-Jones/Steven E. Miller (eds.) (1998), *Theories of War and Peace: An International Security Reader*. Cambridge, MA: MIT Press.

Brzoska, Michael (2004), "New Wars" Discourse in Germany, in: *Journal of Peace Research* 41, 1: 107–17.

Buchan, James (2003), *Crowded with Genius: The Scottish Enlightenment; Edinburgh's Moment of the Mind*. New York: HarperCollins.

Bull, Hedley (1977), *The Anarchical Society: A Study of Order in World Politics*. London: Macmillan.

Burkhardt, Johannes (1997), Die Friedlosigkeit der frühen Neuzeit. Grundlegung einer Theorie der Bellizität Europas, in: *Zeitschrift für Historische Forschung* 24, 1: 509–74.

Büsch, Otto/Michael Erbe (eds.) (1983), *Otto Hintze und die moderne Geschichtswissenschaft*. Ein Tagungsbericht. Berlin: Colloquium Verlag.

Caillois, Roger (1963), *Bellone ou la pente de la guerre*. Brussels: La Renaissance du Livre.

—— (1980 [1939]), War and the Sacred [La Guerre et le sacré], in: Caillois, *Man and the Sacred*. Westport, CT: Greenwood Press, 163–80.

Calhoun, Craig/Frederick Cooper/Kevin W. Moore (eds.) (2006), *Lessons of Empire: Imperial Histories and American Power*. New York: New Press.

Camic, Charles (1983), *Experience and Enlightenment: Socialization for Cultural Change in Eighteenth-Century Scotland*. Chicago: University of Chicago Press.

Capaldi, Nicholas (2003), Introduction, in: Etienne Hofmann (ed.), *Benjamin Constant: Principles of Politics Applicable to All Governments*. Indianapolis, IN: Liberty Fund, xvii–xxii.

Carrithers, David W./Patrick Coleman (eds.) (2002), *Montesquieu and the Spirit of Modernity*. Oxford: Voltaire Foundation.

Carter, Christine Jane (1987), *Rousseau and the Problem of War*. New York: Garland.

Cassirer, Ernst (1951 [1932]), The *Philosophy of the Enlightenment* [Die Philosophie der Aufklärung]. Princeton, NJ: Princeton UP.

Centeno, Miguel Angel (2002), *Blood and Debt: War and the Nation-State in Latin America*. University Park: Pennsylvania State UP.

Chan, Steve (1997), In Search of Democratic Peace: Problems and Promise, in: *Mershon International Studies Review* 41, 1: 59–91.

Chojnacki, Sven (2004), Wandel der Kriegsformen?—Ein kritischer Literaturbericht, in: *Leviathan* 32, 3: 402–24.

Clausewitz, Carl von (1968), *On War* [Vom Kriege]. Harmondsworth: Penguin.

Cohen, Raymond (1994), Pacific Unions: A Reappraisal of the Theory That "Democracies Do Not Go to War with Each Other," in: *Review of International Studies* 20: 207–23.

Collins, Randall (1986), *Weberian Sociological Theory*. Cambridge: Cambridge UP.

—— (1995), German-Bashing and the Theory of Democratic Modernization, in: *Zeitschrift für Soziologie* 24, 1: 3–21.

Comte, Auguste (1875 [1822]), *System of Positive Polity* [Système de politique positive]. Vol. 4, part 2. London: Longmans.

—— (1903 [1844]), *A Discourse on the Positive Spirit* [Discours sur l'esprit positif]. London: William Reeves.

—— (1933), *Die Soziologie. Die positive Philosophie im Auszug*. Herausgegeben von Friedrich Blaschke. Leipzig: Alfred Kröner Verlag.

—— (1973 [1822]), *Plan der wissenschaftlichen Arbeiten, die für eine Reform der Gesellschaft notwendig sind*. Einleitung von Dieter Prokop. Munich: Carl Hanser Verlag.

—— (1998 [1822]), Plan of the Scientific Work Necessary for the Reorganization of Society [Plan des travaux scientifiques nécessaires pour réorganiser la société], in: H. S. Jones (ed.), *Early Political Writings: Auguste Comte*. Cambridge: Cambridge UP, 47–144.

Condorcet (1955 [1795]), *Sketch for a Historical Picture of the Progress of the Human Mind* [Esquisse d'un tableau historique des progrès de l'esprit humain]. London: Weidenfeld & Nicolson.

Constant, Benjamin (1988 [1814]), The Spirit of Conquest and Usurpation and Their Relation to European Civilization [De l'esprit de conquête et de l'usurpation dans leurs rapports avec la civilisation européenne], in: Constant, *Political Writings*, translated and edited by Biancamaria Fontana. Cambridge: Cambridge UP.

—— (2003 [1810]), *Principles of Politics Applicable to All Governments* [Principes de politique applicables à tous les gouvernements]. Edited by Etienne Hofmann. Indianapolis, IN: Liberty Fund.

Conway, Stephen (1989), Bentham on Peace and War in: *Utilitas* 1, 1: 82–101.

—— (1990), Bentham, the Benthamites, and the Nineteenth-Century British Peace Movement, in: *Utilitas* 2, 2: 221–43.

Cooper, Frederick (2005), *Colonialism in Question: Theory, Knowledge, History.* Berkeley/Los Angeles: University of California Press.

Coser, Lewis (1967), *Continuities in the Study of Social Conflict.* New York: Free Press.

Cotkin, George (1994), *William James—Public Philosopher.* Urbana: University of Illinois Press.

Creveld, Martin van (1991), *The Transformation of War.* London: Brassey's.

Curtis, Bruce (1978), William Graham Sumner and the Problem of Progress, in: *New England Quarterly* 51, 3: 348–69.

Czempiel, Ernst-Otto (1992), Governance and Democratization, in: James N. Rosenau/Ernst-Otto Czempiel (eds.), *Governance without Government: Order and Change in World Politics.* Cambridge: Cambridge UP, 250–71.

Daase, Christopher (2004), Demokratischer Frieden—Demokratischer Krieg. Drei Gründe für die Unfriedlichkeit von Demokratien, in: Christine Schweitzer/Björn Aust/Peter Schlotter (eds.), *Demokratien im Krieg.* Baden-Baden: Nomos, 53–71.

Dahrendorf, Ralf (1968 [1966]), In Praise of Thrasymachus [Lob des Thrasymachos. Zur Neuorientierung von politischer Theorie und politischer Analyse], in: Dahrendorf, *Essays in the Theory of Society.* London: Routledge, 129–50.

—— (1972), Zur Theorie und Analyse von Konflikten, in: Dahrendorf, *Konflikt und Freiheit. Auf dem Weg zur Dienstklassengesellschaft.* Munich/Zurich: Piper, 11–93.

Dandeker, Christopher (1994), New Times for the Military: Some Sociological Remarks on the Changing Role and Structure of the Armed Forces of the Advanced Societies, in: *British Journal of Sociology* 45, 4: 637–54.

Dietze, Anita/Walter Dietze (eds.) (1989), *Ewiger Friede? Dokumente einer deutschen Diskussion um 1800.* Leipzig/Weimar: Gustav Kiepenheuer Verlag.

Dion, Stéphane (1990), Durham et Tocqueville sur la colonisation libérale, in: *Revue d'Études Canadiennes/Journal of Canadian Studies* 25, 1: 60–77.

Domhoff, G. William (2006), Mills's *The Power Elite* 50 Years Later, in: *Contemporary Sociology* 35, 6: 547–50.

Downing, Brian M. (1992), *The Military Revolution and Political Change: Origins of Democracy and Autocracy in Early Modern Europe*. Princeton, NJ: Princeton UP.

Doyle, Michael (1983), Kant, Liberal Legacies, and Foreign Affairs, in: *Philosophy and Public Affairs* 12, 3 and 4: 205–35 and 323–53.

———— (1986), Liberalism and World Politics, in: *American Political Science Review* 80, 4: 1151–69.

———— (1997), *Ways of War and Peace: Realism, Liberalism, and Socialism*. New York: Norton.

Dülffer, Jost (1990), Joseph Görres und Friedrich Gentz—Modelle der Friedenssicherung in Deutschland seit der Französischen Revolution, in: Jost Dülffer/ Bernd Martin/Günter Wollstein (eds.), *Deutschland in Europa. Kontinuität und Bruch. Gedenkschrift für Andreas Hillgruber*. Berlin. Propyläen, 52–72.

Durkheim, Émile (1915a), *Who Wanted War? The Origin of the War according to Diplomatic Documents* [Qui a voulu la guerre? Les Origines de la guerre d'après les documents diplomatiques]. Paris: Colin.

———— (1915b), Germany Above All [L'Allemagne au-dessus de tout], in: Durkheim, *Studies and Documents on the War*, Paris: Colin.

———— (1957 [1950]), *Professional Ethics and Civic Morals* [Leçons de sociologie physique des mœurs et du droit]. London: Routledge.

———— (1961 [1902]), *Moral Education* [L'Éducation morale, cours dispensé à la Sorbonne]. New York: Free Press.

———— (1973 [1898]), Individualism and the Intellectuals [L'Individualisme et les intellectuels], in: Robert N. Bellah (ed.), *Émile Durkheim on Morality and Society*. Chicago: University of Chicago Press, 43–57.

Dwyer, John (1998), *The Age of the Passions: An Interpretation of Adam Smith and Scottish Enlightenment Culture*. East Linton: Tuckwell Press.

Earle, Edward Mead (1952), Adam Smith, Alexander Hamilton, Friedrich List: The Economic Foundations of Military Power, in: Earle (with the collaboration of Gordon A. Craig and Felix Gilbert) (ed.), *Makers of Modern Strategy: Military Thought from Machiavelli to Hitler*. Princeton, NJ: Princeton UP, 117–54.

Ehrke, Michael (2003), Von der Raubökonomie zur Rentenökonomie. Mafia, Bürokratie und internationales Mandat in Bosnien, in: *Internationale Politik und Gesellschaft* 2: 123–54.

Elias, Norbert (1978 [1939]), *The Civilizing Process* [Über den Prozeß der Zivilisation. Soziogenetische und psychogenetische Untersuchungen]. New York: Urizen.

Elman, Miriam Fendius (1997), Introduction: The Need for a Qualitative Test of the Democratic Peace Theory, in: Elman (ed.), *Paths to Peace: Is Democracy the Answer?* Cambridge, MA: MIT Press, 1–57.

Elwert, Georg (1997), Gewaltmärkte. Beobachtungen zur Zweckrationalität der Gewalt, in: Trutz von Trotha (ed.), *Soziologie der Gewalt*. Sonderheft 37 der Kölner Zeitschrift für Soziologie und Sozialpsychologie. Opladen: Westdeutscher Verlag, 86–101.

Emerson, Roger (2003), The Context of the Scottish Enlightenment, in: Alexander Broadie (ed.), *The Cambridge Companion to the Scottish Enlightenment*. Cambridge: Cambridge UP, 9–30.

Engels, Friedrich (1975 [1878]), *Herr Eugen Dühring's Revolution in Science* [Herrn Eugen Dührings Umwälzung der Wissenschaft (Anti-Dühring)]. London: Lawrence & Wishart.

——— (1990 [1893]), Can Europe Disarm? [Kann Europa abrüsten?], in: *Karl Marx, Friedrich Engels. Collected Works*. Vol. 27. Moscow: Progress, 372–93.

Enloe, Cynthia (2000), *Maneuvers: The International Politics of Militarizing Women's Lives*. Berkeley/Los Angeles: University of California Press.

Erdmann, Gero (2003), Apokalyptische Trias: Staatsversagen, Staatsverfall und Staatszerfall—strukturelle Probleme der Demokratie in Afrika, in: Petra Bendel/Aurel Croissant/Friedbert Rüb (eds.), *Demokratie und Staatlichkeit. Systemwechsel zwischen Staatlichkeit und Staatskollaps*. Opladen: Leske + Budrich, 267–92.

Ertman, Thomas (1997), *Birth of the Leviathan: Building States and Regimes in Medieval and Early Modern Europe*. Cambridge: Cambridge UP.

Etges, Andreas (1999), *Wirtschaftsnationalismus. USA und Deutschland im Vergleich (1815–1914)*. Frankfurt/M./New York: Campus.

Euchner, Walter (1979), *Naturrecht und Politik bei John Locke*. Frankfurt/M.: Suhrkamp.

Evans, Peter/Dietrich Rueschemeyer/Theda Skocpol (eds.) (1985), *Bringing the State Back In*. Cambridge: Cambridge UP.

Evera, Stephen van (1998), Offense, Defense, and the Causes of War, in: Michael E. Brown et al. (eds.), *Theories of War and Peace: An International Security Reader*. Cambridge, MA: MIT Press, 55–93.

Fanon, Frantz (1963 [1961]), *The Wretched of the Earth* [Les Damnés de la terre]. London: Penguin.

Ferguson, Adam (2006 [1767]), *An Essay on the History of Civil Society*. Charleston, SC: BiblioBazaar.

Ferguson, Niall (2004), *Colossus: The Price of America's Empire*. New York: Penguin.

Fetscher, Iring (1979), Einleitung, in: *Auguste Comte. Discours sur l'esprit positif—Rede über den Geist des Positivismus*. Hamburg: Felix Meiner Verlag, xv–xliv.

——— (1990), *Rousseaus politische Philosophie. Zur Geschichte des demokratischen Freiheitsbegriffs*. Frankfurt/M.: Suhrkamp.

Fichte, Johann Gottlieb (2001 [1796]), Review of Immanuel Kant, *Perpetual Peace: A Philosophical Sketch* [Zum ewigen Frieden—Ein philosophischer Entwurf von Immanuel Kant], in: *Philosophical Forum* 32, 4: 311–21.

Finer, Samuel E. (1962), *The Man on Horseback: The Role of the Military in Politics*. London: Pall Mall Press.

Flasch, Kurt (2000), *Die geistige Mobilmachung. Die deutschen Intellektuellen und der Erste Weltkrieg*. Berlin: Alexander Fest Verlag.

Fletcher, Andrew (1997 [1698)]), A Discourse of Government with Relation to Militias, in: Fletcher, *Political Works*. Edited by John Robertson. Cambridge: Cambridge UP, 1–31.

Fligstein, Neil (2001), *The Architecture of Markets: An Economic Sociology of Twenty-First-Century Capitalist Societies*. Princeton, NJ: Princeton UP.

Förster, Stig (2000), "Vom Kriege." Überlegungen zu einer modernen Militärgeschichte, in: Thomas Kühne/Benjamin Ziemann (eds.), *Was ist Militärgeschichte?*. Paderborn/Munich/Vienna/Zurich: Ferdinand Schöningh, 265–81.

Francis, Mark (2007), *Herbert Spencer and the Invention of Modern Life*. Stocksfield: Acumen.

Fredrickson, George M. (2000), Race and Empire in Liberal Thought: The Legacy of Tocqueville, in: Fredrickson, *The Comparative Imagination: On the History of Racism, Nationalism, and Social Movements*. Berkeley/Los Angeles: University of California Press, 98–116.

Freyer, Hans (1925), *Der Staat*. Leipzig: Ernst Wiegandt—Verlagsbuchhandlung.

Friedberg, Aaron L. (2000), *In the Shadow of the Garrison State: America's Anti-Statism and Its Cold War Grand Strategy*. Princeton, NJ: Princeton UP.

Fries, Helmut (1994), *Die große Katharsis. Der Erste Weltkrieg in der Sicht deutscher Dichter und Gelehrter. Band 1: Die Kriegsbegeisterung von 1914: Ursprünge—Denkweisen—Auflösung*. Konstanz: Verlag am Hockgraben.

Fuchs-Heinritz, Werner (1998), *Auguste Comte. Einführung in Leben und Werk*. Opladen/Wiesbaden: Westdeutscher Verlag.

Gallie, W. B. (1978), *Philosophers of Peace and War: Kant, Clausewitz, Marx, Engels and Tolstoy*. London: Cambridge UP.

Galtung, Johan (1996), *Peace by Peaceful Means: Peace and Conflict, Development and Civilization*. London: Sage.

Gates, Scott/Torbjörn L. Knutsen/Jonathon W. Moses (1996), Democracy and Peace: A More Skeptical View, in: *Journal of Peace Research* 33, 1: 1–10.

Genov, Nikolai (1989), Gesellschaftliche Gemeinschaft und internationale Spannungsverhältnisse. Talcott Parsons über Krieg und Frieden im System der modernen Gesellschaften, in: Hans Joas/Helmut Steiner (eds.), *Machtpolitischer Realismus und pazifistische Utopie*. Frankfurt/M.: Suhrkamp, 261–82.

Gentz, Friedrich (1989 [1800]), Über den Ewigen Frieden, in: Anita Dietze/Walter Dietze (eds.), *Ewiger Friede? Dokumente einer deutschen Diskussion um 1800*. Leipzig/Weimar: Gustav Kiepenheuer Verlag, 377–91.

Gephart, Werner (1996), Die französische Soziologie und der Erste Weltkrieg. Spannungen in Emile Durkheims Deutung des Großen Krieges, in: Wolfgang Mommsen (ed.), *Kultur und Krieg. Die Rolle der Intellektuellen, Künstler und Schriftsteller im Ersten Weltkrieg*. Munich: R. Oldenbourg Verlag, 49–63.

Gerhard, Dietrich (1970), Otto Hintze: His Work and His Significance in Historiography, in: *Central European History* 3: 17–48.

Gerhardt, Volker (1995), *Immanuel Kants Entwurf "Zum Ewigen Frieden." Eine Theorie der Politik*. Darmstadt: Wissenschaftliche Buchgesellschaft.

Gershman, Sally (1976), Alexis de Tocqueville and Slavery, in: *French Historical Studies* 9, 3: 467–83.

Geuna, Marco (2002), Republicanism and Commercial Society in the Scottish Enlightenment: The Case of Adam Ferguson, in: Martin van Gelderen/Quentin Skinner (eds.), *Republicanism: A Shared European Heritage*. Cambridge: Cambridge UP, 177–95.

Geyer, Michael/Charles Bright (1996), Global Violence and Nationalizing Wars in Eurasia and America: The Geopolitics of War in the Mid-Nineteenth Century, in: *Comparative Studies of Society and History* 38, 4: 619–57.

Giddens, Anthony (1984), *The Constitution of Society: Introduction of the Theory of Structuration*. Berkeley: University of California Press.

────── (1985), *The Nation-State and Violence: Volume Two of a Contemporary Critique of Historical Materialism*. Cambridge: Polity Press.

Giddings, Franklin (1918), *The Responsible State: A Re-examination of Fundamental Political Doctrines in the Light of the War and the Menace of Anarchism*. Boston: Houghton Mifflin.

Gilbert, Felix (1975), Introduction, in: Gilbert (ed.), *The Historical Essays of Otto Hintze*. New York: Oxford UP, 3–30.

Görres, Joseph (1979 [1798]), Der allgemeine Friede, ein Ideal, in: Zwi Batscha/Richard Saage (eds.), *Friedensutopien*. Frankfurt/M.: Suhrkamp, 111–72.

Gowa, Joanne (1999), *Ballots and Bullets: The Elusive Democratic Peace*. Princeton, NJ: Princeton UP.

Greenleaf, W. H. (1988), *The British Political Tradition*. Vol. 2: *The Ideological Heritage*. Cambridge: Routledge.

Großheim, Michael (1999), Politischer Existenzialismus, in: Günter Meuter/Henrique Ricardo Otten/Hannes Siegrist (eds.), *Der Aufstand gegen den Bürger. Antibürgerliches Denken im 20. Jahrhundert*. Würzburg: Königshausen und Neumann, 127–63.

Haakonssen, Knud (2006), Introduction: The Coherence of Smith's Thought, in: Haakonssen (ed.), *The Cambridge Companion to Adam Smith*. Cambridge: Cambridge UP, 1–21.

Habermas, Jürgen (1997 [1996]), Kant's Idea of Perpetual Peace, with the Benefit of Two Hundred Years' Hindsight [Kants Idee des ewigen Friedens—aus dem historischen Abstand von zweihundert Jahren], in: James Bohman/Matthias Lutz-Bachmann (eds.), *Perpetual Peace: Essays on Kant's Cosmopolitan Ideal*. Cambridge, MA: MIT Press, 113–54.

────── (2008 [2005]), A Political Constitution for the Pluralist World Society? [Eine politische Verfassung für die pluralistische Weltgesellschaft?], in: Habermas, *Between Naturalism and Religion*. Cambridge: Polity, 312–52.

Haines, Valerie A. (1998), Spencer and His Critics, in: Charles Camic (ed.), *Reclaiming the Sociological Classics: The State of the Scholarship*. Malden, MA: Blackwell, 81–111.

Halévy, Elie (1972 [1928]), *The Growth of Philosophic Radicalism* [La Formation du radicalisme philosophique]. With a Preface by John Plamenatz. London: Faber and Faber.

Hall, John A. (1981), *Diagnoses of Our Time: Six Views on Our Social Condition*. London: Heinemann Educational Books.

———— (1987), War and the Rise of the West, in: Colin Creighton/Martin Shaw (eds.), *The Sociology of War and Peace*. London: Macmillan, 37–53.

Haltiner, Karl W. (1998), The Definitive End of the Mass Army in Western Europe?, in: *Armed Forces and Society* 25, 1: 7–36.

Hanson, Donald W. (1984), Thomas Hobbes' "Highway to Peace," in: *International Organization* 38, 2: 329–54.

Hassner, Pierre (1961), Les Concepts de guerre et de paix chez Kant, in: *Revue Française de Science Politique* 11, 1: 642–70.

———— (1997), Rousseau and the Theory and Practice of International Relations, in: Clifford Orwin/Nathan Tarcov (eds.), *The Legacy of Rousseau*. Chicago: University of Chicago Press, 200–19.

Hegel, G.W.F. (1986 [1803–6]), Aphorismen aus Hegels Wastebook, in: Hegel, *Jenaer Schriften 1801–1807*. Werke 2. Frankfurt/M.: Suhrkamp, 540–67.

———— (1991 [1821]), *Elements of the Philosophy of Right* [Grundlinien der Philosophie des Rechts oder Naturrecht und Staatwissenschaft im Grundrisse]. Cambridge: Cambridge UP.

———— (1999a [1800–1802]), The German Constitution [Die Verfassung Deutschlands], in: Hegel, *Political Writings*. Cambridge: Cambridge UP, 6–101.

———— (1999b [1802/3]), On the Scientific Ways of Treating Natural Law, On Its Place in Practical Philosophy, and Its Relation to the Positive Sciences of Right [Über die wissenschaftlichen Behandlungsarten des Naturrechts, seine Stelle in der praktischen Philosophie und sein Verhältnis zu den positiven Rechtswissenschaften], in: Hegel, *Political Writings*. Cambridge: Cambridge UP, 102–80.

Heilbron, Johan (1995), *The Rise of Social Theory* [Ontstaan van de sociologie]. Minneapolis: University of Minnesota Press.

———— (1998), French Moralists and the Anthropology of the Modern Era: On the Genesis of the Notions of "Interest" and "Commercial Society," in: Johan Heilbron/Lars Magnusson/Björn Wittrock (eds.), *The Rise of the Social Sciences and the Formation of Modernity: Conceptual Change in Context, 1750–1850*. Dordrecht/Boston/London: Kluwer Academic Publishers, 77–106.

Hein, Wolfgang (2005), Vom Entwicklungsstaat zum Staatszerfall, in: *Aus Politik und Zeitgeschichte* 28–29: 6–11.

Heins, Volker/Jens Warburg (2004), *Kampf der Zivilisten. Militär und Gesellschaft im Wandel*. Bielefeld: transcript.

Hellmuth, Eckart/Christoph von Ehrenstein (2001), Intellectual History Made in

Britain: Die *Cambridge School* und ihre Kritiker, in: *Geschichte und Gesellschaft* 27, 1: 149–72.

Hennis, Wilhelm (1984), Max Weber in Freiburg. Zur Freiburger Antrittsvorlesung in wissenschaftsgeschichtlicher Sicht, in: *Freiburger Universitätsblätter* 23, 83: 33–45.

—— (1988), Eine "Wissenschaft vom Menschen." Max Weber und die deutsche Nationalökonomie der Historischen Schule, in: Wolfgang J. Mommsen/Wolfgang Schwentker (eds.), *Max Weber und seine Zeitgenossen*. Göttingen/Zurich: Vandenhoeck & Ruprecht, 25–58.

—— (2000a [1996]), *Max Weber's Science of Man* [Max Webers Wissenschaft vom Menschen]. Newbury: Threshold.

—— (2000b [1987]), *Max Weber's Central Question* [Max Webers Fragestellung]. Newbury: Threshold.

Herberg-Rothe, Andreas (1999), Die Entgrenzung des Krieges bei Clausewitz, in: Johannes Kunisch/Herfried Münkler (eds.), *Die Wiedergeburt des Krieges aus dem Geist der Revolution. Studien zum bellizistischen Diskurs des ausgehenden 18. und beginnenden 19. Jahrhunderts*. Berlin: Duncker & Humblot, 185–209.

—— (2007 [2001]), *Clausewitz's Puzzle: The Political Theory of War* [Das Rätsel Clausewitz]. Oxford: Oxford UP.

Herbst, Jeffrey (2000), *States and Power in Africa: Comparative Lessons in Authority and Control*. Princeton, NJ: Princeton UP.

Hereth, Michael (1986 [1979]), *Alexis de Tocqueville: Threats to Freedom in Democracy* [Alexis de Tocqueville. Die Gefährdung der Freiheit in der Demokratie]. Durham, NC: Duke UP.

Herman, Arthur (2002), *The Scottish Enlightenment: The Scots' Invention of the Modern World*. London: Fourth Estate.

Hess, Andreas (1995), *Die politische Soziologie C. Wright Mills. Ein Beitrag zur politischen Ideengeschichte*. Opladen: Leske + Budrich.

Hibou, Béatrice (1998), Retrait ou redéploiement de l'État?, in: *Critique internationale* 1: 151–68.

Hill, Lisa (1996), Anticipation of Nineteenth and Twentieth Century Social Thought in the Work of Adam Ferguson, in: *European Journal of Sociology* 37, 1: 203–28.

—— (1998), The Invisible Hand of Adam Ferguson, in: *European Legacy* 3, 6: 42–64.

—— (2006), *The Passionate Society: The Social, Political and Moral Thought of Adam Ferguson*. Dordrecht: Springer.

Hintze, Otto (1914), Unser Militarismus. Ein Wort an Amerika, in: *Internationale Monatsschrift für Wissenschaft, Kunst und Technik* 9, 4: 209–20.

—— (1925), Rezension zu Oswald Spengler *Der Staat u.a.*, in: *Zeitschrift für die gesamte Staatswissenschaft* 79: 541–47.

—— (1964 [1929]), Der moderne Kapitalismus als historisches Individuum:

Ein kritischer Bericht über Sombarts Werk, in: Hintze, *Soziologie und Geschichte. Gesammelte Abhandlungen zur Soziologie, Politik und Theorie der Geschichte.* Herausgegeben und eingeleitet von Gerhard Oestreich. Göttingen: Vandenhoeck & Ruprecht, 374–426.

―――― (1975a [1902]), The Formation of States and Constitutional Development: A Study in History and Politics [Staatenbildung und Verfassungsentwicklung. Eine historisch-politische Studie], in: Felix Gilbert (ed.), *The Historical Essays of Otto Hintze.* New York: Oxford UP, 159–77.

―――― (1975b [1906]), Military Organization and the Organization of the State [Staatsverfassung und Heeresverfassung], in: Felix Gilbert (ed.), *The Historical Essays of Otto Hintze.* New York: Oxford UP, 180–215.

―――― (1975c [1929]), Economics and Politics in the Age of Modern Capitalism [Wirtschaft und Politik im Zeitalter des modernen Kapitalismus], in: Felix Gilbert (ed.), *The Historical Essays of Otto Hintze.* New York: Oxford UP, 424–52.

Hirschman, Albert O. (1977), *The Passions and the Interests: Political Arguments for Capitalism before Its Triumph.* Princeton, NJ: Princeton UP.

―――― (1986), Rival Views of Market Society, in: Hirschman (ed.), *Rival Views of Market Society and Other Recent Essays.* New York: Viking, 105–41.

Hobbes, Thomas (1996 [1651]), *Leviathan.* Oxford: Oxford UP.

Hobden, Stephen (1998), *International Relations and Historical Sociology: Breaking Down Boundaries.* London: Routledge.

Hobden, Stephen/John M. Hobson (eds.) (2002), *Historical Sociology of International Relations.* Cambridge: Cambridge UP.

Hobsbawm, Eric J. (1994), *The Age of Extremes: The Short Twentieth Century, 1914–1991.* London: Michael Joseph.

Hobson, John M. (2000), *The State and International Relations.* Cambridge: Cambridge UP.

Hoeres, Peter (2004), *Krieg der Philosophen. Die deutsche und die britische Philosophie im Ersten Weltkrieg.* Paderborn: Ferdinand Schöningh.

Höffe, Otfried (2006 [2001]), *Kant's Cosmopolitan Theory of Law and Peace* ["Königliche Völker." Zu Kants kosmopolitischer Rechts- und Friedenstheorie]. Cambridge: Cambridge UP.

Hoffmann, Stanley (1963), Rousseau on War and Peace, in: *American Political Science Review* 57, 2: 317–33.

Hoffmann, Stanley/David P. Fidler (eds.) (1991a), *Rousseau on International Relations.* Oxford: Clarendon Press.

―――― (1991b), Introduction, in: Hoffmann/Fidler (eds.), *Rousseau on International Relations.* Oxford: Clarendon Press, xi–lxxvii.

Hofmann, Hasso (2002), *Legitimität gegen Legalität. Der Weg der politischen Philosophie Carl Schmitts.* Vierte Auflage mit einer neuen Einleitung. Berlin: Duncker & Humblot.

Hollier, Denis (ed.) (1987 [1979]), *The College of Sociology* [Le Collège de Sociologie]. Minneapolis: University of Minnesota Press.

Holsti, Kalevi J. (1996), *The State, War, and the State of War*. Cambridge: Cambridge UP.

—— (2004), *Taming the Sovereigns: Institutional Change in International Politics*. Cambridge: Cambridge UP.

Hont, Istvan (1983), The "Rich Country—Poor Country" Debate in Scottish Classical Political Economy, in: Istvan Hont/Michael Ignatieff (eds.), *Wealth and Virtue: The Shaping of Political Economy in the Scottish Enlightenment*. Cambridge: Cambridge UP, 271–315.

Hont, Istvan/Michael Ignatieff (1983), Needs and Justice in the Wealth of Nations: An Introductory Essay, in: Istvan/Ignatieff (eds.), *Wealth and Virtue: The Shaping of Political Economy in the Scottish Enlightenment*. Cambridge: Cambridge UP, 1–44.

Howard, Michael (1977), *War and the Liberal Conscience*. The George Macaulay Trevelyan Lectures in the University of Cambridge. London: Temple Smith.

—— (1983), *Clausewitz*. Oxford: Oxford UP.

Huebner, Daniel R. (2008), Toward a Sociology of the State and War, in: *European Journal of Sociology* 49, 2, 65–90.

Hübinger, Gangolf (1988), Staatstheorie und Politik als Wissenschaft im Kaiserreich: Georg Jellinek, Otto Hintze, Max Weber, in: Hans Maier et al. (eds.), *Politik, Philosophie, Praxis. Festschrift für Willhelm Hennis zum 65. Geburtstag*. Stuttgart: Klett, 143–61.

Hughes, Everett (1942), The Impact of War on American Institutions, in: *American Journal of Sociology* 48, 3: 398–403.

Hume, David (1964 [1752]), Idea of a Perfect Commonwealth, in: Hume, *The Philosophical Works* (in 4 vols.). Vol. 3. ed. Thomas Hill Green/Thomas Hodge Grose. Aalen: Scientia, 480–93.

—— (1987a [1741]), Of the Balance of Power, in: Hume, *Essays, Moral, Political and Literary*. Indianapolis, IN: Liberty, 332–41.

—— (1987b [1752]), Of Refinement in the Arts, in: Hume, *Essays, Moral, Political and Literary*. Indianapolis, IN: Liberty, 268–80.

Huntington, Samuel P. (1967 [1957]), *The Soldier and the State: The Theory and Politics of Civil-Military Relations*. Cambridge, MA: Belknap Press of Harvard UP.

—— (1996), Democracy's Third Wave, in: Larry Diamond/Marc F. Plattner (eds.), *The Global Resurgence of Democracy*. 2nd ed. Baltimore: Johns Hopkins UP, 3–25.

Huntley, Wade L. (1996), Kant's Third Image: Systemic Sources of the Liberal Peace, in: *International Studies Quarterly* 40, 1: 45–76.

Hurrell, Andrew (1990), Kant and the Kantian Paradigm in International Relations, in: *Review of International Studies* 16, 3: 183–205.

Hynes, Samuel (1990), *A War Imagined: The First World War and English Culture*. London: Bodley Head.

Ignatieff, Michael (1983), John Millar on Individualism, in: Istvan Hont/Michael

Ignatieff (eds.), *Wealth and Virtue: The Shaping of Political Economy in the Scottish Enlightenment*. Cambridge: Cambridge UP, 317–43.

Ionin, Leonid G./Alla I. Cernych (1989), Krieg und Frieden in der frühen russischen Soziologie, in: Hans Joas/Helmut Steiner (eds.), *Machtpolitischer Realismus und pazifistische Utopie. Krieg und Frieden in der Geschichte der Sozialwissenschaften*. Frankfurt/M.: Suhrkamp, 117–52.

Jackson, Robert H./Carl G. Rosberg (1982), Why Africa's Weak States Persist: The Empirical and the Juridical in Statehood, in: *World Politics* 35, 1: 1–24.

Jäger, Thomas/Gerhard Kümmel (eds.) (2007), *Private Military and Security Companies: Chances, Problems, Pitfalls and Prospects*. Wiesbaden: Verlag für Sozialwissenschaften.

James, William (1971 [1910]), The Moral Equivalent of War, in: *William James: The Essential Writings*. New York: Harper & Row, 349–61.

Janowitz, Morris (1964), *The Military in the Political Development of New Nations: An Essay in Comparative Analysis*. Chicago: University of Chicago Press.

——— (1976), Military Institutions and Citizenship in Western Societies, in: *Armed Forces and Society* 2: 185–204.

Jardin, André (1962), Tocqueville et l'Algérie, in: *Revue des Travaux de l'Académie des Sciences Morales & Politiques* 115, 1: 61–70.

Jean, François/Jean-Christophe Rufin (eds.) (1999), *Ökonomie der Bürgerkriege* [Economie des guerres civiles]. Hamburg: Hamburger Edition.

Jehn, Christopher/Zachary Selden (2002), The End of Conscription in Europe?, in: *Contemporary Economic Policy* 20, 2: 93–100.

Jervis, Robert (1988), Realism, Game Theory, and Cooperation, in: *World Politics* 40, 3: 317–49.

Joas, Hans (1985 [1980]), *George Herbert Mead: A Contemporary Re-examination of His Thought* [Praktische Intersubjektivität. Die Entwicklung des Werkes von George Herbert Mead]. Cambridge, MA: MIT Press.

——— (1996), Die Modernität des Krieges. Die Modernisierungstheorie und das Problem der Gewalt, in: *Leviathan* 24, 1: 13–27.

——— (1999a), The Postdisciplinary History of Disciplines [Postdisziplinäre Disziplingeschichte], in: *European Journal of Social Theory* 2: 109–22.

——— (1999b), Die Soziologie und das Heilige. Schlüsseltexte der Religionssoziologie, in: *Merkur* 53, 605/6: 990–98.

——— (2003 [2000]), *War and Modernity* [Kriege und Werte. Studien zur Gewaltgeschichte des 20. Jahrhunderts]. Oxford: Polity.

——— (2005), Max Weber and the Origin of Human Rights: A Study of Cultural Innovation, in: Charles Camic/Philip S. Gorski/David M. Trubek (eds.), *Max Weber's Economy and Society*. Stanford, CA: Stanford UP, 366–82.

——— (2007), Versuch einer Befreiung. Joachim Radkaus Biographie über Max Weber, in: *Merkur* 61, 1: 62–68.

——— (2008a [2004]), *Do We Need Religion? On the Experience of Self-*

Transcendence [Braucht der Mensch Religion? Über Erfahrungen der Selbsttranszendenz]. Boulder, CO: Paradigm.

——— (2012), *Glaube als Option*. Zukunftsmöglichkeiten des Christentums. Freiburg: Herder Verlag.

Joas, Hans/Wolfgang Knöbl (2009 [2004]), *Social Theory: Twenty Introductory Lectures* [Sozialtheorie. Zwanzig einführende Vorlesungen]. Cambridge: Cambridge UP.

Joas, Hans/Helmut Steiner (eds.) (1989), *Machtpolitischer Realismus und pazifistische Utopie. Krieg und Frieden in der Geschichte der Sozialwissenschaften*. Frankfurt/M.: Suhrkamp.

Johnson, James Turner (1987), *The Quest for Peace: Three Moral Traditions in Western Cultural History*. Princeton, NJ: Princeton UP.

Kaldor, Mary (1999), *New and Old Wars: Organized Violence in a Global Era*. Stanford, CA: Stanford UP.

Kalyvas, Andreas/Ira Katznelson (1998), Adam Ferguson Returns: Liberalism through a Glass, Darkly, in: *Political Theory* 26, 2: 173–97.

Kalyvas, Stathis N. (2001), "New" and "Old" Civil Wars: A Valid Distinction?, in: *World Politics* 54, 1: 99–118.

Kant, Immanuel (1991a [1784]), Idea for a Universal History with a Cosmopolitan Purpose [Idee zu einer allgemeinen Geschichte in weltbürgerlicher Absicht], in: H. S. Reiss (ed.), *Kant: Political Writings*. Cambridge: Cambridge UP, 41–53.

——— (1991b [1786]), Conjectures on the Beginning of Human History [Mutmaßlicher Anfang der Menschengeschichte], in: H. S. Reiss (ed.), *Kant: Political Writings*. Cambridge: Cambridge UP, 221–34.

——— (1991c [1793]), On the Common Saying: "This May Be True in Theory, but It Does Not Apply in Practice" [Über den Gemeinspruch: Das mag in der Theorie richtig sein, taugt aber nicht für die Praxis], in: H. S. Reiss (ed.), *Kant: Political Writings*. Cambridge: Cambridge UP, 61–92.

——— (1991d [1795]), Perpetual Peace: A Philosophical Sketch [Zum Ewigen Frieden. Ein Philosophischer Entwurf], in: H. S. Reiss (ed.), *Kant: Political Writings*. Cambridge: Cambridge UP, 93–130.

——— (1991e [1797]), Metaphysics of Morals [Die Metaphysik der Sitten], in: H. S. Reiss (ed.), *Kant: Political Writings*. Cambridge: Cambridge UP, 131–75.

——— (2007 [1790]), *Critique of Judgement* [Kritik der Urteilskraft]. Oxford: Oxford UP.

Keck, Margaret/Kathryn Sikkink (eds.) (1998), *Activists Beyond Borders*. Ithaca, NY: Cornell UP.

Keene, Edward (2002), *Beyond the Anarchical Society: Grotius, Colonialism and Order in World Politics*. Cambridge: Cambridge UP.

Kehr, Eckart (1970 [1930]), Zur Soziologie der Reichswehr, in: Kehr, *Der Primat der Innenpolitik*. Berlin: de Gruyter, 235–43.

Keohane, Nannerl O. (1972), Virtuous Republics and Glorious Monarchies: Two Models in Montesquieu's Political Thought, in: *Political Studies* 20, 4: 383–96.

Kernic, Franz (2001), *Sozialwissenschaften und Militär. Eine kritische Analyse.* Wiesbaden: Deutscher Universitäts-Verlag.

——— (2004), Demokratie und Wehrform—Anmerkungen zum Verhältnis von Staatsverfassung und Heeresverfassung, in: Ines-Jacqueline Werkner (ed.), *Die Wehrpflicht und ihre Hintergründe. Sozialwissenschaftliche Beiträge zur aktuellen Debatte.* Wiesbaden: Verlag für Sozialwissenschaften, 65–86.

Kersting, Wolfgang (2002), *Thomas Hobbes zur Einführung.* Hamburg: Junius.

Kippenberg, Hans G. (2011 [2008]), *Violence as Worship: Religious Wars in the Age of Globalization* [Gewalt als Gottesdienst. Religionskriege im Zeitalter der Globalisierung]. Stanford, CA: Stanford UP.

Klein, Thoralf/Frank Schumacher (2006), Einleitung, in: Klein/Schumacher (eds.), *Kolonialkriege. Militärische Gewalt im Zeichen des Imperialismus.* Hamburg: Hamburger Edition, 7–13.

Knöbl, Wolfgang (1998), *Polizei und Herrschaft im Modernisierungsprozeß. Staatsbildung und innere Sicherheit in Preußen, England und Amerika 1700–1914.* Frankfurt/M./New York: Campus.

——— (2001), *Spielräume der Modernisierung. Das Ende der Eindeutigkeit.* Weilerswist: Velbrück.

——— (2006a), Zivilgesellschaft und staatliches Gewaltmonopol. Zur Verschränkung von Gewalt und Zivilität, in: *Mittelweg 36*, 15 (Feb./Mar.): 61–84.

——— (2006b), Krieg als Geschäft. Gewaltmärkte und ihre Paradoxien, in: *Westend—Neue Zeitschrift für Sozialforschung* 3, 1: 88–98.

——— (2007), *Die Kontingenz der Moderne. Wege in Europa, Asien und Amerika.* Frankfurt/M.: Campus.

——— (2008), Staatsbildung und staatliche Gewalt aus soziologischer Perspektive, in: Hans Joas (ed.), *Die Anthropologie von Macht und Glauben. Das Werk Wolfgang Reinhards in der Diskussion.* Göttingen: Wallstein, 45–61.

——— (2011), Die Gleichursprünglichkeit verschiedener Machtquellen und das Internationale Staatensystem, in: Tobias ten Brink (ed.), *Globale Rivalitäten. Staat und Staatensystem im globalen Kapitalismus.* Stuttgart: Franz Steiner Verlag, 67–85.

Knöbl, Wolfgang/Gunnar Schmidt (2000), Warum brauchen wir eine Soziologie des Krieges, in: Knöbl/Schmidt (eds.), *Die Gegenwart des Krieges. Staatliche Gewalt in der Moderne*, Frankfurt/M.: Fischer TB, 7–22.

Kocka, Jürgen (1973), Otto Hintze, in: Hans-Ulrich Wehler (ed.), *Deutsche Historiker.* Vol. 3. Göttingen: Vandenhoeck, 275–98.

Kojève, Alexandre (1969 [1947]), *Introduction to the Reading of Hegel: Lectures on the Phenomenology of Spirit* [Introduction à la lecture de Hegel. Leçons sur la Phénoménologie de l'esprit]. New York: Basic.

Kondylis, Panajotis (1996), *Montesquieu und der Geist der Gesetze.* Berlin: Akademie Verlag.

Koselleck, Reinhart (1988 [1973]), *Critique and Crisis: Enlightenment and the Pathogenesis of Modern Society* [Kritik und Krise. Eine Studie zur Pathogenese der bürgerlichen Welt]. Oxford: Berg.

Kracauer, Siegfried (1915), Vom Erleben des Krieges, in: *Preußische Jahrbücher* 161, 3: 410–22.

Krakau, Knud (1967), *Missionsbewußtsein und Völkerrechtsdoktrin in den Vereinigten Staaten*. Frankfurt/M./Berlin: Alfred Metzner.

Kramer, Alan (2007), *Dynamic and Destruction: Culture and Mass Killing in the First World War*. Oxford: Oxford UP.

Kreienbaum, Jonas (2010), Koloniale Gewaltexzesse—Kolonialreiche um 1900, in: Alain Chatriot/Dieter Gosewinkel (eds.), *Koloniale Politik und Praktiken Deutschlands und Frankreichs 1880–1962*. Stuttgart: Franz Steiner, 155–72.

Krohn, Claus-Dieter (1995), Wien-Heidelberg-Berlin-New York. Zur intellektuellen Biographie Emil Lederers, in: *Emil Lederer. Der Massenstaat. Gefahren der klassenlosen Gesellschaft*, Herausgegeben und mit einem Vorwort versehen von Claus-Dieter Krohn. Graz/Vienna: Nausner & Nausner, 9–40.

Kruse, Wolfgang (ed.) (1997), *Eine Welt von Feinden. Der Große Krieg 1914–1918*. Frankfurt/M.: Fischer TB.

Kuhn, Helmut (1933), Rezension zu C. Schmitt, Der Begriff des Politischen, in: *Kant-Studien* 38: 190–96.

Kunisch, Johannes (1999), Die Denunzierung des Ewigen Friedens. Der Krieg als moralische Anstalt in der Literatur und Publizistik der Spätaufklärung, in: Johannes Kunisch/Herfried Münkler (eds.), *Die Wiedergeburt des Krieges aus dem Geist der Revolution. Studien zum bellizistischen Diskurs des ausgehenden 18. und beginnenden 19. Jahrhunderts*. Berlin: Duncker & Humblot, 57–73.

Lake, David A. (1992), Powerful Pacifists: Democratic States and War, in: *American Political Science Review* 86, 1: 24–37.

Lal, Deepak (2004), *In Praise of Empires: Globalization and Order*. New York: Palgrave.

Lasswell, Harold D. (1940), The Garrison State, in: *American Journal of Sociology* 46, 3: 455–68.

Layne, Christopher (1998), Kant or Cant: The Myth of the Democratic Peace, in: Michael E. Brown et al. (eds.), *Theories of War and Peace: An International Security Reader*. Cambridge, MA: MIT Press, 176–220.

Leander, Anna (2002), *Global Ungovernance: Mercenaries, States and the Control over Violence*. Working Papers 4. Copenhagen Peace Research Institute.

——— (2005), The Market for Force and Public Security: The Destabilizing Consequences of Private Military Companies, in: *Journal of Peace Research* 42, 5: 605–22.

Lederer, Emil (1979 [1920]), Die ökonomische Umschichtung im Krieg, in: Lederer, *Kapitalismus, Klassenstruktur und Probleme der Demokratie in Deutschland 1910–1940*. Göttingen: Vandenhoeck & Ruprecht, 145–54.

—— (2006 [1915]), On the Sociology of World War [Zur Soziologie des Weltkrieges], in: *European Journal of Sociology* 47, 1: 241–68.

Leed, Eric J. (1979), *No Man's Land: Combat and Identity in World War I.* Cambridge: Cambridge UP.

Lenger, Friedrich (1994), *Werner Sombart, 1863–1941. Eine Biographie.* Munich: C. H. Beck.

—— (1996), Werner Sombart als Propagandist eines deutschen Krieges, in: Wolfgang Mommsen (ed.), *Kultur und Krieg. Die Rolle der Intellektuellen, Künstler und Schriftsteller im Ersten Weltkrieg.* Munich: R. Oldenbourg Verlag, 65–76.

Lenin, V. I. (1996 [1916]), *Imperialism: The Highest Stage of Capitalism; A Popular Outline.* London: Junius.

Leonhard, Jörn (2008), *Bellizismus und Nation. Kriegsdeutung und Nationsbestimmung in Europa und den Vereinigten Staaten 1750–1914.* Munich: Oldenbourg.

Leonhard, Nina/Ines-Jacqueline Werkner (eds.) (2005), *Militärsoziologie—Eine Einführung.* Wiesbaden: Verlag für Sozialwissenschaften.

Lepenies, Wolf (1988 [1985]), *Between Literature and Science: The Rise of Sociology* [Die drei Kulturen. Soziologie zwischen Literatur und Wissenschaft]. Cambridge: Cambridge UP.

Lichtblau, Klaus (1996), *Kulturkrise und Soziologie um die Jahrhundertwende. Zur Genealogie der Kultursoziologie in Deutschland.* Frankfurt/M.: Suhrkamp.

List, Friedrich (1885 [1841]), *The National System of Political Economy* [Das nationale System der politischen Ökonomie]. London: Longmans.

Llanque, Marcus (2000), *Demokratisches Denken im Krieg. Die deutsche Debatte im Ersten Weltkrieg.* Berlin: Akademie Verlag.

Lock, Peter (2003), Kriegsökonomien und Schattenglobalisierung, in: Werner Ruf (ed.), *Politische Ökonomie der Gewalt. Staatszerfall und die Privatisierung von Gewalt und Krieg.* Opladen: Leske + Budrich, 93–123.

Long, Douglas (2006), Adam Smith's Politics, in: Knud Haakonssen (ed.), *The Cambridge Companion to Adam Smith.* Cambridge: Cambridge UP, 288–318.

Lübbe, Hermann (1963), *Politische Philosophie in Deutschland. Studien zu ihrer Geschichte.* Basel/Stuttgart: Benno Schwabe.

Lukes, Steven (1973), *Émile Durkheim: His Life and Work; A Historical and Critical Study.* London: Penguin.

Luttwak, Edward N. (1999), Give War a Chance, in: *Foreign Affairs* 78, 4: 36–44.

Lutz-Bachmann, Matthias/James Bohman (eds.) (1996), *Frieden durch Recht. Kants Friedensidee und das Problem einer neuen Weltordnung.* Frankfurt/M.: Suhrkamp.

MacPherson, C. B. (1962), *The Political Theory of Possessive Individualism: Hobbes to Locke.* Oxford: Clarendon.

Malinowski, Stephan (2009), Modernisierungskriege. Militärische Gewalt und koloniale Modernisierung im Algerienkrieg (1954–1962), in: Anja Kruke (ed.), *Dekolonisation. Prozesse und Verflechtungen 1945–1990*. Bonn: Dietz, 213–48.

Mann, Michael (1986), *The Sources of Social Power*. Vol. I: *A History of Power from the Beginning to A.D. 1760*. Cambridge: Cambridge UP.

———— (1988a [1977]), States, Ancient and Modern, in: Mann, *States, War and Capitalism: Studies in Political Sociology*. Oxford: Blackwell, 33–72.

———— (1988b [1977]), State and Society, 1130–1815, in: Mann, *States, War and Capitalism: Studies in Political Sociology*. Oxford: Blackwell, 73–123.

———— (1993), *The Sources of Social Power*. Vol. II: *The Rise of Classes and Nation-States, 1760–1914*. Cambridge: Cambridge UP.

———— (1997), Has Globalization Ended the Rise of the Nation State?, in: *Review of International Political Economy* 4, 3: 472–96.

———— (1998), Is There a Society Called Euro?, in: Roland Axtmann (ed.), *Globalization and Europe: Theoretical and Empirical Investigations*. London: Pinter, 184–207.

———— (2003), *Incoherent Empire*. London: Verso.

———— (2004), *Fascists*. Cambridge: Cambridge UP.

———— (2005), *The Dark Side of Democracy: Explaining Ethnic Cleansing*. Cambridge: Cambridge UP.

Mansfield, Edward D./Jack Snyder (1998), Democratization and the Danger of War, in: Michael E. Brown et al. (eds.), *Theories of War and Peace: An International Security Reader*. Cambridge, MA: MIT Press, 221–54.

Manuel, Frank E. (1962), *The Prophets of Paris: Turgot, Condorcet, Saint-Simon, Fourier, Comte*. New York: Harper Torchbooks.

Maoz, Zeev (1997), The Controversy over the Democratic Peace: Rearguard Action or Cracks in the Wall?, in: *International Security* 22, 1: 162–98.

Maoz, Zeev/Bruce Russett (1993), Normative and Structural Causes of Democratic Peace, 1946–1986, in: *American Political Science Review* 87, 3: 624–38.

Marcuse, Herbert (1968 [1934]), The Struggle against Liberalism in the Totalitarian View of the State [Der Kampf gegen den Liberalismus in der totalitären Staatsauffassung], in: Marcuse, *Negations: Essays in Critical Theory*. Harmondsworth: Penguin, 3–42.

Marschak, Jakob, et al. (1941), Emil Lederer, the Economist, in: *Social Research* 8, 1: 79–105.

Marshall, Jonathan (1979), William Graham Sumner: Critic of Progressive Liberalism, in: *Journal of Libertarian Studies* 3, 3: 261–77.

Mazower, Mark (2006), An International Civilization? Empire, Internationalism and the Crisis of the Mid-Twentieth Century, in: *International Affairs* 82, 3: 553–66.

McDonald, Lynn (1997), Classical Social Theory with the Women Founders Included, in: Charles Camic (ed.), *Reclaiming the Sociological Classics: The State of Scholarship*. Oxford: Blackwell, 112–41.

McSweeney, Bill (1999), *Security, Identity and Interests: A Sociology of International Relations*. Cambridge: Cambridge UP.

Mead, George Herbert (1918), Review of Thorstein Veblen's *The Nature of Peace and the Terms of Its Perpetuation*, in: *Journal of Political Economy* 26: 752–62.

——— (1929), National-Mindedness and International-Mindedness, in: *International Journal of Ethics* 39: 385–407.

Mearsheimer, John (1998a), Back to the Future: Instability in Europe after the Cold War, in: Michael E. Brown et al. (eds.), *Theories of War and Peace: An International Security Reader*. Cambridge, MA: MIT Press, 3–54.

——— (1998b), The False Promise of International Institutions, in: Michael E. Brown et al. (eds.), *Theories of War and Peace: An International Security Reader*. Cambridge, MA: MIT Press, 329–83.

Medick, Hans (1973), *Naturzustand und Naturgeschichte der bürgerlichen Gesellschaft. Die Ursprünge der bürgerlichen Sozialtheorie und Sozialwissenschaft bei Samuel Pufendorf, John Locke und Adam Smith*. Göttingen: Vandenhoeck & Ruprecht.

Mehta, Uday Singh (1999), *Liberalism and Empire: A Study in Nineteenth-Century British Liberal Thought*. Chicago: University of Chicago Press.

Meinecke, Friedrich (1957 [1924]), *Machiavellism: The Doctrine of Raison d'État and Its Place in Modern History* [Die Idee der Staatsräson in der neueren Geschichte]. London: Routledge.

Menzel, Ulrich (2001), *Zwischen Idealismus und Realismus. Die Lehre von den Internationalen Beziehungen*. Frankfurt/M.: Suhrkamp.

——— (2004), *Paradoxien der neuen Weltordnung. Politische Essays*. Frankfurt/M.: Suhrkamp.

Mill, James (1808), *Commerce Defended: An Answer to the Arguments by which Mr. Spence, Mr. Cobbett and Others, have Attempted to Prove that Commerce is not a Source of National Wealth*. London: C. and R. Baldwin.

——— (1824), Colony, in: *Supplement to the Fourth, Fifth, and Sixth Editions of the Encyclopedia Britannica*. Edinburgh: Archibald Constable, 257–73.

——— (1825), *Law of Nations: Reprinted from the Supplement to the Encyclopedia Britannica*. London: J. Innes, 257–73.

Mill, John Stuart (1965 [1848]), *Principles of Political Economy*. London: Routledge.

——— (1977a [1858]), On Liberty, in: Mill, *Essays on Politics and Society*, London: Routledge, 213–310.

——— (1977b [1861]), Considerations on Representative Government, in: Mill, *Essays on Politics and Society*, London: Routledge, 371–577.

——— (1977c [1836]), Civilization, in: Mill, *Essays on Politics and Society*, London: Routledge, 117–47.

——— (1984 [1859]), A Few Words on Non-Intervention, in: J. M. Robson (ed.), *Collected Works of John Stuart Mill*. Vol. 21: *Essays on Equality, Law and Ed-*

ucation. Introduction by Stefan Collini. Toronto: University of Toronto Press/ Routledge & Kegan Paul, 111–24.

Millar, John (1793 [1771]), *The Origin of the Distinction of Ranks*. Basel: Tourneisen.

—— (1796), *Letters of Crito, on the Causes, Objects, and Consequences, of the Present War*. http://oll.libertyfund.org/EBooks/Millar_1317.pdf.

Mills, C. Wright (1956), *The Power Elite*. New York: Oxford UP.

—— (1959 [1958]), *The Causes of World War Three*. London: Secker & Warburg.

—— (1966 [1951]), *White Collar: The American Middle Classes*. New York: Oxford UP.

Misch, Georg (1969 [1901]), *Zur Entstehung des französischen Positivismus*. Darmstadt: Wissenschaftliche Buchgesellschaft.

Mizuta, Hiroshi (1980), Two Adams in the Scottish Enlightenment: Adam Smith and Adam Ferguson on Progress, in: Haydn Mason (ed.), *Transactions of the Fifth International Congress on the Enlightenment II*. Oxford: Voltaire Foundation at the Taylor Institution, 812–19.

Moebius, Stephan (2006), *Die Zauberlehrlinge. Soziologiegeschichte des Collège de Sociologie (1937–1939)*. Konstanz: UVK.

Mommsen, Wolfgang J. (1984 [1959]), *Max Weber and German Politics, 1890– 1920* [Max Weber und die Deutsche Politik, 1890–1920]. Chicago: University of Chicago Press.

—— (1994), *Bürgerliche Kultur und künstlerische Avantgarde, 1870–1918. Kultur und Politik im deutschen Kaiserreich*. Frankfurt/M./Berlin: Propyläen.

—— (1995 [1990]), Public Opinion and Foreign Policy in Wilhelmine Germany, 1897–1914 [Außenpolitik und öffentliche Meinung im Wilhelminischen Deutschland 1897–1914], in: Mommsen, *Imperial Germany, 1867–1918: Politics, Culture and Society in an Authoritarian State*. London: Arnold, 189–204.

Montesquieu, Charles Louis (1733/34), *Réflexions sur la monarchie universelle en Europe*. Bibliothèque municipale de Bordeaux, manuscript collection.

—— (1989 [1748]), *The Spirit of the Laws* [De l'esprit des lois]. Cambridge: Cambridge UP.

—— (2005 [1733/34]), Betrachtungen über die universale Monarchie in Europa, in: Effi Böhlke/Etienne François (eds.), *Montesquieu. Franzose—Europäer—Weltbürger*. Berlin: Akademie-Verlag, 225–38.

Moore, Barrington (1966), *Social Origins of Dictatorship and Democracy: Lord and Peasant in the Making of the Modern World*. Harmondsworth: Penguin.

Morgan, T. Clifton/Sally Howard Campbell (1991), Domestic Structure, Decisional Constraints, and War: So Why Kant Democracies Fight?, in: *Journal of Conflict Resolution* 35, 2: 187–211.

Mori, Massimo (1989), Krieg und Frieden in der klassischen deutschen Philosophie, in: Hans Joas/Helmut Steiner (eds.), *Machtpolitischer Realismus und pazifistische Utopie. Krieg und Frieden in der Geschichte der Sozialwissenschaften.* Frankfurt/M.: Suhrkamp, 49–91.

——— (1999), Das Bild des Krieges bei den deutschen Philosophen, in: Johannes Kunisch/Herfried Münkler (eds.), *Die Wiedergeburt des Krieges aus dem Geist der Revolution. Studien zum bellizistischen Diskurs des ausgehenden 18. und beginnenden 19. Jahrhunderts.* Berlin: Dunker & Humblot, 225–40.

Mueller, John E. (1988), *Retreat from Doomsday: The Obsolescence of Major War.* New York: Basic Books.

Müller, Hans-Peter (1991), Die Moralökologie moderner Gesellschaften. Durkheims "Physik der Sitten und des Rechts," in: Émile Durkheim, *Physik der Sitten und des Rechts. Vorlesungen zur Soziologie der Moral.* Frankfurt/M.: Suhrkamp, 307–41.

Müller, Harald (2004), Demokratien im Krieg—Antinomien des demokratischen Friedens, in: Christine Schweitzer/Björn Aust/Peter Schlotter (eds.), *Demokratien im Krieg.* Baden-Baden: Nomos, 35–52.

Münkler, Herfried (1987), *Im Namen des Staates. Die Begründung der Staatsraison in der Frühen Neuzeit.* Frankfurt/M.: S. Fischer.

——— (1992), *Gewalt und Ordnung. Das Bild des Krieges im politischen Denken.* Frankfurt/M.: Fischer TB.

——— (1993), *Thomas Hobbes.* Frankfurt/M./New York: Campus.

——— (1999), "Wer sterben kann, wer will denn den zwingen"—Fichte als Philosoph des Krieges, in: Johannes Kunisch/Herfried Münkler (eds.), *Die Wiedergeburt des Krieges aus dem Geist der Revolution. Studien zum bellizistischen Diskurs des ausgehenden 18. und beginnenden 19. Jahrhunderts.* Berlin: Duncker & Humblot, 241–59.

——— (2001), Der gesellschaftliche Fortschritt und die Rolle der Gewalt. Friedrich Engels als Theoretiker des Krieges, in: Volker Gerhardt (ed.), *Marxismus. Versuch einer Bilanz.* Berlin: Edition Humboldt, 165–91.

——— (2002), *Über den Krieg. Stationen der Kriegsgeschichte im Spiegel ihrer theoretischen Reflexion.* Weilerswist: Velbrück.

——— (2005 [2002]), *The New Wars* [Die neuen Kriege]. Oxford: Polity.

——— (2007 [2005]), *Empires: The Logic of World Domination from Ancient Rome to the United States* [Imperien. Die Logik der Weltherrschaft—vom Alten Rom bis zu den Vereinigten Staaten]. Cambridge: Polity.

Muthu, Sankar (2003), *Enlightenment Against Empire.* Princeton, NJ: Princeton UP.

Myers, Gerald E. (1986), *William James: His Life and Thought.* New Haven, CT.: Yale UP.

Nef, John U. (1943), Limited Warfare and the Progress of European Civilization, 1640–1740, in: *Review of Politics* 6, 3: 275–314.

——— (1950), *War and Human Progress: An Essay on the Rise of Industrial Civilization.* Cambridge, MA: Harvard UP.

Neff, Bernhard (2005), "Dekorationsmilitarismus." Die sozialdemokratische Kritik eines vermeintlich nicht kriegsgemäßen Militärwesens (1890–1911), in: Wolfram Wette (ed.), *Schule der Gewalt. Militarismus in Deutschland 1871–1945.* Berlin: Aufbau Verlag, 91–110.

Neumann, Sigmund (1952), Engels and Marx: Military Concepts of the Social Revolutionaries, in: Edward Mead Earle (with the collaboration of Gordon A. Craig and Felix Gilbert) (ed.), *Makers of Modern Strategy: Military Thought from Machiavelli to Hitler.* Princeton, NJ: Princeton UP, 155–71.

Niesen, Peter/Benjamin Herborth (2007), *Anarchie der kommunikativen Freiheit. Jürgen Habermas und die Theorie der internationalen Politik.* Frankfurt/M.: Suhrkamp.

Novalis (1844 [1799]), *Christianity, or Europe* [Die Christenheit oder Europa]. London: Chapman.

Nowosadtko, Jutta (2002), *Krieg, Gewalt und Ordnung. Einführung in die Militärgeschichte.* Tübingen: Edition diskord.

Oestreich, Gerhard (1964), Otto Hintzes Stellung zur Politikwissenschaft und Soziologie, in: Otto Hintze, *Soziologie und Geschichte, Gesammelte Abhandlungen.* Vol. 2. Göttingen: Vandenhoeck & Ruprecht, 7–67.

Onuf, Nicholas Greenwood (1998), *The Republican Legacy in International Thought.* Cambridge: Cambridge UP.

Oren, Ido (1995), The Subjectivity of the "Democratic" Peace: Changing U.S. Perceptions of Imperial Germany, in: *International Security* 20, 2: 147–84.

Osterhammel, Jürgen (1987), Varieties of Social Economics: Joseph A. Schumpeter and Max Weber, in: Wolfgang J. Mommsen/Wolfgang Schwentker (eds.), *Max Weber and His Contemporaries.* London: Allen & Unwin, 106–20.

Owen, John M. (1997), *Liberal Peace, Liberal War: American Politics and International Security.* Ithaca: Cornell UP.

——— (1998), How Liberalism Produces Democratic Peace, in: Michael E. Brown et al. (eds.), *Theories of War and Peace: An International Security Reader.* Cambridge, MA: MIT Press, 137–75.

Oz-Salzberger, Fania (2002), Scots, Germans, Republic and Commerce, in: Martin van Gelderen/Quentin Skinner (eds.), *Republicanism: A Shared European Heritage.* Cambridge: Cambridge UP, 197–226.

Paine, Thomas (1976 [1776]), *Common Sense.* London: Penguin.

——— (1992 [1791/92]), *The Rights of Man.* Indianapolis, IN: Hackett.

Papcke, Sven (1985), Dienst am Sieg: Die Sozialwissenschaften im Ersten Weltkrieg, in: Papcke, *Vernunft und Chaos. Essays zur sozialen Ideengeschichte.* Frankfurt/M.: Fischer, 125–42.

Parekh, Bhikhu (1995), Liberalism and Colonialism: A Critique of Locke and Mill, in: Jan Nederveen Pieterse/Bhikhu Parekh (eds.), *The Decolonization of Imagination: Culture, Knowledge and Power.* London: Zed Books, 81–98.

Park, Robert E. (1940), The Social Function of War: Observations and Notes, in: *American Journal of Sociology* 46, 3: 551–70.

Parker, Geoffrey (1988), *The Military Revolution: Military Innovation and the Rise of the West, 1500–1800*. Cambridge: Cambridge UP.

Parsons, Talcott (1968 [1937]), *The Structure of Social Action: A Study in Social Theory with Special Reference to a Group of Recent European Writers*. 2 vols. New York: Free Press.

——— (1971), *The System of Modern Societies*. Englewood Cliffs, NJ: Prentice-Hall.

Peel, J.D.Y. (1971), *Herbert Spencer: The Evolution of a Sociologist*. London: Heinemann.

Perkins, Merle L. (1960), Voltaire and the Abbé de Saint-Pierre, in: *French Review* 34, 2: 152–63.

Pettenkofer, Andreas (2010), *Radikaler Protest. Zur soziologischen Theorie politischer Bewegungen*. Frankfurt/Main: Campus.

Pettit, Philip (1997), *Republicanism: A Theory of Government*. Oxford: Clarendon Press.

Pickering, Mary (1993), *Auguste Comte: An Intellectual Biography*. Vol. 1. Cambridge: Cambridge UP.

——— (1997), A New Look at Auguste Comte, in: Charles Camic (ed.), *Reclaiming the Sociological Classics: The State of the Scholarship*. Oxford: Blackwell, 11–44.

Pitts, Jennifer (2005), *A Turn to Empire: The Rise of Imperial Liberalism in Britain and France*. Princeton: Princeton UP.

Pocock, John G. A. (1975), *The Machiavellian Moment: Florentine Political Thought and the Atlantic Republican Tradition*. Princeton, NJ: Princeton UP.

——— (1985a), The Mobility of Property and the Rise of Eighteenth-Century Sociology, in: Pocock, *Virtue, Commerce and History: Essays on Political Thought and History, Chiefly in the Eighteenth Century*. Cambridge: Cambridge UP, 103–23.

——— (1985b), Authority and Property: The Question of Liberal Origins, in: Pocock, *Virtue, Commerce and History: Essays on Political Thought and History, Chiefly in the Eighteenth Century*. Cambridge: Cambridge UP, 51–72.

Radkau, Joachim (2005), *Max Weber. Die Leidenschaft des Denkens*. Munich/Vienna: Hanser Verlag.

——— (2009), *Max Weber: A Biography*. Cambridge: Polity.

Ray, James Lee (1997), The Democratic Path to Peace, in: *Journal of Democracy* 8, 2: 49–64.

Reinhard, Wolfgang (1986), Staat und Heer in England im Zeitalter der Revolutionen, in: Johannes Kunisch (ed.), *Staatsverfassung und Heeresverfassung in der europäischen Geschichte der frühen Neuzeit*. Berlin: Duncker & Humblot, 173–212.

——— (1999), *Geschichte der Staatsgewalt. Eine vergleichende Verfassungsge-schichte Europas von den Anfängen bis zur Gegenwart.* Munich: C. H. Beck.

Reiter, Dan/Allan C. Stam (2002), *Democracies at War.* Princeton, NJ: Princeton UP.

Rengger, N. J. (2000), *International Relations, Political Theory and the Problem of Order: Beyond International Relations Theory?* London: Routledge.

Richter, Melvin (1963), Tocqueville in Algeria, in: *Review of Politics* 25, 3: 362–98.

——— (1997), Europe and *the Other* in Eighteenth-Century Thought, in: *Politisches Denken. Jahrbuch 1997.* Stuttgart/Weimar: J. B. Metzler, 25–47.

Robertson, John (1983a), The Scottish Enlightenment at the Limits of the Civic Tradition, in: Istvan Hont/Michael Ignatieff (eds.), *Wealth and Virtue: The Shaping of Political Economy in the Scottish Enlightenment.* Cambridge: Cambridge UP, 137–78.

——— (1983b), Scottish Political Economy beyond the Civic Tradition: Government and Economic Development in the *Wealth of Nations*, in: *History of Political Thought* 4, 3: 451–82.

——— (1985), *The Scottish Enlightenment and the Militia Issue.* Edinburgh: John Donald Publishers.

Robinson, Ronald (1977), Non-European Foundations of European Imperialism: Sketch for a Theory of Collaboration, in: Roger Owen/Bob Sutcliffe (eds.), *Studies in the Theory of Imperialism.* London: Longman, 117–42.

——— (1986), The Excentric Idea of Imperialism, With or Without Empire, in: Wolfgang J. Mommsen/Jürgen Osterhammel (eds.), *Imperialism and After: Continuities and Discontinuities.* London: Allen & Unwin, 267–89.

Robson, John (1998), Civilization and Culture as Moral Concepts, in: John Skorupski (ed.), *The Cambridge Companion to Mill.* Cambridge: Cambridge UP, 338–71.

Rogers, Clifford J. (ed.) (1995), *The Military Revolution Debate: Readings on the Military Transformation of Early Modern Europe.* Boulder, CO: Westview Press.

Rohbeck, Johannes (1990), Turgot als Geschichtsphilosoph, in: Turgot, *Über die Fortschritte des menschlichen Geistes.* Frankfurt/M.: Suhrkamp, 7–87.

Roosevelt, Grace G. (1987), A Reconstruction of Rousseau's Fragments on the State of War, in: *History of Political Thought* 8, 2: 225–32.

Röpke, Jochen/Olaf Stiller (2005), Einführung zum Nachdruck der 1. Auflage Joseph A. Schumpeters "Theorie der wirtschaftlichen Entwicklung," in: Joseph Schumpeter. *Theorie der wirtschaftlichen Entwicklung.* Berlin: Duncker & Humblot, v–xliii.

Rotberg, Robert I. (2004), The Failure and Collapse of Nation-States: Breakdown, Prevention, and Repair, in: Rotberg (ed.), *When States Fail: Causes and Consequences.* Princeton, NJ: Princeton UP, 1–49.

Rothermund, Dietmar (1998), *Delhi, 15. August 1947. Das Ende kolonialer Herrschaft*. Munich: dtv.

Rousseau, Jean-Jacques (1991a), Fragments on War, in: Stanley Hoffman/David Fidler (eds.), *Rousseau on International Relations*. Oxford: Clarendon, 48–52.

—— (1991b [1761]), Abstract and Judgement of Saint-Pierre's Project for Perpetual Peace (1756), in: Stanley Hoffman/David Fidler (eds.), *Rousseau on International Relations*. Oxford: Clarendon, 53–100.

—— (1994), Geneva Manuscript (First Version of Social Contract) [Du Contrat Social ou Essai sur la Forme de la République (Première Version)], in: Roger Masters/Christopher Kelly (eds.), *Collected Writings of Rousseau IV: Social Contract, Discourse on the Virtue Most Necessary for a Hero, Political Fragments and Geneva Manuscript*. Hanover, NH: University Press of New England, 76–224.

—— (1997a [1758]), Discourse on Political Economy [Discours sur l'économie politique], in: Victor Gourevitch (ed.), *Rousseau, the "Social Contract" and Other Later Political Writings*. Cambridge: Cambridge UP, 3–38.

—— (1997b [1755/56]), The State of War [L'État de guerre], in: Victor Gourevitch (ed.), *The "Social Contract" and Other Later Political Writings*. Cambridge: Cambridge UP, 162–76.

—— (1997c [1772]), Considerations on the Government of Poland and on Its Projected Reformation [Considérations sur le gouvernement de Pologne], in: Victor Gourevitch (ed.), *Rousseau, the "Social Contract" and Other Later Political Writings*. Cambridge: Cambridge UP, 177–260.

—— (2004a [1755]), *Discourse on the Origin of Inequality* [Discours sur l'origine et les fondements de l'inégalité parmi les hommes]. Mineola, NY: David & Charles.

—— (2004b [1765]), *Constitutional Project for Corsica* [Projet de constitution pour la Corse]. Whitefish, MT: Kessinger.

—— (2005 [1761]), Judgment of the Plan for Perpetual Peace [Jugement du projet de paix perpétuelle], in: Roger Masters/Christopher Kelly (eds.), *Collected Writings of Rousseau II: The Plan for Perpetual Peace, On the Government of Poland and Other Writings on History and Politics*. Hanover, NH: University Press of New England, 53–60.

Roxborough, Ian (1994), Clausewitz and the Sociology of War, in: *British Journal of Sociology* 45, 4: 619–36.

Ruf, Werner (2003), Private Militärische Unternehmen (PMU), in: Ruf (ed.), *Politische Ökonomie der Gewalt. Staatszerfall und die Privatisierung von Gewalt und Krieg*. Opladen: Leske + Budrich, 76–89.

Rummel, R. J. (1975–81), *Understanding Conflict and War*. Vols. 1–4. Beverly Hills, CA: Sage.

—— (1983), Libertarianism and International Violence, in: *Journal of Conflict Resolution* 27, 1: 27–71.

Rürup, Reinhard (1984), Der "Geist von 1914" in Deutschland. Kriegsbegeisterung und Ideologisierung des Krieges im Ersten Weltkrieg, in: Bernd Hüppauf (ed.), *Ansichten vom Krieg. Vergleichende Studien zum Ersten Weltkrieg in Literatur und Gesellschaft*. Hainstein: Forum Academicum, 1–30.

Russett, Bruce (1993), *Grasping the Democratic Peace: Principles for a Post–Cold War World*. Princeton, NJ: Princeton UP.

——— (1995), And Yet It Moves, in: *International Security* 19, 4: 164–75.

Russo, Elena (2002), The Youth of Moral Life: The Virtue of the Ancients from Montesquieu to Nietzsche, in: David W. Carrithers/Patrick Coleman (eds.), *Montesquieu and the Spirit of Modernity*. Oxford: Voltaire Foundation, 101–23.

Salomon, Albert, et al. (1940), Emil Lederer, the Sociologist, in: *Social Research* 7, 3: 337–58.

Schaffer, Ronald (1991), *America in the Great War: The Rise of the War Welfare State*. New York: Oxford UP.

Schäffle, Albert (1878), *Bau und Leben des socialen Körpers. Encyclopädischer Entwurf einer realen Anatomie, Physiologie und Psychologie der menschlichen Gesellschaft mit besonderer Rücksicht auf die Volkswirthschaft als socialen Stoffwechsel*. Zweiter Band. Tübingen: Verlag der H. Laupp'schen Buchhandlung.

——— (1899), Zur sozialwissenschaftlichen Theorie des Krieges, in: *Zeitschrift für die gesamte Staatswissenschaft* 55: 218–78.

Scharff, Robert C. (1995), *Comte after Positivism*. Cambridge: Cambridge UP.

Scheler, Max (1916), Der Krieg als Gesamterlebnis, in: Scheler, *Krieg und Aufbau*. Leipzig: Verlag der Weißen Bücher, 1–20.

——— (1955 [1914]), Der Bourgeois und die religiösen Mächte, in: Scheler, *Vom Umsturz der Werte. Abhandlungen und Aufsätze. Gesammelte Werke Bd. 3* (4. durchgesehene Aufl. Herausgegeben von Maria Scheler). Bern: Francke, 362–81.

Schlegel, Friedrich (1996 [1796]), Essay on the Concept of Republicanism Occasioned by the Kantian Tract "Perpetual Peace" [Versuch über den Begriff des Republikanismus veranlaßt durch die Kantische Schrift "Zum Ewigen Frieden"], in: Frederick C. Beiser (ed.), *The Early Political Writings of the German Romantics*, Cambridge: Cambridge UP, 93–112.

Schmidt, Gunnar (2000), Die konstruierte Moderne. Thorstein Veblen und der Erste Weltkrieg, in: *Leviathan* 28, 1: 39–68.

Schmitt, Carl (1991 [1932]), *Der Begriff des Politischen. Text von 1932 mit einem Vorwort und drei Corollarien*. 3rd ed. of the 1962 ed. Berlin: Duncker & Humblot.

——— (1994a [1927]), Der Begriff des Politischen, in: Schmitt, *Positionen und Begriffe im Kampf mit Weimar-Genf-Versailles*. 3rd ed. Berlin: Duncker & Humblot, 75–83.

——— (1994b [1928]), Völkerrechtliche Probleme im Rheingebiet, in: Schmitt,

Positionen und Begriffe im Kampf mit Weimar-Genf-Versailles. 3rd ed. Berlin: Duncker & Humblot, 111–23.

—— (1994c [1939]), Der Reichsbegriff im Völkerrecht, in: Schmitt, *Positionen und Begriffe im Kampf mit Weimar-Genf-Versailles*. 3rd ed. Berlin: Duncker & Humblot, 344–54.

—— (1996 [1938]), *The Leviathan in the State Theory of Thomas Hobbes: Meaning and Failure of a Political Symbol* [Der Leviathan in der Staatslehre des Thomas Hobbes. Sinn und Fehlschlag eines politischen Symbols]. Westport, CT: Greenwood.

—— (1999 [1938]), Neutrality according to International Law and National Totality [Völkerrechtliche Neutralität und völkische Totalität], in: Schmitt, *Four Articles, 1931–1938*. Washington DC: Plutarch, 37–45.

—— (2000 [1925]), The Status Quo and the Peace [Der Status quo und der Friede], in: Arthur Jacobson (ed.), *Weimar: A Jurisprudence of Crisis*. Berkeley: University of California Press, 290–94.

—— (2003a [1950]), *The Nomos of the Earth in the International Law of the Jus Publicum Europaeum* [Der Nomos der Erde im Völkerrecht des Jus Publicum Europaeum]. New York: Telos.

—— (2003b [1938]), *Die Wendung zum diskriminierenden Kriegsbegriff*. 3rd ed. Berlin: Duncker & Humblot.

—— (2007a [1927/32]), *The Concept of the Political* [Der Begriff des Politischen]. Chicago: University of Chicago Press.

—— (2007b [1963]), *Theory of the Partisan: Intermediate Commentary on the Concept of the Political* [Theorie des Partisanen. Zwischenbemerkungen zum Begriff des Politischen]. New York: Telos.

—— (2011 [1932]), Forms of Modern Imperialism in International Law [Völkerrechtliche Formen des modernen Imperialismus], in: Stephen Legg (ed.), *Spatiality, Sovereignty and Carl Schmitt. Geographies of the Nomos*. London: Routledge, 29–45.

Schmitter, Philippe C. (1991), *The European Community as an Emergent and Novel Form of Political Domination*. CEACS Madrid. Working paper 26.

Schnädelbach, Herbert (1984 [1983]), *Philosophy in Germany, 1831–1933* [Philosophie in Deutschland 1831–1933]. Cambridge: Cambridge UP.

Schröder, Hans-Christoph (1973), *Sozialistische Imperialismusdeutung. Studien zu ihrer Geschichte*. Göttingen: Vandenhoeck & Ruprecht.

Schumacher, Frank (2006), "Niederbrennen, plündern und töten sollt ihr": Der Kolonialkrieg der USA auf den Philippinen (1899–1913), in: Thoralf Klein/ Frank Schumacher (eds.), *Kolonialkriege. Militärische Gewalt im Zeichen des Imperialismus*. Hamburg: Hamburger Edition, 109–44.

Schumpeter, Joseph (1934 [1912]), *The Theory of Economic Development* [Theorie der wirtschaftlichen Entwicklung]. Cambridge, MA: Harvard UP.

—— (1951 [1919]), The Sociology of Imperialism [Zur Soziologie der Imperialismen], in: *Imperialism and Social Classes*. Oxford: Blackwell, 3–130.

Schuyler, Robert Livingston (1922), The Rise of Anti-imperialism in England, in: *Political Science Quarterly* 37, 3: 440–71.

Schwabe, Klaus (1965), *Wissenschaft und Kriegsmoral. Die deutschen Hochschullehrer und die politischen Grundfragen des Ersten Weltkriegs.* Göttingen: Musterschmidt-Verlag.

Semmel, Bernard (1961), The Philosophic Radicals and Colonialism, in: *Journal of Economic History* 21, 4: 513–25.

——— (1970), *The Rise of Free Trade Imperialism: Classical Political Economy, the Empire of Free Trade and Imperialism, 1750–1850.* Cambridge: Cambridge UP.

Senghaas, Dieter (1994), *Wohin driftet die Welt? Über die Zukunft friedlicher Koexistenz.* Frankfurt/M.: Suhrkamp.

——— (2000), Wissenschaftsbiographische Notizen, in: Ulrich Menzel (ed.), *Vom Ewigen Frieden und vom Wohlstand der Nationen. Dieter Senghaas zum 60. Geburtstag.* Frankfurt/M.: Suhrkamp, 607–22.

——— (2001 [1998]), *The Clash within Civilizations: Coming to Terms with Cultural Conflicts* [Zivilisierung wider Willen. Der Konflikt der Kulturen mit sich selbst]. New York: Routledge.

——— (2007 [2004]), *On Perpetual Peace: A Timely Assessment* [Zum irdischen Frieden. Erkenntnisse und Vermutungen]. New York: Berghahn.

——— (2010), Gerechter Friede statt gerechter Krieg. Die Lehre der letzten Dekade, in: *Blätter für deutsche und internationale Politik* 55, 9: 89–96.

Shaw, Martin (1991), *Post–Military Society: Militarism, Demilitarization and War at the End of the Twentieth Century.* Philadelphia: Temple UP.

——— (2003), *War and Genocide: Organized Killing in Modern Society.* Cambridge: Polity.

Sher, Richard B. (1989), Adam Ferguson, Adam Smith, and the Problem of National Defense, in: *Journal of Modern History* 61, 2: 240–68.

Shils, Edward A./Morris Janowitz (1948), Cohesion and Disintegration in the Wehrmacht in World War II, in: *Public Opinion Quarterly* 12, 2: 280–315.

Shklar, Judith N. (1987), *Montesquieu.* Oxford: Oxford UP.

Sieferle, Rolf Peter (1995), *Die konservative Revolution. Fünf biographische Skizzen.* Frankfurt/M.: Fischer TB.

Silberner, Edmund (1946), *The Problem of War in Nineteenth Century Economic Thought.* Princeton, NJ: Princeton UP.

Silver, Allan (1990), Friendship in Commercial Society: Eighteenth-Century Social Theory and Modern Sociology, in: *American Journal of Sociology* 95, 6: 1474–1504.

Simmel, Georg (1999 [1917]), Der Krieg und die geistigen Entscheidungen, in: Simmel, *Der Krieg und die geistigen Entscheidungen. Grundfragen der Soziologie. Vom Wesen des historischen Verstehens. Der Konflikt der modernen Kultur. Lebensanschauung.* Collected works vol. 16. Frankfurt/M.: Suhrkamp, 9–58.

Sindjoun, Luc (2002), Sociology Meets International Relations: The True Story of Cinderella and the Prince, in: *International Review of Sociology* 12, 3: 403–16.

Skinner, Quentin (1966), The Ideological Context of Hobbes's Political Thought, in: *Historical Journal* 9, 3: 286–317.

—— (1998), *Liberty before Liberalism*. Cambridge: Cambridge UP.

Skocpol, Theda (1973), A Critical Review of Barrington Moore's *Social Origins of Dictatorship and Democracy*, in: *Politics and Society* 4, 1: 1–34.

—— (1979), *States and Social Revolutions: A Comparative Analysis of France, Russia, and China*. Cambridge: Cambridge UP.

—— (1985), Bringing the State Back In: Strategies of Analysis in Current Research, in: Peter B. Evans et al. (eds.), *Bringing the State Back In*. Cambridge: Cambridge UP, 3–37.

—— (1992), *Protecting Soldiers and Mothers: The Political Origins of Social Policy in the United States*. Cambridge, MA: Belknap Press of Harvard UP.

Slotkin, Richard (1976), *Regeneration through Violence: The Mythology of the American Frontier, 1600–1860*. Middletown, CT: Wesleyan UP.

Small, Albion (1917), Americans and the World Crisis, in: *American Journal of Sociology* 23, 1: 145–73.

Smith, Adam (2007 [1776]), *An Inquiry into the Nature and Causes of the Wealth of Nations*. Petersfield: Harriman.

Smith, Bruce James (1985), *Politics and Remembrance: Republican Themes in Machiavelli, Burke, and Tocqueville*. Princeton, NJ: Princeton UP.

Smith, Michael Joseph (1986), *Realist Thought from Weber to Kissinger*. Baton Rouge, LA: Louisiana State UP.

Sörensen, Georg (1992), Kant and Processes of Democratization: Consequences of Neorealist Thought in: *Journal of Peace Research* 29, 4: 397–414.

Solingen, Etel (1996), Democracy, Economic Reform and Regional Cooperation, in: *Journal of Theoretical Politics* 8, 1: 79–114.

Sombart, Werner (1902), *Der moderne Kapitalismus*. 2 vols. Leipzig: Duncker & Humblot.

—— (1913a), *Krieg und Kapitalismus*. Munich/Leipzig: Duncker & Humblot.

—— (1913b), *Der Bourgeois. Zur Geistesgeschichte des modernen Wirtschaftsmenschen*. Munich/Leipzig: Duncker & Humblot.

—— (1915), *Händler und Helden. Patriotische Besinnungen*. Munich/Leipzig: Duncker & Humblot.

—— (1923), Die Anfänge der Soziologie, in: Melchior Palyi (ed.), *Hauptprobleme der Soziologie. Erinnerungsgabe für Max Weber*. Vol. 1. Munich/Leipzig: Duncker & Humblot, 3–19.

—— (1967 [1912]), *Luxury and Capitalism* [Luxus und Kapitalismus]. Ann Arbor: University of Michigan Press.

—— (1987 [1928]), *Der moderne Kapitalismus*. Munich: dtv.

Sorel, Georges (1950 [1908]), *Reflections on Violence* [Réflexions sur la violence]. With an introduction by Edward A. Shils. Glencoe, IL: Free Press.

Sorokin, Pitirim (1928), Sociological Interpretation of the "Struggle for Existence" and the Sociology of War, in: Sorokin, *Contemporary Sociological Theories*. New York: Harper, 309–56.

———— (1937), *Social and Cultural Dynamics*. Vol. III: *Fluctuations of Social Relationships, War and Revolutions*. New York: Bedminster Press.

———— (1943/44), The Conditions and Prospects for a World without War, in: *American Journal of Sociology* 49, 5: 440–49.

———— (1945), War and Post-War Changes in Social Stratifications of the Euro-American Population, in: *American Sociological Review* 10, 2: 294–303.

Speier, Hans (1939), Class Structure and "Total War," in: *American Sociological Review* 4, 3: 370–80.

———— (1940), The Social Types of War, in: *American Journal of Sociology* 46, 3: 445–54.

———— (1948), The Future of Psychological Warfare, in: *Public Opinion Quarterly* 12, 1: 5–18.

———— (1979), Emil Lederer: Leben und Werk, in: Emil Lederer. *Kapitalismus, Klassenstruktur und Probleme der Demokratie in Deutschland 1910–1940*. Ausgewählte Aufsätze mit einem Beitrag von Hans Speier und einer Bibliographie von Bernd Uhlmannsiek herausgegeben von Jürgen Kocka. Göttingen: Vandenhoeck & Ruprecht, 253–72.

———— (1986 [1933]), *German White-Collar Workers and the Rise of Hitler* [Die Angestellten vor dem Nationalsozialismus. Zur deutschen Sozialstruktur 1918–1933]. New Haven, CT: Yale UP.

———— (1989a), Introduction: Autobiographical Notes, in: Speier, *The Truth in Hell and Other Essays on Politics and Culture, 1935–1987*. New York: Oxford UP, 3–32.

———— (1989b [1936]), Militarism in the Eighteenth Century, in: Speier, *The Truth in Hell and Other Essays on Politics and Culture, 1935–1987*. New York: Oxford UP, 70–96.

———— (1989c [1943]), Ludendorff: The German Concept of Total War, in: Speier, *The Truth in Hell and Other Essays on Politics and Culture, 1935–1987*. New York: Oxford UP, 97–116.

Spencer, Herbert (1885), *Political Institutions: Being Part 5 of the Principles of Sociology*. London: Williams & Norgate.

Spreen, Dierk (2008), *Krieg und Gesellschaft. Die Konstitutionsfunktion des Krieges für moderne Gesellschaften*. Berlin: Duncker & Humblot.

Steinmetz, George (2003), "The Devil's Handwriting." Precolonial Discourse, Ethnographic Acuity, and Cross-Identification in German Colonialism, in: *Comparative Studies in Society and History* 45, 1: 41–95.

———— (2005), Return to Empire: The New U.S. Imperialism in Comparative Perspective, in: *Sociological Theory* 23, 4: 339–67.

Sternhell, Zev (with Mario Sznajder and Maia Asheri) (1994), *The Birth of Fas-*

cist Ideology: From Cultural Rebellion to Political Revolution. Princeton, NJ: Princeton UP.

Stouffer, Samuel A., et al. (1949), The American Soldier. 4 Vols. Princeton, NJ: Princeton UP.

Strange, Susan (1996), The Retreat of the State: The Diffusion of Power in the World Economy. Cambridge: Cambridge UP.

Strauss, Leo (2007 [1932]), Notes on Carl Schmitt, The Concept of the Political [Anmerkungen zu Carl Schmitt. Der Begriff des Politischen], in: Carl Schmitt, The Concept of the Political. Chicago: Chicago UP, 81–108.

Stromberg, Roland N. (1982), Redemption by War: The Intellectuals and 1914. Lawrence: The Regents Press of Kansas.

Sumner, William Graham (1919a [1903]), War, in: Albert Galloway Keller (ed.), William Graham Sumner: War and Other Essays. New Haven, CT: Yale UP, 3–40.

——— (1919b [1881]), Sociology, in: Albert Galloway Keller (ed.), William Graham Sumner: War and Other Essays. New Haven, CT: Yale UP, 167–92.

——— (1919c [1896]), The Fallacy of Territorial Expansion, in: Albert Galloway Keller (ed.), William Graham Sumner: War and Other Essays. New Haven, CT: Yale UP, 285–93.

——— (1919d [1898]), The Conquest of the United States by Spain, in: Albert Galloway Keller (ed.), William Graham Sumner: War and Other Essays. New Haven, CT: Yale UP, 297–334.

Swedberg, Richard (1991), Joseph A. Schumpeter: His Life and Thought. Oxford: Polity.

Swingewood, Alan (1970), Origins of Sociology: The Case of the Scottish Enlightenment, in: British Journal of Sociology 21, 2: 164–80.

Taylor, Charles (1975), Hegel. Cambridge: Cambridge UP.

Taylor, M. W. (1992), Men versus the State: Herbert Spencer and Late Victorian Individualism. Oxford: Clarendon Press.

Thomas, William (1985), Mill. Oxford: Oxford UP.

Thompson, William R. (1996), Democracy and Peace: Putting the Cart before the Horse?, in: International Organization 50, 1: 141–74.

Tilly, Charles (ed.) (1975a), The Formation of National States in Western Europe. Princeton, NJ: Princeton UP.

——— (1975b), Reflections on the History of European State-Making, in: Charles Tilly (ed.), The Formation of National States in Western Europe. Princeton, NJ: Princeton UP, 3–83.

——— (1975c), Western State-Making and Theories of Political Transformation, in: Charles Tilly (ed.), The Formation of National States in Western Europe. Princeton, NJ: Princeton UP, 601–38.

——— (1985), War Making and State Making as Organized Crime, in: Peter

B. Evans et al. (eds.), *Bringing the State Back In*. Cambridge: Cambridge UP, 169–91.

—— (1990), *Coercion, Capital, and European States, AD 990–1990*. Oxford: Blackwell.

Tiryakian, Edward A. (1999), War: The Covered Side of Modernity, in: *International Sociology* 14, 4: 473–89.

Tocqueville, Alexis de (1856), *On the State of Society in France before the Revolution of 1789* [L'Ancien Régime et la Révolution]. London: John Murray.

—— (2001a [1837]), First Letter on Algeria [Deux Lettres sur l'Algérie], in: Jennifer Pitts (ed.), *Writings on Empire and Slavery*. Baltimore: Johns Hopkins UP, 5–13.

—— (2001b [1837]), Second Letter on Algeria [Deux Lettres sur l'Algérie], in: Jennifer Pitts (ed.), *Writings on Empire and Slavery*. Baltimore: Johns Hopkins UP, 14–26.

—— (2001c [1841]), Essay on Algeria, in: Jennifer Pitts (ed.), *Writings on Empire and Slavery*. Baltimore: Johns Hopkins UP, 59–116.

—— (2007 [1835/40]), *Democracy in America* [De la démocratie en Amérique]. New York: Norton.

Todd, Emmanuel (2003 [2002]), *After the Empire: The Breakdown of the American Order* [Après l'empire: Essai sur la décomposition du système américain]. New York: Columbia UP.

Tönnies, Ferdinand (1916), Naturrecht und Völkerrecht, in: *Die Neue Rundschau* 27, 5: 576–87.

—— (1925 [1896]), *Thomas Hobbes. Leben und Lehre*. Stuttgart: Fr. Frommanns Verlag (H. Kurtz).

—— (2002 [1887]), *Community and Society* [Gemeinschaft und Gesellschaft. Grundbegriffe der reinen Soziologie]. Mineola, NY: Dover.

Toulmin, Stephen (1990), *Cosmopolis: The Hidden Agenda of Modernity*. New York: Free Press.

Trotha, Trutz von (1994), *Koloniale Herrschaft. Zur soziologischen Theorie der Staatsentstehung am Beispiel des Schutzgebietes Togo*. Tübingen: J.C.B. Mohr.

—— (1999), "The Fellows Can Just Starve": On Wars of "Pacification" in the African Colonies of Imperial Germany and the Concept of "Total War," in: Manfred F. Boemeke/Roger Chickering/Stig Förster (eds.), *Anticipating Total War: The German and American Experiences, 1871–1914*. Cambridge: Cambridge UP, 415–35.

—— (2000), Die Zukunft liegt in Afrika. Vom Zerfall des Staates, von der Vorherrschaft der konzentrischen Ordnung und vom Aufstieg der Parastaatlichkeit, in: *Leviathan* 28, 2: 253–79.

—— (2003a), Die präventive Sicherheitsordnung, in: Werner Ruf (ed.), *Politische Ökonomie der Gewalt. Staatszerfall und die Privatisierung von Gewalt und Krieg*. Opladen: Leske + Budrich, 51–75.

—— (2003b), Genozidaler Pazifizierungskrieg. Soziologische Anmerkungen zum Konzept des Genozids am Beispiel des Kolonialkriegs in Deutsch-Südwestafrika, 1904–1907, in: *Zeitschrift für Genozidforschung* 2: 28–57.

—— (2005), Der Aufstieg des Lokalen, in: *Aus Politik und Zeitgeschichte* 28–29: 32–38.

Tuck, Richard (1999), *The Rights of War and Peace: Political Thought and the International Order; From Grotius to Kant*. Oxford: Oxford UP.

—— (2002), *Hobbes*. Oxford: Oxford UP.

Turgot, Anne Robert Jacques (1973), *Turgot on Progress, Sociology and Economics*. Translated, edited, and with an introduction by Ronald L. Meek. London: Cambridge UP.

—— (1990), *Über die Fortschritte des menschlichen Geistes*. Herausgegeben von Johannes Rohbeck und Lieselotte Steinbrügge. Frankfurt/M.: Suhrkamp.

Turner, Jonathan (1984), Durkheim's and Spencer's Principles of Social Organization: A Theoretical Note, in: *Sociological Perspectives* 27, 1: 21–32.

—— (1985), *Herbert Spencer: A Renewed Appreciation*. Beverly Hills, CA: Sage.

—— (2003), Herbert Spencer, in: George Ritzer (ed.), *The Blackwell Companion to Major Classical Social Theorists*. Oxford: Blackwell, 69–92.

Vagts, Alfred (1937), *A History of Militarism: Romance and Realities of a Profession*. New York: Norton.

Veblen, Thorstein (1912 [1899]), *Theory of the Leisure Class: An Economic Study of Institutions*. New York: Macmillan.

—— (1954 [1915]), *Imperial Germany and the Industrial Revolution*. New York: Viking Press.

—— (1964 [1917]), *An Inquiry into the Nature of Peace and the Terms of Its Perpetuation*. New York: August M. Kelley.

Voltaire (2005 [1761]), Rescript of the Emperor of China on the Occasion of the Plan for Perpetual Peace [De l'empereur de la Chine à l'occasion du projet de paix perpétuelle], in: Jean-Jacques Rousseau, *The Plan for Perpetual Peace, On the Government of Poland, and Other Writings on History and Politics*. Hanover, NH: Dartmouth College Press, 50–52.

Vortkamp, Wolfgang (2003), *Partizipation und soziale Integration in heterogenen Gesellschaften. Louis Wirths Konzeption sozialer Organisation in der Tradition der Chicagoer Schule*. Opladen: Leske + Budrich.

Wachtler, Günther (ed.) (1983), *Militär, Krieg, Gesellschaft. Texte zur Militärsoziologie*. Frankfurt/M.: Campus.

Waldmann, Peter (1999 [1995]), Societies in Civil War [Gesellschaften im Bürgerkrieg. Zur Eigendynamik entfesselter Gewalt], in: Georg Elwert/Stephan Feuchtwang/Dieter Neubert (eds.), *Dynamics of Violence: Processes of Escalation and De-Escalation in Violent Group Conflicts* (Supplements to Sociologus 1): 61–83. Berlin: Duncker & Humblot.

—— (2002), *Der anomische Staat. Über Recht, öffentliche Sicherheit und Alltag in Lateinamerika*. Opladen: Leske + Budrich.

——— (2003), *Terrorismus und Bürgerkrieg. Der Staat in Bedrängnis*. Munich: Gerling Akademie Verlag.

——— (2007), *Guerra civil, terrorismo y anomia social. El caso colombiano en un contexto globalizado*. Bogota: Grupo Editorial Norma.

Wallace, Stuart (1988), *War and the Image of Germany: British Academics, 1914–1918*. Edinburgh: John Donald Publishers.

Walter, Dierk (2006), Warum Kolonialkrieg?, in: Thoralf Klein/Frank Schumacher (eds.), *Kolonialkriege. Militärische Gewalt im Zeichen des Imperialismus*. Hamburg: Hamburger Edition, 14–43.

Waltz, Kenneth (1959), *Man, the State and War: A Theoretical Analysis*. New York: Columbia UP.

——— (1962), Kant, Liberalism, and War, in: *American Political Science Review* 56, 2: 331–40.

Weart, Spencer R. (1998), *Never at War: Why Democracies Will Not Fight One Another*. New Haven, CT: Yale UP.

Weber, Alfred (1925), *Die Krise des modernen Staatsgedankens in Europa*. Berlin: Deutsche Verlags-Anstalt Stuttgart.

Weber, Max (1923), *General Economic History* [Wirtschaftsgeschichte. Abriß der universalen Sozial- und Wirtschaftsgeschichte]. London: Allen & Unwin.

——— (1964 [1920]), *The Religion of China: Confucianism and Taoism* [Gesammelte Aufsätze zur Religionssoziologie I]. London: Macmillan.

——— (1978 [1922]), *Economy and Society* [Wirtschaft und Gesellschaft]. Berkeley: University of California Press.

——— (1988 [1918]), Deutschlands künftige Staatsform, in: Weber, *Gesammelte Politische Schriften*. Tübingen: UTB, 448–83.

——— (1999 [1895]), The National State and Economic Policy [Der Nationalstaat und die Volkswirtschaftspolitik], in: *Essays in Economic Sociology*. Princeton, NJ: Princeton UP, 120–37.

——— (2003), *Max Weber Gesamtausgabe*: Band II/8: *Briefe 1913–1914*. Ed. W. Mommsen and M. R. Lepsius. Tübingen: Mohr Siebeck.

Weiss, Linda (1999), *The Myth of the Powerless State*. Ithaca, NY: Cornell UP.

Welch, Cheryl B. (2003), Colonial Violence and the Rhetoric of Evasion: Tocqueville on Algeria, in: *Political Theory* 31: 235–64.

Wendt, Alexander (1992), Anarchy Is What States Make of It: The Social Construction of Power Politics, in: *International Organization* 46, 2: 391–425.

——— (2010 [1999]), *Social Theory of International Politics*. Cambridge: Cambridge UP.

Wesseling, H. L. (1997), Colonial Wars: An Introduction, in: Wesseling, *Essays on the History of European Expansion*. Westport, CT: Greenwood Press, 3–11.

Westbrook, Robert (1991), *John Dewey and American Democracy*. Ithaca, NY: Cornell UP.

Williams, Andrew (2006), *Liberalism and War: The Victors and the Vanquished*. New York: Routledge.

Williams, Michael C. (1989), Rousseau, Realism and Realpolitik, in: *Millennium: Journal of International Studies* 18, 2: 185–203.

Willms, Bernard (1987), *Thomas Hobbes. Das Reich des Leviathan*. Munich/Zurich: Piper.

Winch, Donald (1988), Adam Smith and the Liberal Tradition, in: Knud Haakonssen (ed.), *Traditions of Liberalism*. Sydney: Centre for Independent Studies, 359–77.

——— (1997), Bentham on Colonies and Empire, in: *Utilitas* 9, 1: 147–54.

Winter, Jay Murray (1975), The Economic and Social History of War, in: Winter (ed.), *War and Economic Development: Essays in Memory of David Joslin*. Cambridge: Cambridge UP, 1–10.

Wirth, Louis (1938), Urbanism as a Way of Life, in: *American Journal of Sociology* 44, 1: 1–24.

——— (1948), International Tensions as Objects of Social Investigation, in: Lyman Bryson/Louis Finkelstein/R. M. MacIver (eds.), *Learning and World Peace*. Eighth Symposium. New York: Harper & Brothers, 45–53.

——— (1956 [1928]), *The Ghetto*. Chicago: University of Chicago Press.

Wittrock, Björn (2001), History, War and the Transcendence of Modernity, in: *European Journal of Social Theory* 4, 1: 53–72.

Wolin, Sheldon S. (2001), *Tocqueville between Two Worlds: The Making of a Political and Theoretical Life*. Princeton, NJ: Princeton UP.

Wolfe, Alan (1999), *The Power Elite* Now, in: *The American Prospect* (May/June): 90–96.

Wright, Quincy (1942), *A Study of War*. Chicago: University of Chicago Press.

NAME INDEX

SUBJECT INDEX